Message–Attitude–Behavior Relationship

THEORY, METHODOLOGY, AND APPLICATION

HUMAN COMMUNICATION
RESEARCH SERIES

PETER R. MONGE, Editor

Monge and Cappella:
MULTIVARIATE TECHNIQUES IN
HUMAN COMMUNICATION RESEARCH 1980

Cushman and McPhee:
MESSAGE-ATTITUDE-BEHAVIOR
RELATIONSHIP 1980

Woelfel and Fink:
MEASUREMENT OF COMMUNICATION
PROCESSES 1980

Message–Attitude–Behavior Relationship

THEORY, METHODOLOGY, AND APPLICATION

Edited by

DONALD P. CUSHMAN

*Department of Rhetoric and Communication
State University of New York at Albany
Albany, New York*

ROBERT D. McPHEE

*Department of Speech Communication
University of Illinois at Urbana–Champaign
Urbana, Illinois*

1980

ACADEMIC PRESS

A Subsidiary of Harcourt Brace Jovanovich, Publishers

New York   London   Toronto   Sydney   San Francisco

ACADEMIC PRESS, INC.
111 Fifth Avenue, New York, New York 10003

United Kingdom Edition published by
ACADEMIC PRESS, INC. (LONDON) LTD.
24/28 Oval Road, London NW1 7DX

Library of Congress Cataloging in Publication Data
Main entry under title:

Message—attitude—behavior relationship.

    (Human communication research series)
    Includes bibliographies and index.
    1. Interpersonal communication. 2. Attitude
(Psychology) I. Cushman, Donald P. II. McPhee,
Robert. III. Series.
BF637.C45M48   153.6   80–529
ISBN 0–12–199760–X

PRINTED IN THE UNITED STATES OF AMERICA

80 81 82 83   9 8 7 6 5 4 3 2 1

Contents

List of Contributors

Numbers in parentheses indicate the pages on which the authors' contributions begin

Joseph N. Cappella (149), Center for Communication Research, Department of Communication Arts, University of Wisconsin–Madison, Madison, Wisconsin 53706

Robert T. Craig (273), Department of Communication, University of Illinois at Chicago Circle, Chicago, Illinois 60680

Donald P. Cushman (1), Department of Rhetoric and Communication, State University of New York at Albany, Albany, New York 12222

Joseph P. Folger (149), Department of Communication, University of Michigan, Ann Arbor, Michigan 48109

Norman E. Fontes (303), Department of Communication, Michigan State University, East Lansing, Michigan 48824

Dean E. Hewes (43), Department of Communication Arts, University of Wisconsin–Madison, Madison, Wisconsin 53706

John E. Hunter (245), Department of Psychology, Michigan State University, East Lansing, Michigan 48824

Thomas J. Larkin (289), Department of Rhetoric and Communication, State University of New York at Albany, Albany, New York 12222

Robert D. McPhee (1), Department of Speech Communication, University of Illinois at Urbana-Champaign, Urbana, Illinois 61801

Gerald R. Miller (319), Department of Communication, Michigan State University, East Lansing, Michigan 48824

Barbara O'Connor (303), Department of Speech Communication, California State University, Sacramento, California 95817

Daniel J. O'Keefe (117), Department of Speech Communication, Pennsylvania State University, University Park, Pennsylvania 16802

Marshall Scott Poole (245), Department of Speech Communication, University of Illinois at Urbana–Champaign, Urbana, Illinois 61801

David R. Seibold (195), Department of Speech Communication, University of Illinois at Urbana–Champaign, Urbana, Illinois 61801

Jennifer L. Shelby (303), Department of Communication, Michigan State University, East Lansing, Michigan 48824

Joseph Woelfel (89), Department of Rhetoric and Communication, State University of New York at Albany, Albany, New York 12222

Preface

For many years, there has been a need in the social and behavioral sciences for a single volume providing a precise and careful treatment of axiomatic, causal processes, and sets-of-laws approaches to theory construction. In this volume, we have brought together applications of stochastic, path analytic, and multidimensional scaling research methodologies to advance understanding of one of the behavioral sciences' most troublesome problems: the defining of the relationship between messages, attitudes, and behaviors. Specifically, the material presented here has important implications for ongoing controversies in communication, psychology, social psychology, sociology, and anthropology regarding the relationship of alternative methods of theory construction and mathematical modeling techniques. This volume will advance understanding of alternative conceptualizations of various message strategies, cognitive and information processing models, and their relevance to the study of behavior. Social scientists engaged in behavioral research will find this comparative and integrative approach both interesting and powerful.

The introductory chapter sets the stage within the research tradition involving messages, attitudes, and behaviors, and provides a perspective and an overview of the theoretical and methodological contributions of each chapter. Chapters 2–6 provide in-depth justification, supported by data analysis, for the use of various theoretical and methodological approaches to the message–attitude–behavior relationship. Chapters 7–10 discuss various theoretical issues involved in the previous inquiries. The final chapter, by a distinguished researcher who has spent most of this life confronting the various issues raised by this volume, provides some afterthoughts regarding the entire enterprise.

The majority of chapters in this volume were motivated by a series of classes in theory construction and mathematical modeling offered at Michigan State University between 1972 and 1977 and realized in research set up to pursue the issues raised by these seminars. However, as so often happens in intellectual inquiry, ideas and issues raised at one institution or in one domain are advanced by scholars at other institutions and in other domains. In that sense, intellectual inquiry is both exciting and mind stretching as one discovers the variety of theoretical and methodological perspectives that can illuminate a common problem and provide insight into a common set of issues.

Despite the enthusiasm, excitement, and energy created by a productive group of scholars, there is need for the type of caution, tentativeness, and precision fostered by the introduction of multiple perspectives in theory and methodology. An awareness of the strengths and weaknesses of one's own point of view is encouraged in such an environment. So this volume is offered as both a challenge and a caution to young and old scholars who think they have something to contribute to the scientific enterprise. It provides a challenge to think and see in new ways and a caution to those who approach problems from a single perspective.

We have included extensive treatments of innovative mathematical models reflecting stochastic and deterministic mathematical operators case in coextensive, sequential, and multidimensional arrays of systems state. Message strategies have been cast in terms of social, psychological, and information processing constructs.

We are grateful to all who assisted in the preparation of this volume. We thank them for their time, patience, and effort. In particular, we wish to thank Paul Lisnek for his assistance in preparing the indexes.

1

Attitudes, Behaviors, and Messages: An Introductory Overview

ROBERT D. McPHEE
DONALD P. CUSHMAN

In this introductory chapter, we seek to provide an overview and background for the remaining chapters in the book by describing the vast theoretical and empirical literature on the relationship between attitudes and behaviors, and by summarizing the contributions of the later chapters to the understanding of relations among messages, attitudes, and behaviors. We begin by considering the attitude–behavior literature, detailing the major advances and issues informing that literature to the present. Next, we recount the theoretic forms and content within each chapter in this volume, descriptively and critically. Third, we deal with the mathematical and statistical methodology used by several of the authors, and especially with how their methodological choices have conditioned their theories and findings. Finally, we focus on the communicative implications of these chapters, especially the promise of applications for the design of messages and the prediction of their effects.

Review of Theoretical and Empirical Progress and Issues in the Attitude–Behavior Literature.

In this first section, though it is called a "review" of literature, we will not simply summarize and critique the numerous extant attitude–behavior

1

MESSAGE–ATTITUDE–BEHAVIOR RELATIONSHIP
Theory, Methodology, and Applications

studies: Worthy reviews exist outside this book (Ajzen & Fishbein, 1977; Eagly & Himmelfarb, 1978; Schuman & Johnson, 1976; Seibold, 1975) and several of our chapters contain summary reviews. Rather, we seek to place the accomplishments of later chapters in perspective, against a ground of past social scientific problems and accomplishments in constructing theory to support explanations of attitude–behavior relationships.

We view theory construction—the art of specifying and systematizing propositions and theories—as a central constituent of scientific method, nearly always involved when scientists move from a body of extant knowledge or belief toward more precise, general, or necessary hypotheses suitable for testing. The art of theory construction has been the subject of several recent texts (Blalock, 1969; Dubin, 1978; Hague, 1972; Reynolds, 1971; Stinchcombe, 1968). The chapters that follow are intended as examples of that art, revealing its power and utility.

We begin our overview by analyzing the classic origin of the problem of attitude–behavior relations, in traditional social psychology, and especially in the work of LaPierre (1934). The conceptually tangled origins of the problem provide a baseline for a survey of progress in theory construction along four fronts: conceptualization of the problem itself, conceptual and operational definition of variables, specification of relationships between variables, and the systematic organization of propositions into theories. This survey will provide a context for our discussion of the remaining chapters in the book.

Wellsprings of the Problem

Attitudes traditionally have been the object of social scientific research; even as early as 1935, Gordon Allport's notable review listed 17 influential conceptual definitions of attitude. Although they differed substantially among themselves, these definitions overlapped in regarding "the essential feature of attitude as a *preparation or readiness for response* [1935, p. 805]." In this, all the authors surveyed cohered with the dominant "Chicago School" of social psychology, within which an attitude was an incipient or preparatory stage of behavior. Thus, when a baseball player steps into the batter's box, digs in his spikes, lifts his bat, and stares at the pitcher, he would be said to assume the attitude (or posture) of batting. Notice that in this view, attitudes are directly and definitionally tied to behavior, but need not be expressive of any affect or positive or negative orientation. Even by 1935, however, an additional feature of attitudes had attained such prominence that Allport could refer to it as their "most distinctive feature": affective or evaluative directionality. Thurstone's definition of attitude as "the affect for or against a psychological object [1959, p. 297]" was an early version of the conception that was to dominate most later theorizing about attitude and attitude change.

Bogardus' Social Distance scale, the first widely used measure of social attitudes, exemplifies the early direct tie of attitudes to behaviors: Its items were what are now called behavioral intentions rather than relatively pure expressions of evaluation or affect. But subsequent developments in the operational measurement of attitudes, by Thurstone, Likert, Guttman, and others seemed to bring with them a slow change in the "attitude" concept, which began to be thought of as internal, unidimensional, abstract, and evaluative. The logical culmination of this development appears in the work of Osgood and his colleagues, wherein attitude is described as an aspect of semantic meaning, linked to behavior only as a broad dimension of internalized mediatory response. But in this evaluation, social psychology merely imitated common sense as reflected in etymology: In the Oxford English Dictionary (OED, 1971, p. 139) the derivation and first three definitions of "attitude" refer to physical disposition and behavior; only the fourth refers to a "mode of thought."

The *general* origin of the attitude–behavior problem can be traced to this schizophrenia of definition: "Attitude" is thought of both as a predisposition causing consistency in behavior, and also as a general evaluation of an object, measurable by questionnaire. Typically, theorists begin by discussing the behavioral significance of attitudes, but as they move to the actual construction and justification of theory, or to the construction of attitude measures, they take the most important properties of attitude to be the direction and intensity of affect felt toward an object, describable on a questionnaire (for a review that illustrates this move toward concentration on degree of affect, see Scott, 1968, especially page 208). Now clearly, if attitude is defined as a predisposition or a preparation to behave, it is at least a necessary condition for behavior; the link between attitude and behavior is necessary and must exist empirically if valid measures of attitude and behavior are used. But if attitude is affective orientation, it is hard to find any compelling reason to expect behavior to reflect or even be consistent with an attitude: People might or might not act on the basis of their feelings, and if they do, why, that is an interesting phenomenon requiring an explanation in its own right. Unfortunately, most theorists assumed that the predisposition to act and the affective evaluation were one and the same, and used that assumption in justifying and discussing questionnaire research.

The *specific* wellspring of the attitude–behavior problem is a paper by Richard LaPiere (1934), "Attitudes versus Actions." LaPiere traveled the western United States in the company of a young Chinese couple; 6 months after the trip, he sent a questionnaire to many of the establishments that served them, asking whether or not they would accept members of the Chinese race as customers; over 90% of those establishments answered "No" (see Schuman & Johnson, 1976, p. 165 ff., for additional useful discussion). Because this study has been misdescribed and incorrectly criticized so often, it seems useful to quote from the rationale LaPiere supplied:

> Nothing could be used as a more accurate index of color prejudice than the admission or non-admission of colored people to hotels. For the proprietor must reflect the group attitude in his policy regardless of his own feelings in the matter. Since he determines what the group attitude is toward Negroes through the expression of

that attitude in overt behavior and over a long period of actual experience, the results will be exceptionally free from those disturbing factors which inevitably affect the effort to study attitudes by direct questioning.

But in [making that assumption] I overlooked the fact that what I was obtaining from the hotel proprietors was still a "verbalized" reaction to a symbolic situation. The response to a Negro's request for lodging might have been an excellent index of the attitude of hotel patrons toward living in the same hotel as a Negro. Yet to ask the proprietor, "Do you permit members of the Negro race to stay here?" does not, it appears, measure his potential response to an actual Negro [1934, p. 231].

That is, the attitudes at issue here are general social attitudes of customers, which are supposed to be indexed by well-established hotel policies. It seemed, and still seems, reasonable to expect that such policies would govern both responses to questionnaires and behavior in actual situations.

Now let us consider carefully LaPiere's findings. First, the Chinese couple he accompanied presented themselves at various establishments. Practically without exception, they were accommodated; moreover, they were served, often by several employees of one establishment, with such efficiency, interest, and consideration as to indicate the complete absence of a negative attitude among the hotel's staff and customers (see pp. 232–233). Second, LaPiere's questionnaire elicited uniformly negative descriptions of hotel behavior toward "members of the Chinese race"—but in the only case LaPiere observed, one hotel refused *over the telephone* to accommodate "a distinguished Chinese gentleman." The following summary seems accurate: LaPiere found uniformly favorable behavior toward an actual Chinese couple, but also strong indications of favorable attitudes toward those customers; he found uniformly negative attitudes evinced in answers to questions about the symbolic entity, "member of the Chinese race," and some slight indication that behavior toward such symbolic entities (talked *about* rather than *to* over the telephone) might be uniformly negative as well. LaPiere's data directly show a complete dichotomy between responses to symbolic "Chinese" and real Chinese people; they also contain evidence for an almost complete consistency between attitudinal and behavioral responses toward either entity.

LaPiere's study was taken, however, as an attack on the assumption that attitudes have causal or predictive relevance to behavior, and was the subject of numerous critical responses, and of several partial replications that supported the finding of inconsistency between attitudes and behaviors. The attack on "attitudes" as a behaviorally relevant concept crested in 1969, with Wicker's review of 31 studies and his conclusion that attitudes are more likely than not to be unrelated or minimally related to behavior. However, recent conceptual and methodological advances have led to consensus on a more favorable view of the causal relevance of attitudes to behaviors. The accumulated empirical literature to date is well-summarized by Schuman and Johnson's statement (1976, p. 168) that "attitudes and behaviors are related to an extent that ranges from small to moderate in degree," except for the special cases of cheating in school and interracial buyer–seller transactions, in which attitude–behavior correlations are especially low, and voting, where attitudes predict behavior unusually well.

Of course, this general characterization reflects considerable progress in research design and understanding of attitude–behavior relations. Moreover, while recent research has uncovered, and attempted to explain, clear moderate relationships between appropriately chosen measures of attitudes and behaviors, researchers have also established and analyzed very low attitude–behavior relations under a variety of other circumstances. The theoretic progress in explaining when attitudes are or are not consistent with behaviors will be our next concern.

Advances in Conceptualization

We shall make what is probably a counterfactual assumption: That social scientists typically begin by noticing a phenomenon and trying to understand and verify their understanding of it (rather than noticing a paradigm or line of research and trying to extend it or deviate from it). Given this assumption, a logically initial step in the process of theory construction is to specify and purify the scientist's conception of the phenomenon of interest. In reviewing developments at this level in the attitude–behavior literature, we must attend to two aspects: the interpretation chosen for "attitude–behavior relationship," and the development, or lack thereof, of a hypothesized underlying causal process.

Research Strategies

As noted earlier, conceptual ambiguity is an original sin of the attitude–behavior question; thus it is not surprising to discover that researchers have derived and used several distinct interpretations of the question. The deepest division is between theorists who have focused on the explanation of behavioral variability in general, and those who have sought to explain attitude–behavior inconsistency.

Some researchers have attacked the attitude–behavior question by building theoretical models for the prediction of behavior. The most famous such model is Fishbein's (Fishbein, 1967; Fishbein and Ajzen, 1975), but many such models exist to explain behavior in specific domains such as consumer buying (Hughes & Ray, 1974), altruistic behavior (Schwartz, 1977; Schwartz & Tessler, 1972), and health-care behavior (for a summary, see Seibold & Roper, 1979). All these model builders are searching for a complete set of behavioral predictors. Rather than limit themselves to traditional attitudinal predictors, they are free to seek out other variables, modify and narrow attitude concepts (by concentrating on attitudes toward acts), or even ignore attitudes altogether.

Insights and issues relevant to this approach, and to the next, are detailed later in this chapter.

Other researchers have worked to alleviate their puzzlement about attitude–behavior relations in particular. They have followed the course described by Liska: "Researchers have reconceptualized the problem as that of identifying the conditions which affect the extent and direction of the relationship . . . [1974, p. 262]." Liska describes the major issues focused on by these researchers as "problems of measurement, the role of other competing attitudes, and the role of social support." Clearly, the concern here is to explain why attitude–behavior consistency is often low, more than to explain why such consistency exists at all.

As one point of comparison between these approaches, we should note that the first approach seems more likely to be useful to students of communication than the second. Success in building a model explaining differences in behavior presumably would provide direct information to communication researchers about how to construct messages that affect behavior, presumably by affecting first the determinants of behavior (i.e., Ajzen, 1971). Findings under the second approach would be most directly useful to practitioners of brainwashing or assertiveness training, in uncovering ways to influence others' behavior to be more isolated from or reflective of their actual feelings. But we must not exaggerate the clarity or importance of this difference between approaches, since each is contributory to the other. Finding variables that determine behavior also involves finding out the causes forcing that behavior to be inconsistent with attitudes.

Generative Mechanisms

Research approach aside, the assumed goal of scientific research is to understand *why*, for example, behavior is or is not consistent with attitude. Such an understanding, philosophers have recently argued, depends heavily on a conception of what attitudes and behaviors *are*, that one should affect the other (Harré & Madden, 1975). Such a conception is usually set forth in research papers as the justification for whatever hypotheses are tested, as the process or mechanism which should cause the hypothesis to be true. Conception of that sort have been termed "generative mechanisms" by Rom Harré and his associates.

The set of clear generative mechanisms cited in the attitude–behavior literature is surprisingly small, perhaps because of the ambigious conception of attitude from which the whole problem has grown. We can find only three distinct mechanisms underlying the bulk of that literature; several others having had some influence.

The first traditional mechanism underlying presumed attitude–behavior consistency was just discussed as a general wellspring for the whole controversy, and is distantly related to the "probability" conception of DeFleur and Westie

(1963). We shall label it the "definitional explanation" of consistency, and the argument it involves is approximately the following. An attitude, by definition, is a consistent tendency to respond evaluatively to an object. A behavior, *if* it has evaluative implications for an object, *is* such a response. Therefore, *if* a person has an attitude at all, his behavior must generally be consistent with it by definition (for an example of the use of this argument, see Schuman & Johnson, 1976, p. 186). A simple argument, yet much of the progress in theory and research detailed in what follows had been rooted in ever-stricter observance of the "if" clauses in it.

A second common mechanism underlying attitude–behavior consistency is the "latent process" notion of DeFleur and Westie (1963); an attitude is an unobservable cognitive state underlying various modes of verbal and behavioral response, forcing them to be consistent. Note the difference between the latent process idea and the definitional explanation: For the former, attitude is an observable tendency, whereas for the latter, attitude is an underlying force creating the observable tendency. This conception has the same peril and promise as unobservable physical concepts like phlogiston or gravity. If its strength, and the liability of various types of behavior to its influence, can be consistently and generally ascertained, it will have tremendous explanatory power; otherwise, its pseudoexplanatory appeal will lead to tremendous obfuscation. Miller's remarks in the Afterword to this volume caution against the danger of this approach; Seibold's chapter is an attempt to harness the notion as rigorously as possible.

The final common explanatory mechanism underlying attitude–behavior research was popularized most clearly by McGuire's influential essay (1969); Eagly and Himmelfarb (1978) cite it as the basis of almost all current research on attitude change. The mechanism can be labeled "information processing": its proponents try to identify precisely various cognitive states, mechanisms, and processes, and to characterize attitudes and behaviors in the light of their informational determinants. Realistically, this "mechanism" is a label for a conglomeration of approaches, and can be applied to at least the chapters of Woelfel, Poole and Hunter, Cappella and Folger, O'Keefe, and perhaps even Seibold. If anything unifies "information processing" adherents, it is a joint indebtedness to developments in cognitive psychology, the most diverse, dominant, and fast-growing subfield in contemporary psychology.

Aside from the three underlying generative mechanisms already mentioned, several others have had some influence and deserve mention here. First among them is the "action" view of behavior, which springs from several philosophically based approaches to social science (Cushman & Pearce, 1977; Harré & Secord, 1973; von Wright, 1972). Within this view, people act on reasons in situations as they interpret them; these reasons and interpretations are not causes of action, but grounds justifying the decision to act. This perspective seems to have been used very rarely in the study of the attitude–behavior question, although it underlies, in part, the general focus on behavioral intention, as well as the work of O'Keefe, Craig, and Larkin in this book. A second hypothesized mechanism which is widely known but exercises little deep theoretical influence is Bem's notion of "self-perception" (1968). In opposition to the latent process approach of dissonance theory, Bem argued that people's attitudes are "self-descriptions of . . . affinities and aversions," and that in discovering their affinities and aversions, people use their own past behavior as a primary source of evidence. Thus attitudes should be consistent with behavior because they are derived from [past] behavior. Although this notion seems to have broad potential influence, Bem described it in the vocabulary of behavioristic learning theory. Behaviorists have described an array of psychological processes that also might serve as a generative mechanism for use by attitude–behavior theorists. Indeed, behaviorism seems to have had some influence on the views of Martin Fishbein (1967).

Before we leave the subject of possible generative mechanisms, one general point requires discussion. All of these mechanisms are potentially very broad in scope. Theories involving them have been tested for, or used to explain, an extremely wide range of types of behavior, in many different situations. But it certainly seems possible that social scientists might do better generating theories "of the middle range" (Merton, 1949), attempting to describe the processes causing only certain classes or types of behaviors and their relations to attitudes.

One theorist who has pursued this strategy is Shalom Schwartz (1977; Schwartz & Tessler, 1972). He has dealt extensively with the explanation of *altruistic* behavior, paying special attention to the influence of moral norms and perceptions on such behavior. Using a model especially derived to reflect typical processes of moral reasoning, he was able to explain variations in such behavior more successfully than by using Fishbein's more general model (Schwartz & Tessler, 1972). Schwartz's reasoning and procedures probably could not be extended to all sorts of behavior (cf. Fishbein & Ajzen, 1975, pp. 305–306), and a moral normative construct would probably be relatively unimportant in determining other behavior types. Nonetheless, Schwartz's concentration on one type of behavior probably lets us understand that type better than a more general scheme could, and it produced some evidence for typal differences in behavior determination.

Definition of Variables

Many researchers have contributed to the gradual increase in precision and sophistication of definitions of attitudinal and behavioral variables. However, a veritable revolution in conceptualization, bringing many earlier developments into prominence, was wrought by Martin Fishbein (1967) in his stipulation and testing of a widely influential model of behavior and behavioral intention. It is easiest to begin our discussion of variable definition by focusing on the work of Fishbein and his associate Icek Ajzen (1975; Ajzen & Fishbein, 1977).

The Fishbein model is nested in a series of empirically significant conceptual considerations, and we turn our attention first to these. A major distinction among variables is suggested by the title of Fishbein and Ajzen's *Belief, Attitude, Intention, and Behavior* (1975). Rejecting a tricomponential view of attitude, Fishbein initially defined attitude, following Thurstone, as "the amount of affect for or against a psychological object [1967, p. 478]." The usual cognitive component is redefined as belief: "the subjective probability of a relation between the object of the belief and some other object, value, concept, or attribute [Fishbein & Ajzen, 1975, p. 131]." The conative component of attitude is termed behavioral intention, defined as "a person's location on a subjective probability dimension involving a relation between him and some action [p. 288]." Fishbein separates these "components" of attitude in order to stipulate a causal chain involving them and behavior. *Behaviors* (or volitionally controlled behaviors) are determined by behavioral *intentions*, which are functions of *attitudes toward the acts* in question (along with a special class of social normative *beliefs*, to be dealt with later). Attitudes themselves are functionally related to *beliefs*, which, as initial psychological variables in this chain, are determined by (interpreted) experience and messages.

"Attitude toward the act" is one expression of Fishbein's general movement toward conceptual sophistication, summarized most recently in Ajzen and Fishbein (1977). These authors argue that attitudes and behaviors may be specified by considering them as "consisting of four different elements: the *action*, the *target* at which action is directed, the *context* in which action is performed, and the *time* at which it is performed [p. 889]." Particular behaviors usually have specific values for each of these elements; to index behavior more generally, a researcher may form a multiple-act criterion by summing over varying values of one or more of the four elements mentioned. Often, attitude items specify only the target object of the attitude, thus constituting a measure of general *attitude toward the object*; but attitudes toward highly specific actions, precise on all four constituent elements, also may be measured. The major conceptual argument advanced by Ajzen and Fishbein is that attitudes should predict behaviors best under conditions of high *correspondence*—the elements constituting attitude and behavior should be the same, and should be defined at the same level of specificity, for highest correlations to appear empirically. Ajzen and Fishbein array impressive empirical support for this view.

Corresponding to this conceptual development is another, which is primarily operational. Fishbein (1967; 1973; Fishbein & Ajzen, 1974) has followed commentators like Campbell (1963) in noting that behaviors are *items* just like those contained in attitude scales. Any particular behavior may be subjected to psychometric analysis, may turn out to be more or less reliably and validly linked to any particular object, and may turn out to be like items on either a

Likert, a Thurstone, a Guttman, or some other type of scale. A psychometric mismatch between attitude items and behavior items may produce low empirical correlations or "pseudoinconsistency" as a methodological artifact.

Given this complex of concepts, the determinative models within Fishbein's position may be quickly described (we will analyze them in more detail), following Eagly and Himmelfarb's account:

> Fishbein's . . . model for predicting single acts regards behavior as a consequence of intention to act and behavioral intention as a linear regression function of (a) attitude toward the act. and (b) normative pressures that regulate behavior. Attitude toward act may be assessed directly or through the sum of a person's beliefs about the consequences of the act, with the evaluation of each consequence multiplied by the likelihood that the consequence will result from the behavior (i.e. an expectancy–value formulation). The normative component is the sum over referent persons of the product of the belief that a particular referent thinks the person should perform the behavior times the person's motivations to comply with that particular referent's expectations [1978, pp. 529–530].

Three of the conceptual developments that characterize Fishbein's approach have been the objects of significant attention and controversy.

First, Fishbein's use of behavioral intention as a mediating variable between other psychological variables and behavior, although widely accepted and influential, has been questioned by Schuman and Johnson (1976), who argue that in many cases, people's intentions are inchoate until they act, and in still other cases, their behaviors are *direct* responses to situational forces (pp. 169, 173, 194–195), so that intention may be a redundant or unnecessary predictor of behavior. Triandis' alternative attitude–behavior model (1976) also indicates the need to supplement an intention-centered model by attention to habit, ability, and situational constraints.

Another of the conceptual developments brought to prominence by Fishbein is the move toward specificity in attitude and behavior measurement, and in particular, the emphasis on attitude toward the act, Fishbein and Ajzen argue persuasively that any particular behavior may be relatively independent of an attitude toward the target of the behavior, for numerous reasons, but that the average tendency over numerous behaviors with the same target but of different sorts should relate closely to attitude toward their common target. Therefore, they examine attitudes toward objects primarily in their relation to multiple-act indices, and look to attitude toward the act when they consider affective force on behavior. As O'Keefe points out in Chapter 4 of this volume, the original or genuinely puzzling "attitude–behavior question" is about behavior consistency with attitudes toward *objects*—why do people's actions toward objects not reflect their feelings toward those objects? Although Fishbein and Ajzen never (to our knowledge) explicitly derive the relation of an attitude toward an object with particular behaviors, that relation is readily deducible from Fishbein's various models. Apart from chance or highly indirect causal connections, attitude toward the object will relate to behavior through its link with (and therefore less strongly than) attitude toward the act; those two attitudes will be strongly related to the greatest degree when the attributes and objects to which the target object is tied by strong beliefs are the same as those to which the action under consideration also is strongly tied. In other words, behavior will be strongly related to attitude toward its object when the context of meaning for the object is the same as the context of meaning of the behavior. Behavior will be "evaluatively inconsistent," according to Fishbein's model, when it has meaning or consequences not typically connected with the object. Schuman and Johnson describe the case of high consistency as one where "object and act are closely intertwined . . . [1976, p. 173]."

A final conceptual development that has received substantial recent discussion is the issue of scale types of attitude and behavior measures. As noted previously, Fishbein followed Campbell (1963) in describing both attitude and behavior "items" as possessing various psychometric properties; Campbell used this insight to propose an alternative to the common associational approach to consistency. Campbell argued that apparent or pseudoinconsistency might arise when a behavior possesses a relatively high attitudinal threshold: it might take very strong approval of organ donation for a person to actually serve as a transplant donor, so that those whose attitudes are weakly positive appear inconsistent, although they are responding just as they would to a very strong or stringent attitude item. Campbell used this notion to "explain" the finding of La Piere—a moderate level of prejudice might show up on questionnaires but not in overt behavior. As Schuman and Johnson point out, this explanation leaves open the question of why the behavior is more difficult, or has a higher threshold, than the attitude in question; in addition, an empirical examination of pseudoinconsistency as an explanation of observed inconsistency has been published recently by Raden (1977). Reanalyzing data from a variety of studies where only moderate attitude–behavior consistency was observed, Raden came to three conclusions: (a) if one adjusts for pseudoinconsistency or different item difficulty levels on a Guttman scale, observed levels of association or "consistency" increase rather substantially; (b) much of this increase may be due to chance, and would be observed even if attitude and behavior were totally independent variables; and (c) the adjustment for pseudoinconsistency may conceal one possible type of inconsistency—that in which a person's attitude is strongly positive but he still does not act. Raden concludes that more rigorous study is necessary before the pseudoinconsistency account is accepted by attitude–behavior theorists.

This concludes our discussion of developments in the conceptual and operational definitions of attitude, behavior, and related variables. Clearly, controversy still exists over the choice and nature of even central explanatory variables in the attitude–behavior literature; just as clearly, researchers may exercise their powers of choice upon an array of options whose advantages and disadvantages have been explored in some depth.

Specification of Relationships among Variables

The next logical step in theory construction, after precisely defining variables, is that of specifying relationships between them. If we accept the empirical finding of a moderate relationship between attitudes and behaviors, and ignore the possibility that that relationship is spurious or indirect, we face the considerable challenge of deciding what *type* of relationship it is. Several typologies of variable relationships have been developed, of which the best known is Zetterberg's (1963). In the literature of the attitude–behavior relationship, two issues involving specification that have received considerable attention are the necessity or contingency of the relationship, and the direction of causal impact between attitude and behavior.

The broad observed fluctuation in attitude–behavior relationships has led investigators to assume the contingency of the relationship, and to explore the sources or reasons for differences in the relationship's strength. The usual question is, "On what is the attitude–behavior relationship contingent?" The answers fall into three broad groups; antecedent variables, moderating variables, and "other variables." The last group actually involves a pseudoanswer to the question. Other variables are those which, like social normative pressure in Fishbein's model, have an independent additive effect on behavior or behavioral intention. If variance in such a variable increases, the correlation of attitude with intention or behavior will decrease; we nevertheless hesitate to say that such a variable changes the *relationship* between attitude and intention, as opposed to certain *measures* of *size* of relationship.

Antecedent variables or conditions are those that are presupposed by theory, and which must be present (or have a certain value) for a relationship to hold. Examples of such variables are ability and situational facilitation, in Fishbein's theory. But the most significant antecedent variable, for the purposes of this book, is *time of measurement*. Many researchers have noted that, the further apart in time attitudes (or intentions) and behaviors are measured, the lower the intercorrelation between them. Because Fishbein's and other prominent models are static models, not taking time specifically into account, they presuppose that the model's variables are measured over as short a time interval as possible, and they can make no *theoretical* predictions about the consequences as the measurement interval broadens. One innovation of underrated importance (probably initiated by Alwin, 1973), carried through in several chapters of this book is the explicit inclusion of time in attitude–behavior models. As Alwin (1973) and Seibold and McPhee (1979) demonstrate, the inclusion of temporal considerations alters the methods and outcomes of tests of attitude–behavior models significantly; Schwartz (1978) has produced an initial demonstration of the substantive impact of such a change of perspective.

Unlike antecedent variables, moderating variables can be and usually are explicitly included in models in a very specific way. They change the nature of the relationship between more central model variables: That is to say, they *interact* with one variable to produce an effect on another. Several groups of such variables have been advanced; the two most important groups are "attitude-nature" variables and social-pressure variables.

Seibold (1975) and Schuman and Johnson (1976) have reviewed empirical literature that explores variables such as the strength, certainty, and interval consistency of attitudes as moderators of attitude effects on behavior. The argument underlying all these variables, as well as Schwartz's (1978) "stability," and perhaps Regan and Fazio's (1977) "methods of attitude formation," is that people's answers on attitude questionnaires may reflect no real underlying affect. People may have no integrated conception of the object, or may simply not have taken any simple evaluative stand toward it. Thus their "attitude scores" reflect social pressures, or a complex or ambivalent stance not well reflected by one score, or an answer made up on the spot. Such scores would be spuriously related to behavior; therefore, attitude *validity* (to create a label) should determine the strength of the attitude–behavior relationship. This line of argument seems sound and well grounded, even though the variety of un-clearly related conceptual and operational approaches to "validity" defies easy synthesis.

The moderating effects of social pressure have been explored by proponents of the "contingent consistency hypothesis" (Warner & DeFleur, 1969) that social support moderates the strength of the attitude–behavior relationship. Schuman and Johnson provide an insightful review of this area (1976, pp. 186–189), concluding that "only limited and uncertain evidence" exists for the hypothesis. Since that review, Andrews and Kandel (1979) have produced some clearer evidence for an interaction of attitude and social support (although their study may not have avoided a problem, implicit in Shuman and Johnson's account, of a spurious interaction due to a "floor effect" in behavior).

These two sets of moderating variables have dominated the empirical literature on attitudes and behaviors. Other factors also are known to affect the attitude–behavior relationship, most notably as a result of research on the Fishbein model. In that model, attitude toward the act, and social normative beliefs, are directly and linearly related to behavior; however, the weight or causal impact of each variable may shift radically "with the type of behavior under consideration, with the situation in which the behavior is to be per-formed, with the target, and with individual differences between actors [Fish-bein & Ajzen, 1975, p. 314]." The lack of a systematic description and account of these model variations is a source of dissatisfaction with the model, and is taken by some as evidence of its lack of generality and empirical precision (cf. Songer-Nocks, 1976). To rely on empirical regression analysis to determine a different equation for each form of behavior in each situation, seems to indi-cate a fundamental lack of knowledge about why attitudes or social pressures have the impact they do on any particular behavior. But the clear existence of situational and other differences in the attitude–behavior relationship makes the search for moderator variables a promising research focus.

Authors concerned with attitude–behavior relations, including those in this volume, typically have assumed that attitudes cause behaviors, and not the reverse. But the idea that behavior exerts a reverse impact on attitudes, at least in certain situations, has a great deal of research support, and is a central phenomenon explained by dissonance, attribution, and other theories. Indeed, behavioral sources of attitude change are the foundation of an alternative emphasis or paradigm for studying social persuasion (Miller & Burgoon, 1973). Whereas the reverse causal path from behavior to attitude undoubtedly exists, several qualifying points can be made about it. First, this sort of causation seems to derive from the more commonly assumed attitude–behavior chain: We feel, for example, dissonance after counter–attitudinal behavior because we should (and normally do?) act consistently with our attitudes. Second, it seems possible to control reverse causation by dealing with behavior that is new to the subject, or (to eliminate the more obvious and immediate effects) by measuring attitude before behavior (Schuman & Johnson, 1976, pp. 198–199). Nevertheless, it seems desirable to explore two-way causation in the development of long-run attitude–behavior consistency, and it is pleasing to note that most of our authors allow, more or less overtly, for the impact on attitude of elements within (behavioral) experience.

Systematic Ordering of Propositions

After specifying the most important relationships between pairs of variables, one final necessary step remains: the systematic ordering of propositions of the theory. Generally, this step involves bringing the theory into conformity with the requirements for one of several distinct types of theory, which will be outlined in the next section. In the literature on attitude–behavior relationships, the systematic ordering of propositions has involved primary emphasis on two controversial moves: the closure of the system of propositions, and the stipulation of relationships as direct, indirect, or spurious. A nice example of both moves is provided in Fishbein's model. Message variables, and most psychological variables, are hypothesized to affect intentions and behavior first by affecting attitudes toward the act or social normative belief; the last two variables are a closed and complete set of immediate determinants of intention. This closure of the variable "system" (commonly called the completeness hypothesis) seems to possess no theoretic rationale (certainly none in the theory's central statement [Fishbein & Ajzen, 1975]); moreover, Schwartz and Tessler (1972) have produced convincing evidence that, for some sorts of behavior, *personal* normative beliefs, attitudes toward relevant objects, and other variables have powerful unmediated effects on intention. The apparent failure of the completeness hypothesis is indicative of the state of the attitude–behavior literature generally: Whereas theory developments at the levels of variable definition and simple propositions have been frequent, these developments only rarely have been combined and ordered systematically, and then, unsuccessfully.

Theory Types and Present Developments in Message–Attitude–Behavior Theory

In this section of the review, we attempt to describe the remaining chapters in the book, and to place them within the context of advances in theory construction about message–attitude–behavior relationships. Several of our authors overtly tried, in developing their perspectives, to provide an instance of one of several types of classical scientific theory structure that have been distinguished by several authors (McDermott, 1975; Reynolds, 1971). We have designated, therefore, many of the chapters as instances of one or another theory type; an initial discussion describing and contrasting the types is followed by summaries of the applicable chapters. The last three chapters are aimed more at conceptual analysis and development than at specific theory promulgation, and therefore are separately treated. The summary of each chapter is intended both to precis the chapter, and to provide an initial estimate of its strengths and weaknesses. However, we state what will be obvious upon study of the chapters: Our criticisms indicate limitations rather than indictments, and very often the best chapters (in our view) are the ones that are criticized most sharply (since they offer the most incisive ideas for criticism).

Classical Types of Theory

Rarely are any two theories isomorphic—corresponding exactly in concepts and relations among concepts. But theories have been classified on the basis of broad similarities in structure and in central problems encountered. Knowledge of such theory types is profitable because a theorist, conforming to a type in developing and formalizing a theory, gains assurance that his effort avoids many problems by its very structure; he also gains insight into the nature of the real problems his theory will face and the range of solutions to those problems attempted in the past. Thus he can use results from the philosophy of science, and other empirical fields, to improve his particular paradigm.

In Chapter 6 in this volume, Seibold clearly outlines one standard system of distinctions among theories. Within that system, we focus on the three types of classical theory elucidated by Reynolds (1971) and McDermott (1975): axiomatic theory, set-of-laws theory, and causal process theory. All three types are related on various levels to developments in the philosophy of science and empirical social scientific research; with an eye to those developments, we will explain the contrast among the three types, to emphasize their distinct structures, advantages, and problems.

But first, they have similarities. The three classical theory types are alike in claiming generality (within specified limits) and necessity of results. For all three types, necessity is analyzed, most fundamentally, at the level of particular relationships between pairs of variables. These basic relationships generally involve either the causal force one variable exerts on another, or the limitation on a variable imposed by the means used to achieve variation in it. Thus, attitude may affect behavior predictably either by exerting a motivating force that causes the behavior, or by structuring perspective so that we cannot "see our way clear" to act counterattitudinally. (Two other nonclassic forms of theory, systems theory and rules theory, analyze necessity at the level of the whole set of variables attended to, either by claiming isomorphism of an empirical "system" to a web of reflexively related variables, or by explaining variable correlations as practically necessary relations between means to a common goal.) But since classical theories analyze necessary relations between variables pair by pair, they face the common central problem of determining how the pair relations unite into a common whole. This problem emerges and is addressed in three different ways in the three theory types.

Axiomatic theories must be defined in a broad context, ranging from "axiomatics" as a broad formalization movement common to mathematics, logic, and science (Blanche, 1962) to "axiomatic theory" as a very narrow mode of theory construction enunciated by Zetterberg (1963). For us, axiomatic theories are those in which empirical propositions may be deduced directly from axioms in combinations, without the need for construction of a *model* midway between theory and data. Such a theory is equivalent to the *statement* set, axioms plus theorems. In such a theory, formalization is a direct benefit, since it increases deductive power without sacrificing flexibility—the theory is cast so that flexibility in adapting it to applications is not needed. Thus, the problem of arranging and combining intervariable relations is solved by address-ing phenomena in such a light that the structure of variables remains constant and is described by a formal rule for combination of axioms to generate deduc-tions. Since the system of propositions constituting the theory is a whole, tight-knit by the rule of combination, empirical evidence for any part of the theory, whether that part be theorems or axioms, is more or less direct evidence for the whole (Bailey, 1970). But the standard and formal nature of the axioms and rules of combination means that a new problem may arise: change in sys-tematic structure. For example, Hewes, in Chapter 2, describes an axiomatic theory of choice, among a finite set of distinct behavior choices, and portrays messages as suggesting patterns of change in weight afforded to these choices. If behavior is chosen, as a rate, from numbers on the rational number "line," or if the real possibility exists that messages may suggest new choices or establish ambiguity among old choice options, the system of axioms and deductions breaks down (although the ideas underlying the system may not).

Set-of-laws theories have ordinarily been related to the positivistic deduc-tive model of explanation of Hempel and Oppenheim (1948). But Stegmuller (1976) argues that scientific theory is not merely a set of general and particular statements, but a "relatively complicated conceptual instrument [p. vii]," which must be applied to any particular instance to achieve explanation or empirical test. We shall define a *model* as an applied or situated theory. The concern of set-of-law theorists becomes, then, not the arrangement of statements into valid deductive patterns, but the choice and arrangement of concepts so that they achieve a scientific representation or model from which inference can follow. Here, the problem of arranging and combining intervariable relations becomes the problem of constructing a model that adequately reflects a situation. Since models are situation specific, they may be discarded when they fail empirically, without effect on the underlying theory, simply because they may have been inadequate representations of the particular situation. Changes in basic situation structure are challenges to design new models, rather than cause to abandon the theory (as such changes may be for axiomatic theorists), but a new pair of problems surface to haunt the set-of-laws theorists: the model construction problem, and the flexibility problem. The model construction problem is that the only final criterion for model fit is that the model works. Without an algorithm for model construction, the researcher may search forever for an adequate model, either because (*a*) the situation is so complex or unclear that it defies the modeler's intuitive attempts; or (*b*) the theory is incorrect—*cannot* adequately model the situation, even given perfect situational understanding. Thus, failure to find a model that works does not indict the theory, so the theory can never be rejected on the basis of empirical evidence. The flexibility problem is that the theory may be so rich that literally *anything* can be modeled: The theory, as opposed to any particular model, has no empirical import.

Examples of these problems can be stated in terms of the set-of-laws chapters of this book. Practical measurement limitations prevent users of Woelfel's (Chapter 3) approach from "exhaustively" depicting cognitive space and determining the whole range of effects any message might have. Therefore, any empirical failure of prediction might be "explained" by reference to an unmodeled mass or force (which might indeed exist, as did planets like Uranus that produced motions in other planets apparently disconfirming Newton's laws): The problems of model construction and flexibility reinforce one another here. It is hard to imagine a cognitive phenomenon that could not be explained or modeled by the advocates of "information processing" (e.g., Cappella and Folger, Chapter 5). As Anderson (1976) points out, the necessity for combinations of structure and processing assumptions allows almost any structure or process, combined with an appropriate counterpart, to "explain flexibly" practically any empirical findings. Finally, the constructivist position of O'Keefe (Chapter 4) is itself immensely complex, both in the range of possible perceptions of any given research situation or stimulus it allows, and in the range of integrative mechanisms it recognizes (cf. Kaplan & Crockett, 1968). In his study, O'Keefe did find predicted differences in attitude–behavior consistency between subjects of low versus high cognitive development; but both groups produced very high attitude–behavior correlations so that high attitude–behavior consistency is not, in itself, impossible for *any* level of cognitive development.

Causal process theories seem in many ways to be a subtype of set-of-laws theories. Related on one level to realistic philosophies of science (Harré &

Madden, 1975) and on another, more direct level to path analytic methodology (Blalock, 1971), they too accept a modeling approach to theory testing, but one that places special emphasis on the underlying processes explaining inter-variable relationships. In its most usual form, this concern is translated into a search for a proper causal structure among variables, with special reference to indirect and spurious causation and to causal direction. Spurious causation involves a common causal antecedent of two variables; indirect causation in-volves an intervening variable, causing one variable and caused by the other. This approach organizes relationships between variables by building causal models that stipulate whether any given relationship is direct, mediated, or spuriously dependent upon unmeasured or other measured variables. Correlative to the two problems of set-of-laws theories, is the *identification* problem for causal process theories. If we assume too many direct causal links among variables, or stipulate certain prohibited interwoven patterns of causation, our model will be underidentified: The relative strength and even the existence of many causal paths will be undeterminable by *any* empirical evidence. The challenge to the causal theorist is to construct, implement, and argue for the validity of powerful overidentifying restrictions on the model, allowing the accumulation of empirical support. In Chapters 6 and 7, respectively, Seibold, and Poole and Hunter, use constancy of structure and concatenation of process over time to allow empirical test of their theories.

We believe that knowledge of these types of theories, with their generality of form and problems, allows the construction of rigorous theories and the immediate location of key problem areas in the theory. But a closer look at each theory proposed in the following chapters now seems called for.

Axiomatic Theory: Dean Hewes

Hewes set out specifically to construct an axiomatic theory to deal with message–attitude–behavior relationships. Moreover, his theory describes the determination of behavior as a stochastic process—an approach demanding difficult and nonintuitive mathematical description. Nevertheless, his final result seems to have been quite successful, and his account of it very clear. We will concentrate on three central aspects of Hewes' paradigm: his description of behavior and expectations, his stability matrix and the process it describes, and his account of message effects.

Hewes assumes that any single instance of behavior is the outcome or instantiation of a stochastic variable: That is, if we put the same person in an identical situational context 100 times, his behavior will vary over a range of possibilities; therefore, we cannot explain any single instance of behavior, but only the probability that any single possibility will actually occur. Like Fish-bein, Hewes identifies a single intervening variable to "determine" behavioral probability, but calls the variable *behavioral expectation*, thereby taking seriously Fishbein's definition of intention (cited earlier) as the subjective probability of behavior. We should note here that for Hewes, the behavioral "range of possibilities" is discrete and finite: There are a limited and specific number of distinct possible behaviors, each with some actual probability (possible zero) *and* with some perceived probability or expectation level.

Our expectations naturally change over time, even without any environmental influence, says Hewes, so he introduces a stability matrix **S** to describe the pattern of such changes. **S** resembles a traditional marker chain matrix to govern expectations; like such a matrix, it may be empirically determined by analyzing how peoples' expectation distributions change. **S** is not a subjective matrix—it fits real change, not subjects' perceptions of how their expectations change. The concept of **S** as describing "change patterns" is difficult and unfamiliar, but is very important. On this account, whereas expectations are almost never static, patterns of change in expectation, from one act to another, *are* static apart from environmental effects.

But typically the environment does have an influence on behavior—such influences include the effects of communications. To represent such effects, Hewes uses two notions. The first is his (diagonal) matrix of *retention parameters*. Each retention parameter relates to a particular behavior option and governs the stability of change patterns involving change *away* from that option. That is, some particular behaviors are inherently "tractable to direction"— environmental influences can powerfully affect the directions in which our expectations shift from such behaviors. But the external influences themselves are described in an *environmental cue matrix* **C**. **C** can be thought of as the **S** matrix suggested by the environment—that is, it is the set of regular change-of-expectation patterns we would observe if we slavishly followed the environment's directions and suggestions. The main rule of combination, and the empirically significant central proposition for this theory is given in Axiom 2: A new **S** matrix is generated, at each transition time, as the weighted (by *M*) sum of the old **S** and **C**. We will discuss this axiom in depth.

Using that rule, and other axioms, Hewes derives a variety of formal and informal theorems, which explain certain standard findings in the attitude— behavior literature. He also presents the results of an empirical study of the model, in which a series of strenuous statistical tests produced mixed but generally favorable results. More impressive than the empirical support, though, is the careful and rigorous design and justification of this model. It is typical for stochastic modelers to use a standard well-known process description with no particular relation to a theory, fit it to data, and then attempt to draw from the resulting parameter estimates, and other results, a shaky conceptual relevance. (The Markov chain is the object of special abuse by such practitioners.) Hewes has taken a precisely opposite tack: Working from the empirical finding that behavioral data do not conform to a first-order stationary Markov process, he creates a unique model (within our knowledge) that reflects in its structure a theoretical understanding of the crucial processes of behavior determination and of the reasons the Markov chain failed. Hewes' model is a meaningful, purposeful adaptation and rigorous exposition of his stochastic axiomatic theory.

But the model also possesses, we believe, two flaws. One is in the idea that behavior is (stochastically) determined by behavioral expectations. While expectations may predict behavior adequately, they seem inadequate conceptually to *explain* it. One does not act because he expects to; rather, he expects accurately to act because intention or habit or situational constraint has predetermined, in part, his future behavioral choice. So, even if the model works, it may give us no clear understanding of people's reasons for behaving as they do.

The second weakness in the model concerns its representation of externally induced change. Hewes' model is aimed quite precisely at accounting for the nonstationarity of behavior observed in past stochastic research, but its fit to this aim renders it rather contrary to common sense. We generally think of messages and other influences as suggesting optimal or desired courses of behavior, and not as suggesting desired patterns for changing our behavior from one course to another—yet the latter is the description given in Hewes' model. Moreover, the outcome of this model choice is controversial, as is best shown in the context of the following thought-experiment (which is not too unlike several actual attitude-change experiments): Subjects receive a message suggesting a particular course of behavior. After that they receive no relevant external information at all. Hewes' model predicts, generally, that expectations and behavior will continue slowly changing, in the direction advocated, long after the message is received, and that they will never change back toward original, habit-bound values. Hewes cites evidence supporting this view for the attitude-change context, but seemingly broader evidence favoring the *decay* of message effects exists and is supplemented by the work and review of Poole and Hunter (Chapter 7) in this volume. Despite these possible problems, Hewes' work fully conveys the strength of axiomatic theory construction in its power and rigor.

Set-of-Law Theories

Joseph Woelfel

Woelfel's article describes the rationale, development, and findings of an extensive and innovative program of research and theorizing undertaken by him and his colleagues (Danes, Hunter, & Woelfel, 1978; Saltiel & Woelfel, 1975; Woelfel & Danes, 1979; Woelfel, 1971; Woelfel & Saltiel, 1974) Woelfel's rationale for his approach centers on the notions of precision and continuity of measurement, on the use of multidimensional space as a representation for cognitive relationships and processes, and on theoretical principles governing cognitive change in such spaces.

For Woelfel, a prerequisite to progress in social science is an adequate conceptual system. The scheme we use to describe attitudinal or other psychological phenomena places limits on what can be described, as an observed result or a theoretical prediction. In particular, our traditional emphasis on categorical schemes for the conception and measurement of attitudes and behaviors lead us to gross descriptions of their relationship: Behaviors are "attitude-relevant" or not; attitudes and behaviors are "evaluatively consistent" or not, depending on the similarity of their signs. More generally, focusing on the description of attitude objects and behaviors rather than on the *relationships* among these variables, leads to a considerable decrease in the precision with which we can describe those relationships and changes in them. Woelfel views present social scientific conceptual and measurement schemes in precise analogy to pre-Galilean physics: A perspectival breakthrough is a necessary precondition to meaningful empirical progress.

Both his early empirical results and his quest for conceptual and methodological precision lead Woelfel to adopt the real number system as a descriptive system, and to use it to describe psychological similarity or difference between objects as distance between those objects. Standard psychometric techniques are adapted by Woelfel to elicit estimates of perceived difference or distance between pairs of objects; these estimates are then analyzed using a special variant (the Galileo system) of the highly developed psychometric device of multidimensional scaling (MDS). The output of MDS is a redescription of the various objects in terms of their location (on coordinate axes) in a sort of "psychological space," through which objects may "move" as our conceptions of them change.

The similarity of this psychological space to the physical space of Galileo and Newton led Woelfel to use the concepts and equations of Newtonian physical theories as models for an approach to message-induced cognitive change. He proposed that the total amount of information a person has about a concept functions analogously to "inertial mass," with greater mass implying that the concept is more resistant to message-induced attitude (or other cognitive) change. This hypothesis has received impressive empirical support (e.g., Danes *et al.*, 1978). In addition, Woelfel suggests that persuasive messages act as forces on the concepts to which they refer, producing changes in psychological space in ways that resemble physical forces in rules of combination. Of course, Woelfel does not hold that the system of Newtonian laws applies isomorphically to psychological phenomena; a highly persuasive argument for his system is that its precision and flexibility of psychological representation allow and facilitate the discovery of empirical laws of psychological change.

The position espoused here by Woelfel is a genuine innovation in social science, and its suggestiveness and beauty are of great value. In addition, its flexibility allows for considerable creativity in the representation of messages and attitude change phenomena (Craig, 1974; Marlier, 1974). However, the general status of multidimensional space as an isomorphic and sufficient description of cognitions and messages is still very controversial. For one thing, it is not clear that distances in "psychological space" can capture the range of possible meanings and arguments: A message to a prospective bridegroom *C*, "You can't marry *A*—she's already married to *B*," seems incompatible with any spacial representation involving *A*, *B*, and *C* (or even more concepts as well). "Married to" is a *type of relation* between *A* and *B*, and cannot be represented using an essentially different type of relation, similarity or perceived "closeness (but the empirical force of this logical objection is as yet undetermined)." More seriously, Craig (1976) tested a basic presumption of the spacial model—that motion in the space involves general change of position relative to other concepts in the space—and found evidence which challenged the spacial model. Although a number of alternative accounts for his findings exist (as he reports), his explanation itself has not been reevaluated empirically. But whether psychological space is a general model for psychological reality, or is merely a useful paramorphic tool for the understanding of some cognitive and communicative processes, Woelfel's arguments and description reward close study.

Daniel O'Keefe

O'Keefe's chapter is firmly rooted in the theoretical and research paradigm of constructivism (Delia, 1977; Kelly, 1955). Basic to this approach is the principle that people act in an interpreted world, and interpretation is accomplished by applying a structure of personal constructs to distinguish among and bring meaning to phenomena. Constructs are conceptual dimensions or contrasts; we develop beliefs about objects by construing them along these dimensions.

Most constructivist research has focused on developmental differences in construct systems and their effects. People's construct systems change systematically, in complexity and organization, as the people grow in age and experience; changes in our systems for construing other people have been shown to bring with them changes in communicative abilities and other social cognitions. One locus of developmental change is the significance and function of evaluative attitudes. At early levels of development, attitude is a primary mode of cognitive integration—of relating and resolving contradictions among beliefs. But the importance of attitude as an integrative scheme declines with growth in age and experience (O'Keefe reviews a body of literature supporting this contention).

For the constructivist position, behavior is based on beliefs, not in terms of any simple mathematical function, but in terms of the content of each belief as employed in the process of deciding to behave. But for "attitude-relevant" behaviors, the affective value implicit in each relevant belief ought to have some impact on behavior. More importantly, where general attitude underlies and organizes a pattern of beliefs, attitude ought to be a strong determinant of behavior. O'Keefe argues that attitude most clearly underlies and organizes beliefs for persons low in cognitive development; attitude ought to be especially effective as a predictor of behavior for such persons. The research findings he reports powerfully support this argument: less cognitively complex persons (in the interpersonal domain) tended to behave in a much more attitudinally consistent manner than highly complex (i.e., more developed) persons, with respective attitude–behavioral intention correlations of .95 and .75 for a multiact intention index. This finding is consistent with supporting analyses of particular behaviors, and of the relative roles of attitude and net belief positivity.

O'Keefe's arguments and findings represent strong support for the discovery of a new *mediator* of attitude–belief consistency: cognitive development, or complexity. This finding is especially interesting because it clashes in a sense with findings supportive of other mediators such as attitude stability. Stability (Schwartz, 1978) seems to increase attitude–behavior consistency; yet O'Keefe's findings and his literature review suggest that complexity both increases stability and decreases consistency. Of course, no contradiction is implied by these findings; on the contrary, the *joint* study of complexity and attitude "validity" (as defined earlier) might be extremely profitable.

O'Keefe's chapter is both persuasive and suggestive in its arguments, its methods, and the support it arrays for its conclusions. Particularly provocative is its implication that the *way* in which behavior is determined may change across developmental levels. As attitude's integrative function shrinks, people combine and reconcile their beliefs in new ways; the result may be both a different model of behavior determination, and a different meaning for the phrase, "attitude-relevant behavior." Indeed, the central limitation we see to this chapter rests on our desire to know more about the determination of behavior, at any developmental level, in O'Keefe's view. The "immediate determinants of behavior are context-relevant beliefs [p. 10]" on that view; then why does attitude relate *more* strongly to intention than to an index of belief affectivity, for subjects low in complexity, and equally strongly, for highly complex subjects. (Of course, O'Keefe clearly indicates that the index in question does not capture the content or context-relevance of beliefs [p. 45]?) The problem is that the relationships among attitudes, as one belief or as an integrative mechanism, beliefs, and intentions are left unclear, even for specifically "attitude-relevant behaviors." Whereas complexity fairly clearly affects the *strength* of the attitude–behavior relationship, the effects of that mediator on the *processes* underlying the relationship beg for further research.

Capella and Folger

In a rather unusual approach to the problem of attitude–behavior consistency, Cappella and Folger examine presently available evidence on cognitive organization and processing, highlighting the implications of information-processing theory and experimentation for relations among messages, attitudes, and behaviors. As they note, many social psychological theories having relevance to the attitude–behavior question are based on loose or implicit conceptions of cognitive structure and processing. An explicit cognitive focus ought, then, to provide at least a firmer and more formal backdrop for such theorizing by attitude–behavior theorists. Moreover, they make some reference to an argument central to the human information-processing paradigm—an interdisciplinary perspective to which they relate their own effort. Information processing theorists argue that the most important problem facing social scientists is, not (empirical) theory demonstration, but theory development (Miller, 1978). In their view, no understandings of human cognition and behavior current today are clearly *sufficient* to explain behavior, in terms of their internal consistency, realism of processing subassumptions, and generality. Such theorists value work in artificial intelligence because it provides evidence that the theories it adumbrates are at least *possibly* true, since they are workable. Whereas Cappella and Folger do not attempt to produce a program instantiating their theory, they are unusually sensitive to the possibility of fit among the various conceptions they advance to describe cognitive processes and structures, as well as to the empirical evidence for the truth of those conceptions.

Cappella and Folger separate their basic discussion into two parts, one dealing with storage of information in long-term memory, and the second with retrieval of information from long-term memory. The first part of their discussion concerns the structure of memory, which can be described as a network of (meaningful rather than associative) relations among concepts, split into episodic and semantic memory. Attribution of a network structure to memory implies that all the information we have about, for example, a concept, can be represented as relations, or analogously as propositions, involving the concept in question with other concepts or events. Cappella and Folger argue that this view of memory allows us to determine the affective value of any object of memory, as a relatively simple function of the affective values of concepts to which it is connected. Attitude, then, is a function of a network of propositions or beliefs in memory. (It is obvious that, taken as a fully general position, this view cannot stand alone—if the affective value of every concept is a function of the affective values of all other concepts and has no independent existence in memory, then one could never "determine" his attitude toward anything (without the endless solution of equation systems).) But Cappella and Folger use the idea of informational determination of attitude only to deal with situationally cued objects, toward attitudes that vary with situations. Presumably the objects to which these situationally cued objects are tied in memory have standard or context-neutral attitude values from which cued values are derived. The other idea about memory structure, which Cappella and Folger emphasize, is the distinction between episodic and semantic memory. Episodic memory is of experiences and events, specific in space and time; semantic memory is of general information, not directly tied to particular biographical incidents. Evidence is presented that episodic memory is organized and "tagged" or labelled for future recall by situation, so that our memory of an object will be different if we recall a different set of situations in which it was involved.

People act on the information at their disposal at the time of action, argue Cappella and Folger; but what is at their disposal, or in other words can be retrieved from memory, depends on the present situational cues that guide the retrieval process. Thus, the stock of information we use when deciding to act or not includes both semantic information—relevant to the act more or less by definition—and episodic information, cued by the particular past situations and experiences that the present decision brings to mind. On this general ground, Cappella and Folger can explain some attitude–behavior and cross-behavior inconsistency: If, when the attitudinal or behavioral responses are made, the situations and their relevant cues differ, so does the information remembered and acted upon. But Cappella and Folger go beyond the relatively bare notion of situational cues to consider the decision process in some detail. For them, people decide to act by evaluating the goal of action in general, then generating and evaluating various strings of subacts which will let them reach that goal. A major criterion for evaluating goals and subacts is affective value: we will act only if we value the goal and can fashion an acceptable plan for achieving it.

The authors use their perspective to list the various possible grounds of attitude–behavior (in)consistency. Moreover, they draw several rather unusual implications for message construction by describing the sort of message-construction strategies that most probably should stimulate the memory process in such a way as to facilitate a favorable decision about action. We regard their chapter as ground-breaking work of very high quality and great suggestiveness. As the idea of information processing develops in appeal and sophisticated usage within the attitude–behavior literature, we predict that the ideas Cappella and Folger present will become central to research interest.

Our caveats to the Cappella–Folger perspective mainly have to do with what is also one of its strong points: the particular ways in which attitude theories are made relevant to the information-processing theory. For instance, the application of linear and quasi-linear models to evaluate the attitudinal implications seems dubitable: Those models were developed to describe either experimental results stimulated by relatively short, clearly structured messages, or to the output of requested memory "dumps," where memory was described as an experimental requirement. It is not clear that such models apply to relatively raw memory structures. Similarly, the emphasis on contextual evaluation processes that "produce" attitudes in each new situation, seem to vitiate the distinction between "valid" and "invalid" attitudes described previously, which has demonstrated significance as a mediator of attitude–behavior consistency. These problems do not seem insurmountable or essential: Whatever its detailèd final substructure, the perspective presented in this chapter seems clearly worthy of further research attention.

Causal Process Theories

David Seibold

The first exemplar of causal process theory in this book lies in Chapter 6 by Seibold. His chapter represents a reintegration, after considerable research, of a point of view first articulated in 1975 (Seibold, 1975). As it now stands, the theory is enormously complex and interwoven; in this summary we can only attempt to present its essential structure.

Basic to the theory is a distinction between verbal reports and behaviors. Verbal reports are questionnaire answers that reveal (or indicate) some (but apparently not all) of the underlying psychological states determining behavior. Behavior occurs outside the verbal report situation, and, although the underlying states determine it, they do so in ways that can vary according to the superstructure of the theory.

Central to the superstructure of the theory is a conception of personal control or satisfaction. Almost by definition, people act to maximize control; but in doing so, they may act in accord with (or as determined by) one of several different directive forces. *Which* directive force governs behavior is determined by the *locus of control*, which may be personal, social, or situational (thus, it is a discrete trichotomous variable). People act according to that "directive force" (or locus of control category) that maximizes "personal control" (the central drive, not the locus of control category); which directive force or category that will be, depends on a number of factors.

Each directive force can facilitate or hinder any given behavior, more or less intensely—situations make the behavior difficult or difficult to avoid, or social norms may favor or disapprove of the behavior. If the various directive forces are consistent (all facilitating or all hindering behavior), the person will appear to himself to act according to personal directive forces; if not, the determinants of locus of control are unclear (with one exception to be mentioned). One sort of personal directive force is an individuals' personal normative beliefs; another, and the critical one, is *attitude* or underlying attitude. The most important part of Seibold's theoretic substructure, and the focus of his research, is his tricomponential approach to attitude.

Underlying attitude is unmeasureable but has three measureable components; desirability (an affectively oriented variable), likelihood (belief that an act will have valued consequences), and intention (a generalized self-perceived propensity to act). All three of these components have behavior as their target—they are components of "attitude toward the act," so to speak. Underlying attitude can be thought of as a second-order factor underlying these component dimensions, or as a principle of consistency among the components insofar as they are consistent. Each component is a causal function of attitude, and behavior, in turn, is a causal function of these three components (when, presumably, they are under the sway of the personal directive force). The central causal process thesis of Seibold's position is that the three components are equivalent in causal priority—no one causes any other, but relationships among them are a result of common causation by unmeasured attitude. This thesis has support, notably in Seibold and McPhee (1979), Bagozzi (1978), and Bentler and Speckart (1979).

The three components have impact on behavior only contingently. Seibold lists six moderators of causal force: informational base, salience, ease of control, consistency among components, temporal stability, and correspondence in level of generality. Unfavorable levels of moderator variables may lead another directive force to "hold sway" over behavior (this is the exception already mentioned).

The evidence Seibold arrays for his theory is of two general sorts. The evidence for the tricomponential view of attitude is broad and quite convincing. The evidence cited makes tricomponential consistency a very likely model for causal interrelations among likelihood, desirability, and intention; and evidence exists of a strong link from intention to behavior, and of more tenuous behavioral links from desirability and likelihood. On the other hand, the evidence adduced to cast this view within a general framework of antecedent and moderator variables seems somewhat weaker. It seems clear that many of those variables are relevant to attitude–behavior relations, but the exact structure of, or reason for, that relevance remains unclear, in part due to the complexity and nascent character of his formulation.

Seibold himself characterizes it as evolving rather than finished, and his purpose is to place the range of relevant nonattitudinal variables within a causal process framework, rather than to deduce tightly all the relations among moderator and other variables. Even given the relations that are clearly expected among variables, a rigorous exploration that took into account causation among moderator variables, and from main theoretical variables to moderators, would require statistical methods and programs far more sophisticated than those available to social researchers today. What Seibold provides here is strong support for the tricomponential approach to attitude, and a synthetic foundation for further research into conditions for attitudinal effects on behavior.

Poole and Hunter

Poole and Hunter present and test a causal process theory that is quite different, in theory and method, from that of Seibold. Their theory must be explained in terms of key notions of an attitude hierarchy and an information-processing model of attitude influence.

For these authors, at least some psychological objects have meaning for people primarily within the context of a hierarchy of related objects. Objects in the hierarchy are less general or less abstract than those above them, and are related to objects directly above them be generalization or logical inclusion—they are members or parts or types of the upper objects in the hierarchy. As the authors note, substantial research indicates that logical deduction of beliefs does occur in such hierarchies; if someone thinks the federal government is inefficient, he is likely to conclude that its departments and agencies are inefficient as well. Poole and Hunter (Chapter 7) explore the correlative notion that *logical* generalization of attitudes takes place as well: Substitute "good" or "bad" for "inefficient" in the above example. And the notion of logical generalization is key: Attitude toward an object does not influence attitudes toward more general objects, or even equally general objects. Interattitude influence flows *down* the hierarchy only. Moreover, such generalization does not "skip levels"; interattitude influence from a very general object to a very specific one is mediated by attitudes at "intermediate" hierarchial levels. This precise patterning of influence in the attitude hierarchy constitutes the "causal process" central to the theory.

The functional form describing this causal process is a linear discrepancy or "information-processing model" of attitude change. According to this model, change in an attitude, in the simplest case, is a constant proportion of the difference between the given attitude and another that influences it. The "constant proportionality" idea implies that an attitude in a hierarchy will move toward, and eventually equal, the one just above it; and that, over any particular time interval, attitude change will be greatest if the initial difference between the given attitude and the one just above it is very large.

To this model of intrahierarchy processing is added a *message* model: People may change their attitudes because they receive a persuasive message recommending a different attitude. This model too is a linear discrepancy model—the amount of message-induced change is proportional to the amount of difference between present and recommended attitude. In the original article proposing this set of models, Hunter, Levine, and Sayers (1976) suggested that the personality traits of dogmatism and persuasability could be thought of as related to the proportionality constants of the internal change and message models, respectively. But this should not be taken to indicate that hierarchial models characterize all attitude interrelations; Poole and Hunter state that hierarchy is only one possible attitude structure, and researchers should provide evidence that a hierarchy exists before using the models describing hierarchical change.

Poole and Hunter used what seem to us to be extremely thorough and sophisticated methods to test the model of attitude change posited here. They actually developed a set of models based on different assumptions about the type and order of processing a person undertakes on various occasions (described in full in Poole, 1976). Among the strengths of their methodology were care in dealing with and attempting to eliminate sampling error from matrices derived from the raw data, their recognition of extratheoretic sources of model change, their methodological modifications to deal with these (described under "Complications of the Hierarchical Model"), and the strict correspondence between theory and model constraints imposed in testing the model.

The authors link this discussion of attitude change directly to the attitude—behavior literature by focusing on the central idea of attitude specificity. On any single occasion, people behave toward one particular object, so that a specific attitude toward that object should be most closely related to behavior; Poole and Hunter persuasively review the research favoring this view. However, we feel their enthusiasm for specific attitudes should be tempered: People can act with reference to *general* objects, as when a person pays bills on a particular day, or votes for Democrats, and not some particular candidate, by voting a straight ticket. Moreover, they step into controversy by seeming to assume that attitudes toward *acts* are logically related to attitudes toward objects: logically, acts never fall under logical inclusion relations with their objects. They skirt this problem by looking at objects, within situational contexts, toward which behavior is actually directed (as in their Figure 7.2), but such situated objects seem particularly unlikely to fall under the influence of a simple hierarchy: I strongly approve of "a 16-ounce medium-rare steak," but cannot stomach "a 16-ounce medium-rare steak *now*." Of course, as they note, hierarchies of *acts* may exist to which their model clearly would apply. Poole and Hunter do apply their attitude-change model skillfully to the discussion of message effects on behavior, and draw two central conclusions: Messages directed at specific attitude objects will have the greatest immediate behavioral consequences, but such changes are likely to decay rapidly; messages directed at more general objects will be likely to have a long-term, but delayed and often limited, impact on behavior.

We should note two caveats to this research; the first is methodological, the second more substantive. Poole and Hunter, predicting correlations among a whole range of attitudes at different times (as well as generally examining mean values of attitudes at different times, in other writings), use broad-based tests of the accuracy of their model.

It would be useful to have available, in addition, tests specifically designed to measure two key assumptions of the hierarchy theory: that message-induced attitude changes at the bottom of the hierarchy do not generalize immediately upward, and that changes induced at the top of the hierarchy reach the bottom only by passing through intermediate levels. The tests actually used surely would have detected gross violations of these assumptions, but their sensitivity to each assumption seems likely to have been rather limited.

Second, the hierarchical image itself seems oddly connected to the information-processing model of attitude change. As Sally Jackson has noted (personal communication), the Poole–Hunter model entails the destruction of affective differentiation throughout the hierarchy: Over time, all attitudes in the hierarchy become approximately equal to the one at the top (messages may temporarily reverse such a trend). If I hate vegetables, eventually I will grow to hate corn. But if I really like corn, such a theory seems implausible: I should, it seems, be able to regard corn as a distinctive or unusual vegetable, one to which I will not generalize my hatred. Poole and Hunter would presumably reply that such a case is one either of multiple, overlapping hierarchies, or a nonhierarchical structure. But such breakdowns of simple hierarchy seem most likely to occur whenever an attitude is very different from the one just above it in the hierarchy; yet in just such cases the information-processing model predicts the greatest short-term decay in the lower-level attitude. Thus the information-processing model seems unsuited to cases where the simple hierarchy idea is approximately true, since it predicts maximum change in concepts over which hierarchy is likely to have least sway. This objection resembles Whittaker's (1967) caveat to the information-processing model: It works only when the discrepancy being dealt with is quite limited in size. And in an earlier draft of this chapter, Poole and Hunter cited Whittaker's finding as a limit to the scope of their model. But these criticisms should not obscure the innovative power of the authors' synthesis of theory, method, and data; the chapter constitutes a major advance in our understanding of attitudinal phenomena and their relations to behavior and messages.

Contributions to Conceptualization

Robert Craig

Craig advocates an alternative method for the study of attitude–behavior relationships. He begins by identifying three problems with the more usual social–scientific approach to attitude–behavior (in)consistency: Simple intuitive attempts by researchers to match a behavior with the attitude to which it is relevant are unsystematic and liable to failure; more refined attempts to solve this problem using scaling techniques are still intuitively based, and often assume that subjects have particular cognitive structures; and the results of attitude–behavior studies are inadequate because they fail to reveal *why* a given behavior is (in)consistent with attitude toward its target.

These problems can be alleviated, Craig argues, by the systematic investigation of accounts in the sense of Harré and Secord (1973). This method involves inducing the subject to justify an action, or an evaluative attitude which he holds. Such a justification will often involve reference to another or higher-order attitudes, for which a further account is sought. The series of accounts generated should indicate the validity of an attitude–behavior link, if it exists, give some indication of the true cognitive structure in which the attitude or behavior of interest is embedded, and provide clues about *why* consistency or inconsistency is present.

Craig seems to regard this method as, not a replacement for, but a necessary supplement to, "traditional" methods for studying attitude–behavior consistency. Craig himself notes limits to this method in the limited consciousness subjects have of their own cognitive and affective processes, in the idiosyncratic nature of accounts which may fail to reveal important and meaningful intersubject differences, and in the necessity for researchers to interpret and formalize even the most complete and revealing account data when generating new theory or research. Nevertheless, the investigation of accounts is presented as a method that can clearly enrich and validate research generated in nearly all theoretical traditions. In particular, the cognitive structuring it reveals would seem valuable to researchers like Poole and Hunter, who study processes within structures, but who therefore need prior validating evidence that a particular structure is generally present.

We regard Craig's argument as careful, well balanced, and compelling, and our only caveat would be to his advocacy of the study of purely *justificatory* accounts. Asking people to justify attitudes or acts may introduce an excessive rational and socially adapted flavor to the results. In the attempt to make their actions seem reasonable, subjects may neglect the emotional or processual elements, which are possibly causes of action, but rarely reasons for acting. So the collection of justifications might be supplemented by attention to deep *descriptions* of attitude objects and of decision and behavior processes. Such descriptions might be especially likely to reveal the difference between, for example, preexisting attitudes and attitudes deductively derived "on the spot."

T. J. Larkin

In Larkin's Chapter 9, he extends the Wittgensteinian position on meaning to the concepts of intention and attitude. Briefly, Wittgenstein (1953) argues that knowing the meaning of a word is not a matter of mentally "having" an image or conception that corresponds to the word—having such an image or conception is neither necessary nor sufficient for correctly understanding and using the word. We know a word's meaning if and only if we can respond to it correctly and use it correctly in social interaction—the occurrence or possession of some sensed image or state is entirely beside the point. Wittgenstein analyzes numerous examples to show that meaning involves, and can involve, nothing beyond this given the nature of language as a social institution.

After expounding Wittgenstein's position on meaning, Larkin applies similar reasoning to the concepts of attitude and intention. Basically, the argument for intention is that intending is a social act with social significance. It could not have that significance if it were purely or essentially a matter of a private psychological state—we could not consider *intentional* misconduct particularly blameworthy or illegal if having an intention was, essentially, equivalent to a private psychological state. On the contrary, the criteria of having an intention are essentially public—a socially competent person, in a situation where his abilities and will are not unnaturally restricted, can act intentionally, and typically does; any accompanying mental phenomena should be regarded as strictly derivative.

A similar stand can be taken on the topic of attitude. We learn, through social interaction, what having a positive or negative attitude is, and we simultaneously learn the functions of "having an attitude" in social discourse (Larkin lists several). To claim to hate the United Way, yet still volunteer to collect money in its service, is almost a self-contradiction; if we cannot account for such a behavior, we are thought to be either insane or ignorant of the meaning of a negative attitude.

Larkin applies this position to criticize the typical approach to research on attitudes and behaviors. If we try to purify our measures of attitude and intention by removing them from the interactive context and other categories of meaningful social interaction, we also remove them from the source of their essential significance. If we ask subjects about their attitudes in a way that can make no direct sense to them, they will try to invent an interpretation of the questions to guide their answers, by analogy or by guesswork. Our questionnaires thus typically generate a contaminated version of information readily available and regularly used in everyday life.

Philosophers influenced by Wittgenstein have mounted broad-ranging attacks on empirical social science, so to reply in depth to his philosophical position would involve opening issues far beyond the scope of this review. We have two comments: First, the problems Larkin raises seem to have been recognized by researchers at some level, and the advocacy of more valid research methods by, for example, Schuman and Johnson (1976) is in part a response to such problems. Second, we should note that an attitude's meaning and social significance do not necessarily exhaust its consequences. Empiricists such as Daniel Katz and philosophers such as Nietzsche have noted the human tendency to subvert learned structures of thought and feeling to ends that emerge in social interaction only in disguised and distorted forms. To assume that social form exhausts reality is to underestimate the complexity of human behavior.

Fontes, Shelby, and O'Connor

Fontes, Shelby, and O'Connor, in Chapter 10, argue for the viability of structural–functional theory as a base for the analysis of attitude–behavior relationships. Structural–functional theories are systems theories, different from the classical theory types previously discussed in that they are rooted in an approximate isomorphism of reality to a closed and reflexively defined system of concepts. Structural–functional theories are distinctive in the pattern of concepts they identify: an ultimate goal-state G, functions f_i, which are necessary and collectively sufficient for the attainment or preservation of G, and traits t_i, which are mechanisms contributing to and patterned by the functions. All three concepts have ranges of acceptable operation–operation of a t_i, or deviation of an f_i, outside these ranges, threaten or destroy G. The system explains phenomena on the assumption that the phenomena are patterned so that the traits (physical mechanisms) contribute to the functions (subgoals) in order, and in just such a way as, to attain or maintain G at a prescribed or desired level.

Although the example given by Fontes *et al.* is one of a message *sender* rather than of a receiver as is more common throughout this book, it is fairly straightforward to describe a structural–functional receiver model. Let the goal G be "low psychological tension"; let one function require for that goal-state be "high perceived consistency"; let one trait contributing to that function be "evaluative consistency of attitudes and behaviors." Then, if we can assume that a person adjusts his attitudes and behaviors to maintain or attain G, we can predict that, within a certain range and subject to the substitutability of traits under the consistency function, a person's attitudes will be consistent with his or her behaviors. Attitude–behavior inconsistency could be explained either by showing that the goal-state had been abandoned, or that the trait's range of acceptable deviation had expanded, or that another trait (e.g., one of the developmentally higher integrative mechanisms of O'Keefe's chapter) had been substituted by the person to achieve psychological consistency. The potential of such models seems bright, but as Fontes *et al.* note, none as yet has been substantiated as an explanation of attitude–behavior relations.

Theory and Quantitative Relationships: Methods

Many of the following chapters are complex and innovative in theoretical and operational methodology—they use mathematics to treat issues relevant to message–attitude–behavior relations in rather unusual ways. But mathematical forms are not mere instruments in these articles—they exert a return impact on the theoretical presumptions they embody. Several of the authors (Woelfel, Hewes, Poole and Hunter) seem committed to certain operational forms for reasons they discuss; others (Seibold, O'Keefe) use methods that have some history of application with "established" attitude–behavior theories. Rather than join the debate about the best or most appropriate mathematical form, we shall discuss some of the impacts of method on theory that appear repeatedly throughout the book.

There are at least three important consequences that follow from an individual's choice of methodology. These choices powerfully influence the choice and array of theoretic variables, the theorist's conception of time and change, and the treatment of imprecision of fit or error.

One's choice of methodologies influences the particular characterization given to the structure of messages, attitude, and behaviors. A methodology consists of an *operation* performed on *states* or sets of variables. An operation can consist of a simple, uniform transformation yielding one set of states from the same set of variables at an earlier time, or a rule of combination, which yields values on some new set of variables. Or, finally, these two modes of operation can be combined in various ways yielding different transformational modes allowing for different descriptive states—that is, different types and arrays of variables.

Just as methodological choices influence the structure of variables in a theory, they also have substantial impact on the ways in which time and change are dealt with by theorists. Time has been conceived of in at least two ways within this volume. First, several theorists present time as a sequence of points at which the system reaches equilibrium by rapid cognitive processing. The methods used to analyze data, and the operations used to predict attitudes and behavior, thus may depend primarily on other variables at the same point in time. The second orientation assumed by theorists is that time-points are stages in a dynamic development, possibly toward a distant equilibrium. Prediction of attitudes and behavior thus depends on operating on past states and projecting the trajectory of the dynamic forward to the time-point of prediction.

The third impact of methodology on theorizing concerns the conception within theories of theory-relevant error. Errors in prediction and control are often ignored by theorists, but a powerful theory should be capable of improvement when its errors are interpreted within a theoretical perspective. Errors can be dealt with by treating them as an incomplete closure of the theoretic system, incorrect specification of relationships between variables in correct construction of operators, incorrect *sequencing* of theoretical operations, or measurement inadequacies.

Only four of the authors specify and implement methodological operations to accompany their theories. Hewes, Seibold, Poole and Hunter, and Woelfel unite theory and methodology in such a manner that they fall within the categories of this discussion.

Hewes' chapter, in dealing with probabilistic expectations as determinants of behavior, adopts a Markov chain methodology by considering how message reception might theoretically impact Markov attitude processes. He describes cognition as consisting of two components: behavioral expectations and a Markov transformational operator governing *changes* in expectations. Then the impact of messages on cognition is calculated using a second-order transformation which changes the prior, cognitive transformation operator. That is, messages do not change expectations, but change the habitual change patterns of expectations. His theory is like Seibold's in the complexity of its assumptions about time: Messages have their full impact immediately at the upper level of his model, but have a gradual and diminishing impact at the lower level. Since his model is stochastic, he can ignore errors of prediction for individual cases, whereas at a distributional or population level, he interprets discrepancies from his model as indicative of parameter differences between populations. This interpretation is not an empty change of theory to match data; instead, it is a move in the direction of the parametric characterization of populations.

Seibold's chapter develops his theory that attitude has three dimensions with separate impacts on behavior, and which attain their greatest impact when they converge. The general form of the path analytic operator that Seibold adopts allows him to assume that (unmeasured) global attitude, its three dimensions, and behavioral choice are separate variables characterizing his subjects. His specific operator is quite complex: The attitudinal dimensions, and behavior, are in part, time-specific additive combinations of higher-order variables and time-specific error, and, in part, transformations of the same variables from earlier times. Obviously, his assumptions about time and change must be quite complex, but his basic assumption is that equilibrium is reached at each point in time where behavior is required or measurement is conducted. His choice of path analysis allows him to separate measurement unreliability from more substantively significant types of deviations from the model. In particular, he finds his three dimensions of attitude as differentiated, within the structure of the model, to contain large extrasystematic disturbances, that have impact on them. For instance, his finding that intention is by far the most powerful determinant of behavior seems a promising heuristic finding because it indicates that extrasystematic forces that disturb the convergence between intention and other attitudinal dimensions are just those forces that most powerfully influence behavior.

Poole and Hunter's chapter argues for, and uses systems of difference (later differential) equations as fundamental operators in the study of attitude change within an attitudinal hierarchy. Because, in difference equations, a linear combination rule calculates quantitative *change* in system states as a function of the values of those states themselves, and because they are mainly interested in impacts *among* attitudes and messages, their variables are unidimensional, quantitative, and continuous. Their methodology allows attitude change to be a continuing process, while allowing for immediate and transitory message impacts: Messages are modeled in exactly the same way as are temporary higher-level attitudes. Thus they assume that cognitive processing, when it is stimulated, is diffused throughout the hierarchy, but that the impact on any one attitude is extremely limited. Poole and Hunter's theory is most interesting, because it is so intensively linked to difference operators, allowing them to respond to error by restructuring and resequencing operators in ways that dramatically increase their accuracy of prediction.

Woelfel argues for modeling cognitive processes as spatial motions. Basic to his argument is the existence and precision of a class of operators—the algebra and calculus of vectors. Since he advocates, not a particular theory, but a method for empirically discovering theoretic propositions, he allows for the possibility of a variety of types and arrays of cognitive and message variables, and both orientations toward time are compatible with this theory-building strategy. Whereas Woelfel allows for both orientations toward time, he is precise in his conception of deviations of data from expectations. His data are collected using procedures of high reliability, thus discrepancies are attributable to incorrect cross-observer or overtime transformations. Therefore, he designs his propositions to maximally fit properly transformed data.

Mathematical and statistical techniques can be more than tools of social science research: They can serve, just as the classical theory types do, to unify and invigorate the construction and testing of theory. In a sense, researchers can respond to the variety of methods they know: They can conform slavishly to a method, stretching their research topics and propositions into a procrustean fit with their favorite research technique. Better, they can choose on reasoned grounds among the variety of available statistical descriptions, selecting the most suitable and interpreting the results with an eye to the original theory. Finally, they may incorporate mathematical and statistical ideas into the core of their theories, so that the reasoning involved in the theory is mathematical and formal as well as conceptual and meaningful. The last approach has the advantage that the interpretive leap from theory to statistics is less broad: The proper statistical operations are directly derivable from theory, and the outcomes of estimation and statistical testing have direct theoretical meaning. Insofar as our authors move toward meaningful interrelation of theory and methods, we believe they are introducing a vital theory-building resource to the message–attitude–behavior area.

Messages, Attitudes, and Behaviors: Implications

Since this book is about the message–attitude–behavior relationship, we are both obliged and anxious to repair the relative neglect that the "message" concept has received so far in this review. However, that state of neglect duplicates the state of the attitude–behavior literature—a relatively small part of that literature considers the notion of change, and still fewer studies concern themselves explicitly with messages as sources of attitude and behavior change.

The most suggestive study of message-induced attitude and behavior change, in our judgment, is that by Ajzen (1971). He used a Prisoner's Dilemma experimental paradigm to explore the effects of various types of persuasive messages on game behavior. Working within the Fishbein paradigm, two types of messages were used: attitudinal, aimed at attitude toward the act; and normative, aimed at the social normative belief component of Fishbein's model. For each message type, messages of two valences were constructed— urging either cooperation or competition as strategies. Moreover, one other possible message variable was manipulated in the study: In the instructions on playing the game, players were given either a competitive or a cooperative motivational orientation (i.e., they were told that the point of the game was to play either as opponents or as partners). Three findings were rather straightforward, though interesting: The motivational orientation instruction strongly influenced the weighting each component of Fishbein's behavioral intention model received; each message type could change behavior significantly if it were directed at the more heavily weighted model component, but not otherwise; and messages affected behavior primarily by affecting the model component they were aimed at. Two unexpected findings also emerged: When aimed at a heavily weighted model component, messages produced (a) more change; and (b) change that generalized to the other model component as well.

The most useful feature of this study is the frame it provides for discussing message effects on attitudes and behaviors. There are two types of message effects, more or less clearly distinguishable, which have dominated discussion in the general literature and in the following chapters. The first type is the *structural* effect—in a sense this is a complete misnomer. The logic of this sort of effect has been most clearly articulated by Craig (1974): A cognitive structure is a model of thought, or a mapping of attitudes and beliefs. Correlatively, a message can be said to have, or project, or be interpreted to have, a suggested cognitive structure—the set of attitudes and beliefs that its author seems to intend that its hearers should adopt as a result of hearing (or reading) the message. Generally speaking, a structural model of message effects involves the assumption that the message will have its impact either by introducing new information into the recipient's old cognitive structure, or by bringing to light internal contradictions and implications, which the recipient will process by changing his attitude. This model is widely present in attitude-change theory, as well as in the message recommendations of many of the authors represented in this book.

One clear relevance of the attitude–behavior literature to persuasion theory is the new direction it gives to this "structural effects" approach to messages. If "plain old attitude" is irregularly and contingently related to behavior, then constructing messages specifically to change "plain old attitude" is inefficient at best. Rather, we should determine exactly what variables are the most direct determinants of behavior, and design our messages to project desired values of *those* variables. The clearest exemplar of this strategy in the following chapters is that by Woelfel. If the truest cognitive map is a multidimensional space in which cognitive change is concept motion, then we should, when seeking to persuade others to behave, design messages that will produce just the conceptual motions we desire, and no others. Several studies cited in Woelfel's chapter were designed to discover and certify methods for producing specific cognitive changes.

Thus, one response to attitude–behavior inconsistency is to find and specify the cognitive variables with which behavior *is* regularly consistent, then aim for structural effects in those variables. Another approach to attitude–behavior inconsistency is to discover moderating variables, which determine *when* attitude is a powerful determinant of behavior: The structural message effect correlate of this approach would be to discover which persons in a population were likely to be characterized by high attitude–behavior consistency, and send attitude-directed messages just to them. Thus, on O'Keefe's findings, we would use attitudinal messages when the persons we sought to influence were low in cognitive complexity (e.g., children). But this suggests yet another approach: Rather than, or in addition to, controlling direct determinants of behavior, we could design messages to control or influence the mediating variables governing consistency. In just that way, Ajzen (1971) was most successful in persuasion when he sent a message designed to affect, say, attitude toward the act, following his instruction, which elevated the importance of that component in the overall model.

This final approach we might label as one which concentrates on *functional* effects of messages—but here the word functional has not the purposive sense given it by Fontes *et al.*, referring instead to the manner in which the human cognitive system "functions," or works. Under this approach, messages do not overtly project a desired cognitive structure for the receiver's cognitions to mimic for one reason or another; rather, the message is designed with a view to how it will change the receiver's mode of cognitive functioning, inducing him to respond to his present attitude level, more or less consistently. Thus, Poole and Hunter suggested messages that might change a receiver's attitude hierarchy; Seibold suggested messages that play on the receiver's dissonance and attribution processes. The clearest exemplar of this approach, though, is Chapter 5, by Cappella and Folger. Their message suggestions allow the student of persuasion to affect, not the receiver's specific attitude, but the likelihood that the receiver's style of cognitive processing will retrieve information supporting a decision in favor of action.

Of course, both these approaches may be used in conjunction; and both require further research and theoretical specification. But the attitude–behavior literature, as much or more than any other, has been responsible for broadening the range of ideas and processes to which the theorist of influence and persuasion appeals for explanation and practical guidance; the chapters that follow are systematic both in extending that literature and in revealing its manifold relevance to communication processes.

REFERENCES

Ajzen, I. Intentional vs. normative messages: An investigation of the differential effects of persuasive communications on behavior. *Sociometry*, 1971, *34*, 263–280.

Ajzen, I., & Fishbein, M. Attitude–behavior relations: A theoretical analysis and review of empirical research. *Psychological Bulletin*, 1977, *84*, 5, 888–918.

Allport, G. Attitudes. In C. Murchinson (Ed.), *A handbook of social psychology*. Worcester, Mass. Clark University Press, 1935. Pp. 798–844.

Alwin, D. F. Making inferences from attitude–behavior correlations. *Sociometry*, 1973, *36*, 253–278.

Anderson, J. R. *Language, memory, and thought*. Hillsdale, N.J.: Erlbaum, 1976.

Andrews, K. H., & Kandel, D. B. Attitudes and behavior: Specification of the contingent consistency hypothesis. *American Sociological Review*, 1979, *44*, 298–310.

Bagozzi, R. P. The construct validity of the affective, behavioral, and cognitive components of attitude by analysis of covariance structures. *Multivariate Behavioral Research*, 1978, *13*, 9–31.

Bailey, K. D. Evaluating axiomatic theories. In E. F. Borgotta & G. W. Bohrnstedt (Eds.), *Sociological methodology*. San Francisco: Jossey–Bass, 1970. Pp. 48–69.

Bem, D. J. Attitudes as self-descriptions: Another look at the attitude–behavior link. In A. G. Greenwald, T. C. Brock & T. M. Ostrom (Eds.), *Psychological foundations of attitudes*. New York: Academic Press, 1968. Pp. 197–215.

Bentler, P. M., & Speckart, G. Models of attitude–behavior relations. *Psychological Review*, 1979, *86*, 452–464.

Blalock, H. M. *Theory construction*. Englewood Cliffs, N.J.: Prentice-Hall, 1969.

Blalock, H. M. (Ed.). *Causal models in the social sciences*. Chicago: Aldine–Atherton, 1971.

Blanche, R. *Axiomatics*. London: Routledge & Kegan Paul, 1962.

Campbell, D. T. Social attitudes and other acquired behavioral dispositions. In S. Koch (Ed.), *Psychology: A study of a science* (Vol. 6). New York: McGraw-Hill, 1963. Pp. 94–172.

Craig, R. Models of cognition, models of messages, and theories of communication effects: Spacial and network paradigms. Unpublished manuscript, Michigan State University, 1974.

Craig, R. An investigation of communication effects in cognitive space. Unpublished Ph.D. dissertation, Michigan State University, 1976.

Cushman, D., & Pearce, W. B. Generality and necessity in three types of human communication theory, with special attention to rule theory. *Human Communication Research*, 1977, *3*, 344–352.

Danes, J., Hunter, J., & Woelfel, J. Mass communication and belief change: A test of three mathematical models. *Human Communication Research*, 1978, *4*, 243–252.

DeFleur, M. L., & Westie, F. R. Attitude as a scientific concept. *Social Forces*, 1963, *42*, 17–31.

Delia, J. G. Constructivism and the study of human communication. *Quarterly Journal of Speech*, 1977, *62*, 361–375.

Dubin, R. *Theory building* (2nd ed.). New York: Free Press, 1978.

Eagly, A. H., & Himmelfarb, S. Attitudes and opinions. *Annual Review of Psychology*, 1978, *29*, 517–554.

Fishbein, M. Attitude and the prediction of behavior. In M. Fishbein (Ed.), *Readings in attitude theory and measurement*. New York: Wiley, 1967. Pp. 477–490.

Fishbein, M. The prediction of behavior from attitudinal variables. In C. D. Mortensen & K. K. Sereno (Eds.), *Advances in communication research*. New York: Harper & Row, 1973.

Fishbein, M., & Ajzen, I. Attitudes towards objects as predictors of single and multiple behavioral criteria. *Psychological Review*, 1974, *81*, 59–74.

Fishbein, M., & Ajzen, I. *Belief, attitude, intention and behavior: An introduction to theory and research*. Reading: Mass.: Addison–Wesley, 1975.

Hage, J. *Techniques and problems of theory construction*. New York: Wiley, 1972.

Harré, R., & Madden, E. *Causal powers*. Totowa, N.J.: Rowman & Littlefield, 1975.

Harré, R., & Secord, P. F. *The explanation of social behavior*. Totowa, N.J.: Littlefield, Adams, 1973.

Hempel, C. G., & Oppenheim, P. Studies in the logic of explanation. *Philosophy of Science*, 1948, *15*, 135–175.

Hughes, G. D., & Ray, M. L. (Eds.), *Buyer/consumer information processing*. Chapel Hill: University of North Carolina Press, 1974.

Hunter, J., Levine, R., & Sayers, S. Attitude change in hierarchical belief systems and its relationship to persuasibility, dogmatism and rigidity. *Human Communication Research*, 1976, *3*, 3–28.

Kaplan, B., & Crockett, W. H. Developmental analysis of modes of resolution. In R. P. Abelson *et. al.* (Eds.), *Theories of cognitive consistency: A sourcebook*. Chicago: Rand McNally, 1968.

Kelly, G. A. *The psychology of personal constructs* (2 vols.). New York: Norton, 1955.

LaPiere, R. T. Attitudes vs. actions. *Social Forces*, 1934, *13*, 230–237.

Liska, A. E. Emergent issues in the attitude–behavior consistency controversy. *American Sociological Review*, 1974, *39*, 261–272.

Marlier, J. Procedures for a precise test of social judgment predictions of assimilation and contrast. Paper presented at the annual meeting of the Speech Communication Association, Chicago, December, 1974.

McDermott, V. The literature on classical theory construction. *Human Communication Research*, 1975, *2*, 83–102.

McGuire, W. The nature of attitudes and attitude change. In G. Lindzey & E. Aronson (Eds.), *The handbook of social psychology* (Vol. 3). Reading, Mass.: Addison–Wesley, 1969. Pp. 136–314.

Merton, R. *Social theory and social structure*. New York: Free Press, 1949.

Miller, G. R., & Burgoon, M. *New techniques of persuasion*. New York: Harper & Row, 1973.

Miller, L. Has artificial intelligence contributed to an understanding of the human mind? A critique of argument for and against. *Cognitive Science*, 1978, *2*, 111–128.

Oxford English Dictionary, The Compact Edition of the, New York: Oxford University Press, 1976.

Poole, M. S. An experimental test of some mathematical models of change in hierarchies of attitudes. Unpublished M.A. Thesis, Michigan State University, 1976.

Raden, D. Situational thresholds and attitude–behavior consistency. *Sociometry*, 1977, *40*(2), 123–129.

Regan, D. T., & Fazio, R. On the consistency between attitudes and behavior: Look at the method of attitude formation. *Journal of Experimental Social Psychology*, 1977, *13*, 28–45.

Reynolds, P. D. *A primer in theory construction*. Indianapolis: Bobbs–Merrill, 1971.

Saltiel, J., & Woelfel, J. D. Inertia in cognitive process: The role of accumulated information in attitude change. *Human Communication Research*, 1975, *1*, 333–344.

Schuman, H., & Johnson, M. P. Attitudes and behavior. *Annual Review of Sociology*, 1976, *2*, 161–207,

Schwartz, S. H. Normative influences on altruism. In L. Berkowitz (Ed.), *Advances in experimental social psychology* (Vol. 10). New York: Academic Press, 1977. Pp. 221–279.

Schwartz, S. Temporal instability as a moderator of the attitude–behavior relationship. *Journal of Personality and Social Psychology*, 1978, *36*, 715–724.

Schwartz, S., & Tessler, R. C. A test of a model for reducing measured attitude–behavior discrepancies. *Journal of Personality and Social Psychology*, 1972, *24*, 225–236.

Scott, W. A. Attitude measurement. In G. Lindsay & E. Aronson (Eds.), *The handbook of social psychology* (Vol. 2), Reading, Mass.: Addison–Wesley, 1968. Pp. 204–273.

Seibold, D. R. Communication research and the attitude–verbal report–overt behavior relationship. A critique and theoretical reformulation. *Human Communication Research*, 1975, *2*(1), 3–32. (a)

Seibold, D., & McPhee, R. Attitude–behavior processes: Test of alternative longitudinal models. Paper presented at the annual convention of the Eastern Communication Association, Philadelphia, April, 1979.

Seibold, D. R., & Roper, R. E. Psychosocial determinants of health care intentions: Test of Triandis and Fishbein models. In I. D. Nimmo (Ed.). *Communication Yearbook 3*, New Brunswick, N.J.: Transaction Books, 1979.

Songer-Nocks, E. Situational factors affecting the weighting of predictor components in the Fishbein model *Journal of Experimental Social Psychology*, 1976, *12*, 56–69. (a)

Stegmuller, W. *The structure and dynamics of theories*. New York: Springer-Verlag, 1976.

Stinchcombe, A. L. *Constructing social theories*. New York: Harcourt, Brace & World, 1968.

Thurstone, L. L. *The measurement of values*. Chicago: University of Chicago Press, 1959.

Triandis, H. C. *Interpersonal behavior*. Monterey, California: Brooks/Cole Publishing, 1976.

Warner, L., & DeFleur, M. Attitude as an interaction concept: Social constraint and social distance as intervening variables between attitudes and action. *American Sociological Review*, 1969, *34*, 153–169.

Whittaker, J. O. Resolution of the communication discrepancy issue in attitude change. In C. Sherif & M. Sherif (Eds.), *Attitude, ego-involvement, and change.* New York: Wiley, 1967. Pp. 159–177.

Wittgenstein, L. *Philosophical investigations.* Oxford: Blackwell, 1953.

Woelfel, J. *Sociology and science.* Unpublished manuscript, Michigan State University, 1971.

Woelfel, J., & Danes, J. Multidimensional scaling models for communication research. In P. Monge & J. Cappella (Eds.), *Multivariate research techniques in human communication research.* New York: Academic Press, 1979.

Woelfel, J., & Saltiel, J. Cognitive Processing Motions in a multidimensional space: A general linear model. Unpublished manuscript, Michigan State University, 1974.

von Wright, G. H. *Explanation and understanding.* Ithaca, N.Y.: Cornell University Press, 1972.

Zetterberg, H. *On theory and verification in sociology.* New York: Bedminster Press, 1963.

2

An Axiomatized, Stochastic Model of the Behavioral Effects of Message Campaigns

DEAN E. HEWES

The history of scientific inquiry tends to substantiate the commonsense notion that the way people choose to look at the world influences what they see (Feyerabend, 1970; Hanson, 1961; Kuhn, 1970). For example, the theoretical framework one chooses to study an empirical phenonemon may partially shape what one sees empirically. The potential danger of these "theory-laden" perceptions (Hanson, 1961) requires a theorist to make a rational choice among theoretical frameworks based on cost–benefits analysis of each framework. Does the theoretical framework unduly restrict the way the theorist can view the phenomenon? Can this restriction in perception be compensated for by the power of the explanations that can be generated within that framework?

The first portion of this chapter is devoted to such a cost–benefits analysis of alternative theoretical frameworks. This is accomplished by examining (*a*) the general flexibility and explanatory power of the axiomatic approach; and (*b*) the relative merits of a stochastic process approach to the message-mediating variable–behavior problem, as contrasted with a deterministic approach. Following the cost–benefits analysis, an axiomatic theory of the relationships among messages, mediating variables, and behaviors is elaborated and linked to research.

43

MESSAGE–ATTITUDE–BEHAVIOR RELATIONSHIP
Theory, Methodology, and Applications

Why Choose an Axiomatic Theory?

A theory is axiomatic if it contains a *dictionary*, which precisely defines the variables in the theory, a set of *axioms*, which formally state the relationships among those variables, and a *calculus*, which permits formal deductions (Bunge, 1973). No assumption is made about the nature of the relationship posited in the axioms (logical, causal, stochastic, etc.), nor is a particular calculus required for a theory to be called axiomatic. No assumption is made that the axiomatic relationships are to be taken as true, nor is there any requirement that all these relationships be either empirically verified or verifiable (Blanché, 1962; Reynolds, 1971).

Described in this manner, an axiomatic theory is nothing more than a theory that comes close to the ideal form of a "scientific" theory (Turner, 1967, pp. 228–229). Of course, even natural science theories seldom reach this ideal; however, the process of attempting to achieve it results in certain advantages that make the effort worthwhile. Bunge (1973) outlines 13 such advantages that flow from the process of axiomatizing theories in physics. Several of these advantages can be compressed into two, which are potentially important for theorizing in the social sciences.

The first of these advantages is *rigor*. Axiomatizing a theory promotes rigor in the definition of variables, in the specification of the properties of these variables, in the identification of the types of relationships that are hypothesized to exist between those variables, and in making deductions. Examples provided by Seibold (Chapter 6, this volume), Duncan (1963), Costner and Leik (1964) support the value of rigor in social science theorizing. For instance, Seibold (Chapter 6, this volume) has correctly assessed the deleterious effects of definitional ambiguity on the study of the attitude–behavior relationship, whereas Dundan as well as Costner and Leik have documented the unfortunate consequences to deductive rigor that result from a nonrigorous specification of relationships among variables.

On a broader scale, a rigorous specification of axioms and a commensurate precision in deduction facilitates economy and parsimony (Einstein, 1934; Kaplan, 1964). By contrast, an alternative theory construction stratagem attempting to "retroduce" (Hanson, 1961) theoretical relationships from a firm data base (Seibold, 1975) does not generally provide as logically consistent a theory (Einstein, 1934) nor does it produce a theory which allows as clear a visualization of the phenomenon (Apostel, 1961). In short, axiomatization can improve the quality of deductions, the precision with which those deductions can be tested, and the overall parsimony and clarity of the theoretical formulation.

Axiomatization also brings with it a second advantage; *suggestiveness*, where "suggestiveness" refers to that property of a theoretical framework that facilitates change in the face of disconfirming evidence. As noted in the description of an axiomatic theory, the axioms are not presumed to be true. Instead, an axiomatic theory "by exhibiting all its assumptions, tempts the bold scientist to suspend some of them, with replacement or without, just to see what 'happens', i.e., how the set of consequences is affected [Bunge, 1973, p. 170]." The suggestiveness of axiomatic theories increases a theorist's options for modification.

Suggestiveness (or heuristic value) in theories has always been considered a value, particularly in the social sciences (for example, see McGuire, 1969; Simons, 1971). The provocativeness of axiomatic theories in the physical and mathematical sciences bodes well for the utility of axiomatization in the social sciences (Bunge, 1973; Blanché, 1962); however, the real value of the suggestiveness of axiomatic theories can best be seen when they are compared to the single law theories (congruity theory, cognitive dissonance, etc.) often employed in the social sciences (for an unusually rigorous example see Saltiel & Woelfel, 1975). An example may help to demonstrate the point.

Suppose that a theorist hypothesizes that human behavior conforms to a proposition of the form "$A \rightarrow C$," where A and C are variables and "$\rightarrow$" implies some relationship, for instance, causation.[1] If the data do not support this proposition, the theorist is immediately confronted with two areas of difficulty. First, there is no other recourse to modify this relationship through direct application of logic. Only intuition is applicable. While intuition is not to be shunned, nothing in the *structure* of the proposition aids the theorist, and it is the advantages of particular structures of theories that are under discussion here.

Second, if the theorist attempts to use inductive techniques to modify the form of the proposition (for instance, to change the mathematical specification of the relationship to improve fit), there is a danger of capitalizing on chance variations in the data. In the long run, induction can lead to serious logical problems, not the least of which is the difficulty in maintaining the parsimony of the theory (Hempel, 1966; Popper, 1959). In general, creation and testing of single propositions (or laws) of human behavior may raise serious practical and logical problems for theory construction.

Many of these difficulties can be softened by the suggestiveness and rigor of the axiomatic approach. By positing a number of underlying relationships that function within an interlocking network of axioms, the axiomatic theory facilitates theory development. As an overly simplistic illustration, suppose instead of one proposition, we couch our explanation of human behavior in an interlocking network of propositions:

$$A \rightarrow B \quad B \rightarrow C \quad B \rightarrow D \quad C \rightarrow E$$

where A, B, C, D, and E are variables and "$\rightarrow$" is as before. In such a network, not only can one deduce that $A \rightarrow C$ but also that $A \rightarrow D$, $A \rightarrow E$, and $B \rightarrow E$. If some of the propositions and deductions are found empirically invalid, the axiomatic theory may help to suggest modifications of itself; something a single

---

[1] This argument is not intended to be limited to causal relationships. A causal framework is used only for purposes of illustration.

proposition cannot do.[2] More importantly, *even if some of the axioms are not empirically testable*, the network of axioms may make it possible to modify the system so that the data become comprehensible.[3] Once the axiomatic structure has been altered, the hypothesized relationships can be logically derived again, leaving the theory rigorous at the definitional, relational, and deductive levels.

Of course, it may not be possible to make such alterations. A crucial variable may have been excluded from the dictionary; a set of axioms may be limited by their logical structure so that they cannot be modified within the existing framework; too few of the axioms and deductions may receive empirical support. In any of these instances, an axiomatic theoretical structure may face the same difficulties as a single proposition. When these problems are not encountered, the axiomatic theory offers greater advantages than a single proposition (or single law) approach. Thus, the *structure* of axiomatic theories aids in theory development by facilitating suggestiveness and rigor.

Why a Stochastic Process Theory?

In the previous section we addressed the question of the general flexibility and explanatory power of axiomatic theories. Such theories were found to be highly flexible in their ability to aid in theory development. Their explanatory power is increased by their rigor. In this section of the chapter, we will concern ourselves with the choice of the particular form of axiomatic theory that is best suited to studying the relationships among messages, mediating variables, and behaviors.[4]

As the title of this chapter suggests, the theory to be presented here is based on a stochastic process model. To determine whether or not this theoretical framework has maximum explanatory power and minimum perceptual restriction, the stochastic approach must be compared with the most obvious alternative perspective; the deterministic approach underlying most covering laws theories in the social sciences (for instance, Saltiel & Woelfel, 1975) and the vast majority of causal theories (Seibold, Chapter 6, this volume). Each approach (deterministic and stochastic) will be explicated briefly. The intent of

---

[2] If $A \to C$, $A \to E$, $B \to C$, $B \to D$, and $C \to E$ are verified, but $A \to B$ and $A \to D$ are not, the system can easily be modified to conform to this new data by positing that $A \to C$, $B \to C$, $B \to D$, and $C \to E$. This modification is not the *only* formulation that will account for these data, but it is the most parsimonious reformulation *of this axiomatic system*.

[3] If $B \to D$ is untestable, $A \to D$ is not empirically verified, and all other axioms and deductions are verified, one can reasonably, but not uniquely, modify the system to explain these data by dropping $B \to D$ from the axioms.

[4] As a point of clarification, the arguments presented to this point do not advocate either a deterministic or a stochastic model; either type of model can be cast in an axiomatic framework. My only point in the previous section was to advocate formal axiomatization over alternative forms of theory. In this section, I shall advance arguments in support of stochastic theories.

these arguments will be to demonstrate the viability of the often neglected stochastic perspective.

The Deterministic Approach

In a deterministic law, two or more variables are related in such a way that, in principle, knowledge of the values of some of those variables in a given instantation logically entails knowledge of the values of the rest of the variables in that same instantiation (Hempel & Oppenheim, 1948). "In principle" means that only measurement error and/or ignorance of other laws prevents perfect prediction (Nagel, 1961). Is this type of theoretical framework applicable to the study of the relationship among messages, mediating variables and behaviors? The answer can be "Yes" only with a number of reservations.

1. At minimum, one must have an interlocking network of deterministic laws to provide a deterministic explanation of any event, even in principle. Unless one is willing to maintain that some domain of human behavior is controlled by one and only one law,[5] a single law cannot yield deterministic explanation in principle or in fact without involving the *ceteris paribus* clause.[6] Once the *ceteris paribus* clause is imposed, other laws must be assumed to be operating in a constant fashion in a given event or to be operating randomly over a series of replications of that event. In the first case, a single, deterministic law can give only an incomplete explanation that can be generalized to other events only if the unknown laws continue to be well behaved; *something one can never know in advance.* In the second case, the explanations generated by the law can only be linked to the event stochastically (McClelland, 1975); consequently, an explanation that is *in principle* deterministic can have no more real explanatory power than one that is *in principle* stochastic.

In short, deterministic explanation requires the identification of a network of deterministic laws to generate deterministic explanations. If even one law applicable to a given event remains unknown, stochastic explanations are as strong as deterministic explanations in principle as well as in practice. Since complete knowledge of the laws of human behavior is far from a reality, it would seem more reasonable to cast our theoretical explanations so that they correspond with our actual ability to explain; that is, we should employ stochastic explanations.

2. Deterministic explanations of human behavior in terms of messages or mediating variables may be possible only under a restricted domain of conditions. Consider the relationship between mediating variables and behaviors: Mediating variables cannot in principle explain the behavior of any single

---

[5] Since even the natural sciences cannot claim a single law that can explain any real event, no matter how simple, it seems highly unlikely that the social sciences will be able to do so.

[6] Roughly, this means that all other things are assumed to be equal.

human being. As von Wright (1971) has clearly demonstrated, the mediating variable "intention to behave" logically cannot entail behavior. Only in rather restricted instances can the environment, in the form of physical obstructions or others' intentions, be counted on to cooperate with one's own intentions. This same argument can be leveled at any mediating variable or combination of such variables one might choose to mention.[7] Since at least one internal mediating variable must stand between a message and a behavior (unless the message and the behavior are temporally coincident), the argument advanced applies to the relationship between messages and behaviors as well. Thus, only when a message is temporally coincident with the behavior it is intended to elicit, *and* when the message is totally effective, *and* when the environment does not inhibit action can one anticipate a direct, deterministic relationship between an individual's behavior and message variables.[8] Thus, messages and internal mediating variables may be deterministically related to behaviors only under conditions in which behavior is highly familiar and/or routinized so that obstructions to intentions can be avoided (see, as support, Crespi, 1971; Tittle & Hill, 1967).

The arguments presented here are not intended to prove that a deterministic laws approach is invalid. They are intended to establish two points which, if accepted, argue for the relatively greater utility of a stochastic perspective.

1. If, in practice, our knowledge of human behavior is likely to remain incomplete for the near future, then our ability to explain that behavior is limited to the stochastic level in principle even if the world is "really" deterministic. Under these conditions, a deterministic approach to theory construction may prove relatively less useful since it will generate predictions not in line with experience, and explanations not in line with actual knowledge.

2. If, in fact, the relationships among messages, mediating variables and behaviors are deterministic only under a restricted domain of conditions, the deterministic laws approach unjustifiably restricts our perceptions outside that domain of conditions. It does so by focusing our endeavors on increasing the strength of empirical relationships *which may not be capable of being strengthened* without the incorporation of other variables.

In those instances in which we can reasonably presume that individual action will be either facilitated or, at least, not inhibited by the environment, a

---

[7] Empirical support for this proposition can be seen in the marked tendency of attitude–behavior studies to find higher correlations when behaviors are measured under normal, familiar, or highly routinized situations where others' opposition and/or physical obstructions are less likely to be found (Crespi, 1971; Tittle & Hill, 1967).

[8] An indirect relationship might exist *if* the message was totally persuasive, and *if* the environment did not block the ability to fulfill an intention to act.

deterministic approach may prove highly useful, since it correctly focuses attention on improved specification and measurement. This is particularly true where a relatively complete knowledge of human behavior is available. Otherwise, stochastic theorizing may prove more appropriate.

The Stochastic Approach

In a stochastic formulation, one or more variables are related in such a way that, in principle, knowledge of the values of some of those variables in a given instantiation may logically entail only approximate knowledge of the values of the rest of the variables. The degree of that approximation may range from perfect prediction of a single case, or accurate prediction with a probability of 1.00, to totally imperfect prediction, or accurate prediction with a probability of .00 (Ayer, 1956). In either case, it is the *probability* of prediction of a single case, not the prediction itself, which is considered generalizably regular in stochastic theories.

Can stochastic formulations be applied to the study of the relationships among messages, mediating variables, and behaviors? The answer is "Yes," given a belief that an adequate description of human behavior and cognition requires the acceptance of a range of indeterminacy. Either or both of the following arguments could serve as a basis for that belief.

1. Any prediction and explanation of individual behavior in a social context, based on intraindividual variables, must incorporate a range of indeterminacy. No individual can reasonably be expected to have complete control of his or her social environment, especially the other people in that environment. To that extent, no prediction of that individual's future behavior made on the basis of goals, attitudes, or expectations should be restricted to the deterministic. This principle has been supported at the philosophical level by von Wright (1971), and at the theoretical and empirical level by Wicker (1971) and Fishbein and Ajzen (1975), among others.

2. Mediating cognitive variables may well be inaccessible at anything other than a stochastic level. For example, Natsoulas' (1970) review of introspection strongly suggests that reflexive self-examination of cognitive processes, though offering important insights into cognition, has a strong component of indeterminacy. The inherent ambiguities in the language of self-expression as well as the apparent inability of humans to explicitly describe their cognitive states and processes (Nisbett & Wilson, 1977; Slovic & Lichtenstein, 1971; pp. 683–684; Smith & Miller, 1978) may be contributory causes of this indeterminacy. In either case, an adequate description of the linkage between messages and behaviors through individual cognitive processes may necessitate a stochastic formulation.

A description of the message, mediating variable, behavior relationship is primarily oriented toward intraindividual variables. Attitudes, beliefs, expectations, and so on, all operate at the level of the individual. Messages are explicitly viewed either in terms of the perceptions of individuals or are implicitly treated that way as in the case of manipulation checks of message differences made against the perceptions of subjects. If explanations and predictions of behavior are to be made from an intraindividual perspective, the two arguments advanced strongly support the use of stochastic formulations. Stochastic theories allow one to represent the full range of predictability from determinacy to total indeterminacy.

Above and beyond arguments over the "true" nature of the empirical relationships in question, there are pragmatic reasons for adopting a stochastic perspective. Let us briefly consider two of those reasons.

First, stochastic models have great flexibility in representing complex theoretical relationships. Whereas a more detailed discussion of this point has been presented elsewhere (Hewes, 1975a), suffice it to say that deterministic models often *assume* certain properties to be true which may, in fact, be of theoretical interest to represent otherwise. For instance, stochastic models can quite easily be adopted to represent developmental trends in variance across time and across other variables, as well as a host of other more complex relationships that cannot be easily or efficiently represented or predicted by deterministic base models. In fact, Bailey (1975) has demonstrated that, for a wide variety of processes, deterministic models are merely simplified versions of more powerful stochastic models.

A second point in favor of probabilistic representations is their success in accurately representing and predicting a wide variety of phenomenon. Occupational mobility (Bartholemew, 1973), intragenerational social mobility (McFarland, 1970), consumer behavior (Massey, Montgomery & Morrison, 1970), attitude change (Hewes, 1978; Hewes & Evans-Hewes, 1974), and voting behavior (Anderson, 1954; Hawkes, 1969; W. Miller, 1972), among other variables all have been successfully analyzed with stochastic models. Although it can be argued that stochastic models have a number of unsolved problems (Coleman, 1973; Ginsberg, 1972a,b), the point remains that they have demonstrated wide and successful application in the extremely short period of time since their inception (Kemeny, 1969). In fact, the success of stochastic models has been such that in many areas of the social sciences with traditionally deterministic leanings, they are enjoying either increasing popularity (Lee, Judge & Zellner, 1970) or have displaced their deterministic counterparts (Greeno, 1974). At the very least, the success stochastic formulations have exhibited elsewhere suggests their potential utility in the investigation of the relationships among messages, mediating variables, and behaviors.

In general, stochastic models may prove highly useful in the prediction and explanation of behavioral choice. Especially in those theories in which explanation is derived from the intraindividual variables, the most realistic framework for theorizing would appear to be stochastic. Both the success in other areas of application and the complexity of potential predictions generated by such models support attempts to utilize stochastic models in the problem under consideration.

It was argued earlier that the form of a theory can influence the way in which a theorist sees empirical phenomena; therefore, a rational decision must be made concerning which among a number of alternative theoretical frameworks is to be chosen. In the ensuing discussion, I conclude that an axiomatic framework is rigorous in ways advantageous to the study of relationships among messages, mediating variables, and behaviors and that the suggestiveness of the axiomatic approach helps guide theory development in ways in which the single-law approach cannot. The discussion proceeded to a consideration of the particular type of axiomatic system that should be adopted. A stochastic process format was contrasted with a deterministic alternative; greater flexibility in perception and equivalent explanatory power were claimed for stochastic formulations in most applications. If these conclusions are valid, a stochastic representation should be a highly productive theoretical framework in which to cast the relationship between messages, mediating variables, and behaviors.

An Axiomatized Stochastic Theory

The arguments just presented are highly general. They are intended to suggest a class of theories which could prove useful in the study of messages, mediating variables, and behaviors. To demonstrate the potency of these arguments, a concrete example of axiomatized stochastic theories is necessary. The development of this theory proceeds through traditional steps; presentation of a dictionary of theoretical terms, explication of the axioms of the theory, application of a calculus to the axioms to produce a set of theorems. A partial defense of the utility of this theory is delineated through a comparison of the predictions of the theory to previous research, and through direct empirical test.

Two strategic considerations are reflected in the following theory construction process. First, a major goal of this process was the development of a theory with maximal capability to predict the impact (both immediate and delayed) of both individual messages and sequences of messages on cognitive structures and, consequently, on behavior. This goal seems to be central to practical applications of persuasion theory. Certainly increasing our ability to predict behaviors is crucial given the failure to find anticipated, large correlations between attitudes and behaviors (Mervielde, 1977; Schuman & Johnson, 1976). Even current improvements in this area (especially Ajzen & Fishbein, 1977; Fishbein & Ajzen, 1974; Snyder & Tanke, 1976; Weigel & Newmann, 1976) are fraught with difficulties. For instance, the use of multiple act criteria (indices created by summing across a set of behaviors hypothetically related to a given attitude, Fishbein & Ajzen, 1974) recently have undergone attack on conceptual and methodological grounds (Cappella & Folger, Chapter 5, this volume; Hewes & Haight, 1979). In general, even substantial improvements in attitude–behavior correlations leave unresolved the issue of how one changes behavior over time (for instance, Alwin, 1973; Cook & Flay, 1978; Mervielde, 1977). This issue becomes increasingly salient given the dearth of theories dealing specifically with the over-time effects of individual messages, or message campaigns, on behavior (Cook & Flay, 1978). Thus, attainment of the goal of increased predictive power requires a theoretical move designed not merely to improve cross-sectional associations between measures of mediating variables (attitudes, beliefs, perceived normative pressure, etc.) and behavior, but, to represent the *cumulative process* of message reception on cognitive and behavioral change.

To specify more precisely what kind of theoretical move is mandated, consider my second major goal; the development of a theory in which variables and axioms are as "historically durable" as possible (Gergen, 1973, p. 318). This goal derives from Kenneth J. Gergen's controversial article, "Social Psychology as History." In that article Gergen advanced the thesis that the generalizations of social sciences are particularly susceptible to cultural change and to the reflexive reaction of individuals in the general culture upon dissemination of those generalizations. Whereas Gergen's evidence can certainly be challenged (Schlenker, 1976), the fact remains that certain variables and relationships among variables are likely to be more sensitive than others to the changing currents of culture. For instance, Craig and Cushman (1976) have argued that the bases of persuasion have been radically altered in the twentieth century, and Reisman (1952) has suggested that the reinforcement value of social approval has markedly increased over this same interval.

What can be done to insulate our theories from the ravages of "historicity"? Two tactics suggest themselves. First, we can cast theoretical axioms at the most general and enduring level possible. Norms governing specific social actions or role restrictions of gender, for example, are likely to be transient; the principles of human learning (Homans, 1971, pp. 40–43), social exchange, and information processing are likely to be more durable. Second, since it is often difficult, if not impossible, to derive rules of correspondence between objective observables and the variables in these more durable theories (Gergen, 1976, pp. 374–375), subjects may be able to serve as "transducers" between theory and objective "reality." For example, operant conditioning theories have always faced a problem of specifying the objective properties of a "reinforcer" in unimpoverished environments without resorting to a tautological relationship between "reinforcer" and "response" (Shaw & Costanzo, 1970, Ch. 2). Yet, subjects' self-reports of those things they find rewarding or the ways in which they behave when faced with different potential reinforcers may provide sufficient information so that, directly or by inference, we can provide a non-tautological definition of "reinforcer" for those subjects at that point in time. Of course this definition must be verified predictively, but if we use this measurement strategy we can test durable operant theories even though the nature of variable "reinforcer" changes from person to person, culture to culture, time to time. Similarly, recent advances in social exchange theory eschew sole reliance on objective payoff matrices in favor of a potentially large "subjective" component (Kelley & Thibaut, 1978), permitting "historicity" of the objective manifestations of "payoff" while leaving the theory intact.

In short, we can side-step some of the problems of "historicity" by relying on abstract, durable theoretical formulations coupled with subjects' direct or indirect estimates of the values of the essential variables at any given point in time. (We may have to avoid direct estimates of subjects' psychological "processes" in favor of estimates of their psychological "states" if Nisbett and Wilson [1977] are correct, although the ballots are not all in on that issue [Smith & Miller, 1978].) If these estimates are close to the "true" values of the variables, the psychological and sociological processes that give rise to these estimates can be temporarily finessed, though they can and should be used to augment a "durable" theory. If the generalizations forming the basis of these psychological and sociological processes are ahistorical, so much the better; if not, none of a theory's predictive power is lost during periods of cultural change. In the discussion to follow, I will attempt to demonstrate that the theory presented here has potentially high predictive power, that it can be augmented by current research so as to increase its explanatory power, and that subjects can make the necessary judgments to operationalize it. Whether or not the theory is really transhistorical must be left to history.

Definition of Variables

In this section, definitions will be provided for the five basic variables to be used in the model. First, let us consider "behavioral expectations" and their relationship to attitudes.

Behavioral Expectation

The "behavioral expectation" variable is an adaptation of the "conative" or behavioral dimension of attitude as operationalized by Triandis (1964), Ostrom (1969), and Kothandapani (1971). A behavioral expectation is *a subjective estimate of the probabilities that one will perform one of a closed set of behaviors under a specified set of conditions.* The behavioral expectation (B_e) of a given point in time ($t + k$) can be represented as a row vector of probabilities where the number of probabilities corresponds to the number of possible behaviors. The vector indicates the probability with which one expects to perform each given behavior.

$$B_e(t + k) = (p_1 \cdot p_2 \cdot p_i \cdot \cdots \cdot p_j) \tag{1}$$

where p_1 is the expected probability, as judged at $t + k$, that one will perform Behavior 1, etc. By this definition $\sum_{i=1}^{j} p_i = 1.00$; the set of behaviors is assumed to be exhaustive, though it need not be mutually exclusive under specifiable conditions (Hewes, 1979, pp. 59–61). Psychologically, I presume that the behavioral options $(1, 2, \ldots, i, \ldots, j)$ contained in $B_e(t + k)$ can be partially ordered along a dimension defined by the subjective evaluation individuals assign to the outcome resulting from a given behavioral option at a given point in time. This general evaluation subsumes traditionally evaluative measures such as "attitude toward object" and "attitude toward act."[9] Its existence is supported by the fact that even the grossest measures of evaluation do rather well in predicting behavior when obtained temporally close enough to the initiation of the behavior so that the various contextual, personal, and attitudinal sources of evaluation (see Calder & Ross, 1973; Kelman, 1974; Mervielde, 1977; Schuman & Johnson, 1976 for reviews) can be taken into account (this point will be documented extensively later). Further, I presume that the magnitudes of the probabilities of the set of options contained in $B_e(t + k)(p_1, p_2,$ etc.) are roughly, positively related to their ranking on the general evaluative dimension.

The term "roughly" is intended to imply certain qualifications. First, there exists the possibility of ties in the rankings. Some or, potentially, all of the behavioral options may be evaluatively equivalent or so nearly so that the behaviors cannot be discriminated (see particularly Fishbein & Ajzen's, 1974,

---

[9] At or very near the moment of choice, a general evaluation of the options is made, implicitly or explicitly. That general evaluation summarizes traditional predictors of behavior such as "attitude toward act," "attitude toward behavior," "perceived normative force," "visibility of the behavior," "situational factors" (Wicker, 1971). I am speculating that each and all of these variables can be translated into potential costs and benefits to be derived from the options of the choice. For instance, the relationship between "attitude toward object" and a particular behavioral option implies costs and/or benefits in terms of cognitive and social consistency; "perceived normative force" has its obvious costs and benefits in social sanctions. Even Wicker's (1971) analysis of "situational factors" in church attendance, could potentially be translated into a subjects' judgments concerning the relative costs and benefits of attendance, *when compared to other options*. Finally, "attitude toward act" is conceptually closest to the general evaluation dimension I am positing since one's evaluation of an act seems to be principally an evaluation of its consequences, both internal and external.

By arguing for the existence of this general evaluative dimension, I am explicitly supporting our intuitions that evaluations must be linked to behavior, and that the correlations between various evaluative measures, both direct and inferred, and behavior will vary as a direct function of their salience in determining a general, cumulative evaluation of the options made at or close to the point of choice. Therefore, we may, with extreme caution, employ evidence from a wide range of attitude–behavior studies to sketch the rough outlines of a theory involving changes in $B_e(t + k)$. These arguments are not meant to imply that attitudes *cause* behavior, nor that a theory of message–behavior change linkages must necessarily take into account directly changes in various evaluative domains. In fact, it is probably simpler to by-pass the issue of the causal relationship between attitude change and behavior change altogether by focusing on the mediating influence of other internal variables such as those to be presented later.

discussion of the "coefficient of linearity" in this regard). Second, in my conception, changes in evaluations do not necessarily imply changes in the subjective expectation of the probability of behavior. The states of $B_e(t + k)$ represent points on a continuum defined by the general evaluative dimension. Depending on the arrangement of those points, it is possible to change evaluations either positively or negatively without changing the subjective probabilities contained in $B_e(t + k)$ (for instance the "threshold effect" discussed in Campbell, 1963; Raden, 1977; Schuman & Johnson, 1976; also see Calder & Ross, 1973, p. 26).[10] For example, one can well imagine instances where those already favoring an issue could be made to evaluate it even more positively (Hovland, Lumsdaine & Sheffield, 1949) without any change in specific behaviors being possible.

The conclusions to be drawn from these qualifications and the definition of B_e are (a) that the relationship between B_e and alternative forms of the evaluative dimension ("toward object," "toward act," etc.) are likely to be mild but potentially exploitable given care in interpretation;[11] (b) that the processes shaping the underlying ordering of the elements of B_e are complex, thus making its *direct* measurement highly desirable to simplify the prediction of behavior; and (c) that many of the barriers that stand between adequate predictions of behavioral expectations (B_e) from attitudes (such as "threshold effects" and "evaluative ties") do not necessarily obstruct the prediction of the probabilities of actual behavior from behavioral expectations. In fact, evidence summarized by Ajzen and Fishbein (1973; Fishbein & Ajzen, 1975), strongly suggest that variables very much like B_e, that is, "behavioral intentions," do rather well in predicting actual behaviors.[12]

---

[10] Whereas Raden's data support my general claim, certain qualifications are necessary. First, though Raden demonstrates small but consistent improvements in attitude–behavior associations through the introduction of the notion of "threshold," the meaning of "small" is unclear in his discussion since no meaningful metric of the improvement is provided. Second, even by his own analysis (p. 126), the data he summarizes may not yield good tests of the threshold hypothesis because of the skewness of the marginal distribution of both attitudes and behaviors (also, Mervielde, 1977). Third, Raden's arguments are directed toward the attitude–behavior relationship per se. It is unclear what they may imply about the attitude and behavior *change* issue presented earlier.

[11] By opting for this explanation, I am intentionally denying the tripartite description of the relationship between attitudes and behaviors advanced by Chein (1948), Katz and Stotland (1959), Krech, Crutchfield, and Ballachy (1962), and others. Hewes (1975b) provides an extensive critique of this alternative approach as does Fishbein (1967; Fishbein & Ajzen, 1975).

[12] Behavioral intentions can be seen as a special case of behavioral expectations, where the number of options are limited to two, and where the inhibiting context variables may not be taken into account. Thus, I may "intend" to do something, but I could reasonably anticipate (expect) that I might not be able to complete the action (Hewes, 1975b). Of course, the correlational evidence offered by Ajzen and Fishbein leaves open the possibility that changes in B_e might not be associated with changes in behavior.

The Stability Matrix

The B_e vector indicates the perceived likelihood that a person will respond in any of a number of ways at a specific point in time. Bellamy and Thompson (1967), McNemar (1946), and Wiggins (1973), among others, have noted that a description of predisposition to act (usually defined as an "attitude" in these works) is incomplete without some notion to its stability. One might expect to act in a particular manner at one point in time but be so uncertain or unconfident in the choice of that behavior that it would be a poor guide to predicting subsequent behavior (see Warland & Sample, 1973 for empirical support).

Clearly we must have some way to represent the stability of behavioral choices in the absence of message input. Without this representation we would be unable to account for indecisive or inconsistent behavior. Further, any such representation must be able to account for "localized instability" in behavior (i.e., instability associated with only a few of the possible options). For example, I may have found the choice between Hubert Humphrey and Richard Nixon difficult as I filled out a questionnaire prior to the election, since I felt both candidates were evaluatively equivalent. On the other hand, I might have found choosing to vote or not to vote for George Wallace to have been quite easy. My choice in Wallace's case would be a better indicator of my subsequent voting behavior with respect to Wallace than would my choices with respect to Nixon and Humphrey. Similar problems might be expected to occur in any instance involving the choice among behavioral options.

This notion of "localized instability" can be linked to the discussion of behavioral expectations (B_e). As I noted, alternative elements of B_e might not scale directly onto an evaluative dimension due to "ties." Some behavioral options may prove to be evaluatively similar or even identical. What we would have in this case are the behavioral analogues of the "regions of acceptance," "neutrality," and "rejection" in social judgment theory (Sherif, Sherif, & Nebergall, 1965). Choices of behaviors scaled *within* each of these evaluative regions might be expected to be highly unstable since they are evaluatively similar. On the other hand, the probabilities of changes (transitions) between behaviors in differing regions might be expected to be quite stable. Although I do not wish to take on all the problematic theoretical baggage of social judgment theory (Kiesler, Collins, & Miller, 1969), the notion of regions of evaluative similarity does provide a useful psychological rationale for the importance of localized instability.

Finally, in order to capture fully the dynamics of behavioral stability–instability, a cognitive representation would have to incorporate *internally driven trends* in behavior change. From the example of localized instability, one could infer that an individual forced by circumstances to perform an evaluatively negative behavior would not be likely to continue without behavioral support (message input) from the environment. A representation of behavioral stability must capture not only the simple equivalence or lack of equivalence of a set of options, but also the likely direction of behavioral change unsupported by messages. That such internally driven trends are important can be gleaned directly from Festinger's (1964) classic analysis of long-term behavior change as well as empirically from some of the fear–appear research (Leventhal, Watts, & Pageno, 1967). If my earlier analysis concerning the relationship attitudes and behavioral expectations is correct, we may also derive indirect support from research employing attitudes as the dependent variables. For example, the per-suasion literature also reveals support for the existence of both decay processes (for instance McGuire, 1973) and, more recently, for long-term increases in attitude change unsupported by message input (Cook & Flay, 1978; Gruder, Cook, Hennigan, Flay, Alessis, & Halamaj, 1978; Tesser, 1978). If behavioral expectations (B_e) can be interpreted as belief statements, then McGuire's (1960a,b,c) early work on "inertial" change in beliefs would reinforce the im-portance of capturing internally generated change in B_e.

The stability matrix S is intended to capture these aspects of cognitive change.[13] S is defined as *the cognitive mechanism which maps the values of B_e at one point in time to those at the next point in time*. In particular, S controls the *amount* and *direction* of stochastic change in B_e. The matrix S is conceived as being susceptible to change from forces from the environment, particularly messages. Further, in the event that no messages are received, S controls the amount and direction of stochastic change in B_e in the same way that a transition matrix in a Markov chain controls mappings of initial probability vectors into a posteriori probability vectors (Kemeny & Snell, 1960). In that sense, S repre-sents the internal predisposition for change in B_e in the *absence* of messages.

The B_e vector aids in the construction of the S matrix. This is done by performing an experiment where one observes B_e at time zero and again at some later point in time from the same sample. The construction of S is a simple matter once the two values of B_e are obtained. This procedure has been described elsewhere (Hewes & Evans-Hewes, 1974; Hewes, 1975a). The result of the procedure is a $j \times j$ matrix of probabilities where j is the number of behaviors included in B_e.

The stability matrix S thus has elements $\{s_{ij}\}$ where s_{ij} is the probability of behavior option i at $t + k$ being followed by option j at $t + k + 1$.

---

[13] A note of caution needs to be inserted here. The evidence presented above for the inclusion of S *only* justifies the inclusion of *some* mechanism to control internally generated or maintained behavioral change. Each of these sources of evidence posits a different mechanism. For instance Cook and Flay (1978) advanced the disassociative cue hypothesis to explain the "absolute sleeper effect," while Tesser (1978) appeals to attitudinal schemata. The value of the stability matrix is that it is flexible enough to capture all of these patterns of change. This flexibility is also a potential disadvantage since it makes disconfirmation difficult; however, the S matrix can be operationalized with sufficient precision so that it can lead to a testable alternative explanation of the absolute sleeper effect. I assert without proof that S is considerably more precise than Tesser's attitudinal schemata.

A perfectly stable B_e where $j = 3$ would have associated with it an S of

$$S = \begin{pmatrix} 1 & 0 & 0 \\ 0 & 1 & 0 \\ 0 & 0 & 1 \end{pmatrix}$$

indicating that $B_e(t + 0) = B_e(t + 1)$, or that there is no tendency for the probabilities in B_e to change in a systematic fashion.[14]

An S illustrating local instability for $j = 3$ would have the form

$$S = \begin{matrix} & 1 & 2 & 3 \\ 1 & .33 & .33 & .33 \\ 2 & .33 & .33 & .33 \\ 3 & .00 & .00 & 1.00 \end{matrix}$$

where Options 1 and 2 are perfectly unstable but Option 3 is highly stable.

Finally, an example of an S matrix indicating perfect negative stability with highly systematic change of behavioral expectation would appear as

$$S = \begin{pmatrix} 0 & 0 & 1 \\ 1 & 0 & 0 \\ 0 & 1 & 0 \end{pmatrix}$$

Of course, stability matrices less extreme than these examples are more likely to occur.

Environmental Cues to Action

Von Wright (1971) clearly indicates that environmental factors may mediate between intentions and actual behavior. This point was emphasized by Fishbein (1967) in discussing the failure of his model to establish consistently high correlations between behavioral intentions and actual behaviors. He noted that changes in such environmental conditions as "normative climate" may have attenuated the relationship between intentions and behavior. Empirical evidence supplied by Warner and DeFluer (1969) and Wicker (1971), and many others (e.g., Cathcart, 1974; Craig & Cushman, 1975; McPhee, 1975; Schwartz & Tessler, 1972) supports the notion that the intervening effects of environmental cues are important to formation and change of behavioral expectations. Behavioral expectations should incorporate dynamic input from the environment.

---

[14] Another example would occur when $B_e(t + 0)$ and S are at "stable equilibrium" (Kemeny & Snell, 1960). In this case the distribution of probabilities in $B_e(t + 0)$ and in any and every row of S are equal.

To include environmental cues in the model, a matrix **C** is introduced with the following characteristics: (*a*) **C** is of the same order as the **S**, that is, a $j \times j$ matrix; (*b*) **C** is allowed to change over time; (*c*) the **C** matrix summarizes the cues to behavior as *perceived* by the individual.[15] *The elements in a* **C** *matrix indicate the probabilities for changing behavior as suggested by the environment conditional upon a person's current behavior or behavioral expectations.* A **C** matrix indicating a strong set of perceived cues to perform Behavior .1 in a 3×3 matrix would be

$$\mathbf{C} = \begin{pmatrix} 1.0 & .0 & .0 \\ 1.0 & .0 & .0 \\ 1.0 & .0 & .0 \end{pmatrix}$$

whereas a **C** matrix indicating no change in behavioral expectations would appear as

$$\mathbf{C} = \begin{pmatrix} 1.0 & .0 & .0 \\ .0 & 1.0 & .0 \\ .0 & .0 & 1.0. \end{pmatrix}$$

The **C** matrices described above summarize the whole range of input received from the environment including changes in normative input, environmental conditions, and many others. At this point in the discussion, no attempt to disaggregate **C** into its component parts is made, though this could certainly be done as an extension of the present formulation. This issue is addressed in somewhat greater depth later.

The Retention Parameter Matrix

Until now, no mechanism has been introduced to permit messages (environmental cues) to be integrated into the cognitive structure of an individual. Surely something of this kind is crucial since as Miller (1969) noted,

> [m]ost scientifically useful generalizations concerning human information processing will have to take account of both environmental stimuli available to the individual (Information 1) and the background experiences that he brings with him to the situation (Information 2) [p. 52].[16]

If we are to take both these sources of "information" into account, some

---

[15] This second condition eliminates the need to consider the attentional process itself. Only the cues actually filtered through the perceptual system are of interest at this point in the theoretical development.

[16] Miller seems to identify Information 1 with *objective* rather than *perceived* environmental stimuli. In that sense, my reliance on the latter forms of stimuli differs from Miller's intended argument.

mechanism to integrate them into behavior change is necessary. The retention parameter matrix, $\mathbf{M}$, is such a mechanism. $\mathbf{M}$ is defined *as a matrix of deterministic constants which control the degree to which changes in behavior or behavioral expectations are controlled by the stability matrix or the environmental cues matrix.* Psychologically, the existence and function of $\mathbf{M}$ implies that individuals must somehow integrate their own internal tendencies toward constancy or change with those cues toward constancy or change perceived in the environment. Thus $\mathbf{M}$ provides, in principle at least, a way of integrating external cues to action, what Miller (1969) has labeled "Information 1," with internal mechanisms governing stability or change in behavior choice, what Miller has labeled "Information 2."

More precisely, $\mathbf{M}$ is used to create new values for the elements of the stability matrix $\mathbf{S}$ at $t + k$ by constructing a weighted average between the immediately previous values of $\mathbf{S}$ (at $t + k - 1$) and the elements of the cues matrix, $\mathbf{C}$, received at $t + k$. The matrix $\mathbf{M}$ is *not* used in the absence of an input from the environment. (The details of this process are summarized in Axioms 2 and 3 to follow.) Since we reasonably assume that the weight accorded to internally or externally derived sources of change is potentially conditional upon current behavior or behavioral expectation,[17] $\mathbf{M}$ is a $j \times j$ matrix whose states conform to those appearing in B_e, $\mathbf{S}$ and $\mathbf{C}$. The elements of $\mathbf{M}$, $\{m_{ij}\}$, are constrained such that $0 \leq m_{ij} \leq 1.00$, $m_{ij} = 0$ if $i \neq j$; therefore, $\sum_{i=1}^{k} m_{ij} \leq 1.00$ where k = the number of behaviors or states in B_e.[18] The elements of the $\mathbf{M}$ matrix are assumed to be relatively stable across time and to vary with the topic of messages and specified characteristics of the cognitive styles of individuals. As such, the intellectual ancestors of $\mathbf{M}$ are the concept of "persuasibility" (Janis & Hovland, 1959) and the k_{ij} parameter appearing in the attitude change models of Abelson (1964) and Taylor (1968). As used in the current model, $\mathbf{M}$ stands for an underspecified psychological process. That is, it represents an intuitively appealing process for which the antecedents are unknown.

There are several plausible hypotheses which one might advance to explain the necessity of placing a variable set such as $\mathbf{M}$ in a model of the message–mediating variable–behavior relationship. For example, one might argue that individuals vary in the extent to which they typically rely on internal as opposed to external sources of information to determine this behavior. Early formula-

---

[17] Waly and Cook (1965; also Brigham & Cook, 1970) provide indirect support for this conclusion when they observed that messages will be judged more plausible to the degree that they are consistent with a person's attitudes. To the extent that B_e, or one's actual behavior, reflects one's evaluative position, one's perception of the strength of a message in changing B_e or behavior should be influenced by the current state one holds in B_e or in actual behavior. Hewes *et al.* (1977) tested this hypothesis and found support for it within the context of the current model.

[18] This means that $\mathbf{M}$ is a diagonal matrix—a condition imposed by the mathematical requirement that $\mathbf{M}$ is to function as a weighting procedure in a weighted averaging process.

tions of Snyder's "self-monitoring" variable (1972, 1974)[19] stressed this differential reliance on information sources as a cognitive style variable that might serve as a moderator between evaluations of behavioral options and behavior. Subsequent research (Snyder & Swann, 1976; Snyder & Tanke, 1976; see Snyder, 1979, for a particularly thorough summary) seems to have borne out this hypothesis. In the context of the theory presented here, one could argue that some of the variability in the elements of the **M** matrix would be conditional upon the degree to which an individual was a high or low self-monitor. Other individual difference variables such as "cognitive complexity" (O'Keefe, Chapter 4, this volume) and self-esteem (see Wells & Marwell, 1976, pp. 24–28) also might explain variability in the elements of **M**. In addition topic-related variables, such as "ego involvement" (Sherif, Sherif & Nebergall, 1965), might influence the magnitude of the elements of **M**, with highly involved individuals placing less emphasis on environmental cues than those less involved. Note, however, that the elements of **M** do not directly affect behavioral expectations or behaviors; they do so only indirectly through the joint effects of internal driving forces for stability–change (i.e., **S**, and the particular configuration of perceived environmental cues). Thus **M** is a somewhat more complex mechanism than "persuasibility" as it has been operationalized (Janis & Hovland, 1959). On the other hand, McGuire's (1968a,b) five-step "susceptibility" model suggests that **M** might have to be broken down into subcomponents such as "attention to the communication," "comprehension of its contents," "yielding to what is comprehended" (integration into **S** in my terms). Of the last two subcomponents proposed by McGuire ("retention of the agreed upon position" and "acting on that position"), the first is not dealt with in the current formulation[20] and the second is subsumed under other components of the model.[21] Progress in the explication of the theory presented here will undoubtedly require more specificity in the antecedents and internal structure (subcomponents) of the **M** matrix.

Behavior Probability Distribution Variable

With the behavior probability distribution variable, B_h, we have come almost full circle in the kinds of variables specified in this theory. B_h is highly

---

[19] More recent formulations (1977; in press) of self-monitoring seem to place less emphasis on the information source preference aspect of this variable and more on it as a measure of social facility.

[20] The current model does not incorporate a memory assumption. This is probably undesirable, since highly divergent time intervals between messages may have differential effects even for the same messages. I am currently undertaking to include a retention component in the model, although I am not including it directly in the **M** matrix.

[21] The translation of message integration into action is accomplished through the joint effects of **C**, **S**, and **M** (see Axioms 1–4 to follow).

similar to B_e. B_h summarizes the probability that an individual will *actually perform* a particular behavior at some specified point in time.

Formally, B_h is a row vector with j states, each state corresponding to a behavior included in the exhaustive set of behaviors specified in B_e:

$$B_h(t + k) = b_1 b_2 \cdots b_i \cdots b_j)$$

where b_i is actual probability of performing behavior i at $t + k$. By this definition, $\sum_{i=1}^{j} b_i = 1.00$; the set of behaviors is assumed to be exhaustive.

B_h is the clearest presentation of the meaning of the previous defense of the stochastic framework of this theory. The definition of B_h allows for the possibility that a range of indeterminacy exists in our ability to formulate an intraindividual prediction behavior. Thus, whereas it is possible that entry b_i of B_h may be 1.00 indicating perfect predictability, it is also possible that all j entries of B_h will be equal indicating that no particular behavior can be predicted on an intraindividual basis. Such a conclusion is fully consistent with the rationale for stochastic modeling presented at the beginning of this chapter.

The five variables described here (B_e, S, M, C, and B_h) represent the basic units from which the model is constructed. The way in which these five variables are related is the subject of the next section of this paper.

The Axiomatic Structure

At several points in the definition section of this paper mention was made of the relationships among two or more of the variables in the theory. In this section, those relationships are formalized into a set of axioms. Since the calculus of this model employs probability theory and matrix algebra, the axioms will be stated in comparable language and then verbally explicated.

Axiom 1

$$\text{Prob}[v(t + k) = i \,|\, v(t + k - 1) = j, v(t + k - 2) = m, \ldots, v(t + 0) = p]$$
$$= \text{Prob}[v(t + k) = i \,|\, v(t + k - 1) = j]$$

where $v(t + k)$ is a "state" variable indicating that at time $t + k$, an individual would expect to perform behavior i with the ith probability in the B_e vector, and so on for $v(t + k - 1)$, $v(t + k - 2)$, and so on. The symbols $i, j, m, \ldots$, and p are integers between 1 and n where n is the number of behaviors in B_e. The symbol k is a positive integer or zero.

Stated verbally, Axiom 1 implies that the process being described is of the "first order," that is, predicting a future event is assumed to require no more information than that contained in the immediately prior event and the method of mapping one event onto the other. Axiom 1 is the "order" assumption made in Markov chain analysis (Hewes, 1975a).

Since the conventional notation used in this theory is matrix notation, Axiom 1 will be phrased in that form; $B_e(t + k) = B_e(t + k - 1)S_k$.

Corollary 1.1

$$B_e(t + k) = B_e(t + 0) \prod_{i=1}^{k} S_i$$

This corollary can be established by the informal use of mathematical induction. Let us start with the matrix form of Axiom 1 for $t + 1$ and restate Axiom 1 in the same form for $t + 2, t + 3$ and so on.

$$B_e(t + 1) = B_e(t + 0)S_1$$
$$B_e(t + 2) = B_e(t + 1)S_2 = B_e(t + 0)S_1S_2$$
$$B_e(t + 3) = B_e(t + 2)S_3 = B_e(t + 0)S_1S_2S_3$$
$$\vdots$$
$$B_e(t + k) = B_e(t + k - 1)S_k = B_e(t + 0)S_1S_2S_3 \cdots S_k$$

or, for simplicity,

$$B_e(t + k) = B_e(t + 0) \prod_{i=1}^{k} S_i$$

Psychologically, Axiom 1, and its associated corollary, operationalize the cognitive processes discussed previously in conjunction with the stability matrix; that is, Axiom 1 describes how a behavioral expectation at one point in time might be used to predict subsequent behavioral expectations. Thus Axiom 1 incorporates all the internal mechanisms governing change in behaviors and behavioral expectations including general predispositions toward behavioral change, one's confidence in behavioral expectations and/or future behavior and evaluative equivalence of alternative behavioral options.

Axiom 2

$$s_{ij}(t + k) = m_{ii}s_{ij}(t + k - 1) + (1 - m_{ii})c_{ij}(t + k)$$

except when no message is received at $t + k$ where $s_{ij}(t + k - 1)$ is the probability of changing from expectation i to expectation j during the period of time from $t + k - 1$ to $t + k$, m_{ii} is the retention parameter for state i and $c_{ij}(t + k)$ is the perceived change in behavioral expectations being received from the environment.

Verbally, Axiom 2 states that an individual weighs prior information and new input in creating his or her cognitive structure for mapping $B_e(t + k - 1)$ into $B_e(t + k)$. A weight of m_{ii} is applied to the prior stability matrix in the mapping procedure while a weight of $(1 - m_{ii})$ is applied to changes perceived as coming from the environment. *This weighted average process occurs only when a message is perceived at $t + k$.*

In matrix notation Axiom 2 becomes $S_k = MS_{k-1} + (I - M)C_k$. Cognitively, Axiom 2 represents the mental integration of internal and external change processes described in the previous discussion of the retention parameter matrix M. Axiom 2 merely states in mathematical form the commonsensical assumption that individuals attempt to guide their behavior by both internal and external change processes although they may differ in the salience they impute to those two sources of information. In effect, Axiom 2 makes the model "open" to the message environment and thus potentially superior to even the elaborate closed system sequential models currently in vogue in the attitude change and marketing literature (for instance Hawkes, 1969; Herniter & Magee, 1961; Hewes & Evans-Hewes, 1974; Massy, Montgomery, & Morrison, 1970; Miller, 1972; but cf. Ginsberg, 1972a,b; Singer & Spilerman, 1974; Spilerman, 1972, for other ways of "opening" stochastic models to input).

Corollary 2.1

$$S_k = M^k S_0 + (I - M) \sum_{i=1}^{k} M^{k-i} C_i$$

except when no message is received at any time i, $1 \leq i \leq k$. All symbols are previously defined.

This corollary can be supported by the informal use of mathematical induction applied to Axiom 2. Starting with Axiom 2 applied to $t + 1$ and proceeding from there,

$$S_1 = MS_0 + (I - M)C_1$$
$$S_2 = MS_1 + (I - M)C_2 = M(MS_0 + (I - M)C_1) + (I - M)C_2$$
$$S_3 = MS_2 + (I - M)C_3 = M(M(MS_0 + (I - M)C_1) + (I + M)C_2)$$
$$\quad + (I - M)C_3$$
$$S_3 = M^3 S_0 + M^2(I - M)C_1 + M(I - M)C_2 + (I - M)C_3$$

In general,

$$S_k = M^k S_0 + (I - M) \sum_{i=1}^{k} M^{k-i} C_i$$

Axiom 3

$$s_{ij}(t + k) = s_{ij}(t + k - 1)$$

when no message is received at $t + k$ where s_{ij} is as before.

Verbally, Axiom 3 is the logical complement of Axiom 2. Axiom 3 simply states that if no cues from the environment are received at $t + k$ then the preexisting cognitive structure for change is reinserted in Axiom 1. In matrix notation $S_k = S_{k-1}$ when no message is received at $t + k$. Axiom 3 simply indicates that, in the absence of external sources of stability–change, the internal change processes begun at $t + k - 1$ will continue uninterrupted at $t + k$.

Axiom 4

$$be_i(t + k) = b_i(t + k)$$

where $b_i(t + k) =$ the probability of performing Behavior i at $t + k$, $be_i(t + k) =$ the probability of holding behavioral expectation i at $t + k$ and the i's refer to corresponding behaviors. The symbol be_i is the ith element of vector B_e. Stated verbally, Axiom 4 suggests that an individual's expectations are isomorphic (at the stochastic level) to the probabilities of behavioral choice of the point when those behaviors are to be performed.[22] In matrix notation $B_e(t + k) = B(t + k)$ where $B(t + k)$ is a row vector of b_i's with the same number of entries as B_e.

Deduction from the Axioms

Two classes of deductions can be made from the axioms just presented. The first type is formal deductions, or theorems, derived from the axioms through application of the logical calculus of the theory. The second type of deduction is of a less formal sort. In effect, this type employs a good bit of verbal reasoning and is intended primarily to help provide an intuitive understanding of the workings of the theory. Both types of deductions are presented in what follows.

Formal Deductions

The theorems listed below are not a complete set of possible deductions from the four axioms. Without exception, these theorems place no constraints on the values of the variables other than those imposed in the definitions. Obviously, when constraints are imposed, a host of special cases of these theorems could be derived. And, in fact, placing a priori theoretical constraints on the values or configurations of values of the parameters would increase the explanatory power of this theory (see Hewes, 1979, pp. 69–73).

Theorem 1

$$B_e(t + k) = B_e(t + 0) \prod_{i=1}^{k} \left(\mathbf{M}^i \mathbf{S}_0 + (\mathbf{I} - \mathbf{M}) \sum_{j=1}^{i} \mathbf{M}^{i-j} \mathbf{C}_j \right)$$

when messages are received for all j, $1 \leq j \leq k$.

Theorem 1 can be established directly by substitution of Corollary 2.1 into

---

[22] This axiom may be more complex than it appears. For instance, there are different implications to Axiom 4 when the behavioral choice must be made at a specified time (for example, voting) and when the choice can be made at some free-floating time period. In the latter case, one must know the expectations for behavioral choice and expectations of time of choice. Alternatively, the time of choice could be incorporated in the expectation. For example, "What is the probability that you will buy a car *next week?*"

Corollary 1.1. Corollary 1.1 defines the mapping of $B_e(t + 0)$ onto $B_e(t + k)$.
Corollary 2.1 amplifies on the structure of S_i in Corollary 1.1 by relating S_i to C_i.

Theorem 1 provides the basis for prediction of values of B_e at any future time
$t + k$ knowing only S_0, **M** and the various values of **C** which are perceived at
each point in time from $t + 1$ to $t + k$. Theorem 1 represents the individual as
an information processing mechanism which must constantly weigh predisposition based on prior information with new information perceived to flow
from the environment. The weighing process is consciously or subconsciously
undertaken at each point in time when a message is received. The individual is
thus seen as being in a process of active adaptation to his or her *perceived*
environment. The rate of adaptation is determined by the elements of **M**.

Theorem 2

$$B_e(t + k) = B_e(t + 0)S_1^k$$

when no message is received at $t + i$ where i is any number between 1 and k.

Corollary 1.1 and Axiom 3 form the basis of Theorem 2. Corollary 1.1 states
that $B_e(t + k) = B_e(t + 0)\prod_{i=1}^{k} S_i$. According to Axiom 3, $S_i = S_{i-1}$ when no
message is received at $t + i$. Since no message is received at $i = 1$ through k,
$S_1 = S_2 = \cdots = S_k$; therefore, by substitution, $\prod_{i=1}^{k} S_i = S_1^k$.

Theorem 2 provides the same kind of basis for prediction as does Theorem
1; however, Theorem 2 makes prediction much simpler since there is no need to
know **M** or the various values of **C**. Instead, Theorem 2 describes changes in B_e
in terms of a simple first-order Markov chain. The chain is first order because of
Axiom 1 and stationary because of Axiom 3.

Theorem 2 describes the cognitive processing of information by the
individual as potentially dynamic *even if no new information is received*. By
raising S_1 to successively higher powers, B_e will change across time until it
reaches stable equilibrium under most conditions.[23] Such changes are entirely
in accordance with the empirical evidence mustered in support of the inclusion
of **S** in this theory.

Theorem 3

$$B_e(t + k) = B_e(t + 0) \prod_{j=1}^{k} \left[\partial\left(M^j S_0 + (I - M) \sum_{i=1}^{j} M^{j-i} C_i \right) + (I - \partial)S_{j-1} \right]$$

---

[23] To be more precise, if **S** is an "irreducible, aperiodic" transition matrix (Derman, Gleser,
& Olkin, 1973, Ch. 12), that is, if for some power or powers of **S**, one can get from any state to
any other state, and if those powers are *not* whole number multiples of one another, then B_e will
achieve stochastic equilibrium. This may also happen even if **S** is "reducible," that is even if some
states cannot be reached directly or indirectly from other states, but having a reducible **S** is highly
unlikely empirically.

where ∂ is an identity matrix when a message is received at time $t + j$ and a matrix of zeros otherwise.

In one sense Theorem 3 is not a true theorem at all but rather a combination of the contingencies inherent in Corollaries 1.1 and 2.1. Those contingencies involve whether or not a message is received at some point in time. The ∂ matrix allows for that contingency to be explicitly included in Theorem 3 so that the deductions presented in Theorems 1 and 2 can be combined. Theorem 3 merely indicates that when a message C_k is received at $t + k$, a weighted average is made. That average is composed of S_{k-1} and C_k. When no message is received at $t + k$, S_{k-1} becomes S_k by default. Thus, Theorem 3 reduces to Theorem 1 when ∂ equals an identity matrix at all points in time; it reduces to Theorem 2 when ∂ equals a matrix of zeros for all points in time.

Theorem 4

$$B_h(t + k) = B_e(t + 0) \prod_{j=1}^{k} \left[\partial\left(M^j S_0 + (I - M) \sum_{i=1}^{j} M^{j-i} C_i \right) + (I - \partial)S_{j-1} \right]$$

where ∂ is an identity matrix when a message is received at $t + j$ and a matrix of zeros otherwise.

The proof for Theorem 4 is simple, for all we must do is to make a substitution of $B_h(t + k)$ for $B_e(t + k)$ in Theorem 3. The substitution is legitimate due to the relationship posited between B and B_h in Axiom 4.

The import of Theorem 4 far exceeds the simplicity of its proof. By the application of Theorem 4 it is possible, assuming the theory is correct, to make predictions of behavioral probability distributions for any point in the future if the values of $B_e(t + 0)$, M and the C's are known. Since some of these values may not be known, Theorem 4 also illustrates the limits of the predictive power of the theory. That Theorem 4 contains such limits is merely a reflection of the central theme of this paper; predictions of individuals from intraindividual theories are likely to be inherently limited.

Theorem 5

$$B_h(t + k) = B_h(t + 0) \prod_{j=1}^{k} \left[\partial\left(M^j S_0 + (I - M) \sum_{i=1}^{j} M^{j-i} C_i \right) + (I - \partial)S_{j-1} \right]$$

where ∂ is an identity matrix when a message is received at $t + j$ and a matrix of zeros otherwise.

Theorem 6

$$B_e(t + k) = B_h(t + 0) \prod_{j=1}^{k} \left[\partial\left(M^j S_0 + (I - M) \sum_{i=1}^{j} M^{j-i} C_i \right) + (I - \partial)S_{j-1} \right]$$

where ∂ is an identity matrix when a message is received at $t + j$ and a matrix of zeros otherwise.

Theorems 5 and 6 are presented together since they are simple modifications of Theorem 4 based on Axiom 4. Theorem 5 permits predictions from behavioral distributions to behavior distributions while Theorem 6 reverses the direction of prediction presented in Theorem 4. The value of Theorems 5 and 6 is that they demonstrate the flexibility of prediction that can be made by the theory presented here.

In general, all of the theorems facilitate prediction in ways that are particularly useful to the communication researcher. First, they posit a complex but precise linkage between internal mediating variables (**M** and **S**) and behaviors. The precision of that linkage increases the testability of the theory while the complexity helps to explain the disconcerting diversity of empirical results found in attitude–behavior studies. Second, Theorems 1–6 explicitly incorporate communication into the process of cognitive and behavioral change; consequently, the theory permits predictions of the cumulative effects of messages. Such considerations are missing from the vast majority of research on the relationships among messages, mediating variables, and behaviors, and are central to a realistic theory of persuasion (Cook & Flay, 1978, p. 45; Hewes et al., 1977).[24]

Both of these advantages will come to nothing if the formalisms presented until now cannot be made intuitively meaningful. Without a "feeling" for the implications of the theory, it is doubtful that an understanding of the uses or abuses of it would be clear. Four illustrative deductions will be presented in order to help make the theory more meaningful at the intuitive level.

Informal Deductions

In this part of the chapter, four informal deductions will be made from the theory. The purpose of these deductions is twofold; to aid the reader in gaining an intuitive understanding of the basic implications of this theory which may have been obscured by the formal notation, and to illustrate the theory's capacity to make commonsensical predictions, thus enhancing its face validity. To simplify the interpretation of these deductions, it will be assumed that a message is being received at all points in time.

1. *The longer the time between the measurement of behavioral expectations and the actual behavior, the greater the potential impact of external influences on changes in behavioral expectations.*[25] This follows directly from the $\mathbf{M}^k\mathbf{S}_0$ term

---

[24] In Seibold's (1974) extensive review of this literature, not a single study was reported employing a multiple message approach to behavioral change. Some recent research in this area is summarized by Woelfel (Chapter 3, this volume).

[25] The word "potential" is inserted here because if $\mathbf{C}_k = \mathbf{S}_{k-1}$, there will be no apparent change impact of $\mathbf{C}_k$ on $\mathbf{S}_k$.

in Theorem 1. Since each entry of $\mathbf{M}$ is generally less than 1.00, raising $\mathbf{M}$ to increasing powers decreases each entry's size. The smaller the values of the elements of $\mathbf{M}^k$, the greater must be the potential impact from environment cues to action.[26] This conclusion is linked to empirical evidence of attitude–behavior relationships in the next section of this chapter.

2. *The impact of a persuasive message on behavior change is inversely related to the length of time between the message and the actual behavior unless that message is reinforced by subsequent messages.* This second conclusion is a logical extension of the first, where the focus is now placed on the effect of messages rather than on the effects of prior information on B_e. The most impact that a persuasive message contained in $\mathbf{C}$ can have on the ith entry of B_e is $1 - m_{ii}$. As that time between the insinuation of that message, $t + n$, and the performance of the behavior, $t + k$, increases, the impact of that particular message decreases by $m_{ii}^{k-n}(1 - m_{ii})$.[27] Since m_{ii} is generally less than 1.00, $m_{ii}^{k-n}(1 - m_{ii})$ rapidly converges on .00 unless each successive message received by the individual reinforces the previous message.

3. *The more recent the message, the greater the impact of that message on behavior change.* This conclusion can be derived from the expression after the "$+$" sign in Theorem 4, for as the value of n increases, the value of m_{ii}^{k-n} also increases. Since n is a time index, the more recent inputs from the environment will have the greatest impact on the value of $\mathbf{S}_k$. For instance, if we express this reasoning in matrix form for $k = 3$,

$$\mathbf{S}_3 = \mathbf{M}^3\mathbf{S} + (\mathbf{I} - \mathbf{M})\mathbf{M}^2\mathbf{C}_1 + (\mathbf{I} - \mathbf{M})\mathbf{M}\mathbf{C}_2 + (\mathbf{I} - \mathbf{M})\mathbf{C}_3 \qquad (36)$$

The impact of $\mathbf{C}_3$ is obviously greater on $\mathbf{S}_3$ than the other set of cues since its weight $(\mathbf{I} - \mathbf{M})$ is greater than the weights of the other cues, $([\mathbf{I} - \mathbf{M}]\mathbf{M})$ and $([\mathbf{I} - \mathbf{M}])\mathbf{M}^2$, assuming, of course, that $\mathbf{M} \neq \mathbf{I}$ or a matrix of zeros.

4. *If the environmental cues to action consistently suggest a pattern of behaviors, in the long run the individual will conform to those cues.* Mathematically, the statement above requires that $\mathbf{C}_i = \mathbf{C}_j$ for all i and j. In other words, $\mathbf{C}$ is a constant. It also requires that k become very large. This can be accomplished by taking the limit of Corollary 2.1[28]

$$\lim_{k \to \infty} \mathbf{S}_k = \lim_{k \to \infty}(\mathbf{M}^k\mathbf{S}_0) + \left((\mathbf{I} - \mathbf{M}) \sum_{i=1}^{k} (\mathbf{M}^{k-i})\mathbf{C}\right)$$

$$= \lim_{k \to \infty}(\mathbf{M}^k\mathbf{S}_0) + \lim_{k \to \infty}\left((\mathbf{I} - \mathbf{M}) \sum_{i=1}^{k} (\mathbf{M}^{k-i})\mathbf{C}\right)$$

$$= 0 - \mathbf{C}(\mathbf{I} - \mathbf{M})(\mathbf{I} - \mathbf{M})^{-1}$$

$$= \mathbf{C}$$

---

[26] As noted above, we have assumed that messages are received at all points in time. Theorem 1 contains that assumption.

[27] This conclusion comes directly from the right-hand expression of Theorem 4.

[28] See Levine and Burke (1972, p. 45) for the algorithm that permits the simplification in step three of this deduction.

Stated verbally, this means that in the long run, each S_i will approach C. The net result will be that the behavioral expectations of the individual will come under control of the environment since the S matrices control the changes in behavioral expectations.[29] The more consistent the C matrices are in indicating that only one behavior is being supported by environmental cues, the more likely will the individual anticipate and perform that behavior.[30]

Summary

The process of theory construction is now complete. Theorems 1–6 represent the culmination of all the steps taken to define and axiomatize the relationships in the theory. The theory also led to four illustrative theoretic deductions. These conclusions are not a complete set of all the deductions that can be made from this model.

The next significant question concerns the validity of the model which generated the conclusion. In the next section of this chapter, the question of validity will be investigated. Although this model was not constructed with an immediate predictive application in mind, research from some rather diverse areas lends support to it.

Validation of the Theory

The validation process will proceed in two stages. Initially, the theory is examined both with and without consideration of particular configurations of probabilities in the C matrix. Particular configurations of probabilities in C are examined as they relate to communication–mediating variable–behavior change relationships. The predictions of the theory under each of these conditions is compared to the results of empirical inquiry. In the second stage of validation, the results of a pilot empirical test of the theory are reported.

Two notes of caution need to be inserted before proceeding. First, all but one of the studies on which these validational efforts rely were not designed to test the theory posited here. In particular, studies reporting attitude–behavior

---

[29] The proof for this statement is too long to include in this already over-long chapter; however, intuitively, one can see that each S in Theorem 4 will converge geometrically on the value of C if C is constant. In the long run, $\prod_{i=1}^{k} S_i$ will converge on C^{∞} which is the equilibrium value for C if it is "regular" (see footnote 23). The net result is that B_h will come under the control of C regardless of the values of $B_e(t + 0)$. Further, if C is an absorbing transition matrix, that is, if C indicates that only one behavior is permissible, only that one behavior will be performed in the long run.

[30] Perhaps even more interesting is that deduction 4 is highly similar to the predictions of Woelfel's forced linear aggregate theory (Saltiel & Woelfel, 1975). Despite radically different assumptions about the cognitive responses to input, the two theories reach the same general conclusion, although the theory presented here allows for a range of indeterminacy and predicts the distribution of that range.

correlations must be used circumspectly since, as I have already argued, the correspondence between behavioral expectations and a general measure of outcome evaluation is unlikely to be strong. Further, because typical attitude measures such as "attitude toward act" and "attitude toward object" are likely to tap only partially the evaluative dimension along which the elements of B_e are scaled, attitude behavior correlations can be expected to capture only crudely the relationships posited in Axioms 1–4. Nonetheless, the results of previous research do provide some necessary insights into the grosser requirements of a theory of the cumulative impact of message campaigns.

A second note of caution also must be attached to the kinds of conclusions that are drawn in the validational discussion. In many instances these conclusions seem quite obvious, particularly those dealing with the effects of time on message–behavior or attitude–behavior relationships. The obviousness of the conclusions should not obscure two facts; that *any* theory of the cumulative impact of messages on behavior must be able to encompass these conclusions, and that current theories of the message–mediating variable–behavior relationship do *not* provide any mechanism to explain the kinds of temporal regularities noted in what follows. In effect, I am arguing that the kinds of conclusions discussed represent the minimal facts that must be explained before any process theory of message effects is worthy of future research.

Stage 1: Fit to Previous Research

Without Specifying C

Two sets of predictions generated from the theory are explored here. The first set focuses on the dynamics of attitude and behavior change suggested by this model, whereas the second set relates to inconsistencies in the attitude–behavior literature that can be resolved by this model.

The first test of the model was suggested by its similarity to Markov chains. Theorem 1 could be characterized as a Markov chain without a stationary transition matrix. Put another way, the theory presents a system open to the influence of communication while the Markov chain is a system closed to communication. This description points to a prediction of the theory that can be checked against the data: *That Markov chain models of attitude and behavior change should lead to their least accurate predictions when there is the greatest change in input from the surrounding environment.* If a large change in the composition of the C matrix takes place, then an open system, such as the one posited here, should respond by changing the process. A closed system such as a Markov chain would not take into account the change in the process and thus would produce its worst predictions at the points of changed input. Some evidence for this prediction does exist in both the attitude and behavior change literature.

Anderson (1954) reported a significant departure in the accuracy of predictions of a Markov chain model of voting preferences during the periods following the Democratic and Republican conventions. At all other times the model's predictions were extremely accurate. Anderson explained these results in terms of nonstationarity of the transition matrices for those periods of time. Henry's (1971) reanalysis of that data confirmed Anderson's suspicions. Maffei (1961), in a study on buyer behavior, found that this behavior could be described by a first-order Markov process during periods where no major promotional activity was underway. Once promotional activity was started, the transition matrix became significantly nonstationary. In other marketing research, this nonstationarity appears to be accepted as a fact of life produced by a changing communication environment (Massy *et al.*, 1970; Lipstein, 1965, 1968). Along similar lines, a study by Hewes and Evans-Hewes (1974) indicated that when a message was introduced, a measure of attitude toward socialized medicine validated against behavioral intentions failed to fit a Markov model for the time period immediately following the introduction of that message. Although another explanation for this phenomenon was suggested, reanalysis of the data showed that explanation to be incorrect.[31] The model presented here would explain these results.

The support provided for the prediction above is not conclusive, but it is highly suggestive. In general, the evidence points to the conclusion that some form of stochastic model *with input* provides a good description of attitude and behavior change. The theory presented here describes such a process. While the general form of processes of attitude and/or behavior change lends support to the model advanced here, a higher degree of specificity in validation is desirable. One prediction might be drawn from Informal Deduction 1 of the previous section. If the model is correct, *the longer the time between the measurement of behavioral expectations and the actual behavior, the greater the potential impact of external influences on changes in behavioral expectations.* This leads to the prediction that in studies in which no control is placed on external influences, the relationship between attitude and behavior should decay as the length of time between measures of both variables increases.[32]

To test this prediction, 15 studies which explored the attitude–behavior relation were assigned to two categories based on the degree of association found between the variables.[33] No studies attempting to change environmental cues to action were examined. The median lengths of time between measures

---

[31] The explanation suggested by Hewes and Evans-Hewes (1974) was that the transition matrix was heterogeneous. A more powerful indicator of heterogeneity than the one used in that study was used in a reanalysis of the data. No significant heterogeneity was detected, thus leaving nonstationarity as the more reasonable explanation.

[32] Since few studies report "behavioral expectations," the assumption must be made that "attitudes," as operationalized by the individual researcher, are at least consistently related to behavioral expectations, if not highly so.

[33] The specific criteria for classification were the same as those used in Seibold (1974) and Tittle and Hill (1967).

of attitude and observation of behavior were compared for the studies in the two categories.

For the seven studies reporting low attitude–behavior relationships (Bray, 1950; Corey, 1937; Kutner, Wilkins, & Yarrow, 1952; La Piere, 1935; Pace, 1949; Warland & Sample, 1973; Weinstein, 1972) the median time interval was one week, whereas the range of time intervals ran from several months (La Piere, 1935) to no lag (Pace, 1949).[34] For the seven studies reporting a moderate-to-high relationship between attitudes and behaviors (Ajzen, 1971; Ajzen & Fishbein, 1970; DeVries & Ajzen, 1971; Fishbein, 1966; Kraus, 1966; Silverman & Cochrane, 1971; Udel, 1965) the median time interval was approximately one hour. The range of time intervals was 8 weeks (Silverman & Cochrane, 1971) to no lag in a self-report study by DeVries and Ajzen (1971); however, it should be noted that four out of the seven studies all had the median time interval. Excluding self-report studies, there was only one study in which the time lag and attitude relationship did not conform to the predictions of the model.

This overall consistency in prediction is noteworthy since rather diverse instruments and methodologies were used in those studies.[35] Several of the authors of the studies explained their findings in ways similar to those suggested by the model (see Ajzen & Fishbein, 1973, Bray, 1950, pp. 67–68; Silverman & Cochrane, 1971, pp. 55–56; Warland & Sample, 1973, pp. 182–184). Although one cannot completely confirm the validity of the model on the basis of this evidence, it does suggest some mediating process like the one posited in the model.

Particular Configurations of C

This section describes the effects on a particular configuration of probabilities in C. The C matrices associated with persuasive communication would, in the extreme, appear as below:

$$
C_k = \begin{pmatrix} 1.00 & .00 & .00 \\ 1.00 & .00 & .00 \\ 1.00 & .00 & .00 \end{pmatrix} \tag{38}
$$

---

[34] This median should be considered low since only the lower limits of time were chosen for each study where a range of times was reported. Further, it is doubtful whether the Pace (1940) study should really be described as investigating a situation of no lag between expression of attitude and performance of behavior since his study was of self-reported attitudes and behaviors. If Pace is dropped, the median interval increases to ten days.

[35] Another explanation of these findings is that the "demand characteristics" of the experiment conditions employed by Ajzen, Fishbein, and others artificially inflated the attitude behavior correlations. This explanation is valid only to the extent that demand characteristics are somehow differentiated from the "normative input" variable which is part of C. Orne's (1962) description of demand characteristics leaves no reason to differentiate these two variables; therefore, even though the correlations between attitudes and behaviors found in the short-interval studies may not be due to "true" relationships posited by the authors, the results still support the model presented here.

In general, a persuasive message should result in a perceived C with the probabilities in one column larger than those in any other column of the matrix.

In the section of this chapter dealing with the development of the model, the effects of such messages were discussed. In particular, Informal Deduction 2 predicted that *the impact of a persuasive message on behavior change is inversely related to the length of time between the message and the actual behavior unless that message is reinforced by subsequent messages.* Two qualifications on the method of testing this conclusion must be made. First, the function which determines the decrease in the ability of a message to influence a behavior i is $(1 - m_{ii})m_{ii}^{j}$ where j is the length of time between the messages and the behavior. Obviously, decrease in the strength of influence is highly related to the size of m_{ii}. Thus, a confounding factor in the test of the suggested hypothesis is the differing values of m_{ii} which could be associated with particular behaviors investigated in the studies. A second qualification concerns the perception of the environmental cues to action. Since C includes *all* messages perceived by the individual as relevant to a given set of behaviors, it is difficult in many of these studies to estimate how the C matrix might have appeared to the recipients of the message. The difficulty in assessing the form of C becomes another potentially confounding factor in interpreting the studies below.

Given these qualifications, 14 studies of persuasion, attitude change, and behavior change were divided into two groups—those finding low persuasion–behavior relationships and those finding moderate-to-high relationships.[36] The median amount of time between the introduction of the message and the observation of the behavior was obtained for both groups. For the low relationship group (Chaffee & Linder, 1969; Leventhal et al., 1966; Greenwald, 1966; Leventhal, Jones, & Trembly, 1966; Leventhal, Singer, & Jones, 1965; Leventhal et al., 1967), the median time interval was 9 days with a range of three months to no delay.[37] For the moderate-to-high studies (Ajzen, 1971; Freedman, 1965; Greenwald, 1965; Krauss, 1966; Lehmann, 1970; Leventhal & Niles, 1964; Leventhal & Watts, 1966) the median interval was no time lag, whereas the range was from no lag to four months.

These data tend to support the prediction of the model. Again, the clarity of support is unexpectedly striking. Five out of the seven moderate-to-high relationship studies reported no lag at all between attitudinal measure and behavior. Of the low relationship group only one study (Chaffee & Linder, 1969) reported on lag. The authors of that study characterized the experimental conditions as unusual and Seibold (1974) concurred with that categorization. In

---

[36] Criteria for this division are reported in Seibold (1974).

[37] One study (Leventhal et al., 1967) took behavioral measures at one point in time before, and three points in time after the presentation of the message. Although the overall impact of the message was not statistically significant, smoking behavior reported over time corresponds to the pattern anticipated with this model. Since the values of the elements of M and the value of the C's after the message are unknown, we will consider the similarity between the model's prediction and the data as interesting support for, but hardly proof of, the validity of the model.

short, the data reported in these studies tend to support a general prediction of the model presented here. While this general prediction cannot confirm the validity of the specific form of the model suggested here, it does lend overall support to it.

Conclusions Concerning Indirect Evidence of Validity

The validity of the model remains to be firmly established. Whereas three general hypotheses of the model were tested and supported, these hypotheses were not precise enough to thoroughly test such a precise theory. At best, the consistent success of the predictions of the theory suggests that future research should be directed toward testing the exact predictions of the theory. That task is undertaken in the next section.

Stage 2: A Pilot Test

Hewes, Brazil, and Evans (1977) report a pilot test of certain aspects of the theory presented in this chapter. This section serves as a summary of their results. For a more complete presentation of the methodology and results, consult the original work.

Hewes *et al.* concentrated their attention on two aspects of the theory; the ability of the model to predict behavioral expectations (Theorems 1–3), and the ability of the theory to predict stability matrices (Axioms 2 and 3). Testing of the axioms and theorems relating behavioral expectations to behavior probability distributions (Axiom 4 and Theorems 4–6) were postponed (*a*) because of the difficulty in gathering over-time behavioral data; (*b*) because of the extensive research already linking expectations to behaviors in much the same way as posited in Axiom 4 (Fishbein & Ajzen, 1975; Mischel, 1968); and (*c*) because the validity of Axioms 1–3 and Theorems 1–3 can be established independently of the other axioms and theorems.

Hypotheses and Results

Two hypotheses were advanced based on the formalization of the theory reported in this chapter.[38]
The first prediction is derived directly from Theorem 3. In particular,

$$B_e(t + k) = B_e(t + 0) \prod_{j=1}^{k} \left[\partial \left(\mathbf{M}^j \mathbf{S}_0 + (\mathbf{I} - \mathbf{M}) \sum_{i=1}^{j} \mathbf{M}^{j-i} \mathbf{C}_i \right) + (\mathbf{I} - \partial) \mathbf{S}_{j-1} \right]$$

---

[38] The methodology employed by Hewes *et al.* (1977) adds the auxiliary hypothesis of homogeneity across individuals for values of $\mathbf{M}$, $\mathbf{S}_0$, and the values of the $\mathbf{C}$ matrices. For a complete exposition of the impact of that auxiliary hypothesis, see the original work.

One-hundred-thirty subjects were exposed to three one-sided messages supporting socialized medicine at 3-day intervals. The elements of C for each of these three messages were obtained from a separate sample of 34 subjects. Behavioral expectations were obtained from the audience through a direct measurement at $t + 0$ (1 week prior to the first message) and a validated indirect technique for measurement at $t + 1$ (after the first message) through $t + 4$ (1 week after the third message). Two sets of behavioral expectations were gathered for each subject for each point in time. Subjects reported on their expectations that they would (a) take a member of their family to a socialized medical clinic for treatment given the opportunity; and (b) vote for a nationalized system of socialized medicine if given the opportunity. B_e had two "states," would or would not in each case. Since some of the data in $t + 2$ was needed to estimate M, predictions of B_e were made for $t + 3$ and $t + 4$ (for further details concerning the methodology see Hewes et al., 1977).

For $t + 3$, the predicted distribution for expectations of taking a family member to a socialized clinic was

$$\hat{B}_e(t + 3) = \begin{pmatrix} \overset{\text{would}}{.79} & \overset{\text{would not}}{.21} \end{pmatrix}$$

The actual distribution for that same point in time was

$$B_e(t + 3) = \begin{pmatrix} \overset{\text{would}}{.85} & \overset{\text{would not}}{.15} \end{pmatrix}$$

A goodness-of-fit test ($\alpha = .05$) was not significant ($\chi^2 = 3.315$, df $= 1$, $p > .075$) indicating that the theory accurately predicted the distribution of B_e within the limits of chance.[39] The probability of rejecting a false null hypothesis (the power of this statistic) was approximately .96 for an effects parameter of .10, and .75 for an effects parameter of .05 (Cohen, 1969).[40] In general, the odds of rejecting an incorrect theory were quite good.

A similar prediction of B_e was made for $t + 4$. No message was received by the subjects immediately prior to $t + 4$ so that S_4 was presumed equivalent to S_3 as dictated by Theorem 3. The predicted distribution for expectations at $t + 4$ of taking a family member to a socialized clinic was

$$\hat{B}_e(t + 4) = \begin{pmatrix} \overset{\text{would}}{.77} & \overset{\text{would not}}{.23} \end{pmatrix}$$

The actual distribution for that same point in time was

$$B_e(t + 4) = \begin{pmatrix} \overset{\text{would}}{.75} & \overset{\text{would not}}{.25} \end{pmatrix}$$

---

[39] Note that the statistical procedures associated with model testing utilize the predictions of the model as the *null hypothesis*. This is the reverse of traditional tests of verbal hypotheses where the theory's predictions are associated with largely unquantified *alternative hypotheses*.

[40] Approximately the same power values apply throughout the rest of the results of this hypothesis.

A goodness-of-fit test ($\alpha = .05$) failed to achieve significance ($\chi^2 = .409$, df $= 1$, $p > .85$) indicating that, within the limits of chance, the theory accurately predicted the distribution of $B_e(t + 4)$. The power of this test was the same as the last.

Having tested the ability of the model to predict one set of expectations, it became important to replicate the findings on a different type of expectation. To that end, expectations concerning the subjects' willingness to vote for or against socialized medicine were assessed using the same procedure over the same time periods.

The predicted distribution of expectations for $t + 3$ was

$$\hat{B}_e(t + 3) = \begin{pmatrix} \overset{\text{for}}{.152} & \overset{\text{against}}{.848} \end{pmatrix}$$

The actual distribution was

$$B_e(t + 3) = \begin{pmatrix} \overset{\text{for}}{.103} & \overset{\text{against}}{.897} \end{pmatrix}$$

The goodness-of-fit test was not significant at the .05 level ($\chi^2 = 2.007$, df $= 1$, $p < .15$). For $t + 4$ the distribution predicted by the theory was

$$\hat{B}_e(t + 4) = \begin{pmatrix} \overset{\text{for}}{.173} & \overset{\text{against}}{.827} \end{pmatrix}$$

whereas the actual distribution of voting expectations was

$$B_e(t + 4) = \begin{pmatrix} \overset{\text{for}}{.125} & \overset{\text{against}}{.875} \end{pmatrix}$$

Again, the goodness-of-fit test failed to achieve statistical significance ($\chi^2 = 1.807$, df $= 1, p < .15$). The predictions of the theory for both $t + 3$ and $t + 4$ were well within the limits of chance. Further, as in the previous set of hypotheses, the odds of detecting a violation of the predictions of the theory were relatively high. The predictions of Theorem 3 are tentatively supported by these results. At the very least, there is reason to proceed with more detailed and powerful tests of the aspect of the theory investigated in this study.

The second prediction made by the theory is somewhat more basic than the first, since it is a test of two of the axioms. Axioms 2 and 3 predict the actual values of the stability matrix. Formally,

$$\mathbf{S}_k = \mathbf{MS}_{k-1} + (\mathbf{I} - \mathbf{M})\mathbf{C}_k \qquad \text{for Axiom 2}$$

and

$$\mathbf{S}_k = \mathbf{S}_{k-1} \qquad \text{for Axiom 3.}$$

The values of $\mathbf{S}_2$ through $\mathbf{S}_4$ for both sets of expectations were taken from the same sample employed in the other hypotheses. $\mathbf{S}_1$ was excluded because it was taken as a "given" in the test procedures used by Hewes *et al.*

For expectations about taking a member of one's family to a socialized clinic, the cumulative lack of fit for S_2 through S_4 was statistically significant ($\chi^2 = 9.972$, df $= 3, p < .05$). For expectations about voting, the cumulative lack of fit was also significant ($\chi^2 = 12.195$, df $= 3, p < .05$). In both of these tests the statistical significance of the goodness-of-fit tests indicates that Axioms 1 and 3 do not completely capture the generative mechanisms for the S matrices. On the other hand, care must be taken not to overemphasize the importance of the significance tests. For instance, the percentage of people misclassified in the S matrices for the first set of expectations was very small: 3.8% for S_2, 5.8% for S_3, and 4.7% for S_4. For the second set of expectations, the percentages of people misclassified were 0.9%, 7.7% and 5.4%, respectively. In other words, the actual errors in estimating S were not large even though they were statistically significant. This point is supported by the accuracy in predicting B_e even given the errors in the stability matrices.

These results leave the status of Axioms 2 and 3 questionable. While they were rejected statistically, very little practical significance was observed in the percentages of misclassification. Hewes et al. (1977) suggest that (a) errors in the composition rules of Axiom 2; (b) problems in the estimation of M; (c) excessive heterogeneity in the sample; or (d) some combination of these could have produced the results presented. In any event, the results of all three hypotheses taken together suggest that the theory is more likely to require a "tune-up" than an "overhaul." As ever, future research is necessary to check the validity of this assertion.

Summary, Conclusions, Caveats and Extensions

On the whole, the validation of the theory fared quite well. Previous literature suggests the validity of a theory like the one presented. Whereas support for Axioms 2 and 3 was qualified, more sophisticated estimation procedures and greater care in sampling may well prove to be better solutions to the lack of fit than modification of the theory. Time and testing will tell.

Meanwhile, there are several directions for development and testing of the theory that appear to be particularly important. First, the theory needs to be tested in a competitive communication environment. As I have argued elsewhere (Hewes, 1975b; Hewes et al., 1977) the strongest test of this theory, or of any theory of the cumulative effects of communication, is one which simulates the contradictory and competing influx of messages that pervades our daily lives. Only in such an environment are we likely to see whether or not a theory of message campaigns is strong enough to live up to its promises; only in such an environment can the particular theory of message campaigns presented here be optimally contrasted with the kinds of "closed system" process models of attitude and behavior change that are currently in vogue (see Hewes et al., 1977, p. 207, 212; Lipstein, 1965, 1968; Massy et al., 1970). The series of three one-sided messages used in this study did not stimulate the kind of competitive message environment necessary for conclusive testing of this theory. Research is currently underway that does simulate such message environments.

A second area of necessary theoretical development concerns the retention parameter matrix M. One limiting assumption of Hewes *et al.* (1977) was that the sampled population was homogeneous with respect to the S_k's, C_k's, and M. While Hewes *et al.* did provide partial empirical support for this assumption for the S and C matrices, no such evidence was provided for M. And, as we have already noted, there are theoretical reasons for believing that the elements of M may vary across individuals. Heterogeneity in the elements of M could well explain some, if not all, of the problems encountered in supporting Axioms 2 and 3 empirically. Thus in order both to increase the predictive power of the theory and to provide an unambiguous test of Axioms 2 and 3, the antecedents of the elements of M should be investigated. As noted previously, individual difference variables such as self-monitoring, cognitive complexity, and self-esteem are likely candidates for future investigation. If these or other potential antecedents prove out, the explanatory and predictive power of the theory would be markedly increased.

Perhaps the component of the theory warranting the greatest attention in future conceptual and empirical work is the C matrix, or matrix of "environmental cues to action." Any theory of message campaigns must provide some mechanism for mapping messages onto behavior or attitude change. The only *manipulable* component of the theory serving this function is the C matrix; however, the current formulation of C leaves much to be desired. The weakness in the current formulation, and also one of its greatest strengths, are both reflected in the fact that the elements of C are *perceived* cues to action (i.e., the elements of C not linked theoretically to any *objective* properties of messages). This is a strength in the sense that historical processes are quite likely to alter the linkages between the objective properties of messages and their subjective interpretation. For instance, if Reisman (1952) is correct in his argument that social approval has become a much more salient determinant of support and/or behavior change during the first half of the twentieth century, then any attempt to forge ahistorical linkages between appeals to "normative beliefs" (for instance, Ajzen, 1971; Fishbein, 1967, p. 488) and the elements of C is doomed to failure. Similarly, the strength of association between message strategies in the political arena based on party identification and voting behavior have undergone considerable historical fluctuation (for instance, Goldberg, 1966). As argued earlier, the kinds of abstract cognitive processes captured in Axioms 1–4 are more likely to be ahistorical than are the linkages between particular message strategies and their attitudinal or behavioral consequences.

On the other hand, the fact that C is not linked to objective aspects of messages makes the theory less useful than it might be. Let me make this point by comparison. Both Woelfel's and Seibold's theories (Chapters 3 and 6, this volume) provide direct suggestions concerning the content of messages that should be constructed to produce behavioral change. This is a highly desirable property for a theory to possess, for it simplifies the transition from purely theoretical investigation to real-world application.[41] Since the present definition of **C** precludes this property, what help can the theory provide in designing message campaigns? Two suggestions come to mind.

The most readily available assistance can be gained without the necessity of creating a theoretical link between the objective properties of messages and **C**. One does not need to incorporate such linkages in the theory at this time to be able to design persuasive messages; the literature in persuasion, advertising, and attitude change is full of such advice. Rather, the primary requirements for designing an effective message campaign are (a) the ability to assess the cumulative impact of a set of predesigned messages; and (b) the ability to estimate when such a campaign has reached the point of diminishing returns. Both of these requirements can be met by adopting the strategy implemented by Hewes *et al.* (1977): Design a set of messages employing the prescripts available in the appropriate literature; have an independent sample of subjects drawn from the target population estimate the elements of **C** for the various messages; use the theory to simulate the effects of the message campaign on the target population. Although one may not be able to specify the values of the elements from theory with this strategy, it would permit us to assess the cumulative effects of a message campaign in advance and to determine points of diminishing returns.

A second suggestion for applying the theory to message design problems more directly addresses the nature of the relationship between the object properties of messages and the elements of **C**. This suggestion involves the use of the current literature in attitude change, advertising, and persuasion to suggest the antecedents of the elements of **C**. These antecedents could then be varied systematically and placed in functional relationship to the elements of **C** empirically. Thus, for instance, if "source credibility" (X_1) and "message intensity" (X_2) were linearly and additively associated with the perceived likelihood of changing from behavior i to behavior j (the target behavior) then we might estimate the empirical form of that relationship with a multiple regression equation of the form

$$c_{ij} = \hat{a} + \hat{b}_1 X_1 + \hat{b}_2 X_2 + E$$

Assuming that we can account for a sizable amount of variability in c_{ij} and that we can cross-validate the values of $\hat{b}_1$ and $\hat{b}_2$, the techniques for estimating c_{ij}

---

[41] There are trade-offs suffered by these theorists, too. Woelfel seems to have avoided the problem of historicity by placing the choice of concepts to be localed in his multidimensional spaces *outside* his theoretical formulation. Further, whereas he is certainly right in principle that one needs ratio level measurement to address issues of cognitive change with the power his theory demands, one has to wonder if his measurement in practice ever attains this ideal. Seibold demands less of his data (interval-level measurement) but the potential for "historicity" in both the form and strength of his causal relationships is high. Time will tell which, if any, of these theorists have made the correct trade-off.

for particular values of X_1 and X_2 are well known (for instance Cohen & Cohen, 1975, pp. 113–115; Kmenta, 1971, pp. 374–377).[42] Clearly other variables than "credibility" and "message intensity" could be treated in a like manner.

The point I am trying to make is that there are solutions readily available to the problem of augmenting the current definition of C to include its objective message antecedents. The social influence literature is certainly rich enough to ensure good hunting. There are, however, three caveats which need to be made before we attempt the wholesale importation of social influence variables into predictive equations for the elements of C. First, it should be very clear from the existing literature that attempts to change behavior have been highly ineffective. Consequently, we must recognize that whatever antecedents may exist for the elements of C, we may be unable to structure C matrices such that they can create any large-scale and rapid behavior change. Second, the available literature on persuasion may not be easy to translate into suggestions for the antecedents of C. Most of the literature is concerned with attitude change, while the elements of C are characterized by behavioral options. Thus, for instance, literature suggesting how one might increase the positive evaluation of an attitude object may prove meaningless if that change can be accomplished only for those who already are performing or are willing to perform a particular behavior. A change in an attitude does not necessarily imply anything about a change in behavior. Antecedents of the former, therefore, may not be antecedents of the latter. Finally, there is no reason to assume that the empirical linkages between message variables and C will prove to be ahistorical. The arguments presented earlier would suggest just the opposite.

Despite these caveats, and the obvious difficulty in finding message variables permitting the a priori specification of the values of the elements of C, there is reason to hope that the theory presented here will prove applicable to the design of message campaigns. Certainly it, or subsequent modifications of it, can be used to simulate message campaigns even before the problem of specifying the antecedents of C has been solved. If future empirical work supports these claims, the theory presented here would put us well on the way to having a rigorous, predictive explanation of the cumulative effects of message campaigns.

Above and beyond these extensions of an speculations about the existing theory are a series of issues of equal importance to the successful study of the message–mediating variable–behavior problem. In the introduction of this chapter, it was suggested that the choice of theoretical frameworks could alter the perceptions of a phenomenon and, ultimately, the success in predicting,

---

[42] I am ignoring a whole host of practical issues in this presentation to save space. These issues include the problems created when the values of the dependent variable are theoretically constrained ($0 \le c_{ij} \le 1$), finding an objective scale for "credibility" and "message intensity," and establishing stable estimates of b_1 and b_2.

explaining, and controlling that phenomenon. We have now reached a point where it is possible to reflect on the truth of that claim in light of a particular theory.

Does an axiomatized stochastic approach unduly restrict the way in which we can view the message–attitude–behavior problem? The answer is a tentative "No" in that a range of determinacy among the relationships is allowed *and is predictable from the theory*. The theory does restrict our perception to behaviors that are mutually exclusive and exhaustive, but this limitation can be overcome easily in principle (Hewes, 1979, pp. 59–61). Does an axiomatized, stochastic theory provide explanations of sufficient power to be useful? The answer is a tentative "Yes." In this particular theory the use of finite mathematics and probability theory as theoretical calculi allow for rigorous and mathematically tractable deductions (but see Rescher, 1970, for another view on the limitations of explanation within a stochastic framework). In the end, we have reason to believe that an axiomatized, stochastic framework is a good bet for further development. The arguments presented in favor of the stochastic nature of intraindividual theories and the predictive power of the theory presented here suggest that it is. Even if the choice of a stochastic framework proves unfruitful, the process of axiomatization recommended and demonstrated in this chapter should hold promise for future theorizing. There is sufficient research into the relationship among messages, mediating variables, and behaviors to make axiomatization justifiable. We may not be right in choosing the axioms or the calculus for our theories, but, at least, if we axiomatize, we will have a pretty good idea when we are wrong.

REFERENCES

Abelson, R. Mathematical models of the distribution of attitudes under controversy. In N. Frederiksen & H. Gulliksen (Eds.), *Contributions to mathematical psychology*. New York: Holt, Rinehart & Winston, 1964.

Ajzen, I. Attitudinal vs. normative messages: An investigation of the differential effects of persuasive communication on behavior. *Sociometry*, 1971, *34*, 263–280.

Ajzen, I., & Fishbein, M. The prediction of behavioral intentions in a choice situation. *Journal of Experimental Social Psychology*, 1969, *5*, 400–404.

Ajzen, I., & Fishbein, M. The prediction of behavior from attitudinal and normative variables. *Journal of Experimental Social Psychology*, 1970, *6*, 466–487.

Ajzen, I., & Fishbein, M. Attitudes and normative beliefs as factors influencing behavioral intentions. *Journal of Personality and Social Psychology*, 1972, *21*, 1–9.

Ajzen, I., & Fishbein, M. Attitudinal and normative variables as predictions of specific behavior. *Journal of Personality and Social Psychology*, 1973, *27*, 41–57.

Ajzen, I., & Fishbein, M. Attitude–behavior relationships: A theoretical analysis and review of empirical research. *Psychological Bulletin*, 1977, *84*, 888–918.

Alwin, D. Making inferences from attitude–behavior correlations. *Sociometry*, 1973, *36*, 253–278.

Anderson, T. Probability models for analyzing time changes in attitudes. In P. Lazarsfeld (Ed.), *Mathematical thinking in the social sciences*, Glencoe, Ill.: Free Press, 1954.

Apostel, L. Towards the formal study of models in the non-formal sciences. In B. Kazemeir & D. Vuysje (Eds.), *The concept and the role of model in mathematics and natural and social science.* Dordrecht: D. Reidel, 1961.

Ayer, A. What is a law of nature? *Revue Internationale de Philosophie, 1956,* No. 36, Fasc. 2.

Bailey, N. *The mathematical theory of infectious diseases and its applications* (2nd ed.). New York: Hafner, 1975.

Bartholemew, D. *Stochastic models for social processes.* New York: Wiley, 1973.

Bellamy, M., & Thompson, W. Stability of attitude as a predeterminer of experimental results. *Speech Monographs,* 1967, *34,* 180–184.

Blaché, R. *Axiomatics.* London: Routledge & Kegan Paul, 1962.

Bray, D. The prediction of behavior from two attitude scales. *Journal of Abnormal and Social Psychology,* 1950, *45,* 64–84.

Brigham, J., & Cook, S. The influence of attitude on the recall of controversial material; A failure to confirm. *Journal of Experimental and Social Psychology,* 1969, *5,* 240–243.

Bunge, M. *Philosophy of physics.* Dordrecht: D. Reidel, 1973.

Calder, B., & Ross, M. *Attitudes and behavior.* Morristown, N.J.: General Learning Press, 1973.

Campbell, D. Social attitudes and other acquired behavioral dispositions. In S. Koch (Ed.), *Psychology: A study of a science* (Vol. 6). New York: McGraw-Hill, 1963.

Cappella, J. An introduction to the literature of causal modeling. *Human Communication Research,* 1975, *1* (4), 362–377.

Cathcart, E. The importance of situational factors: An examination and extension of the Fishbein models. Unpublished doctoral dissertation, University of North Carolina, 1974.

Cattell, R. Psychological theory and scientific method. In R. Cattell (Ed.), *Handbook of multivariate experimental psychology.* Chicago: Rand McNally, 1066. Pp. 1–18.

Chaffee, S., & Linder, J. Three processes of value change without behavior change. *Journal of Communication,* 1969, *19,* 30–40.

Chein, I. Behavior theory and the behavior of attitudes: Some critical comments. *Psychological Review,* 1948, *55,* 175–188.

Cohen, J. *Statistical power analysis for the behavioral sciences.* New York: Academic Press, 1969.

Cohen, J., & Cohen, P. *Applied multiple regression–correlation analysis for the behavioral sciences.* New York: Wiley, 1975.

Coleman, J. *Models of change and response uncertainty.* Englewood Cliffs, N.J.: Prentice-Hall, 1964.

Coleman, J. *The mathematics of collective action.* Chicago: Aldine, 1973.

Cook, T., & Flay, B. The persistence of experimentally induced attitude change. In L. Berkowitz (Ed.), *Advances in experimental social psychology* (Vol. 2). New York: Academic Press, 1978.

Corey, S. Professed attitudes and actual behavior. *Journal of Educational Psychology,* 1937, *28,* 271–280.

Costner, H., & Leik, R. Deductions from "axiomatic theory." *American Sociological Review,* 1964, *29* (6), 819–835.

Craig, R., & Cushman, D. An experimental test of certain attitude change implications of Fishbein's model of attitudes. Submitted to the Interpersonal Division of I. C. A., Chicago, 1975.

Craig, R., & Cushman, D. Communication systems: Interpersonal implications. In G. R. Miller (Ed.), *Explorations in interpersonal communication.* Beverly Hills: Sage, 1976.

Crespi, I. What kinds of attitude measures are predictive of behavior? *Public Opinion Quarterly,* 1971, *42,* 30–40.

Dabbs, J., & Leventhal, H. Effects of varying the recommendations in a fear-arousing communication. *Journal of Personality and Social Psychology,* 1966, *4,* 525–531.

DeVries, D., & Ajzen, I. The relationship of attitudes and normative beliefs to cheating in college. *Journal of Social Psychology,* 1971, *83,* 199–207.

Duncan, O. Axioms or correlations? *American Sociological Review,* 1963, *28,* 452.

Einstein, A. *Essays in science.* New York: Philosophical Library, 1934.

Festinger, L. Behavioral support for opinion change. *Public Opinion Quarterly*, 1964, *28*, 404–417.
Feyerabend, P. Against method. In M. Radner & S. Winokur (Eds.), *Minnesota Studies in the Philosophy of Science*. Minneapolis: University of Minnesota Press, 1970. Pp. 17–130.
Fishbein, M. Sexual behavior and propositional control. Presented at the Psychonomic Society Convention, St. Louis, 1966.
Fishbein, M. Attitudes and the prediction of behavior. In M. Fishbein (Ed.), *Readings in attitude theory and measurement*. New York: Wiley, 1967, 477–492.
Fishbein, M. The prediction of behaviors from attitudinal variables. In C. D. Mortensen & K. Sereno (Eds.), *Advances in communication research*. New York: Harper & Row, 1973, 3–31.
Fishbein, M., & Ajzen, I. Attitudes toward objects as predictors of single and multiple behavioral criteria. *Psychological Review*, 1974, *81*, 59–74.
Fishbein, M., & Ajzen, I. *Belief, attitude, intention and behavior*. Reading, Mass.: Addison-Wesley, 1975.
Freedman, J. Long-term behavioral effects of cognitive dissonance. *Journal of Experimental Social Psychology*, 1965, *1*, 145–155.
Gergen, K. Social psychology as history. *Jornal of Personality and Social Psychology*, 1973, *26*, 309–320.
Gergen, K. Social psychology, science and history. *Personality and Social Psychology Bulletin*, 1976, *2*, 373–383.
Ginsberg, R. Critique of probabilistic models: Application of semi-Markov model to migration. *Journal of Mathematical Sociology*, 1972, *2* (1), 63–82. (a).
Ginsberg, R. Incorporating causal structure and exogenous information in probabilistic models: With special reference to choice, gravity, migration and Markov chains. *Journal of Mathematical Sociology*, 1972, *2* (1), 83–104. (b)
Goldberg, A. Discerning a causal pattern among data on voting behavior. *American Political Science Review*, 1966, *60*, 913–922.
Greeno, J. Representation of learning as discrete transition in a finite state space. In D. Krantz, R. Atkinson, R. D. Luce and P. Suppes (Eds.), *Contemporary developments in mathematical psychology* (Vol. 1). San Francisco: W. J. Freeman, 1974. Pp. 1–44.
Greenwald, A. Behavior change following a persuasive communication. *Journal of Personality*, 1965, *33*, 370–391.
Greenwald, A. The effects of prior commitment on behavior change after a persuasive communication. *Public Opinion Quarterly*, 1966, *4*, 595–601.
Gruder, C., Cook, T., Hennigan, K., Flay, B., Alessis, C., & Halamaj, J. Empirical tests for the absolute sleeper effect predicted from the discounting cue hypothesis. *Journal of Personality and Social Psychology*, 1978, *36*, 1061–1073.
Hanson, N. Is there a logic of scientific discovery? In H. Feigl & G. Maxwell (Eds.), *Current issues in the philosophy of science*. New York: Holt, Rinehart & Winston, 1961. Pp. 20–35.
Harding, J., Kutner, B., Proshansky, H., & Chein, I. Prejudice and ethnic relations. In G. Lindzey (Ed.), *Handbook of social psychology*. Reading, Mass.: Addison-Wesley, 1954. Pp. 1021–1061.
Hawkes, A. An approach to the analysis of electoral swing. *Journal of the Royal Statistical Society*, 1969, *A132*, 68–79.
Hempel, C. *Philosophy of natural science*. Englewood Cliffs, N.J.: Prentice-Hall, 1966.
Hempel, C., & Oppenheim, P. Studies in the logic of explanation. *Philosophy of Science*, 1948, *40*, 135–175.
Henry, N. The retention model: A Markov chain with variable transition probabilities. *Journal of the American Statistical Association*, 1971, *66*, 264–267.
Herniter, J., & Magee, J. Customer behavior as a Markov process. *Operations Research*, 1961, *9*, 105–122.
Hewes, D. Finite stochastic modeling of communication processes: An introduction and some basic readings. *Human Communication Research*, 1975, *1* (3), 271–283. (a)
Hewes, D. A stochastic model of the relationship between attitudes and behaviors. Presented to the Information Systems Division of I. C. A., Chicago, 1975. (b)

Hewes, D. Procedures for estimating "m" and "S_0" in a message mediating variable–behavior model. Unpublished paper, Arizona State University, 1976.

Hewes, D. Process models for sequential, cross-sectional survey data. *Communication Research*, 1978, *5*, 455–482.

Hewes, D. The sequential analysis of social interaction. *Quarterly Journal of Speech*, 1979, *65*, 56–73.

Hewes, D., Brazil, A., & Evans, D. A comparative test of two stochastic processes models of messages, mediating variables and behavioral expectations. Presented at I. C. A., Berlin, 1977.

Hewes, D., & Evans-Hewes, D. Toward a Markov chain model of attitude change. Debut paper in the Interpersonal and Small Group Division of the S. C. A. Convention, Chicago, 1974.

Hewes, D., & Haight, L. Multiple act criteria in the validation of communication traits: What do we gain and what do we lose? Paper presented to the International Communication Association, Philadelphia, 1979.

Homans, G. *Social behavior: Its elementary forms* (2nd ed.). New York: Harcourt Brace Jovanovich, 1971.

Hornik, J. Two approaches to individual differences in cooperative behavior in an expanded prisoner's dilemma game. Unpublished Masters thesis, University of Illinois, 1970.

Hovland, C., Lumsdaine, A., & Sheffield, F. *Experiments on mass communication*. Princeton, N.J.: Princeton University Press, 1949.

Hovland, C., & Weiss, W. The influence of source credibility on communication effectiveness. *Public Opinion Quarterly*, 1951, *15*, 635–650.

Janis, I., & Hovland, C. An overview of persuasibility research. In I. Janis & C. Hovland (Eds.), *Personality and persuasibility*. New Haven: Yale University Press, 1959. Pp. 1–16.

Kaplan, A. *The conduct of inquiry*. San Francisco: Chandler, 1964.

Katz, D., & Stotland, E. A preliminary statement to a theory of attitude structure and change. In S. Koch (Ed.), *Psychology: A study of a science* (Vol. 3). 1959. New York: McGraw-Hill. Pp. 423–475.

Kelley, H., & Thibaut, J. *Interpersonal relations*. New York: Wiley, 1978.

Kelman, H., & Hovland, C. "Reinstatement" of communicator in delayed measurement of opinion change. *Journal of Abnormal and Social Psychology*, 1953, *48*, 327–335.

Kelman, H. Attitudes are alive and well and gainfully employed in the sphere of action. *American Psychologist*, 1974, *29*, 310–324.

Kemeny, J. The social sciences call on mathematics. In the committee on support of research in the mathematical sciences (Ed.), *The mathematical sciences*. Cambridge, Mass.: M. I. T. Press, 1969, pp. 21–36.

Kemeny, J., & Snell, J. *Finite Markov chains*. New York: Van Nostrand, 1960.

Kiesler, C., Collins, B., & Miller, N. *Attitude change*. New York: Wiley, 1969.

Kmenta, J. *Elements of econometrics*. New York: Macmillan, 1971.

Kothandapandi, V. Validation of feeling, belief, and intention to act as three components of attitude and their contribution to prediction of contraceptive behavior. *Journal of Personality and Social Psychology*, 1971, *19*, 321–333.

Krauss, R. Structural and attitudinal factors in interpersonal bargaining. *Journal of Experimental Social Psychology*, 1966, *2*, 42–55.

Krech, D., Crutchfield, R., & Ballachy, E. *Individual in society*. New York: McGraw-Hill, 1962.

Kuhn, T. *The structure of scientific revolutions* (2nd ed.). Chicago: University of Chicago Press, 1970.

Kutner, B., Wilkins, C., & Yarrow, P. Verbal attitudes and overt behavior involving racial prejudice. *Journal of Abnormal and Social Psychology*, 1952, *47*, 649–652.

LaPiere, R. Attitudes vs. actions. *Social Forces*, 1934, *13*, 230–237.

Lee, T., Judge, G., & Zellner, A. *Estimating the parameters of the Markov probability model from aggregated time series data*. Amsterdam: North-Holland, 1970.

Leventhal, H., & Niles, P. A field experiment on fear arousal with data on the validity of questionnaire measures. *Journal of Personality*, 1964, *32*, 459–479.

Leventhal, H., Jones, J., & Trembly, G. Sex differences in attitude and behavior change under conditions of fear and specific instructions. *Journal of Experimental Social Psychology*, 1966, *2*, 387–399.

Leventhal, H., Singer, R., & Jones, S. Effects of fear and specificity of recommendations upon attitudes and behavior. *Journal of Personality and Social Psychology*, 1965, *2*, 20–29.

Leventhal, H., & Watts, J. Sources of resistance to fear-arousing communication on smoking and lung cancer. *Journal of Personality*, 1966, *34*, 155–175.

Leventhal, H., Watts, J., & Pagano, F. Effects of fear and instructions on how to cope with danger. *Journal of Personality and Social Psychology*, 1967, *6*, 313–321.

Levine, G., & Burke, C. *Mathematical model techniques for learning theories.* New York: Academic Press, 1972.

Lipstein, B. A mathematical model of consumer behavior. *Journal of Marketing Research*, 1965, *2*, 259–265.

Lipstein, B. Test marketing: A perturbation in the market place. *Management Science*, 1968, *14* (8), 437–B448.

Maffei, R. Advertising effectiveness, brand switching and market dynamics. *Journal of Industrial Economics*, 1961, *9* (2), 119–131.

Massy, W., Montgomery, D., & Morrison, D. *Stochastic models of buying behavior.* Cambridge, Mass.: M. I. T. Press, 1970.

McClelland, P. *Causal explanation and model building in history, economics and the new economic history.* Ithaca, N.Y.: Cornell University Press, 1975.

McFarland, D. Intragenerational social mobility as a Markov process: Including a time-stationary Markovian model that explains observed declines in mobility rates over time. *American Sociological Review*, 1970, *35*, 463–476.

McGuire, W. Cognitive consistency and attitude change. *Journal of Abnormal and Social Psychology*, 1960, *60*, 345–353. (a)

McGuire, W. Direct and indirect persuasive effects on dissonance-producing messages. *Journal of Abnormal and Social Psychology*, 1960, *60*, 354–358. (b)

McGuire, W. A syllogistic analysis of cognitive relationships. In M. Rosenberg & C. Hovland (Eds.), *Attitude organization and change.* New Haven: Yale University Press, 1960. (c)

McGuire, W. Personality and susceptibility to social influence. In E. F. Borgatta & W. W. Lambert (Eds.), *Handbook of personality theory and research.* Chicago: Rand-McNally, 1968. Pp. 1130–1187. (a)

McGuire, W. Personality and attitude change; An information-processing theory. In A. Greenwald *et al.* (Eds.), *Psychological foundations of attitudes.* New York: Academic Press, 1968. (b)

McGuire, W. Nature of attitude and attitude change. In G. Lindzey and E. Aronson (Eds.), *Handbook of social psychology.* Reading, Mass.: Addison-Wesley, 1969.

McGuire, W. Persuasion, resistance, and attitude change. In I. Pool and W. Schramm (Eds.), *Handbook of communication.* Chicago: Rand-McNally, 1973. Pp. 216–252.

McNemar, Q. Opinion–attitude methodology. *Psychological Bulletin*, 1946, *4*, 43.

McPhee, R. Derivation and test of a new model of message–attitude–behavior relationship. Presented to the Information Systems Division of Chicago, 1975.

Mervielde, I. Methodological problems of research about attitude–behavior consistency. *Quality and Quantity*, 1977, *11*, 259–281.

Miller, G. A. Finite Markov processes in psychology. *Psychometrika*, 1952, *17*, 149–167.

Miller, G. R. A crucial problem in attitude research. *Quarterly Journal of Speech*, 1967, *53*, 235–240.

Miller, G. R. Communication and persuasion research: Current problems and prospects. *Quarterly Journal of Speech*, 1968, *54*, 268–277.

Miller, G. R. Human information processing: Some research guidelines. In R. Kibler & L. Barker (Eds.), *Conceptual frontiers in speech–communication.* New York: Speech Association of America, 1969.

Miller, W. L. Measures of electoral change using aggregate data. *Journal of the Royal Statistical Association*, 1972, *135*, 122–142.

Mischel, W. *Personality and assessment*. New York: Wiley, 1968.

Nagel, E. *The structure of science*. New York: Harcourt, Brace & World, 1961.

Natsoulas, T. Concerning introspective knowledge. *Psychological Bulletin*, 1970, *73* (2), 89–111.

Nisbett, R., & Gordon, A. Self-esteem and susceptibility to social influence. *Journal of Personality and Social Psychology*, 1967, *5*, 268–276.

Nisbett, R., & Wilson, T. Telling more than we can know: Verbal reports on mental processes. *Psychological Review*, 1977, *84*, 231–259.

Orne, M. On the social psychology of the psychological experiment: With particular reference to demand characteristics and their implication. *American Psychologist*, 1962, *17*, 776–783.

Ostrom, T. The relationship between the affective, behavioral and cognitive components of attitude. *Journal of Experimental Social Psychology*, 1969, *5*, 12–30.

Pace, C. Opinion and action: A study in validity of attitude measurement. *American Psychologist*, 1949, *4*, 242.

Popper, K. *The logic of scientific discovery*. New York: Basic Books, 1959.

Raden, D. Situational thresholds and attitude–behavior consistency. *Sociometry*, 1977, *40*, 123–129.

Reisman, D. *The lonely crowd*. New Haven: Yale University Press, 1952.

Rescher, N. *Scientific explanation*. New York: Free Press, 1970.

Reynolds, P. *A primer on theory construction*. New York: Bobbs-Merrill, 1971.

Saltiel, J., & Woelfel, J. Inertia in cognitive processes: The role of accumulated information in attitude change. *Human Communication Research*, 1975, *1* (4), 1975.

Schlenker, B. Social psychology and science: Another look. *Personality and Social Psychology Bulletin*, 1976, *2*, 384–390.

Schuman, H., & Johnson, M. Attitudes and behavior. *Annual Review of Sociology*, 1976, *2*, 161–207.

Schwartz, S., & Tessler, R. A test of a model reducing measured attitude–behavior discrepancies. *Journal of Personality and Social Psychology*, 1972, *24*, 225–236.

Seeman, M., & Evans, J. Alienation and learning in a hospital setting. *American Sociological Review*, 1962, *21*, 772–783.

Seibold, D. Communication research and the attitude–verbal report–overt behavior relationship: A critique and theoretical reformulation. Presented at the S. C. A. Convention, Chicago, 1974.

Seibold, D. Communication research and the attitude–verbal report–overt behavior relationships: A critique and theoretical reformulation. *Human Communication Research*, 1975, *2*, 3–32.

Shaw, M., & Costanzo, P. *Theories of social psychology*. New York: McGraw-Hill, 1970.

Sherif, C., Sherif, M., & Nebergal, R. *Attitude and attitude change: The social judgment–involvement approach*. Philadelphia: W. B. Saunders, 1965.

Silverman, B., & Cochrane, R. The relationship between verbal expressions of behavioral intentions and overt behavior. *Journal of Social Psychology*, 1971, *84*, 51–56.

Simons, H. Psychological theories of persuasion: An auditor's report. *Quarterly Journal of Speech*, 1971, *57* (4), 383–392.

Singer, B., & Spilerman, S. Social mobility models for heterogeneous populations. In H. Costner (Ed.), *Sociological Methodology 1974*. San Francisco: Jossey-Bass, 1974.

Slovic, P., & Lichtenstein, S. Comparison of Bayesian and regression approaches to the study of information processing in judgment. *Organizational Behavior and Human Performance*, 1971, *6*, 649–744.

Sluzki, C. Transactional disqualifications. *Archives of General Psychiatry*, 1967, *16*, 494–504.

Smith, E., & Miller, F. Limits on perception of cognitive processes: A reply to Nisbett and Wilson. *Psychological Review*, 1978, *85*, 355–362.

Snyder, M. Individual differences in the self-control of expressive behavior. Doctoral dissertation, Stanford University, 1972.

Snyder, M. The self-monitoring of expressive behavior. *Journal of Personality and Social Psychology*, 1974, *30*, 502–517.

Snyder, M. Impression management. In L. S. Wrightsman (Ed.), *Social psychology*. Belmont, Calif.: Brooks–Cole, 1977.

Snyder, M. Self-monitoring processes. In L. Berkowitz (Ed.), *Advances in experimental social psychology* (Vol. 12). New York: Academic Press, 1979.

Snyder, M., & Swann, W., Jr. When actions reflect attitudes: The politics of impression management. *Journal of Personality and Social Psychology*, 1976, *34*, 1034–1042.

Snyder, M., & Tanke, E. Behavior and attitude: Some people are more consistent than others. *Journal of Personality*, 1976, *44*, 510–517.

Spilerman, S. The analysis of mobility processes by the introduction of independent variables into a Markov chain. *American Sociological Review*, 1972, *37*, 277–294.

Suppes, P., & Atkinson, R. *Markov learning models of multiperson interactions*. Stanford, Calif.: Stanford University Press, 1960.

Taylor, M. Towards a mathematical theory of influence and attitude change. *Human Relations*. 1968, *21* (2), 121–139.

Tesser, A. Self-generated attitude change. In L. Berkowitz (Ed.), *Advances in experimental social psychology* (Vol. 11). New York: Academic Press, 1978.

Tittle, C., & Hill, R. Attitude measurement and prediction of behavior: An evaluation of conditions and measurement techniques. *Sociometry*, 1967, *30*, 199–213.

Triandis, H. Exploratory factor analysis of behavioral component of social attitudes. *Journal of Abnormal and Social Psychology*, 1964, *68*, 420–430.

Turner, M. *Philosophy and the science of behavior*. New York: Appleton–Century–Crofts, 1967.

Udell, J. Can attitude measurement predict consumer behavior? *Journal of Marketing*, 1965, *29*, 46–50.

von Wright, G. *Explanation and understanding*. Ithaca, N.Y.: Cornell University Press, 1971.

Waly, P., & Cook, S. Effect of attitude on judgments of plausibility. *Journal of Personality and Social Psychology*, 1965, *2*, 745–749.

Warland, R., & Sample, J. Response certainty as a moderator variable in attitude measurement. *Rural Sociology*, 1973, *38*, 175–186.

Warner, L., & DeFluer, M. Attitude as an interaction concept: Social constraint and social distance as intervening variables between attitudes and action. *American Sociological Review*, 1969, *34*, 153–169.

Weigel, R., & Newman, L. Increasing attitude–behavior by correspondence by broadening the scope of the behavioral measure. *Journal of Personality and Social Psychology*, 1976, *33*, 793–802.

Weinstein, A. Predicting behavior from attitudes. *Public Opinion Quarterly*, 1972, *36*, 355–360.

Wells, L., & Marwell, G. *Self-esteem: Its conceptualization and measurement*. Beverly Hills: Sage, 1976.

Wicker, A. An examination of the 'other variables' explanation of attitude–behavior inconsistency. *Journal of Personality and Social Psychology*, 1971, *19*, 18–30.

Wiggins, L. *Panel analysis: Latent probability models for attitude and behavioral processes*. San Francisco: Jossey–Bass, 1973.

3

Foundations of Cognitive Theory: A Multidimensional Model of the Message–Attitude–Behavior Relationship

JOSEPH WOELFEL

> By the aid of language different individuals can, to a certain extent, compare their experiences. Then it turns out that certain sense perceptions of different individuals correspond to each other, while for other sense perceptions no such correspondence can be established. We are accustomed to regard as real those sense perceptions which are common to different individuals, and which therefore are, in a measure, impersonal. . . . The only justification for our concepts and system of concepts is that they serve to represent the complex of our experiences: beyond this they have no legitimacy [A. Einstein, *The meaning of relativity* (5th ed). Princeton, N.J.: Princeton University Press, 1956. Pp. 1–2].

A fundamental insight of modern communication theory is that we do not view "reality" except through the mediation of our system of concepts. The interaction of "reality" and our concepts makes up "experience." The goal of science is to render "experience" as orderly, informative, and predictable as possible and it does this by modifying the set of symbols by which experience is represented.

In the absence of concepts, there is no experience at all—at least no experience we can remember from moment to moment. When concepts have been ill chosen, the resulting experiences will be inconsistent and unpredictable. Depending on the inappropriateness, this confusion may range from minor to chaotic.

It follows that behavior as a "reality" has no meaning, and that the meaning of behavior as an "experience" is dependent on the concepts by which it is defined. With little modification, the concept of behavior as it is understood by communication scientists (and the concept "attitude" which is derived from it) comes to us from Aristotle. In virtually every branch of science except com-

MESSAGE–ATTITUDE–BEHAVIOR RELATIONSHIP
Theory, Methodology, and Applications

munication and the social sciences, scientists have found Aristotelian concepts incompatible with the symbol system we call "science" and have replaced them with new concepts drawn from Galileo, Newton, Gauss, Einstein, and others.

In this chapter, a non-Aristotelian theory of behavior, based on the works of these thinkers will be presented. Among its advantages will be found (a) an increased level of predictability for any behavior; (b) a logically self-consistent theory that is also consistent with contemporary physical theory; and (c) a relatively well-developed engineering capability.

Behavior, Attitude, and Entelechy

As noted elsewhere (Woelfel, 1977), the structure of Greek thought was heavily categorical, and the notion of the continuum was not well developed. This led to particular difficulties in describing (even prior to explaining) motion or change of any sort. Aristotle's definition of motion, in fact, considers it to be an intermediate semireal state between two "actual" states of being (rather than a quantum physics of subatomic particles, Aristotle describes every entity in experience as a quantum). In Aristotle's view, every body "jumps" from here to there across a semireal state of not actually being anywhere.

Aristotle's thought was not only categorical, but also teleogical. Every object (not only living objects) moved only insofar as it "intended" to be in the place to which it moved. Intention pervaded Aristotle's universe, living and nonliving. It is important to understand that it is not the case that Aristotle generalized his experience of human intention to intentionality for all other things; rather the opposite is true. Aristotle's concept of purpose was developed for nonliving material bodies and applied to human activity subsequently. Aristotle's belief that humans act for ends follows from his belief that the universe acts for ends, and not conversely.

Contemporary attitude theory continues to cling to this Aristotelian model of human activity even though the same model has been found to fail for every other domain of experience to which it has been applied. Behaviors are almost universally conceived of and operationalized as discrete acts, undertaken due to some "purpose" or in order to satisfy some goal, gain a reward, or avoid a punishment (these intentions or predispositions are "attitudes"). What's more, this retention of the Aristotelian theory of human activity is despite consistent, clear, and long-standing failure of the theory in virtually any of its manifest forms to fit observations to even the most generous tolerances. By the late nineteenth and early twentieth century, the deviation of this model from experience was apparent, and, for example, Max Weber posited an Aristotelian rational model for human behavior, but acknowledged its value only as an "ideal type" from which everyday behavior should be expected to deviate (Weber, 1949). Historically, the development of twentieth century social science gave rise to an intensified study of the Aristotelian model, although, to be sure, most social scientists would not have been aware of their debt to Aristotle. The introduction of mathematics into social science in the early decades of this century led to complicated models of internal psychological attitude structures, and the development of the much simpler Likert-type scale and later the very similar semantic differential-type scale led to widespread quantitative studies of human attitudes and their relationship to behavior. The development of the high speed computer, coupled with widespread availability of prepackaged ANOVA (analysis of variance) software during the post war period led to a relatively profuse outburst of what has come to be viewed as the classical model of attitude research: a series of affective orientations toward some attitude object measured by Likert-type or semantic differential-type scales, random assignment of subjects to a message-like treatment, followed by ANOVA checks of the statistical significance of effects. Several dozen such studies have been reported in communication journals, and hundreds may be found in psychology journals.

In spite of the early enthusiasm such studies generated, very little solid theoretical advancement paralleled these researches, and by the early 1970s, such studies reported in the literature had dwindled to only a trickle. The manifest reasons for this disillusionment have been threefold. First, affective conceptions of attitude, that is, measures of the degree to which persons like or favor an attitude object, or perceive likely advantages to accrue to them from the performance of some act, have been very disappointing predictors of later observed behaviors. This has been true virtually regardless of the type of scale employed in their measurement or the type of statistical analysis employed in arraying the data. Second, attitude-change studies have produced a bewildering array of apparently contradictory effects, such as direct changes monotonically related to the change message, nonlinear relations between change stimulus and measured attitude change, delayed changes ("sleeper effect") and even nonmonotone effects ("boomerang effects"). Not only have these changes been widely varied, but seldom is the amount of variance in the change scores explained by the message treatments larger than a few percentage points. Third, and following quite directly from the first two reasons, few efficient or powerful engineering applications have followed from this work. Whereas applications of social science in general have grown rapidly in volume and precision, there is little direct evidence that attitude theory as such has added much additional help to aid in the solution of pervasive and important human problems.

In retrospect, it is easy enough to see that the "classical" approach to the message–attitude–behavior relationship suffers from important methodological problems. First, the universal application of category-type scaling has dramatically restricted the precision of measurement in such studies, thus reducing the amount of reliable variance in attitudes detected in a typical study. This led to a widespread belief that attitudes are hard to change, when in fact only relatively large change could be detected with the imprecise measures used.

Second,   the heavy reliance on the ANOVA design led to a strong tendency to establish only whether or not any variance at all is accounted for by the manipulations, rather than to note that the absolute magnitudes of explained variance have been almost universally negligible. This in turn has often led investigators to conclude that theories have been supported because statistically significant effects have been noted, when quantitative evaluations would have led to more disappointing conclusions. Furthermore, in cases where theories have been rejected, the ANOVA design leaves little guidance as to how or in what directions theory must be modified to produce more acceptable results.

Most importantly, such methodological insufficiencies may have led researchers away from a much more important conclusion, that is, that the underlying model of discrete jumps from one qualitative state of behavior to another discrete state of behavior in response to internal affective orientations to attitude objects may itself be false, or at best applicable to a very small range of human activity.

At the same time, a viable alternative formulation of the message–attitude–behavior relationship was being developed particularly by the philosopher George Herbert Mead (1934) and his followers, most of whom were sociologists. Mead (who, as a philosopher, was a specialist in the study of Aristotle), although concerned with discrete acts, explicitly directed attention toward behavior as a continuing process, rather than as a series of discrete acts. He frequently used the word "ongoing" to describe human activity. To be sure, Mead considered human behavior to exhibit a deliberate, purposeful aspect, but this he considered to emerge only at junctures where the ongoing activity had been interrupted. By far the larger part of human activity consisted of carrying out relatively standardized processes appropriate to a role or set of roles, which together constituted an organized self. An attitude within this model consists of the global relationship of the individual to an object or set of objects, including but not restricted to an affective component. While the subjective utility of adopting an attitude or role was a factor in Mead's account of an actor's assimilation of an attitude or role into the self, by far the larger part of the basis for adoption of an attitude or role was the consistent and repeated definition of those attitudes or roles as consistent with the individual's self by the set of "others" with whom the individual communicated or "interacted."

Insofar as the position of an actor in his or her environment is continually changing due to the ongoing process of activity, attitudes in Mead's theory are in continual flux. Insofar as the behaviors (and situations within which behaviors are enacted) are organized, and insofar as the definitions of the self offered by others around the individual are consistent over time, the self and its constituent attitudes exhibit organization and stability. Depending on which of these two aspects of Mead's thinking they emphasized, two schools of thought emerged from Mead's work. The first, primarily developed by Mead's student Herbert Blumer (1969) emphasized the spontaneity and evaescence of attitudes and the self. This school never developed a quantitative research focus, although it has led to much insightful analysis of human interaction.

A second group, following from the work of other students of Mead, Manford Kuhn and Alfred Lindesmith, and from Lindesmith's student Anselm Strauss (Lindesmith & Strauss, 1956), emphasized the more stable aspects of attitudes and the self. This work was given an initial quantitative form by sociologists for the most part, particularly by Sewell and Haller. Important clarifications of the theory were offered by Mills (1940), who conceived of acts as if they were words, and likened the decision to perform an act to the "decision" to apply an appropriate word in a given linguistic context. A "motive" for Mills was less a driving force toward action than a justification for an action which one has learned as appropriate for a given behavioral context. This view was made more explicit by Nelson Foote (1951), and reached a particularly clear form in the work of Edwin Lemert (1951).

Lemert suggested that individuals, particularly children, often exhibit relatively random and unorganized behaviors, some of which are deviant according to either statistical or moral norms. When observers take note of such behavior and offer consistent role definitions of the individual on the basis of these observations (labeling), the individual may adopt these definitions of self, ascribe the labeled role to themselves, and therefore enact behaviors conceived to be appropriate to the role regardless of their perceived personal utility.

Sewell, Haller, and Portes (1969) extended these notions away from deviant acts and roles, and posed a theory suggesting that the consistent definitions of "significant others" might lead adolescent youth to designate a specific level of educational attainment as appropriate to themselves, and consequently seek an education within this band. Their empirical research was able to explain fully 50% of the variance in the decision of high school seniors to attend college. Later, Haller and the present author (1971) showed that the averaged educational and status expectations of a set of "significant others" for a sample of high school students accounted for about 50% of the variance in the educational and occupational aspirations of those children. (These aspirations are clearly the kind of long-range stable attitudes that lend themselves well to empirical research in the field.)

The Significant Other Project (Woelfel and Haller, 1971) was significant in another unexpected respect. By 1967, the most formal statements of self-theory, in spite of their verbal emphasis on process, were still categorical in form (Kinch, 1963; Woelfel, 1967). Activities, like other objects, were thought to be defined by placing them into categories, and the self was similarly thought to be defined by being placed into categories. (Bruner, 1958; Woelfel, 1967). The resulting relationship between object and self (the attitude) was then either consistent (this is the type of behavior a person like myself might perform) or inconsistent (this is not the type of behavior a person like myself might perform). This categorical form of the theory resisted precise measurement, made mathematization of the theory cumbersome, and led to important theoretical intractability, particularly when dealing with the problem of multiple and disparate sources of influence (such as significant others). If all of a person's significant others held consistent expectations for his or her behavior, prediction of subsequent activity was simple, but how an individual might behave when faced with multiple and disparate expectations remained problematic. In fact, the problem of which behavior to choose reduced to the question of which influence source to accept, which is really the same question pushed back one stage (this same question provided the impetus for the long-term interest of communication scientists in source credibility).

The significant-other project led out of this infinite regress in a purely accidental way. As it turned out, both attitudes measured in that study were attitudes toward levels of attainment (i.e., the level of education students hoped to attain and the level of occupational prestige to which they aspired). Each of the expectations of each of the individual's significant others was thus represented by a value on a continuum. For lack of a more sophisticated alternative suggested by theory, these multiple expectation levels were simply averaged to yield an average level of expected attainment. Surprisingly, this variable alone accounted for more than half the variance in the students' own attitudes. This was higher than other attitude researches had attained, even using extensive multivariate models, by a wide margin.

Careful scrutiny of the logic of averaging then led investigators to realize the potential of the theory implicit in this operation, since it turns out that the average of any set of diverse expectations represents a least-squares balance point at which resulting stresses ought to be at a minimum. Such a theory (sometimes called—somewhat unfortunately, perhaps—Linear Force Aggregation Theory) had many desirable features. First, it lent itself very well to mathematical statement, since the equation for attitude change reduced simply to the expression

$$A_n = (A_0 N_0 + I N_1)/(N_0 + N_1) \qquad (1)$$

where A_n = The new attitude
   A_0 = The old attitude
   N_0 = The number of messages (amount of information) out of which the old attitude was formed
   I = The average value of the new information received
   N_1 = The number of messages in the new information.

Second, the theory predicted unambiguously that the stability of any attitude would be proportional to the amount of information (number of messages) out of which it had been formed. Subsequent research, particularly by Saltiel (Saltiel & Woelfel, 1975) and by Danes, Hunter, and Woelfel (1978) have been strongly supportive of this notion over alternative plausible formulations. Third, the theory could be shown to be identical in form to classical

Newtonian theory. The possibility of a unified theory encompassing conceptions not only of social and psychological changes but physical motion as well has been very exciting. Consider, for example, the implications of the fact that equations from Newton's theory predict human attitude change and human behaviors better than any theory specifically developed to deal with human phenomena by a wide margin (to be sure, this notion still constitutes a formidable barrier to the theory's acceptance by social scientists to whom the fundamental difference of humans from all other aspects of nature remains a basic philosophical and even religious belief).

In spite of the moral outrage caused some workers by a "physical" theory of human behavior, the predictive record of the theory even in this early formulation has been extraordinary. In a previously unreported study, Woelfel and Hernandez (1970) were able to account for 89% of the variance in rate of marijuana smoking in four separate random samples of 341 university students from two countries. This study is particularly interesting because it provides a direct contrast between affective and cognitive attitude theories. The traditionally conceived attitude, measured by the item "What is your attitude toward marijuana?" followed by five response alternatives ranging from very beneficial to very harmful, explained less than 5% of the variance in self-reported rate of use, while the self-concept item "To what extent do you consider yourself the type of person who might smoke marijuana?" followed by five response alternatives accounted for over 80% of the variance in self-reported behavior alone. While one might be tempted to think that this measure is a consequence of one's observation of one's own smoking behavior rather than a cause, the fact that over 70% of the variance in that item itself can be accounted for by the weighted average of expectations for the individual of his or her friends contradicts such a simplistic explanation.

Mettlin (1973) used an identical model to account for about as much variance in cigarette smoking among adults. In a widely different context, the same model did approximately as well in explaining both the formation of attitudes and subsequent behaviors toward French Canadian Separatism among a sample of adult residents of Montreal, Quebec, Canada. (Woelfel, Woelfel, Gillam, & McPhail 1974). Although other examples could be cited, it should suffice to point out that, even in this early form, the theory has never failed a research test, and in fact no alternative theory of which we are aware has accounted for as much variance as has this theory in as wide a variety of contexts.

In spite of these early successes, the theory in this form exhibited important deficiencies. First among these was that the theory did not tie itself unambiguously to a consistent measurement system, but rather relied on the imprecise category-type scales like the Likert-type and semantic differential-type scales then in current vogue among attitude researchers. Researchers have long been aware that the use of such pseudoordinal scaling methods was far less desirable than the use of ratio-type scaling, but few researchers, with the important exception of Stevens (1951) and his student Hamblin (1974), had any real idea of how to move to the level of ratio scaling. Secondly, the theory was restricted to applications in those areas where dependent attitudes and behaviors could be quantified as rates (like rate of cigarette smoking) or pseudorates (like level of occupational prestige). This is not to say that predictions the theory made about the adoption or nonadoption of discrete behaviors were false, but rather that the theory could make no such predictions, since no method for averaging discrete expectations was known. Thus, for example, if one's mother wanted one to be a doctor and one's father wanted him or her to be a lawyer, the theory must predict that he or she would select an occupation "between" these two expectations, but it was not clear what "between" might mean in this context.

Categories and Continua

Of course one does not choose between "doctor" and "lawyer", but rather between one's experience of doctor and lawyer. This experience of doctor or lawyer is an "object" (Blumer, 1966) to the person. An object may be thought of as a category into which a person may or may not fit, and this, of course, is the source of the difficulty. But the object itself may be defined by placing it into still more general categories, such as "occupation," "high-paying," and so forth. Different objects (occupations, in this instance) may be placed into categories on the basis of their similarity in some regard. Similarity (or dissimilarity) however, is not a categorical concept, but rather a continuously variable notion, bounded by identity (no difference) and infinity (infinitely different). This point marks an important interface between the idea of the discrete or categorical and the idea of the continuum, since objects are included into a category when they are "sufficiently" similar to warrant inclusion. In fact the argument can be made that similarity is a prior notion to category, since objects are categorized on the basis of their similarity. The notion of category is, in fact, related to the notions of purpose and interest, since a set of objects may be similar enough to warrant inclusion in the same category for one purpose, yet different enough to fit different categories for other purposes even though their similarity relations remain the same. In such cases, only the purpose or interest changes. Thus if we have a specific ailment, doctors are too different from each other to be included within a single category, but rather a specific doctor is needed, and must be distinguished from all other doctors. Yet if our interest lies in choosing an occupation, all doctors may be safely placed in the category "doctor," even though all the differences among them, of which we were previously aware, still exist. Only the importance of those difference or separation relations for our purposes has changed. Thus, for some purposes, the set of difference relations among a set of objects may be unimportant, and so we may consider the set as a single object, which is itself embedded in a set of difference relations with yet other objects. Each of these may also be subdivided as our need requires, and so on. For our purposes, a set of objects may be considered a single object when the difference relations or separations among its constituent objects are too small to be important for the purpose at hand, even though we understand that the object is not inherently monistic, but has designatable and differentiable internal components.

Our experience consists of such objects, ranging from the smallest objects capable of discrimination from the background of our experience by our sensory apparatus, up to the most global categories. Clearly, no object has existence independent of the human act of categorization. These objects are arbitrarily discrete regions, neighborhoods, or domains of the continuum of experience which are bounded by some interest that makes the neighborhood particularly salient. These neighborhoods or domains are often made to seem even more discrete because they are named or described by recourse to a symbol or set of symbols, such as "Albany" or "happiness," although neither Albany nor happiness have distinct natural boundaries independent of arbitrary human designations. These objects are themselves sufficiently different or far removed from other regions to be designated by different symbols. Objects may then be described as named regions or neighborhoods separated from other such neighborhoods by some distance or dissimilarity. In this sense, it is possible and meaningful to conceive of a region that lies between the region of experience called "doctor" and the region of experience called "lawyer." Overall, therefore, our experience may be thought of as a space within which lie symbols designating regions of our experience which have been salient enough to be designated by symbols. In order to show how such a space may be constructed and calibrated, and to aid in distinguishing it from other spatial renderings of human cognitions like those particularly of Osgood, Suci, and Tannenbaum (1957), it is appropriate to proceed somewhat more formally than previously.

Definitions

We assume that individuals encode observations into symbols, combine and store the symbols in some way, and compare them with other persons and across time by means of language. These processes are cognitive processes. Science, by this definition, is a cognitive process, although a collective cognitive process to be sure. Gauging the state of one's health across the years is also a cognitive process, as is determing one's own political position from day to day. Collective cognitive processes (or cultural processes) are those cognitive processes resulting from the coordinated activity of a system of individual cognitive processes, like science, ensemble music, or election of government officials.

The primary symbol system underlying cognitive processes is assumed to be the vernacular language. Relatively invariant complexes of experiences are symbolized by certain vernacular language words like "red" or "hard" or "disappointed." These several complexes themselves are perceived to differ from each other in some ways; in fact, the minimal comparison between two experiences that can be reported is the dichotomous discrimination of difference versus no difference. The differences or separations among the symbols are considered primitive or fundamental variables in the theory. Any concept in the language has a meaning that is given by its pattern of similarities and differences to the other concepts. Change in these separations over time therefore represents change in meaning or definition of concepts. These changes are cognitive processes.

The Symbol Set

The first step in measurement is the stipulation of a symbol set. We choose the set of positive real numbers (see Suppes and Zinnes, 1963) for several reasons. First, since the set is infinite, there is no minimal interval size as with a finite set, like, for example, the semantic differential 7-interval scale. Moreover, the real number system is systematic, forming new symbols by rules; a very large set of transformations in the set (like addition and multiplicating, for example) are well known, and a very large set of people are already familiar with elements of the real numbers—far more than are familiar with other psychometric devices.

Rules of Correspondence

The second requirement of measurement is the establishment of a clear, consensual, and unambiguous rule for establishing correspondences between observations and symbols. We choose, following Einstein (1961) and others (Campbell, 1928; Ellis; 1966; Hamblin, 1974, Hays, 1967; Krantz, Luce, and Suppes, 1971; Stevens, 1951; Suppes and Zinnes, 1963), a ratio rule. First, an arbitrary element of the set of observations to be measured is designated as a unit standard against which all other observations are compared. As noted earlier, the primitive observations of cognitive processes are the separations among concepts, and one of these separations is chosen as a standard; other separations are compared to this standard as ratios. Formally, the rule is expressed as a conditional statement "if a and b are u units apart, how far apart are x and y?" In the present case, "far apart" is defined to mean "different in meaning" so that increasing numbers represent pairs of concepts of increasingly different meaning. Formally, the rule requires that a pair of concepts S_{ab} whose difference in meaning is perceived to be double that of another pair S_{eb} should be represented by a separation double that of the second pair, or $S_{ab} = 2S_{eb}$. Furthermore, no formal restriction on how small a difference may be reported is established by the scaling procedures: Limitations of precision are given by the observational capabilities of the observer, and not by the scale on which such differences are reported. It is important to understand that the use of a precise scale does itself not guarantee precise measurement, since the actual process by which the scale is employed can add or subtract from precision. Because the length of a bridge, for example, is *reported* in ratio numbers—say, meters—does not guarantee that the measurements have been carefully made. But the use of an imprecise scale—like a semantic differential scale—is sufficient to limit precision of measure.

It is also important to note that this procedure of measuring the dissimilarities in meaning directly is inherently more precise than the indirect procedure recommended by Osgood *et al.* (1957), where the pairwise dissimilarities of any two objects are calculated from their measured dissimilarities from a set of attribute words. Nor is the difference minor. Meyer (1975) shows this with a simple example:

> Suppose one wishes to measure the voltage between two dynodes A and B of a photomultiplier tube.
>
> 1. We may measure $V_A = (2010 \pm 10)$ Volts and $V_B = (1982 \pm 10)$ volts using a voltmeter capable of a relative error $\epsilon \sim 10/2000 = 1/2\%$. The voltage difference $V_A - V_B = 28$ volts with an error of $\epsilon_{(A-B)} = \sqrt{10^2 + 10^2} = 14$ volts yielding $V_A - V_B = 28 \pm 14$ volts. $\epsilon_{(A-B)} = 50\%$
> 2. We may measure the voltage difference directly with a voltmeter good to 10% and get 28 ± 3 volts. It would appear that there is usually a hard way to do business [p. 41].

Note that the use of the indirect procedure increases the error in this simple instance by 500%, even though the measurement instrument employed was 20 times more precise. Communication researchers, like other social scientists, have often been indifferent to precision of measure, and the result often has been that good ideas (like Osgood's notion of semantic space) have failed to yield much more than insights because they are simply too crudely measured to behave lawfully. Although our intentions bear important resemblences to Osgood's, the execution in the present case can be shown to produce results up to several orders of magnitude more precise than are possible by Osgood's methods. Whatever imprecision of measure may exist within this system is not a consequence of the imprecision of the scale on which measurements are reported, and this is a crucial advantage.

Once accomplished, these procedures make possible a mathematically precise definition of the meaning of any concept; since each concept is defined by its relative similarity to all other concepts, any concept C is defined by the $1 \times (k - 1)$ vector of separations from the $k - 1$ other concepts. The interrelationships among any subset of k concepts is similarly given by the $k \times k$ matrix $\bar{S}$ of separations among the k concepts averaged across members of the culture.

An important notion of interactionist theory is that the self may be an object of the individual's experience in the same way as any other concept may be the object of attention. Furthermore, it is quite explicit in virtually every version of Mead's thinking and that of his followers that the self is defined in terms of its relationship to other objects of experience. It is thus completely

TABLE 3.1

Length of All Self-Concept and DHIA Vectors by Adaptor Categories

(Numbers in Parentheses Are The Percentages of Error for the Value Directly above the Percentage Value)

Sample	Accurate information	You	Good	Convenient	Keeping records	Culling	Breeding	Measuring production	Necessary	Profit	Inexpensive	Computers	Useful
								Concepts					
N = 22 Nonadoptors													
You	54	181	39	54	49	51	49	57	40	55	70	148	43
Error	(17)	(20)	(16)	(13)	(19)	(16)	(17)	(18)	(27)	(18)	(22)	(18)	(32)
DHIA	91		114	107	81	91	109	117	142	141	153	137	107
Error	(35)		(31)	(25)	(37)	(37)	(46)	(45)	(39)	(40)	(36)	(41)	(49)
N = 21 Discontinuers													
You	62	138	41	53	45	32	37	73	45	37	46	163	46
Error	(27)	(26)	(20)	(17)	(18)	(21)	(21)	(27)	(44)	(25)	(28)	(32)	(36)
DHIA	93		100	121	93	101	76	63	111	100	109	79	79
Error	(38)		(39)	(26)	(62)	(56)	(38)	(46)	(27)	(31)	(28)	(47)	(40)
N = 81 Adoptors													
You	38	22	40	50	45	41	34	30	43	46	52	89	35
Error	(10)	(17)	(11)	(10)	(15)	(11)	(12)	(19)	(23)	(13)	(13)	(15)	(11)
DHIA	30		30	35	18	24	27	20	26	28	46	36	21
Error	(14)		(14)	(13)	(21)	(17)	(20)	(27)	(22)	(17)	(16)	(26)	(24)

appropriate to define the self by including it among the set of objects in the pair comparisons. Thus the self may be defined as well by its $1 \times (k - 1)$ vector of separations from the $k - 1$ other concepts. For convenience it will be useful to define each of these pairwise dissimilarities, as perceived either by an individual or by a set of individuals as a *belief*. Furthermore, since Mead defines attitudes as the orientation or relationship of the self to some object or set of objects, it is consistent with his position to define *attitude* as a belief about the self, that is, the measured separation between the self and any object or set of objects. All attitudes are beliefs, therefore, but the converse is not true. Within the present model, therefore, attitudes are primarily cognitive structures that may or may not include an affective component.

Since, following Blumer, an object is "anthing which may be designated or referred to [Blumer, 1967]," behaviors or actions may be arrayed as objects in this space. It is therefore possible and sensible to estimate persons' attitudes toward behaviors as distance or separations between the self and those behaviors. These global relationships are entirely consistent with virtually all interactionist writers' views, since they have meaning only within a complete context within which both object and self are defined relative to all other relevent objects.

Conceived of and measured in this way, attitude bears some relationship to more conventionally measured attitudes. Danes and Woelfel (1976), for example, found the correlation between distance from the self to political figures to correlate with conventional favorability measures for the same figures about .9. The same pattern has been repeated in other studies. Important exceptions exist, however. Green, Maheshwari, and Rao (1969) did not find substantial correlations between distances from self and favorability, but many of their objects were "big ticket" items out of economic reach. This indicates people can place an object far from themselves even if they are strongly in favor of it if, on other grounds (such as price) it is "out of reach." In fact, there is substantial evidence from many sources that attitude conceived and measured as distance from the self is a much better predictor of behavior than any other formulation yet devised. Table 3.1, for example, is typical of the relation between distance from self and behavior. It shows the distances among the self and a set of concepts relative to a dairy-herd testing service of three groups, those who have adopted the testing service, those who have not adopted, and those who have discontinued the service. Note particularly the distance between self and the testing service (DHIA) is 181 for nonadopters, 138 for discontinuers, and only 30 for adopters.

The Geometry of Separation

The concept of a geometry of separation capitalizes on the recognition that physical distance is viewed as a special case of separation in general, and thus is isomorphic to conceptual separation in formal structure. Therefore, conceptual separations may be presented in a geometrical format analogous to the depiction of physical distance; the separations in the matrix $\bar{S}$ may be arrayed in a geometrical pattern. Consider the matrix:

$$\bar{S} = \begin{pmatrix} & a & b & c \\ a & 0 & 0 & 0 \\ b & 0 & 0 & 0 \\ c & 0 & 0 & 0 \end{pmatrix}$$

Here, since $\bar{S}_{ab} = \bar{S}_{ac} = \bar{S}_{bc} = 0$, the three concepts lie on a point in a zero (0) dimensional space. In the matrix:

$$\begin{pmatrix} & a & b & c \\ a & 0 & 1 & 3 \\ b & 1 & 0 & 2 \\ c & 3 & 2 & 0 \end{pmatrix}$$

the separations form a line segment in a one-dimensional space which may be geometrically arrayed as the following pattern:

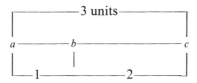

and the matrix:

$$\begin{array}{c c c c} & a & b & c \\ a & 0 & 1 & 2.24 \\ b & 1 & 0 & 2 \\ c & 2.24 & 2 & 0 \end{array}$$

represents a triangle in a two-dimensional Euclidean space.

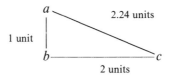

And finally consider the matrix $\bar{S}$ that extends outside the real number domain:

$$\bar{S} = \begin{pmatrix} & a & b & c \\ a & 0 & 1 & 4 \\ b & 1 & 0 & 2 \\ c & 4 & 2 & 0 \end{pmatrix}$$

This geometrical pattern represents a complex, non-Euclidean space of 2 dimensions; one real and one imaginary dimension. The translation of conceptual separations into a geometrical configuration will produce a spatial configuration of r dimensions, where r is always one or more fewer than the number (k) of conceptions judged $(r \leq k - 1)$.

Transformation Rules

Among the most important transformation rules are those describing the symbolic operations by which observations are transformed to correspondence across observers and over time, since these are the transformations by which information is conveyed among individuals. Since the primitive data of the theory consist of the matrix of reported separations S or $\bar{S}$, we will be particularly interested in transformation rules that preserve these separations. Restricting ourselves to transformations that preserve the raw separations guarantees that the data are never distorted. In this way, data provided by measurements may never be "tampered with" and remain the final arbiter of theory.

Frame of Reference. Once the observations have been encoded into the symbols of the theory, we may begin to compare them across observers and over time to discover invariances. The first step in this comparison process is to transform those observations into a convenient frame of reference (Goffman, 1974; Halliday & Resnick, 1966). Although the concept of reference frame has occupied an important place in virtually every social science (and in physics), it has generally resisted precise quantitative treatment in the social sciences. Since this theory is founded on a fundamental variable (separation), which is formally homomorphic with physical distances, it is possible to make use of mathematical procedures developed to establish physical reference systems to generate reference frames for cognitive processes. The procedures used here were developed by Young and Householder (1938) and Torgerson (1958) under the name *metric multidimensional scaling*. First, the matrix of separations S is centered and premultiplied by its transpose to give the scalar product matrix B

$$b_{ij} = \frac{1}{2}\left(\frac{1}{k}\sum_{i}^{k} d_{ij}^2 + \frac{1}{k}\sum_{j}^{k} d_{ij}^2 - \frac{1}{k^2}\sum_{i}^{k}\sum_{j}^{k} d_{ij}^2 - d_{ij}^2\right) \qquad (2)$$

which is then reduced by the Jacobi procedure[1] to an orthogonal matrix of Eigenvectors R. The matrix R represents a rectilinear coordinate system upon which the concepts are projected as vectors. For k concepts, the matrix R is always $k \times r$ where $r \leq k - 1$. Each column vector of R represents one dimension of the space and is orthogonal to all other columns. Each row of R represents the position vector of the concept in the space (Davis & Snider, 1975).

Although it makes little difference for the elementary presentation in this

---

[1] This procedure is formally identical to a complete principle-components factor analysis of the B matrix. It differs from typical factor-analytic procedures in that (*a*) the input matrix consists of ratio-scaled scalar products rather than correlations; and (*b*) all the factors are extracted rather than just a subset. This means that the original distances may be regenerated from R with no error.

chapter, advanced work within this non-Euclidean space is greatly simplified by adopting the convectional tensor notation for these vectors. (McConnel, 1933). Within this notation, any concept is represented by the first rank tensor $\mathbf{R}_{(\alpha)}^{\mu}$ where the α in parentheses represents the αth concept. (It is placed in parentheses to indicate that it is not a tensor index, but rather simply a designation of which tensor we are discussing. The superscript μ ranges from one to r, where r is the number of dimensions in the space and refers to the coordinate value of the tensor on the μth dimension. In this notation, the self is represented by the tensor $\mathbf{R}_{(\alpha)}^{\mu}$,

No information is lost by this transformation, nor of course, is any created. Since the set of reference vectors upon which the concepts are now projected is orthonormal, however, mathematical treatment of processes among the concepts is substantially simplified, since vector equations defined on rectilinear coordinates take on a very convenient algebraic form.

This is in marked distinction to the transformation by which Osgood converts measured dissimilarities into "semantic space." In Osgood's procedure, the covariance matrix derived from the intitial measurements is first standardized, then factored. The resulting factors serve as orthogonal vectors on which each of the concepts is projected. Due to the standardization, however, these eigenvectors are not unit vectors; rather each concept's position vector has been unitized, so that the position vector of each concept in the space is one unit in length regardless of its length in the raw measures. We have already remarked that the indirect measurement procedure used by Osgood costs a great deal in precision, as does the use of the categorical semantic differential-type scale, and that together, these errors in judgment may cost as much as several orders of magnitude of precision. Compared to the distortions resulting from this standardization procedure, however, these earlier problems are small. As shown elsewhere (Woelfel & Danes, 1979) this procedure, when applied to a map of the United States cities, produces distortions in excess of *several thousand kilometers* in the position of many of the cities, and results in absurdities such as the location of Miami several hundred kilometers north of Chicago. The result of these distortions is that the distances among concepts in Osgood's semantic space are virtually randomly related to their distances as measured (the skeptical reader is invited to test these conclusions with data of a known configuration, such as physical distances or the arrangement of objects on his or her desk). In the Galileo™ type procedures described here, however, no information is lost and no distortions incurred whatever, and measured distances may be reproduced to within computational rounding error, which, at default values in the Galileo™ computer program is preset at .001%. Thus whereas the semantic space of Osgood provided an insightful and ingenious way to array concepts, from a computational point of view, it is sufficiently imprecise to be virtually useless for the investigation of attitude changes. This very imprecision, in fact, plays an important role in Osgood's finding of virtually no variation in semantic space even across major cultural boundaries, since the space is too inaccurate to note any but the most overwhelming differences.

While this rectilinear coordinate system shares important characteristics with the familiar 3-dimensional rectilinear coordinate system of classical mechanics, it differs in two important ways, both consequences of the empirically derived structure of the concepts measured to date. First, the rank or dimensionality of the space is higher than 3, although the exact rank varies across concept domains and across time, as well as across individuals. Second, the space is almost always found to be non-Euclidean. In spatial terms, non-Euclidean spaces are warped or bent; in cognitive terms, non-Euclidean separation patterns represent inconsistencies among conceptions.

Non-Euclidean geometric structure is represented in the Galileo configuration by negative characteristics roots (eigenvalues) in the matrix; negative eigenvalues indicate imaginary components of the eigenvectors corresponding to these roots, since the eigenvalue is the sum of the squared components, as

$$\lambda_\mu = \sum_\alpha^k (\mathbf{R}_{(\alpha)}^\mu)^2 \tag{3}$$

While these imaginary components and negative roots were intially considered by many psychometricians to be artifactual or indications of error, their consistent recurrence, stability over time, and generally lawful behavior (e.g., they are generally larger in absolute magnitude for domains not clearly understood by or unfamiliar to respondents) seem to indicate that they should not be disregarded. Furthermore, they add no essential mathematical difficulties as long as care is taken to preserve their signs during numerical computations.

Cross-Observer Transformations

For any observer, these operations performed across k concepts will yield the $k \times r$ matrix $\mathbf{R}$ representing a (non-Euclidean) rectilinear coordinate system upon which are projected k positions vectors $\mathbf{R}_{(\alpha)}^\mu, \mathbf{R}_{(\beta)}^\mu, \ldots, \mathbf{R}_{(k)}^\mu$. The end points of these vectors, as has been shown, constitute a geometric pattern that corresponds to the interrelations among the concepts as seen by the ith individual.

Comparisons of the observations of two or more observers, once those observations have been encoded into this system, constitutes a two-step procedure. First, a transformation on one or both of the reference frames must be identified, which minimizes the discrepancy among the two or more spaces, while preserving the separations within each. Once this has been accomplished, the resulting matrices simply may be compared by subtraction. These distance-preserving transformations are called rigid motions, and consist of rotations and translations on the coordinates.

Translations within the Galileo reference frame are straightforward extensions of translations in the 3-space common to ordinary physical conception. First, some arbitrary point $\mathbf{R}_{(p)}^{\mu}$ is chosen, and its position vector is subtracted from the position vectors of all concepts in the space such that

$$\hat{\mathbf{R}}_{(\alpha)}^{\mu} = \mathbf{R}_{(\alpha)}^{\mu} - \mathbf{R}_{(p)}^{\alpha} \qquad (4)$$

Since $\mathbf{R}_{(p)}^{\mu} - \mathbf{R}_{(p)}^{\mu} = 0$ (the null vector) this has the effect of placing the pth point on the origin of the reference frame. This procedure is carried out for the reference frame of each person in the comparison, so that the reference frames of each observer are centered on the same point.

Next, the two coordinate frames are rigidly rotated to a least-squares best fit on each other. This rotation is accomplished by successive pairwise infinitesimal rotations of the eigenvectors until the total squared distance of concepts from their counterparts across observers is minimized (Woelfel *et al.*, 1975). Since we are concerned only with those transformations that preserve the original separations, rotations must be carried out separately for the positive eigenvectors and the negative eigenvectors. This is required since distance is not invariant under rotation of complex numbers, and is permitted, since each of the positive eigenvectors is orthogonal to each of the negative eigenvectors. (Woelfel, Holmes, & Kincaid, 1979).

Once these operations have been carried out for any two persons, they yield the transformed matrices $\mathbf{R}_i$ and $\mathbf{R}_j$ for the ith and jth individuals. Comparison of space is now given straightforwardly by the subtraction

$$\hat{\mathbf{R}}_i - \hat{\mathbf{R}}_j = \Delta\mathbf{R} \qquad (5)$$

where the matrix $\Delta\mathbf{R}$ represents the difference between the cognitive structures of the ith and jth individuals. Any row $\Delta\mathbf{R}_{(\alpha)}^{\mu}$ of $\Delta\mathbf{R}$ represents the difference between the definition of the αth concept as seen by the ith and jth persons within a now common reference frame.[2] The length $|\mathbf{R}_{(\alpha)}^{\mu}|$ of any row vector of $\Delta\mathbf{R}$ represents the distance between or difference in meaning between the same word as used by the ith and jth person.

Over-Time Transformations

The description of process in the Galileo framework essentially involves the comparison of a time-ordered series of individual coordinate frames $\mathbf{R}_{t0}$, $\mathbf{R}_{t1}, \ldots, \mathbf{R}_{tn}$ or aggregate coordinate frames $\bar{\mathbf{R}}_{t0}, \bar{\mathbf{R}}_{t1}, \ldots, \bar{\mathbf{R}}_{tn}$. As is well known in physical science, there exists no single "privileged" coordinate system against

---

[2] For an interesting alternative procedure for the comparison of individual cognitive structures, see Marlier, 1974. Marlier's procedure involves the projection of the individual cognitive spaces of a series of individuals into an aggregate space based on the average separation matrix $\mathbf{S}$, after which individual differences can be estimated by linear regression techniques. Marlier is able to account for over 72% of the differences in individual perceptions with this model.

which absolute changes may be measured, and the situation is no different in cognitive space. As is clear from the nature of the procedure by which the Galileo coordinate frames are constructed, the orientations of the eigenvectors of any time frame are functions of the state of the configuration at that time, and therefore any change in the configuration over time will result in an artifactual reorientation of the reference axes (eigenvectors). This is equivalent to comparing motions across reference frames which may be "tumbling" (i.e., in non-uniform rotation and translation) relative to each other. The first step in making comparisons, therefore, is a series of rotations and translations as described earlier to bring the time-series of coordinate systems into best-fit with each other (Woelfel *et al.*, 1975). Several such procedures are possible. First, if no information other than that contained within the matrices at each time period is available, rotation and translation to simple least-squares best-fit across the time-series is appropriate. If additional constraints can be determined on other grounds (as, for example, might be the case if the observer were to know that some of the concepts had been implicated in messages across a time interval and others had not) some of the concepts might be differentially weighted into the minimization procedure or even left as free parameters, as is described in detail elsewhere (Woelfel *et al.*, 1979). One such strategy might be to translate the origin of the reference frame onto the concept of self (the "me") at each time interval, then rotate the spaces serially to a least-squares best-fit on those concepts the individual herself or himself reports as relatively unchanging across the time interval measured. For an equivalent cultural solution, the aggregate "me" might be set at the origin of the collective space, and least-squares criteria applied to those concepts collectively judged stable over time. The resulting process would represent the individual cognitive processes or collective cultural processes as seen respectively by the individual, or by the culture as a whole. What is most important, however, is the understanding that the description of the processes—and hence the "laws of nature"—within the spaces will be altered by different choices of a rotation scheme, and that there exists no "correct" choice. Once a choice has been made, however, processes will be wholly determined by observations (data) within that framework, and will be the same for all observers who utilize the same rotation scheme. *Within this consensus*, it makes sense to say the processes are observed and laws discovered; the consensus itself, however, is created by the observers and not discovered.

Velocity and Acceleration. Once a stable reference frame has been defined (by whatever means), it becomes a simple matter to describe cognitive processes relative to that frame. At any instant, the definition of a concept is given by its location in the reference frame, which in turn is given by its position vector $\mathbf{R}_{(\alpha)}^{\mu}$. Changes in the meaning of any concept will be given by a *change* in location, or a change in the position vector $\Delta\mathbf{R}_{(\alpha)}^{\mu}$. For any interval of time Δt, therefore, the average rate of change of meaning or average velocity is given by $\Delta\mathbf{R}_{(\alpha)}^{\mu}\ \Delta t$. At any instant in time, this velocity will be given by the derivative $V_t = d\mathbf{R}_{(\alpha)}^{\mu}/dt$. In the space of reference, R is given by its r components $R_{(\alpha)}^{\mu}$.

Since the reference vectors are orthogonal in the Galileo reference frame, the partial derivatives are linearly additive, giving

$$V_t = \sum_{i=1}^{r} dR_{(\alpha)}^{\mu}/dt \qquad (6)$$

Equation (6) represents the direction and rate at which a given concept is changing in meaning at an instant t. This rate itself may change over time, and this change in the rate of change is formally an acceleration, which is given by the second derivative

$$a_t = d^2 R_{(\alpha)}^{\mu}/dt^2. \qquad (7)$$

It is these accelerations that require explanation and so they are of particular importance. Nevertheless it is important to understand that the accelerations will turn out differently if different rotation and translation strategies are employed earlier in the analysis, and so, also, will the laws that account for them. This suggests an additional strategy for such transformation decision: For completely practical reasons, those distance-preserving transformations should be chosen which produce the simplest laws of motion within the cognitive reference frame.

Explanations of Cognitive Processes

The equations developed in the previous section are powerful descriptive tools, and many even more powerful descriptive equations can be found in physics, engineering, and mathematics books dealing with mechanics and vector and tensor analysis, as long as one is careful to generalize those equations to r dimensions, while paying careful attention to the signs of the roots corresponding to the dimensions. The implication that equations for cognitive processes may be found in physics books has generally been viewed with a combination of suspicion and alarm by social scientists on the ground that psychological or cultural processes are not analogous to physical processes. These arguments are not germane here, since the equations listed do not predict or require any specific processes in the cognitive reference frames, but simply describe those processes whatever they may be. That such equations can describe processes within this system is not an empirical question, but simply a formal consequence of the arbitrary distance rule chosen. The question at issue is not whether equations which describe the processes observed in the system can be found, but rather whether those equations, once found, are sufficiently simple to allow predictability greater than that obtainable with ordinary language. To the extent that such equations yield patterned regularities, they will yield such increased predictive power. As we suggested earlier, such patterned regularities, or invariances, once named, constitute scientific laws valid within the reference system.

Simple Messages

To illustrate what such laws might look like in this system, consider the following example:

Figure 3.1 represents the first principal plane of the space representing (hypothetical) measures of the pairwize dissimilarities among the six concepts α, β, γ, δ, ϵ, ζ. The position of each individual in the space R is given by the position vector $R^\mu_{(\alpha)}$ whose magnitude $\rho_\alpha = (\sum^r_{\mu=1}(R^\mu_{(\alpha)})^2)^{1/2}$ where $R^\mu_{(\alpha)} =$ the μth component of the αth position vector. Each column vector represents a reference vector orthogonal to each other reference vector (eigenvector) whose length is given by

$$\rho_\mu = \left[\sum^k_{\alpha=1} (R^\mu_{(\alpha)})^2 \right]^{1/2} \tag{8}$$

where λ_μ is the μth root of the characteristic equation for B.

After several repeated measures, assume we have established that the concepts are not in motion relative to one another. Assume further that, at this point in time, all n oberservers receive a message which says, in English,

$$S_1 \quad \text{``}\alpha \text{ is } \beta\text{''}$$

This message, the categorical assertion of identity, we call a "simple message." Since it is a categorical assertion of identity, it is the strongest form of simple message. A weaker simple message might say "α and β are similar."

Subsequently a series of additional measures across time are taken. We now must make several assumptions, each of which may be falsified by the observations if they fail. First, we may assume that the message will result in some changes in the configuration of vectors. If this is so, the eigenvalues and eigenvectors of B will be different for the postmessage measurements than for the premessage measures. These differences may be certified within probability parameters by standard statistical procedures; correlations of corresponding eigenvectors across time may be statistically nonunity; cannonical correlations of the $R^\mu_{(\alpha)}$ across Δt may be statistically nonunity by chi-square criteria: mean differences between position vectors may be statistically significant by ANOVA procedures, and so forth. Row interactions and row × column interactions in N way repeated-measures analysis of variance may be performed on either the coordinates of R or the distance matrix $\bar{S}$ to determine whether specific concepts or specific pairs of concepts are differentially affected by the message (see Gillham and Woelfel, 1977; Woelfel et al., 1975, Woelfel & Danes, 1979).

Second, we might assume that only the concepts referred to in the message will be directly affected by the message. If this is true, then a rotation and translation[3] of the coordinates across any interval of time could be found for

---

[3] We are restricted to rotations and translations since these "rigid notions" preserve distances (separations) within time periods.

which all differences $R_{(\alpha)t_1}^{\mu} - R_{(\alpha)t_0}^{\mu} = 0$ where the αth concept is not implicated in the message, but where $R_{(B)t_1}^{\mu} - R_{(B)t_0}^{\mu}$ does not equal zero if concept is mentioned in the message. This transformation is given by translating both R_{t_0} and R_{t_1} to an origin at the centroid of those concepts thought to be unaffected by the message (or on one of those concepts itself), and rotating about this origin until the squared distances among the hypothetically stable concepts are at a minimum. If the hypothesis is correct, these differences will be zero by statistical criteria, whereas the distances between the manipulated concepts will be nonzero by the same criteria. If this hypothesis is false, no such rotation can be found.

A stronger version of the hypothesis would predict not only motion versus stability, but also the direction and magnitude of such motion. Mature, trustworthy hypotheses about the direction and magnitude of resultant motion can only be made after many careful observations within the system, but initial guesses based on our understanding of the meanings of English words and their effects can provide useful starting points.

The meaning of the English words in statement S_1 imply that the observer has overestimated the separation between α and β. If, in general, people attempt to comply with the meaning of the message—that is, adjust their view in the direction of the view expressed in the message—then, in general, the distance between α and β should be reduced by receipt of the message. This relative motion may be differentially attributed to $R_{(\alpha)}^{\mu}$ and $R_{(\beta)}^{\mu}$ in Figure 3.1. By con-

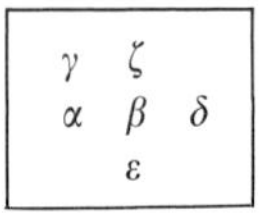

Figure 3.1. Hypothetical representation of first principal plane of the space of 6 concepts α, β, γ, δ, ε, ζ.

vention, the force of this message may be defined as the sum of magnitudes of vectors F_1 and F_2 where $|F_1| = -|F_2|$. Since, by definition, the force F is equally attributed to each concept R^{μ}, differential displacement along the $R_{(\alpha)}^{\mu} - R_{(\beta)}^{\mu}$ vector must therefore be attributed to characteristics of the $R_{(\alpha)}^{\mu}$. That quality of the $R_{(\alpha)}^{\mu}$ which differentially resists acceleration (or displacement) is called *inertial mass*, which is given by

$$\frac{m\beta}{m\alpha} = \frac{|\Delta\mathbf{R}_{(\alpha)}^{\mu}|}{|\Delta\mathbf{R}_{(\beta)}^{\mu}|} \qquad (9)$$

We seek now to determine some distance-preserving transformation such that the ratios of the respective $|\Delta\mathbf{R}_{(\alpha)}^{\mu}|$'s remains invariant across repeated messages and over time or in which the ratios of the $|\Delta\mathbf{R}_{(\alpha)}^{\mu}|$'s are known functions of some measurable events. Such an outcome would be an inertial reference frame, and within this frame, the known values of the ratios of the $|\Delta\mathbf{R}_{(\alpha)}^{\mu}|$'s constitute valuable information about the differential magnitude of the response of the $R_{(\alpha)}^{\mu}$'s to messages.

Strict confirmation of the hypothesis that the message may be represented as a force vector on a line through the two concepts in the message by an observed angel of

$$180° = \cos^{-1}(R_{(\alpha)}^{\mu} \cdot R_{(\beta)}^{\mu}/|\Delta R_{(\alpha)}^{\mu}||\Delta R_{(\beta)}^{\mu}|) \tag{10}$$

to within statistical criteria. Strict confirmation of the inertial hypothesis is given by the criterion

$$\frac{|\Delta R_{(\alpha)}^{\mu}|/|\Delta R_{(\gamma)}^{\mu}|}{|\Delta R_{(\beta)}^{\mu}|/|\Delta R_{(\alpha)}^{\mu}|} = \frac{|\Delta R_{(\alpha)}^{\mu}|}{|\Delta R_{(\beta)}^{\mu}|} \tag{11}$$

for all values of α, β and γ.

Compound Messages

A yet more complex hypothesis might suggest a useful combination rule. We might hypothesize, for example, that English sentences average like vectors, that is, the meaning of the English sentences "α is β" "α is γ" (or perhaps, "α is β and γ." These are called here "compound messages."

If sentences average like vectors, then the resultant vector $\hat{R}_{(\alpha)}^{\mu} = (R_{(\beta)}^{\mu} + R_{(\gamma)}^{\mu})$ can be considered a single message vector resulting in $R_{(\alpha)}^{\mu}$ moving along the vector $\hat{R}_{(\alpha)}^{\mu}$ with an acceleration a inversely proportional to m_{α}.

These hypotheses also are easily falsified, requiring yet more complexities to be allowed in the theory. The important point, however, is to illustrate that the rejection of hypotheses leads directly to the development of successively more accurate, if perhaps more complicated descriptions of processes, and correspondingly more complicated hypotheses which correspond to observations to within increasingly better approximations.

Once the systems has been set into motion, it iteratively improves its fit to observations while providing a consensus among observers within which this increasing pool of comparable observations may be interchanged. The result is a tendency toward individually and collectively enhanced observational capacities, reasoning ability, and access to information for those who use the system.

Once an inertial reference frame has been stipulated, hypotheses consist of statements about the forces generated by different events in the inertial frame. Failure of these hypotheses (e.g., the hypothesis that suggests a message-like S^1 will result in forces along the vector connecting the concepts linked in the message, which in turn results in motion only along this vector) requires stipulation of an additional force (in this case, acting to produce motion out of the anticipated vector). Research must then uncover observed events in the frame corresponding to the residual force vector inferred by the motion out of the predicted vector.

A Current Assessment

Theories are traditionally evaluated in the social sciences on two grounds (*a*) the reliability of their measures; and (*b*) the extent to which outcomes predicted by the theory conform to observed outcomes (validity). In terms of these criteria, this theory compares favorably with competitive theories. Many careful studies have shown reliabilities above those considered requisite by most social scientists (Barnett, 1976; Cody, 1976; Gillham & Woelfel, 1976; Marlier, 1974). Moreover, outcomes predicted by the theory have been in good conformity with observation. Barnett, Serota, and Taylor (1974) interviewed by telephone a small sample of registered voters in a United States congressional district to determine the set of concepts they mentioned most frequently while describing an upcoming congressional race. Sixteen of these concepts were included in a Galileo questionnaire that was administered to a larger sample and the results entered into an early version of the Galileo computer program. Based on the resulting solution, they advised a little known candidate in his first attempt at public office as to the optimal set of messages he should send to the electorate, to move himself closer to the location of the "me" or average voter's position in the space. Two subsequent measures showed that this message had the desired cognitive effects—that is, the candidate moved as predicted. As a consequence, this political newcomer defeated his experienced opponent (the incumbant congressman) with nearly 60% of the vote (Barnett *et al.*, 1974).

Similarly, in a later, more sophisticated laboratory experiment, Cody (1976) entered similar data into the Galileo 3.9 computer program which utilized Eq. (8) through (12) to determine the optimal message strategy to increase successfully the credibility of two moderately well-known political candidates. Similar procedures have been used commercially to aid in the diffusion of educational innovations; the formation of statewide organizations for special education; to aid in the reformation of a state educational system, and to aid in the sale of commercial products and services. In each of these and other cases, the results have been more precise and informative than those yielded by already proven existing procedures, and their dollar value has greatly exceeded the costs of the research.

While the extent to which this system will prove useful in basic attitude–behavior research is still open, Gillham and Woelfel (1976) have shown that it may be used in lieu of much more tedious conventional methods. Barnett (1976) showed that these procedures were able to detect effects of bilingualism on cognitive processing too small to be detected by the most sensitive of conventional scaling methods. Danes *et al.*, (1978) have shown in laboratory experiments that the "inertial mass" hypothesis expressed in the theory (see Saltiel & Woelfel, 1975) accounts for resistance to attitude change far more accurately than plausible conventional models. Marlier (1974, 1976) showed in a laboratory experiment that the set of transformations designated by the theory account very accurately for differences in individual perspectives about railroad nationalization. Brophy (1976) showed that a sizable portion of the variance in perceptions of members of an academic department, as measured by these techniques, could be accounted for by their positions in a communication network. Wakshlag and Edison (1975) showed that these procedures produced measures of the credibility of message sources more precise than conventional semantic differential and factor analytic models. Serota, Fink, Noell, and Woelfel (1975) showed that these procedures provide precise measures of the differential perceptions of the United States power structure across levels of socioeconomic status. Danes and Woelfel (1975) showed that these techniques produce more reliable information for a given sample size than do traditional ordinal scaling methods. Craig (1975) showed the system produced extremely stable measures of the perceptions persons held about nations, although ambiguities in the persuasive messages he generated from the theory precluded unambiguous tests of its dynamic assumptions in his experiment. Mistretta (1975) showed that the system made accurate predictions about the perceptions of crimes and their penalties consistent with Durkheim's (1951) predictions. Barnett (1972) showed that the system yields stable and reliable outcomes even under adverse conditions such as cross-domain scaling and across politically turbulent circumstances. Gordon (1976a) showed that these procedures provide accurate measures of the perceptions of radio stations and their program formats precise enough to predict observed listening patterns, and further showed (Gordon, 1976b) that changes in the metric established by the experimenter yield ratio-level changes in scaling outcomes.

This evidence shows that the theory compares quite favorably with other social science theories in terms of traditional reliability and predictability figures. But such data can be seriously misleading, if one considers only the extent to which the measured data provided by the theory are reliably (reproducibly) measured and the outcomes predicted by the theory are confirmed by these observations. Although the measures yielded by the theory are in the range of the reliabilities of traditional theories (or usually somewhat higher) the fineness of gradation of the measures is usually two or more orders of magnitude better, and the quantity of information yielded is proportionately higher. Clearly, if one measure provides 100 units of information at 90% reliability, and a second provides 10 units of information at 90% reliability, the former measure is preferable by an order of magnitude difference.

This same reasoning applies to the confirmation of predicted outcomes. A proper evaluation of the theory in contrast to others should note that, not only are the outcomes predicted by the theory confirmed to smaller tolerances (usually by about a factor of two or more), but the predicted outcomes themselves are more complicated by far than those derived from earlier theory. The theory presented here, in other words, predicts outcomes about which earlier theories are generally mute or indecisive, and finds these predictions confirmed within smaller tolerances than the cruder predictions of earlier theories are confirmed by methods appropriate to them.

Whereas these experiments support the key premises of the theory, it should be clear from the preceding discussion that the construction of a useful theory is a lengthy collective social process requiring not only causal hypotheses, but the development of symbol systems, logical roles of combination, measurement rules, and a relatively large cadre of trained users even before information substantial enough to warrant hypothesis formulation can be collected.

Ultimately, any theory is to be judged on the extent to which it makes correct, useful, and informative statements about problems of real human interest on the basis of observations that can be made at a cost commensurate with their use value. A good theory, therefore, must make the solution of some class of human problems easier. The more important the problems, and the easier and more certain the solutions, the better the theory.

On first reading, it may be difficult to see how the tedious equations of the preceding pages can make the solution of human problems easy. In fact, however, once mastered, this system does vastly simplify important human activities. Although the derivation of the equations presented earlier was strenuous work, once derived, they need not be derived again for each use. In fact, all of them have been encoded into computer software, which makes the tedious logical manipulations they entail quite automatic. It will be the pragmatic ease with which this theory can enable us to solve difficult and important problems that determines its ultimate acceptability.

REFERENCES

Barnett, G. Reliability and metric multidimension scaling. Unpublished Manuscript, University of Illinois, Urbana, 1972.

Barnett, G. A. Reliability and metric multidimensional scaling. Unpublished research report, Department of Communication, Michigan State University, East Lansing, 1974.

Barnett, G. A. Bilingual information processing: The effects of communication on semantic structure. Unpublished Ph.D. dissertation, Michigan State University, East Lansing, 1976.

Barnett, G., Serota, K., & Taylor, J. A method for political communication research. Presented at the Annual Conference of the Association for Education in Journalism, San Diego, Calif., 1974.

Blumer, H. Commentary and debate. *American Journal of Sociology*, 1966, *71*(5) 535–547.

Blumer, H. Symbolic interactionism: *Perspective and method*, Englewood Cliffs, N.J.: Prentice–Hall, 1969.

Brophy, M. A Study of the interrelationship between the social structure and the cognitive belief system or "culture" of a social unit. Unpublished M.A. thesis, Michigan State University, East Lansing, Michigan, 1976.

Bruner, J. Social psychology and perception. In E. Maccoby, T. Newcomb, & E. Hartley (Eds.), *Readings in social psychology*. New York: Holt, Rinehart & Winston, 1958.

Campbell, N. R. *An account of the principles of measurement and calculation.* London: Longmans Green, 1928.

Campbell, N. R. *What is science?* New York: Dover, 1921. P. 110. (Originally published, 1952.)

Cliff, N. Adverbs as multipliers. *Psychological Review*, 1959, *66*, 27–44.

Cliff, N. Consistencies among judgments of adjective combinations. In N. Shepard, A. K. Romney, & S. B. Nerlove. *Multidimensional scaling: Applications* (Vol. 2). New York: Seminar Press, 1974.

Cody, M. An application of the multiattribute measurement model: Measurement and manipulation of source credibility. Unpublished M.A. thesis, Michigan State University, East Lansing, Michigan, 1976.

Craig, R. An investigation of communication effects in cognitive space. Unpublished Ph.D. dissertation, Michigan State University, East Lansing, 1976.

Danes, J., & Woelfel, J. An Alternative to the traditional scaling paradigm: Ratio judgments of separation. International Communication Association Annual Meeting, Chicago, 1975.

Danes, J., Hunter, J., & Woelfel, J. Mass communication and belief change. *Human Communication Research*, 1978, *4*(3), Spring, 243–252.

Davis, H. F., & Snider, A. D. Introduction to vector analysis, Boston: Allyn and Bacon, 1975.

Durkheim, E., *Suicide*. Glencoe, Ill.: The Free Press, 1951.

Einstein, A. *The meaning of relativity* (5th ed.). Princeton: Princeton University Press, 1956.

Einstein, A. *Relativity: The special and general theory*. New York: Crown, 1961.

Ellis, B. *Basic concepts of measurement*. Cambridge, England: Cambridge University Press, 1966.

Foote, N. Identification as the basis for a theory of motivation, *American Sociological Review*, 1951, 36 10–21.

Gillham, J., & Woelfel, J. D. The Galileo system: Preliminary evidence for precision, stability, and equivalence to traditional measures. *Human Communication Research*, 1977, Fall.

Goffman, E., *Frame analysis: An essay on the organization of experience.*, N.Y., Harper & Row, 1974.

Gordon, T. Subject abilities to use MDS: Effects of varying the criterion pair. Unpublished research paper Temple University, Philadelphia, 1976. (a)

Gordon, T., & Deleo, H. C. Structural variation in "Galileo" space: Effects of varying the criterion pair in multidimensional scaling. Paper presented at the annual meeting of the International Communication Association, Portland, Oregon, 1976. (b)

Green, P., Maheshwari, A., & Rao, V. Self-concept and brand preferences. *Journal of the Market Research Society*, 1969, *11*, 343–360.

Hays, W. *Quantification in psychology*. Belmont: Brooks–Cole, 1967.

Hamblin, R., Social attitudes: Magnitude measurement and theory, In H. Blalock, Jr. (Ed.). *Measurement in the social sciences*, Chicago: Aldine, 1974.

Heisenberg, W. *The physical principles of the quantum theory*. trans. by C. Eckert & F. C. Joyt. Chicago: University of Chicago Press, 1930.

Hertz, H. *The principles of mechanics*. New York: Dover, 1956.

Kinch, J. A formalized theory of the self-concept. *American Journal of Sociology*. 1963, *68*(4), 481–486.

Kramer, E. E. *The nature and growth of modern mathematics* (Vols. 1 & 2). New York: Hawthorn Books, 1970.

Krantz, D. H., Luce, R. D., & Suppes, P. *Foundations of measurement* (Vol. 1). *Additive and polynomial representations*, New York: Academic Press, 1971.

Lemert, E. *Social pathology*. New York: McGraw–Hill, 1951.

Lindesmith, A., & Strauss, A. *Social psychology*. New York: Holt, Rinehart & Winston, 1956.

Marlier, J. Procedures for a precise test of social judgment predictions of assimilation and contrast. Paper presented at the annual meetings of the Speech Communication Association, Chicago, December, 1974.

McConnel, A. *Applications of tensor analysis*, New York: Dover, 1933.

Mead, G. *Mind, self and society*, Chicago: The University of Chicago Press, 1934.

Mettlin, C. Smoking and behavior: Applying a social psychological theory, *Journal of Health and Social Behavior*, 1973 *14*, 144–152.

Meyer, S. *Data analysis for scientists and engineers*. New York: Wiley, 1975.

Michels, W. Malcolm, C., & Patterson, A. L. *Foundations of physics*. Princeton: N.J. D. Van Nostrand, 1968.

Mills, C. Situated actions and vocabularies of motive, *American Sociological Review*, 1940, *5*, 904–13.

Mistretta, M. Criminal law and the collective conscience: Multidimensional scaling of collective cultural perceptions of crime. Unpublished manuscript, University of Illinois, Urbana, 1975.

Osgood, C., Suci, G., & Tannenbaum, P. *The measurement of meaning*, Urbana: University of Illinois Press, 1957.

Piesko, H. Multidimensional scaling in Riemann space. Unpublished Ph.D. dissertation. Department of Psychology, University of Illinois, Urbana–Champaign, 1970.

Poincaré, H. *The foundations of science*. Lancaster, Penn.: Science Press, 1946.

Reichenbach, H. *Space and time*. New York: Dover, 1958.

Saltiel, J., & Woelfel, J. D. Inertia in cognitive processes: The role of accumulated information in attitude changes. *Human Communication*, 1975, *1*, 333–344.

Serota, K. B., Fink, E. L., Noell, J., & Woelfel, J. D. Communication, ideology and political behavior: A multidimensional analysis. Paper presented to the Political Communication Division of the International Communication Association, Chicago, April, 1975.

Sewell, W., Hallez, A., & Portes, A. The educational and early occupational attainment process, *American Sociological Review*. 1969, *34*, 82–92.

Stevens, S. Mathematics, measurement, and psychophysics. In S. Stevens (Ed.), *Handbook of experimental psychology*. New York: Wiley, 1951, p. 1.

Stevens, S. Measurement, statistics, and the schemapiric view. *Science*, 1957, *161*, 849–856.

Suppes, P., & Zinnes, J. L. Basic measurement theory. In R. D. Luce, R. R. Bush, & E. Galanter (Eds.) *Handbook of mathematical psychology*. New York: Wiley 1963, pp. 1–76.

Torgerson, W. S., *Theory and method of scaling*. New York: Wiley, 1958.

Wakshlag, J., & Edison, N. A model for the validation of the source credibility construct. Paper presented at the Speech Communication Association Annual Meeting, December, 1975.

Weber, M., *The methodology of the social sciences*, Glencoe, Ill: Free Press, 1949.

Woelfel, J. The western model. Unpublished manuscript. Honolulu, East West Center, 1977.

Woelfel, J. D., & Danes, J. Multidimensional scaling models for communication research, In P. Menge & J. Capella, *Multivarite methods In communication research*. New York: Academic Press, 1979.

Woelfel, J., & Haller, A. Significant others, the self-reflexive act and the attitude formation process, *American Sociological Review*, 1971.

Woelfel, J., Holmes, R., & Kincaid, L. Rotation to congruence for general Riemann surfaces under theoretical constraints. Unpublished paper. Honolulu, East West Center, 1979.

Woelfel, J. D., Woelfel, J. C., Gillham, J., & McPhail, T. Political radicalization as a communication process, *Communication Research*, 1974, *1*(2).

Woelfel, J., A Paradigm for research on significant others. Paper presented at annual meetings of The American Sociological Association, San Francisco, August, 1967.

Woelfel, J. D., & Hernandez, D. Media and interpersonal influences on attitude formation and change. Unpublished manuscript (mimeo) University of Illinois, Urbana, 1970.

Young, G., & Householder, A. Discussion of a set of points in terms of their mutual distances, *Psychemetrika*, 1938, 3, 19–22.

4

The Relationship of Attitudes and Behavior: A Constructivist Analysis

DANIEL J. O'KEEFE

The concept of attitude has played a central role in explanations of communication phenomena. Most obviously, the concept has enjoyed prominence in explanations of the effects of persuasive messages. But the concept of attitude also has been employed in accounts of, for example, the place of communication in the development of interpersonal relationships. Hence the finding that attitudes typically are not well correlated with behavior has motivated many communication theorists and researchers, as it has investigators in other fields, to address the nature of the attitude–behavior relationship. The present analysis is an attempt to extend an existing general theoretical framework for communication studies—constructivism—to the realm of the attitude–behavior relationship. This chapter offers, in turn, an analysis of the nature of the "attitude–behavior problem," a sketch of the constructivist view of the attitude–behavior relationship (with a summary of relevant research evidence), and a discussion of the relationship of the constructivist view to that of similar approaches.

MESSAGE–ATTITUDE–BEHAVIOR RELATIONSHIP
Theory, Methodology, and Applications

The Nature of the Problem

Because constructivism stresses the joint importance of conceptual analysis and programmatic research (see, e.g., Delia, 1976; D. O'Keefe, 1975), initially I want to pay some attention to exactly what the attitude–behavior problem is, and to the nature of "attitude–behavior consistency."

Of course, the "problem" is that measures of attitude usually are not very closely related to measures of overt behavior. In his well-known review article, Wicker (1969) concluded that the research evidence indicates that "it is considerably more likely that attitudes will be unrelated or only slightly related to overt behaviors than that attitudes will be closely related to actions [p. 65]." Such low correlations represent a problem, for typically it has been assumed that attitudes "have consequences for the way people act toward others, for the programs they actually undertake, and for the manner in which they carry them out. Thus attitudes are always seen as precursors of behavior, as determinants of how a person will actually behave in his daily affairs [A. Cohen, 1964, pp. 137–138]." But what exactly is an "attitude?" And how is "behavior" to be conceptualized? And what would it mean for behavior to be "consistent" with an attitude?

The Concept of Attitude

As with any concept that finds wide application in a number of disciplines, the concept of attitude is one that has received a large number of competing definitions. Indeed, there sometimes seem to be as many ways to categorize definitions of attitude as there are definitions themselves (see McGuire, 1969, pp. 141–149). But there is one central theme that runs throughout most definitions of attitude, and this same theme also is reflected in the most common attitude measurement procedures. The recurrent theme is that an attitude is fundamentally a person's general evaluation of an object (entity, person, policy, etc.). For example, McGuire (1969) concludes his survey of the definitional morass this way:

> This extended discussion of how attitude is best defined from a provocative, heuristic point of view must not obscure the point that, in a given experiment on attitude, the term can very readily be given an operational definition in terms of observable and scorable responses. Typically the person's attitude regarding an object is operationally defined as the response by which he indicates where he assigns the object along a dimension of variability. The dimension of variability is usually an evaluative one like desirability, but may occasionally be another, such as probability of occurrence [p. 149].

Insko (1967) reached a similar conclusion, noting that "the most common contemporary usage" regards "the evaluative dimension as the single defining dimension for attitudes [p. 2]." And, as Fishbein and Ajzen (1975, pp. 53–106) have shown, the standard attitude measurement techniques (Thurstone, Likert,

Guttman, Osgood's semantic differential) are all directed at assessing the respondent's overall evaluation of the attitude object. Because of this recurrent theme in both conceptual and operational definitions of attitude, in this chapter, an attitude will be taken to be a person's general evaluation of some object.

Two points of clarification about this concept of attitude may be useful. First, not infrequently one encounters a tripartite definition of attitude as something involving "affect, cognition, and conation." But the overwhelmingly common operational definition of attitude is one that assesses only evaluation (affect). Hence if the existence of low correlations between attitude measures and behavioral measures is to be explained, it is that operational definition that must be accorded special weight.

Second, because it is attitude toward an object that is involved in the attitude–behavior problem, any genuine solution to the problem must be one that clarifies the relationship between attitude toward an object and behavior toward that object. The attitude–behavior problem cannot be dismissed by suggesting that some other "attitudinal" variable should be studied. For example, a person's attitude toward a particular behavioral *act* may be highly correlated with the person's performance of that act, but this does not solve the original attitude–behavior problem. The source of the attitude–behavior problem is that a person's attitude toward an object is not well correlated with the person's behavior toward that object, and hence it is that relationship (the relationship of attitude toward an object and behavior toward that object) that must be the focus of study.

The Concept of Behavior

In their analysis of the attitude–behavior relationship, Fishbein and Ajzen have made several distinctions concerning the concept of behavior that I simply wish to reemphasize here. The first distinction is between attitude-relevant and attitude-irrelevant behavior (see Fishbein, 1973; Fishbein & Ajzen, 1974). Not every bit of behavior is potentially relevant to one's attitude, argue Fishbein and Ajzen, and hence one ought not expect that attitude measures will be highly correlated with any and all behavioral measures. While this distinction is an important one, it is also a dangerous one, for it raises the possibility of a strong circularity in accounts of the attitude–behavior relationship. One might draw the circle so tightly as to end up arguing that all and only attitude–relevant behaviors are correlated strongly with attitude, and that if a given bit of behavior is not highly correlated with attitude then that behavior must not be attitude-relevant. This, of course, is tantamount to saying "the behaviors one can account for using the concept of attitude are just those behaviors one can account for using the attitude concept." Still, the relevant point emphasized by the distinction is that not just any behavioral measure should necessarily be expected to be closely related to attitude.

But Fishbein and Ajzen also emphasize a distinction between two sorts of behavioral measures: single-act and multiple-act behavioral measures (see Fishbein, 1973; Fishbein & Ajzen, 1974). A single-act measure involves simply the observation of some one particular behavioral act, while a multiple-act measure involves the observation of several different behaviors. Fishbein and Ajzen argue that this distinction is important because, although a person's attitude may not be related very strongly to the performance of any particular act, that attitude may be highly correlated with the overall pattern of behavior as assessed by a multiple-act behavioral criterion (see Fishbein & Ajzen, 1974). I will have more to say in what follows concerning this analysis of the differential relationship of attitude to single- and multiple-act behavioral measures, but for the moment I only want to emphasize the importance of the distinction.

The Concept of Consistency

The absence of high correlations between attitude measures and behavioral measures typically is glossed as indicating "inconsistency" between attitude and act. The point I wish to make here is that the concept of consistency embedded in most treatments of the attitude–behavior relationship is a concept of *evaluative* consistency. As Ajzen and Fishbein (1977, p. 889) point out:

> It is usually considered to be logical or consistent for a person who holds a favorable attitude toward some object to perform favorable behaviors, and not to perform unfavorable behaviors, with respect to the object. Similarly, a person with an unfavorable attitude is expected to perform unfavorable behaviors, but not to perform favorable behaviors.

Hence if the attitude–behavior problem is to be illuminated, what must be explicated is why evaluative (rather than, say, "descriptive" or "psychological") consistency appears not to generally exist between a person's attitude toward some object and that person's behavior toward that object.

The Constructivist Analysis

I now turn to the constructivist view of the relationship of attitudes and behavior. First, the theoretical analysis of this relationship will be offered, and then relevant empirical research will be discussed.

Theoretical Analysis

Constructivism (see Delia, 1976, 1978; B. O'Keefe, 1978; D. O'Keefe, 1978) is a theoretical viewpoint that has proved useful in a number of diverse domains in communication studies: The processes underlying the formation of impressions of others both in laboratory contexts (Delia, 1972; Delia, Gonyea, & Crockett, 1971; B. O'Keefe, Delia, & O'Keefe, 1977) and in informal social interaction (Delia, Clark, & Switzer, 1974), the nature of communicator credibility (Delia, 1977), the development of communication skills in children (Clark & Delia, 1976, 1977; Delia & Clark, 1977; Delia, Kline, & Burleson, 1979; Delia & B. O'Keefe, 1979), developmental differences in communication skills among young adults (B. O'Keefe & Delia, 1979), the perception of political candidates and political communication (Freeman, 1976; S. Jackson, 1977; Swanson & Freeman, 1975), the nature of social class differences in communication (Applegate, 1978; Applegate & Delia, in press), the analysis of interpersonal interaction (Delia, Clark, & Switzer, 1979; B. O'Keefe, Delia, & O'Keefe, in press), and the interrelationships of various features of the social–cognitive system underlying communicative behavior (Delia & B. O'Keefe, 1976; Hale & Delia, 1976; B. O'Keefe & Delia, 1978). Constructivism's focus has been the social–cognitive foundation of communication. The particular conception of the cognitive system underlying human conduct (including communication) is based on a fusion of George Kelly's (1955) personal construct theory and Heinz Werner's (1948) cognitive–developmental views.[1] Persons are seen as having systems of personal constructs: dimensions along which objects and events are construed. A person makes sense of events by placing them along these perceptual dimensions. These bipolar constructs are systematically interrelated and hierarchically organized, permitting the individual to draw inferences and generate predictions. Although persons have constructs for construing all manner of events and objects, constructivism has focused on persons' "interpersonal constructs," that is, the constructs they use for construing the behavior and personalities of other persons.

Within this domain (as in other domains), construct systems are seen to develop in accord with Werner's (1957) orthogenetic principle: "Wherever development occurs, it proceeds from a state of relative globality and lack of differentiation to a state of increasing differentiation, articulation, and hierarchic integration [p. 126]." Applied to personal constructs, this suggests that (within a given domain) relatively more developed construct systems will, compared to relatively less developed systems, contain a larger number of constructs, and that these constructs will exhibit a greater degree of hierarchic organization and integration.

Hence one crude index of the comparative developmental status of a construct system within a given domain is simply the number of constructs the individual possesses for construing events in that domain: The larger the num-

---

[1] Elements of the Chicago school of symbolic interactionism as exemplified in the work of Herbert Blumer (1969) also play a role in constructivism, but these are not germane to the present analysis, and so are not discussed here. For more extensive and complete descriptions of constructivism, see Delia (1977, 1978), B. O'Keefe (1978), and D. O'Keefe (1978).

ber of constructs in a person's system, the more "cognitively complex" he or she is said to be (see Crockett, 1965). It is important to emphasize that cognitive complexity is a domain-specific notion. One might be a complex perceiver of persons and a noncomplex perceiver of, say, art. While a phrase such as "in a given domain" or "within the construct subsystem" will not always be included here, it should be remembered that a person may be cognitively complex in one area while noncomplex in another. Complexity is, however, only one of a number of developmental dimensions along which individuals' construct systems differ. Within a given domain, individuals differ not only in the number of constructs they possess for that domain, but also in the content of the particular constructs they employ, in the organization of their constructs, and in a number of other ways (see, e.g., B. O'Keefe & Delia, 1978). The central point is simply that the constructivist position is a cognitive–developmental view that identifies systematic developmental differences among persons.

The relationship of constructs to behavior is, in the constructivist view, seen as operating through beliefs. Beliefs are conceived of as the application of constructs to events. In employing my construct "honest–dishonest" to construe John, I arrive at some belief about John (say, that John is honest). That belief, and other beliefs I have, then serve as the bases for my behavior. Obviously, differences in construct systems will produce related differences in beliefs. As a simple example, several studies have shown that persons with relatively more complex interpersonal construct systems form more differentiated impressions of others (impressions with larger numbers of beliefs about the other) than do noncomplex perceivers, and that the impressions of complex perceivers exhibit greater internal organization and integration of conflicting information than do those of noncomplex perceivers (Crockett, Gonyea, & Delia, 1970; Nidorf & Crockett, 1965; B. O'Keefe, Delia, & O'Keefe, 1977).

It is perhaps important to emphasize that in the constructivist view beliefs are thought of as substantive cognitions which are connected to behavior by virtue of their content; it is on the basis of the content of their beliefs that persons select certain of these beliefs as relevant to their behavior in a given situation (Delia, Crockett, Press, & O'Keefe, 1975; Delia & D. O'Keefe, 1977). Although all beliefs have an affective dimension (Fishbein, 1967b), the constructivist view emphasizes that it is the substance of the belief that controls its relevance to conduct. Thus persons act as they do because of the content of the context-relevant beliefs that they hold, and these beliefs are the product of the application of systems of personal constructs to events.

Notice that constructivism makes no direct use of the concept of a generalized evaluation of an object (attitude). Although persons do have attitudes, the constructivist analysis denies that attitudes are important direct determinants of behavior; in our view, the immediate determinants of behavior are context-relevant beliefs.

But then what role *do* attitudes play? One might think of an attitude as simply another belief which, along with many other beliefs, is potentially relevant to one's actions. Seen in this way, the relatively poor observed correlation between attitudes and behavior becomes understandable, for one would not expect *any* one belief to predict behavior very successfully.

But although a generalized evaluation can be usefully construed as simply one sort of belief, one should recognize that it is nevertheless a special sort of belief precisely because it reflects the person's general evaluative characterization of the object, and general evaluative considerations have often been thought to be the central basis for the cognitive organization of experience. The key here is the general idea of evaluative consistency. Several accounts of cognitive operations and organization have stressed the role of affective–evaluative considerations in the maintenance of cognitive consistency (e.g., Abelson & Rosenberg, 1958; Heider, 1946; Osgood & Tannenbaum, 1955). The general theme of these approaches is that persons seek to maintain evaluative consistency among their beliefs, and that evaluative inconsistency is a state persons seek to avoid.

This basic theme is itself, of course, not incompatible with the constructivist idea that it is context–relevant beliefs, not attitudes, which are the primary determinants of behavior. Indeed, from a constructivist point of view, the importance of attitudes resides precisely in their role in the organization of belief systems. The critical difference is that within the constructivist view, this role is not a simple one, but depends on the comparative developmental status of the individual's construct system.

Briefly put, the central claims are these. Generalized evaluations of objects can serve as organizing principles for beliefs by providing criteria for evaluative consistency. But evaluation is only one possible belief-organization principle; rather than checking one's belief for evaluative consistency, one instead might employ a principle of, for example, descriptive consistency. And the central claim of the present analysis is that persons systematically differ in the extent to which they rely upon a principle of evaluative consistency: Persons with relatively more developed systems of personal constructs within a given domain will be less likely to rely upon a principle of evaluative consistency within that domain than will persons with relatively less developed cognitive systems in that domain. Moreover, in the constructivist view, this evaluative consistency principle is seen as potentially applicable not only to beliefs, but also to behavior, so that persons with relatively developed systems will be less likely (compared to those with less developed systems) to manifest a uniform evaluative orientation toward the object as reflected in their behavior. As noted earlier, attitude–behavior consistency usually is taken to be evaluative consistency between attitude and act. The constructivist analysis suggests that if attitude–behavior consistency is viewed in this way, systematic differences in attitude–behavior consistency should exist both between persons (of differing developmental levels in a given domain) and within persons (across domains where the person varies in developmental level). The less developed perceiver should, by virtue of his greater reliance on principles of evaluative consistency, exhibit greater evaluative consistency between his generalized attitude and his overt behavior than should the comparatively more developed perceiver.

In a sense, the basic idea advanced here is simply a revision and elaboration of the old saw that "consistency is the hobgoblin of small minds": Evaluative consistency is an important principle of cognitive organization in underdeveloped domains of a person's construct system. Thus the person who says "I don't know art, but I know what I like" is the exemplary noncomplex perceiver of art, and stands in sharp contrast to the perceiver who says "While I don't really much care for this painting, notice the nice way in which the artist has represented the drapery folds." The former's system for construing art is dominated by considerations of evaluative consistency, whereas the latter's is not.

Hence the general claim of the present theoretical analysis is that within a given domain, developmentally more advanced perceivers should place less reliance on principles of evaluative consistency than should relatively less advanced perceivers. And more specifically, the claim is that these developmental differences should be reflected in differential use of evaluative consistency principles both in the organization of beliefs about objects within the domain and in the organization of behavior toward objects within the domain.

Research Evidence

A good deal of existing research bears on these claims, though naturally most of the evidence concerns differences in belief organization, rather than differences in behavioral organization; investigators typically have not seen the need to examine the relevant individual-difference variables in the context of the attitude–behavior problem. And even the existing research generally has not been given the interpretation to be offered here. Still, the extant empirical data give considerable reason to think that the proposed theoretical analysis is viable.

Belief Organization

A number of studies bear on the issue of developmental differences in reliance on evaluative consistency principles in belief organization. The suggested analysis leads directly to the hypothesis that perceivers who differ in developmental advancement in a domain should differ in the univalence of the beliefs they hold about objects in that domain; less advanced perceivers, by virtue of their greater reliance on a principle of evaluative consistency, should be more likely to form evaluatively one-sided sets of beliefs than should developmentally advanced perceivers. Consistent with this prediction, Supnick (1964) found that in the interpersonal domain, noncomplex perceivers give a larger number of univalent impressions than do complex perceivers; her research used free-response impressions which were decomposed by the investigator into different qualities attributed to the person described, and it was the investigator who decided whether a given quality was positive or negative in valence. However, similar findings recently have been reported by Delia (1979) in a study in which subjects decomposed their own impressions and provided their own valence ratings. Delia compared complex and noncomplex subjects' impressions, using the proportion of traits in the dominant valence as an index of evaluative consistency; for example, a subject who wrote an impression in which 60% of the valenced qualities were positive and 40% were negative would be said to have 60% of the traits occurring in the dominant valence, whereas a subject who wrote an impression in which 95% of the qualities were negative and 5% were positive would have 95% of the traits in the dominant valence. Delia found that noncomplex perceivers wrote evaluatively more consistent impressions (i.e., had a significantly higher proportion of traits in the dominant valence) than did complex perceivers—a result directly predicted by the proposed analysis.

Related evidence concerning belief organization can be found in studies of developmental differences in the use of Heiderian balance schemes (Heider, 1946). Such schemes are based directly on considerations of evaluative consistency among a set of beliefs. Consistent with the present theoretical analysis, several studies have found that interpersonally cognitively noncomplex perceivers are more likely than complex perceivers to employ balance schemes in learning social relationships and are also more likely to continue to employ such schemes even when these have been disconfirmed (Delia & Crockett, 1973; Press, Crockett, & Rosenkrantz, 1969). Similar developmental differences in the use of balance schemes have been observed among children. Consistent with our Wernerian prediction, children's interpersonal construct systems become more differentiated, more abstract, and more hierarchically integrated over the course of childhood (Bigner, 1974; Biskin & Crano, 1977; Delia, Burleson, & Kline, in press; Scarlett, Press, & Crockett, 1971)—in short, older children tend to have relatively more developed cognitive systems in the interpersonal domain than do younger children. Hence the present theoretical analysis easily accomodates the findings indicating that whereas young children rely heavily on balance schemes for predicting social relationships, over the course of childhood development, the child comes progressively to rely less and less on such schemes (Atwood, 1969; Saltz & Medow, 1971).

Additional evidence concerning differences in the use of evaluative consistency principles in belief organization is provided by Markus (1977) in her investigation of what she called self-schemata, "cognitive generalizations about the self, derived from past experience, that organize and guide the processing of the self-related information contained in an individual's social experience [p. 63]." She studied females with and without self-schemata along a particular dimension of behavior, independence–dependence. The term "aschematic" was used to refer to persons "without schema on this particular dimension"; Markus obtained data confirming that "the aschematics have no articulated cognitive generalizations or self-schemata along the dimension of independence–dependence [pp. 66, 72]." Two kinds of schematics were identified, independents (those with self-schemata along the dimension who judged themselves to be relatively independent) and dependents (those with self-schemata who judged themselves to be relatively dependent).

Markus made several comparisons between aschematics, independents, and dependents, but the comparison of interest here concerns whether, when given a list of positive and negative trait-words related to the independence–dependence domain, aschematics, independents, and dependents would differ in the extent to which they saw these words as self-descriptive. The analysis proposed here suggests that those perceivers relatively developed in the independence–dependence domain (schematics, whether independent or dependent) should be more likely to check both positive and negative traits as self-descriptive, whereas less developed perceivers (the aschematics) should exhibit greater reliance on evaluative consistency and check adjectives predominantly of one valence (very likely predominantly positive, assuming they have a generally positive attitude towards themselves). Markus' findings are consistent with this prediction. For the aschematics, there was a high correlation ($r = .53$) between the percentage of individuals judging a word to be self-descriptive and the positivity of the word; no such relationship was apparent for dependents ($r = .11$) or independents ($r = .21$). These findings can now be seen as a natural consequence of the schematics' hypothesized lessened reliance (compared to aschematics) on evaluative consistency as a principle of belief organization.

Behavioral Organization

Several studies bear directly on the issue of developmental differences in attitude–behavior consistency. The most straightforward evidence is contained in recent research by D. O'Keefe and Delia (1980). Because the present chapter contains some additional analyses of these data, the procedures employed in the original study bear describing in some detail.

Subjects in this study were 71 students enrolled in small introductory communication classes at a midwestern university. In an initial session, participants completed a version of Crockett's (1965) Role Category Questionnaire measure of interpersonal cognitive complexity. This measure asks the subject to write descriptions of one liked and one disliked peer; approximately 10 minutes were taken for each description. Each impression was scored for the number of interpersonal constructs it contained following the procedures of Crockett, Press, Delia, and Kenny (1974). The number of constructs in the two impressions was then summed to yield a subject's cognitive complexity score. These scores were rank-ordered and broken at the median into groups of complex ($n = 37$) and noncomplex ($n = 34$) subjects.

This measure of interpersonal cognitive complexity has well-established validity and reliability. Crockett (1965), Delia (1978), and Delia, Clark, and

Switzer (1974) summarize considerable evidence bearing on the validity of the present measure; and the superiority of the measure has been demonstrated in direct comparisons with Bieri's (Bieri, Atkins, Briar, Leaman, Miller, & Tripodi, 1966) more generally known measure of cognitive complexity based on ratings of individuals on provided or elicited constructs (Horsfall, 1969; H. Jackson, 1978). Two coders' independent scorings of 27 of the protocols from the present sample yielded an interrater reliability coefficient by Pearson correlation of .94.

Approximately three months after adminstration of the Role Category Questionnaire, subjects participated in the second phase of the study. In this session, subjects completed a questionnaire in which they briefly described and provided ratings of the one individual in the class toward whom the strongest feelings had been developed. All classes in the study were small (roughly 15 class members each), and thus it was reasonable to expect that each individual had developed a generalized evaluation of at least one class member. Subjects were asked to "think of the person in this class toward whom you have developed the strongest feelings (positive or negative)." Then each subject was asked to describe the selected class member in writing, to provide ratings of him or her on general evaluation (attitude) scales, and to indicate behavioral intentions toward the selected class member in nine interpersonal contexts.

The attitude measure consisted of the four 7-step semantic differential evaluative scales developed by Fishbein and Raven (1962): beneficial–harmful, favorable–unfavorable, undesirable–desirable, and bad–good. Each scale was scored $+3$ to -3, with overall attitude determined by summing the ratings on the four scales. Roughly two-thirds of the obtained overall attitude scores were positive; one-third were negative. This distribution was similar for the complex and noncomplex subject groups; and within-valence analyses revealed that complexity groups did not differ in the extremity of their evaluations (e.g., complex and noncomplex subjects who had overall positive attitudes did not differ in the extremity of their evaluations).

The behavioral intentions index was a measure in which nine behavioral situations were described, and participants were asked to assume that an opportunity existed to interact with the selected class member in each of the specified circumstances; participants were asked to indicate the likelihood of the target person being picked as an interactional partner given such opportunity. For example, one item asked participants to "assume you have the opportunity to spend an evening with the person as your companion at a formal social gathering. How likely would you be to pick him or her as your companion for such an evening?" The participant's response to each item was made on a 7-step scale anchored by the phrases "Very Unlikely" and "Very Likely." Each item was scored -3 (unlikely) to $+3$ (likely), and the ratings were summed across the nine situations to yield a multiple-act behavioral intentions index score. The nine situations called for consideration of the other as a companion at a formal social gathering, someone with whom to work out a compromise on an issue where goals conflict, a partner on a major graded out-of-class assignment, someone to spend time talking with at a large party, someone to seek advice from concerning a conflict in an important interpersonal relationship, someone to pool knowledge and skills with in solving a difficult problem, a companion at an informal social gathering, a companion for an afternoon at an amusement park, and a companion for an afternoon spent having a coke or beer and just talking. These nine items had been pretested for their attitude-relevancy using a separate group of subjects drawn from the same population as the subjects participating in the main study; all are highly attitude-relevant (for details, see D. O'Keefe & Delia, 1980).

The impression each subject wrote of the selected class member was also analyzed. Each belief element appearing in a subject's impression was coded as of positive, negative, or neutral–ambiguous evaluation. Such experimenter codings of valence have been found to correlate highly with subjects' own evaluative ratings of the elements in their impressions (see D. O'Keefe & Delia, 1980, for details). Two measures were derived from these codings. One was an index of the evaluative consistency of beliefs about the target person (an index previously employed in Delia, 1979), computed by determining the proportion of elements which appeared in the dominant evaluation (positive or negative) as compared to the total number of valenced elements (positive plus negative). This score ranged from .50 (maximally inconsistent, with an equal number of positive and negative beliefs) to 1.00 (maximally consistent, with all the beliefs of one valence). Two coders' independent codings of the impressions yielded a .96 reliability coefficient (by Pearson correlation) for the index of evaluative consistency of beliefs.

The second measure derived from these codings was the proportion of positive elements in the impression (i.e., number of positive elements divided by total number of elements). This measure (employed previously by Delia, Crockett, Press, & O'Keefe, 1975) provides an index of the overall evaluative tone of the subject's beliefs about the target person as manifested in the written impression. Two coders' independent codings of the impressions yielded a .95 reliability coefficient (by Pearson r) for proportion of positive elements.

The results of this study directly support the present theoretical analysis. In confirmation of previous findings concerning belief organization, a significant difference ($p < .01$) in the evaluative consistency of complex and noncomplex subjects' beliefs was found (means for complex and noncomplex subjects of .75 and .87, respectively); the correlation of cognitive complexity and the index of evaluative consistency of beliefs was $-.26$ ($p < .05$).

Relevant to the issue of developmental differences in behavioral organization, a significant difference ($p < .001$) between complex and noncomplex subjects was found in attitude–behavioral intentions consistency. The correlation of attitude with the multiple-act behavioral intentions index was .95 among noncomplex subjects and .75 among complex subjects, displaying the predicted greater consistency between attitude and behavioral intentions for developmentally less advanced subjects. This same developmental difference also emerged at the level of single-act behavioral intentions (i.e., the nine behavioral intention items considered individually). The mean attitude–behavioral intention correlation (after r to Z transformation) across the nine individual situations was .88 for noncomplex subjects and .65 for complex subjects. In all nine situations, the correlation was higher for noncomplex subjects than for complex subjects, and in eight of the nine situations that difference met or approached the .05 (2-tailed) significance level.

An analysis of complex and noncomplex subjects' comparative variability in behavioral intentions also displayed the expected developmental differences. If noncomplex subjects rely heavily on an evaluative consistency principle for organizing their behavioral intentions, such subjects should exhibit relative evaluative homogeneity in their behavioral intentions toward a particular person; by contrast, of course, complex perceivers should display greater variation in the evaluative direction of their behavioral intentions toward another person. The variance of the nine behavioral intention items was computed for each subject, and the expected difference ($p < .01$) in variability of behavioral intentions was obtained (means for complex and noncomplex subjects of 2.35 and .97, respectively); the correlation of cognitive complexity and variance in behavioral intentions was .37 ($p < .01$). There was also the anticipated negative relationship between the index of evaluative consistency in beliefs and variability in behavioral intentions ($r = -.37, p < .01$); the multiple correlation of cognitive complexity and the evaluative consistency of beliefs with the variability of behavioral intentions was .47.

The differential effect of the evaluative content of subjects' beliefs on behavioral intentions was also present. The correlation between the proportion of positive beliefs in the impression and the multiple-act behavioral intentions index was significantly different ($p < .05$) for complex and noncomplex subjects (correlations of .74 and .92, respectively), again displaying the greater importance of evaluative consistency considerations for noncomplex perceivers.

Additionally, the hypothesized greater importance of overall attitude to noncomplex perceivers was revealed in differential correlations between the proportion of positive elements in the impression and overall attitude (.72 versus .93 for complex and noncomplex subjects, respectively; the difference is significant, $p < .01$). Because generalized evaluative considerations are relatively more important to noncomplex perceivers, their overall attitude more nearly reflects the evaluative tone of their beliefs than is the case for complex perceivers.

One unusual feature of these results is the relative powerfulness of attitude as a predictor. The correlation of attitude with the multiple-act behavioral intentions index for the sample as a whole was .85 ($p < .001$); this, however, is very much in line with Fishbein and Ajzen's (1974) reported range of .70 to .92 for correlations between attitude and multiple-act behavioral criteria. The mean correlation (after r to Z transformation) of attitude with the nine single-act criteria, on the other hand, was .75—rather higher than might have been anticipated on the basis of extant research. But the nature of the research design no doubt contributed to this effect: The target person for each subject was that class member toward whom the strongest feelings had been developed, a mix of positive and negative attitudes was obtained (i.e., there was not a restricted range among attitude scores), and reasonably "clean" measures were used (Fishbein & Raven's attitude scales, and a small set of highly attitude-relevant behavioral intention measures).

Several additional analyses (not contained in the report of D. O'Keefe & Delia, 1980) have subsequently been performed on these data. Several partial correlations were computed; a preliminary word is in order concerning the conceptual status of these partial correlations. One partial correlation was computed between the overall behavioral intentions index and the proportion of positive elements in the impression, with attitude partialled out; conceptually, this represents an estimate of the role (with respect to behavioral intentions) of the evaluative tone of beliefs about the object apart from the overarching importance of the overall attitude. A second partial correlation was computed between the behavioral intentions index and the overall attitude measure, with the proportion of positive elements partialled out; conceptually, this represents an estimate of the role (with respect to behavioral intentions) of overall attitude apart from the evaluative tone of the particular beliefs about the object.

These partial correlations were computed separately for complex and noncomplex subjects. The present theoretical analysis would suggest that for noncomplex subjects the partial correlation of attitude with behavioral intentions (removing the effect of proportion of positive elements) should be fairly substantial, but that the partial correlation of proportion of positive elements with behavioral intentions (removing the effect of overall attitude) should be comparatively low because of the hypothesized importance to noncomplex subjects of overall attitude. For complex subjects, by contrast, the two partial correlations would not be expected to be very different nor unusually large, just because evaluative consistency considerations (whether captured in overall attitude or in the evaluative tone of the impression) are predicted to be relatively unimportant for complex perceivers.

The obtained partial correlations confirm these expectations. For complex subjects, the partial correlation of the behavioral intentions index and the proportion of positive elements, partialling out attitude, was .44 ($F[1,34] = 8.16$, $p < .01$); the partial correlation of the behavioral intentions index and attitude, partialling out proportion of positive elements, was .47 ($F[1,34] = 9.64$, $p < .01$). By contrast, for noncomplex subjects the partial correlation of behavioral intentions and proportion of positive elements, partialling out attitude, was .32 ($F[1,31] = 3.54$, ns); the partial correlation of behavioral intentions and attitude, partialling out proportion of positive elements, was .66 ($F[1,31] = 23.93$, $p < .001$). The varying magnitudes of these partial correlations directly display the greater importance of overall attitude as a determinant of behavioral intentions for noncomplex subjects. It is especially striking that the correlation for noncomplex subjects between the proportion of positive elements and the multiple-act behavioral intentions index drops dramatically, from .92 to .32, once the effect of attitude is partialled out.

It might be noted that (as J. Cohen & Cohen, 1975, p. 108, point out) the significance level achieved by the F for each partial correlation is identical to the significance level that would be obtained for the corresponding semipartial (part) correlation. That is, a significant F-value for a partial correlation here indicates that, in a multiple regression analysis using attitude and proportion of positive elements as two predictors of the behavioral intentions index, a predictor variable for which a significant F is obtained does make a significantly nonzero contribution to the overall R. Thus the present results indicate that for noncomplex subjects, the multiple correlation using attitude and proportion of positive elements as predictors of the multiple-act behavioral intentions index is not significantly better than the prediction that would be obtained using only attitude as a predictor—a result entirely consistent with the hypothesized importance of overall attitude to noncomplex subjects.

This point can be underscored by examining the standardized partial regression coefficients for attitude and proportion of positive elements as predictors of the behavioral intentions index. For complex subjects these coefficients are .45 (attitude) and .42 (proportion of positive elements); for noncomplex subjects the coefficients are .70 (attitude) and .27 (proportion of positive elements). The multiple correlation for complex subjects is .80 ($F[2,34] = 28.44$, $p < .001$) and for noncomplex subjects is .96 ($F[2,31] = 182.20$, $p < .001$). The "shrunken" R is .79 for complex subjects and is .95 for noncomplex subjects.

In sum, D. O'Keefe and Delia's (1980) data are quite supportive of the present theoretical analysis of the attitude–behavior relationship. In a variety of ways, developmentally less advanced perceivers in this study exhibited considerably greater reliance on evaluative consistency principles than did developmentally more advanced perceivers, including greater reliance on such consistency principles in the formation of behavioral intentions.

Additional evidence bearing on the present analysis of differences in behavioral organization is provided by Norman (1975). In a series of studies, he investigated the influence of "affective–cognitive consistency" on the correlation between attitude and behavior. In addition to assessing subjects' overall attitudes and obtaining measures of overt behavior, Norman developed a "cognitive index" of favorability toward the attitude object based on Rosenberg's (1956, 1960) value–instrumentality formulation of attitude. This cognitive index was based on subjects' judgments of the desirability of various goals and judgments of the extent to which each goal would be achieved or blocked by the attitude object; crudely, the larger the number of favorable goals the subject thought the attitude object would help achieve (and the larger the number of undesirable goals the subject thought the attitude object would block), the more favorable the subject's overall attitude toward the object was thought to be.

Two rankings of subjects (according to the degree of favorability toward the object) were then produced, based on (*a*) the overall attitude measure; and (*b*) the cognitive index. The discrepancy between each subject's two ranks was computed; the discrepancy scores were rank-ordered and then split at the median. This produced two groups, one deemed "high" in "affective–cognitive consistency," the other "low."

Notice that the theoretical analysis outlined in the present chapter suggests that Norman's procedure serves to differentiate subjects for whom evaluative consistency seems to be an important principle of cognitive organization (the "high-consistency" group) from those for whom that principle is less important ("low-consistency"). For example, a subject who has a strongly positive attitude as measured by the overall attitude measure, but whose beliefs (as indexed by the value–instrumentality measure) exhibit substantial bivalency (e.g., a subject who holds a roughly equal number of positive and negative beliefs about the object) will be thought to be "lower" in affective–cognitive consistency than a subject with the same overall attitude score but a univalent belief system. On this basis, the constructivist analysis would predict that the overall attitude measure would be more highly correlated with overt behavior for the "high-consistency" group than for the "low-consistency" group. The reason is simply that subjects who place heavy reliance on evaluative consistency as a principle of belief organization in a given domain are also likely to employ a similar principle in judging the relationship between their overall attitude and their overt behavior in that domain. Consistent with this prediction, the attitude–behavior correlations for the high-consistency groups ranged from $+.47$ to $+.62$ (all significant), whereas for the low-consistency groups the correlations ranged from $-.28$ to $+.24$ (none significant).

The continuity between Norman's results and the present theoretical analysis can also be displayed by considering some additional analyses of D. O'Keefe and Delia's (1980) data. As previously reported, D. O'Keefe and Delia found that noncomplex subjects were more likely than complex subjects to have the evaluative tone of their beliefs about the target person reflected in their overall attitude toward that person (as displayed in differential correlations between attitude and the proportion of positive elements in the impression), suggesting that noncomplex subjects display greater "affective–cognitive consistency." To further examine this suggestion, D. O'Keefe and Delia's data were reanalyzed following a procedure that duplicated (in abstract form) Norman's procedures. Subjects were rank-ordered on the basis of the overall attitude measure, and on the basis of the proportion of positive elements in the impression; the absolute difference between the two ranks was computed for each subject; these rank differences were then rank-ordered and broken at the median, yielding one group "high in affective–cognitive consistency" ($n = 36$) and one group "low in affective–cognitive consistency" ($n = 35$).

As expected, there was a significant association between the complexity grouping and the affective–cognitive consistency grouping. The 2 × 2 chi-square (high–low cognitive complexity versus high–low affective–cognitive consistency) was 5.12 (1 df, $p < .05$), with noncomplex perceivers more likely to be high in affective–cognitive consistency (of 34 noncomplex subjects, 22 were high in affective–cognitive consistency; of 37 complex subjects, 23 were low in affective–cognitive consistency). And consistent with Norman's findings, the correlation between attitude and the behavioral intentions index was higher for the high affective–cognitive consistency group ($r = .95$, 34 df, $p < .001$) than for the low affective–cognitive consistency group ($r = .82$, 33 df, $p < .001$); these correlations are significantly different ($z = 2.85, p < .01$).

These additional analyses thus buttress the present interpretation of Norman's (1975) results, and suggest that differential affective–cognitive consistency perhaps may be seen best as a consequence of differences in developmental level. As indicated both by the differential correlations for complex and noncomplex subjects between overall attitude and the proportion of positive elements, and by the significant association of complexity and affective–cognitive consistency, it is developmentally less advanced persons who are most likely to display high affective–cognitive consistency—a result entirely in line with the hypothesized greater reliance of such persons on evaluative consistency principles.

Other Evidence

Evidence not directly concerning belief organization and behavioral organization is also relevant to the present theoretical analysis. Although I shall not discuss this evidence extensively, it does offer further support for the general theoretical claims.

One piece of additional relevant evidence concerns the relative stability of attitudes for complex and noncomplex perceivers. Faced with the task of integrating sequentially presented evaluatively inconsistent information about another person, interpersonally complex perceivers should find it easier to arrive at a stable overall evaluation of the other than should noncomplex perceivers; noncomplex perceivers, as a consequence of their greater reliance on a principle of evaluative consistency, should find it difficult to reconcile the inconsistency, and hence should show greater fluctuations in their overall evaluation of the other (with the fluctuation most likely occurring in the direction of the most recently presented piece of information). Several studies have shown that interpersonally complex perceivers in fact display less shift than noncomplex perceivers (who display recency effects) in sequential evaluations of another person (Klyver, Press, & Crockett, 1972; Mayo & Crockett, 1964).

Similarly, noncomplex perceivers show greater shifts in attitude when one or the other valence of simultaneously (not sequentially) presented bivalent information is made salient (Delia, Crockett, Press, & O'Keefe, 1975); noncomplex perceivers' reliance on evaluative consistency leads their overall attitude to be dominated by whatever valence of the information is salient at the moment. These observed effects are now explicable as natural consequences of the suggested relationship between the developmental level of the construct system and the extent of reliance on evaluative consistency as a principle of cognitive organization.

Another general result that fits nicely into the proposed framework concerns the ways in which perceivers differing in interpersonal cognitive complexity reconcile and integrate evaluatively inconsistent information about another person. Based on Kaplan and Crockett's (1968) theoretical argument that developmentally advanced perceivers utilize more sophisticated modes of resolving evaluative inconsistency, Crockett and his coworkers developed a scoring system for the analysis of impressions written on the basis of bivalent stimulus information (Crockett, Press, Delia, & Kenny, 1974). The system assigns one of 15 levels of organization to each impression, depending on the extent to which (and manner in which) evaluative inconsistency is recognized and reconciled. Impressions organized at lower levels either reproduce the stimulus information with little elaboration, or utilize only one valence of the information so as to produce an evaluatively one-sided impression. At higher levels of organization, evaluative inconsistency is managed through the use of integrative strategies involving (for example) the attribution of underlying motivational characteristics to the stimulus person that lead him to have both positive and negative qualities. What is important here is that higher levels of organization indicate an increasing ability of the perceiver to recognize and cope with evaluative inconsistency in increasingly advanced ways. The implication of the present theoretical analysis is that interpersonal cognitive complexity and level of organization should be related, such that complex perceivers utilize more advanced levels of organization. Developmentally less advanced perceivers should be more prone simply to reproduce the stimulus information (without integrating it) or to produce univalent impressions, whereas more advanced perceivers should find it easier to fit the evaluatively inconsistent information together in some way. Such a relationship has been observed consistently in a number of impression-formation studies (Crockett, Gonyea, & Delia, 1970; Nidorf & Crockett, 1965; B. O'Keefe, Delia, & O'Keefe, 1977; Rosenkrantz & Crockett, 1965).

Evidence concerning the relative effectiveness of one-sided and two-sided persuasive communications provides another indication of the viability of the proposed framework. The present analysis suggests that receivers who are developmentally less advanced in domains relevant to the topic of the communication would find one-sided communications less confusing, easier to understand, and more persuasive (compared to two-sided communications) because the univalent character of the communication would mesh more easily with their univalent cognitive systems; this prediction parallels the results discussed above concerning the integration of bivalent information in impression formation. And there is evidence to suggest that audiences who are relatively knowledgeable about the topic can be more effectively persuaded by two-sided communications, whereas those less knowledgeable are more influenced by one-sided messages (Chu, 1967; Hass & Linder, 1972). Knowledgeability, of course, is not synonymous with developmental advancement, but there is reason to believe that the two are positively related (see Crockett, 1965, pp. 56–63).

Summary

On the whole, the research evidence is quite supportive of the present theoretical analysis. In a variety of investigations, developmentally advanced perceivers have been shown to systematically place less reliance on principles of evaluative consistency than do less advanced perceivers. And consistent with the proposed analysis, such developmental differences have been discovered with respect to both belief organization and the organization of behavior.

Comparison with Fishbein and Ajzen's Analysis

In some ways, the present analysis may be seen as fundamentally similar to the approach offered by Fishbein and Ajzen (Ajzen, 1971; Ajzen & Fishbein, 1969, 1970, 1972, 1973, 1974, 1977; Fishbein, 1967a, 1973; Fishbein & Ajzen, 1974, 1975). But there are also several important differences between the two accounts, best discussed following a brief sketch of Fishbein and Ajzen's analysis.

Fishbein and Ajzen's View

The approach offered by Ajzen and Fishbein is most conveniently described in two parts: the attitude model, and the behavioral intentions model.

The Attitude Model

Consistent with the usage here, Fishbein (1967b) takes an attitude to be a person's overall evaluation of an object. An attitude is hypothesized to be a function of two factors. One consists of the evaluative aspects of the beliefs the person holds about the object; the other is the strength with which the beliefs are held. Mathematically, Fishbein (1967b) expresses this as follows: Attitude =

$\sum b_i a_i$, where b_i represents the strength with which the ith belief about the object is held and a_i represents the evaluation of the ith belief. Fishbein and Raven's (1962) AB scales were developed to assess these two determinants of attitude; the B scales (e.g., likely–unlikely, true–false, probable–improbable) measure belief strength; the A scales (e.g., desirable–undesirable, good–bad, favorable–unfavorable) measure the evaluation of each belief (and can also be used to assess overall attitude). While Fishbein's attitude model is in fact more detailed than this, the present description is sufficient for my purposes here.

The Behavioral Intentions Model

Fishbein and Ajzen's behavioral intentions model (e.g., Ajzen, 1971; Ajzen & Fishbein, 1973; Fishbein, 1967a, 1973) represents their attempt to come to terms with the attitude–behavior problem. Fishbein and Ajzen emphasize the importance of the distinction between single-act and multiple-act behavioral criteria (see, e.g., Fishbein & Ajzen, 1974), and their behavioral intentions model is focused on the problem of predicting single behaviors. Recognizing that most of the behaviors in which social scientists are interested are under volitional control, Ajzen and Fishbein argue that the best predictor of whether a person will perform a particular act is that person's behavioral intention (i.e., the person's intention to perform or not to perform that act); hence the focus of their approach to the attitude–behavior problem concerns the determinants of a person's behavioral intentions (for a discussion of factors influencing the relationship of intention and behavior, see Ajzen & Fishbein, 1974).

One's behavioral intentions are hypothesized to be determined by two factors. The first is one's attitude toward the act. Notice that this is not an attitude in the sense that the term has been used here: One's attitude toward the act is one's overall evaluation of that act (e.g., "buying Oldsmobiles"), not one's evaluation of the object (Oldsmobiles). However, one's attitude toward the act is a function of factors similar to those that determine attitude: the strength with which one holds one's beliefs about the act, and the evaluation associated with each belief.

The second determinant of behavioral intention is a social–normative factor, representing one's judgments about the expectations of particular significant others and one's motivation to comply with those expectations (see Fishbein & Ajzen, 1975, p. 302). This normative component has been variously formulated by Fishbein and Ajzen (see Ajzen & Fishbein, 1973, p. 43; Fishbein, 1967a), but the present description most nearly represents their recent accounts.

The Attitude–Behavior Relationship

In a variety of studies, Ajzen and Fishbein have shown that the behavioral intentions model is a good predictor of single-act behavioral criteria (Ajzen,

1971; Ajzen & Fishbein, 1969, 1970, 1972, 1973). But this does not directly solve the original attitude–behavior problem, for it does not explicate the relationship between attitude (attitude toward an object) and conduct.

In addressing the attitude–behavior relationship, Fishbein and Ajzen (1974) stress the distinction between single-act and multiple-act behavioral measures. Their view is this: "A person's attitude toward an object need not be related to any single behavior that may be performed with respect to the object (i.e., may not permit prediction of single-act criteria). However, it should be related to the overall pattern of his behaviors (i.e., it should predict multiple-act criteria) [p. 61]." Thus "a person's attitude toward an object influences the overall pattern of his responses to the object, but . . . it need not predict any given action [Ajzen & Fishbein, 1977, p. 888]." The data reported by Fishbein and Ajzen (1974, p. 64) directly support this differential relation of attitude to single- and multiple-act criteria; using a variety of attitude measures, the mean correlations of attitude with single-act criteria ranged from .14 to .23, whereas the correlations with multiple-act measures ranged from .70 to .92. Given these high correlations of attitude with multiple-act measures, Fishbein and Ajzen (1974) argue that multiple-act criteria can be viewed best as behavioral attitude measures, that is, as alternative attitude measurement procedures.

Comparison

There are a number of important continuities between the present analysis and that offered by Fishbein and Ajzen. Both views implicitly or explicitly recognize the central role of context-relevant beliefs as determinants of conduct; both views suggest that attitudes are not important direct determinants of behavior; and thus both approaches indicate that, as a rule, attitudes should not be especially highly correlated with single-act behavioral criteria.

Where the two analyses most directly part company is over the issue of exactly what role attitudes do play in the organization of cognition and conduct. The present analysis takes issue with two particular claims contained in Fishbein and Ajzen's approach: that (a) one's attitude toward an object is a function of the evaluation of each belief and the strength with which each belief is held; and (b) one's attitude toward an object should be closely related to the overall pattern of one's behavior toward that object (i.e., to multiple-act criteria), to the point that multiple-act criteria can serve as alternative attitude measurement procedures.

Consider first the question of the determinants of attitude. There is considerable evidence to suggest that the apparent contribution of belief-strength measures to predictions of attitude is a methodological artifact resulting from the use of supplied belief lists. Delia, Crockett, Press, and O'Keefe (1975) had subjects write impressions of a stimulus person and then decompose their impressions into the separate belief components; subjects then rated each belief both for evaluation and for belief strength; a measure of overall attitude was also obtained. As the authors note, the prediction of attitude based simply on a sum of the component evaluations (in Fishbein's terms, $\sum a_i$) was "not improved through the addition of component belief strength weightings [p. 16]." Because each subject's belief-strength ratings were given for beliefs already included in the subject's written impression, only beliefs that the subject already held were rated for belief strength. By contrast, if one had given subjects a list of possible beliefs (e.g., trait attributes) and asked for both belief-strength ratings and evaluations of the belief elements, the belief-strength ratings would likely have contributed significantly to the prediction of attitude, because those ratings would have differentiated those beliefs the subject held from those the subject did not hold.

In fact, Cronen and Conville (1975) conducted a series of studies on just this issue, in which they examined the contribution of belief-strength scores to prediction of attitude under conditions of either free elicitation of subjects' beliefs or employment of supplied belief lists. They consistently found that belief-strength weightings improved the attitude prediction only when supplied belief lists were used. As Cronen and Conville conclude, the earlier findings suggesting the importance of belief strength as a determinant of attitude were likely "an artifact of the employment of standard belief lists [p. 148]." What Cronen and Conville's (1975) and Delia, Crockett, Press, and O'Keefe's (1975) results suggest is that when considering the determinants of attitude, one need take only the evaluative aspects of beliefs into account (as long as supplied belief lists are not the basis for prediction).

But even beyond this, the present analysis suggests that there are important developmental differences in the extent to which persons' attitudes in fact reflect the overall evaluative tone of their beliefs about the object. As D. O'Keefe and Delia (1980) found, persons with developmentally more advanced cognitive systems in the attitude domain exhibited lower correlations between the proportion of positive beliefs about the attitude object and their overall attitude toward the object than did persons with less developed systems. And this evidence is buttressed by the reanalysis of D. O'Keefe and Delia's data, which displayed the expected developmental differences in what Norman (1975) calls "affective–cognitive consistency" (the degree to which one's attitude is consistent with the bivalency of one's beliefs about the object).

These developmental differences make good theoretical sense in light of the relatively unimportant role that attitudes apparently play for persons with developmentally advanced cognitive systems in the attitude domain. Precisely because persons with less developed systems place heavy reliance on evaluative consistency principles, such persons have considerable need to "keep tabs on" their attitudes toward objects, and hence their attitudes closely reflect the evaluative tone of their beliefs. Persons with more advanced systems, because of the vestigial role that evaluation plays in their cognitive systems, need not be particularly concerned about the extent to which their attitudes reflect the overall valence of their beliefs.

This analysis explicates what might be taken to be a puzzling empirical fact (puzzling, at least, for a Fishbeinian conception of the determinants of attitude). If some version of a Fishbein-like model of the determinants of attitude is correct, then to the extent that individuals differ in the bivalency of their beliefs about an object, to that same extent those individuals' attitudes should differ in extremity. For example, if one individual has a univalent set of beliefs about an object, his attitude toward that object presumably should be more extreme than the attitude of a person whose beliefs about the object exhibit a considerable degree of bivalency. The puzzling empirical fact here is that several investigations have shown that interpersonally less complex perceivers are more likely to form univalent impressions of other people than are more complex perceivers, but these two groups do not differ in their evaluations of others (Delia, 1972; Meltzer, Crockett, & Rosenkrantz, 1966; Nidorf & Crockett, 1965; Press, Crockett, & Delia, 1975; Rosenkrantz & Crockett, 1965). If both developmentally advanced and less advanced perceivers follow the same "information integration" model (e.g., a Fishbein-like "sum of the evaluations" model), then the observed differences in bivalency should be accompanied by differences in attitude. The fact that differentially advanced perceivers do not differ in attitude suggests that perceivers at different developmental levels must in some sense be relying on different information integration schemes. The present analysis, of course, explicates why that should be so: Developmentally less advanced perceivers, as a consequence of the heightened importance of considerations of evaluative consistency, should be more likely to have their attitudes more nearly reflect the evaluative pattern contained in their beliefs about the attitude object.

Consider now the second claim mentioned previously, that one's attitude toward an object should be closely related to multiple-act behavioral criteria. Fishbein and Ajzen (1974) present evidence that such is in fact the case, but they do not go far in explaining why this relationship should hold. They simply suggest that these strong relationships indicate that multiple-act criteria can safely "be viewed as an alternative attitude measurement procedure" (Fishbein & Ajzen, 1974, p. 62; also see Fishbein, 1973, p. 22), and thus they account for the relationship as one of a high correlation between different attitude measurement procedures (Fishbein, 1973, p. 22; Fishbein & Ajzen, 1974, p. 64).

Delia, Crockett, Press, and O'Keefe (1975), on the other hand, explained the relationship between attitude and multiple-act behavioral criteria this way:

> The overall attitude is a function of beliefs about the object. When multiple-act criteria are employed, the chance of some particular belief becoming relevant [to a particular action context] increases. To the extent that a variety of contexts are sampled in the multiple-act measure, a large number of beliefs about the object come into play. Thus it is to be expected that the multiple-act criteria (by virtue of the variety of beliefs involved) will be significantly related to the generalized attitude [p. 18].

The present analysis, however, suggests that this explanation is incomplete. Although the general line of reasoning is sound, this account fails to acknowledge important developmental differences—differences both in the extent to which one's attitude reflects the evaluative pattern of one's beliefs about the object, and in the extent to which considerations of evaluative consistency between attitude and act are important. The first sort of difference has been discussed earlier; it is the second difference that is important here.

The evidence discussed from D. O'Keefe and Delia (1980) indicates that multiple-act behavioral criteria are less well correlated with attitude for developmentally advanced persons than for developmentally less advanced persons. The present analysis explains this difference as a consequence of differential reliance on evaluative consistency principles in judging the relationship between attitude and act: Developmentally advanced persons, as a consequence of lessened reliance on such principles, should be more likely to engage in attitude-discrepant behavior. Thus not only does the present analysis suggest that multiple-act behavioral criteria cannot in all cases be taken as sound indices of overall attitude (but only for persons with relatively less advanced cognitive systems in the attitude domain); it also indicates why the overall relationship that does hold between attitude and multiple-act criteria occurs, while simultaneously pointing to the existence of important developmental differences in this relationship.

Thus in two general ways the present analysis departs from the approach offered by Fishbein and Ajzen: The present analysis suggests that Fishbein's claims about the determinants of attitude are flawed, and that Fishbein and Ajzen's analysis of the relationship between attitude and multiple-act behavioral criteria is insufficient. And in both cases, the present analysis emphasizes developmental differences in reliance on evaluative consistency principles in the organization of cognition and conduct.

The constructivist approach also diverges from Ajzen and Fishbein's analysis in other respects. For example, in Fishbein and Ajzen's account, beliefs emerge as insubstantial colorless elements that serve only to add or to subtract increments of affect to some attitude. The viewpoint offered here, by contrast, emphasizes that beliefs are substantive cognitions whose relevance to conduct is controlled by their content (see Delia, Crockett, Press, & O'Keefe, 1975, p. 17). Indeed, the present analysis even departs from Ajzen and Fishbein's view concerning a matter that was earlier conceded as a point of similarity: the question of the relationship of attitude to single-act behavioral criteria. Fishbein and Ajzen suggest that, on the whole, attitudes should not be highly correlated with single-act criteria. While this may be true as a general rule, the present analysis again indicates that developmentally less advanced persons, by virtue of greater reliance on evaluative consistency principles, should exhibit greater attitude–behavior consistency (than should persons with more advanced cognitive systems) even at the level of single-act criteria. And the evidence from D. O'Keefe and Delia (1980) discussed earlier directly supports this claim.

None of this, of course, should be taken as a denigration of Fishbein and Ajzen's accomplishments. The present analysis is indeed similar in broad outline to their approach, and one would not go far wrong in viewing the considerations raised here as elaborations and refinements of Fishbein and Ajzen's approach. But the research evidence discussed here suggests that these refinements are indeed necessary if an adequate understanding of the relationship of attitude to behavior is to be had.

Concluding Remarks

In this concluding section, I wish to address briefly two additional points: the implications of the present analysis for the construction of persuasive messages, and some broader issues concerning the nature of theory development.

Message Construction

The constructivist analysis of the relationship of attitudes, beliefs, and behavior has several direct implications for the construction of effective persuasive messages. One such implication already has been obliquely mentioned: The choice between a one-sided and a two-sided persuasive message should depend (at least in part) on the relative developmental advancement of the receivers with respect to the attitude domain. As discussed earlier, persons who are knowledgeable about the message topic are relatively more influenced by two-sided messages, whereas those less knowledgeable are more influenced by one-sided messages. This suggests a general principle to the effect that persuasive messages should be designed so as to fit the developmental character of the receivers' topic-relevant cognitive systems. Put in this broad way, the present analysis may be seen to have implications beyond "structural" message features (e.g., one- versus two-sided messages) to "content" aspects of persuasive communications. For example, it may be the case that certain *kinds* of arguments are differentially persuasive to persons with differentially advanced cognitive systems in the attitude domain. Although at present no direct empirical evidence bears specifically on this point, one need only think of, for example, Kohlberg's (1969, 1971) analysis of the different types of reasoning that characterize different levels of moral development to see how the present emphasis on developmental differences among receivers suggests the possibility that a given argumentative content may be differentially persuasive to receivers at differing developmental levels.

The present analysis also bears on the issue of the behavioral consequences of attitude change. The existence of low correlations between attitude measures and behavioral indices has convinced many investigators that changing a person's attitude toward an object either will have insignificant consequences for that person's behavior toward the object or (following Fishbein and Ajzen) will influence the overall evaluative pattern of behavior toward the object (as reflected in multiple-act behavioral criteria), although not necessarily producing alterations in the likelihood of performance of any specific act (as indicated by single-act criteria). The developmental emphasis of the present analysis, on the other hand, emphasizes the role of individual developmental differences in attitude–behavior consistency at the level of both single- and multiple-act behavioral measures. A persuasive message that changes a person's attitude toward an object may have substantial and far-reaching consequences for that person's attitude-relevant conduct toward the object if the receiver is a person with a relatively noncomplex cognitive system in the attitude domain. By contrast, a similar change in the attitude of a relatively more complex person may have comparatively little impact on the person's conduct, just because such a person places relatively little emphasis on evaluative consistency principles in judging the relationship between his attitude and his conduct. Hence persuasive messages that are designed to change receivers' attitudes, as opposed to those designed to change particular beliefs or behavioral intentions (for a discussion of the distinction, see Fishbein & Ajzen, 1972), are, if successful, most likely to influence the conduct of receivers who are relatively less developmentally advanced in the attitude domain.

In the same vein, this constructivist analysis suggests that persuasive messages designed to change particular beliefs about an object, even if successful, may not have important consequences for the person's attitude toward that object. Persons with differentially advanced cognitive systems differ in the extent to which their attitudes reflect the evaluative tone of their beliefs about the object: The attitudes of persons with relatively noncomplex systems much more closely represent the evaluative character of the person's particular beliefs about the object than is the case for persons with more complex systems. Thus the common persuasive strategy of "change the receiver's beliefs about the object, thereby changing the attitude toward the object" is one more likely to succeed with receivers who have comparatively less complex systems with respect to the attitude domain.

Theory Development

One popular response to the attitude–behavior problem has been the "other variables" answer. The general idea is that attitude is only one of a large number of variables that influence behavior, and that it is these other variables that explain the discrepancy between attitudes and behavior; hence the researcher's task becomes one of identifying those other variables and specifying their interrelations (for representative other-variable studies, see Jackman, 1976; Petersen & Dutton, 1975; Schofield, 1975; Wicker, 1971; Wicker & Pomazal, 1971). This state of affairs is of course naturally suited to the use of complex regression procedures, including causal-modeling techniques (see, e.g., Alwin, 1973, 1976; Perry, Gillespie, & Lotz, 1976; Seibold, 1975).

However, this other-variables approach is less than ideal, for it embodies a variable–analytic stance toward the research enterprise. What I mean by a variable–analytic orientation is "the examination of communication in terms of the influence of discrete factors (variables) upon communication outcomes (effects)," where the variables to be studied are selected not from their roles in a unified conceptual framework, but on the basis of "ad hoc theoretical considerations" (Delia, 1977, pp. 72, 74). As Delia (1977) indicates, "such an approach necessarily leaves the research enterprise fragmented since different theoretic frames typically serve to generate the conceptualization and measurement of each variable, while still other considerations lead to their hypothesized interrelations [p. 74]." As a consequence, this variable–analytic research strategy too often fails to contribute to general conceptual or theoretical advance. As Swanson (1977) has noted, "a characteristic of variable analysis in communication research has been the absence of any theoretical stance per se; variable analysis functions typically as a system for organizing results rather than as a theoretic system [p. 5]." Without a unitary theoretical framework to guide research, whatever findings result do not (and often cannot) receive unified theoretical treatment and explanation because the initial research effort was not programmatically conducted under the aegis of a single conceptual framework.

By contrast, "within a unified perspective . . . the selection of concepts, and through them, variables, is not based upon ad hoc considerations, but follows from an integrated conceptual analysis. . . . The same system of concepts employed in conceptualizing and measuring variables also serves to generate their hypothesized interrelations [Delia, 1977, p. 74]." This is particularly important in approaching the attitude–behavior problem for, as Liska (1974) has noted, the central problem in the attitude–behavior area is one of formulating "a unitary conceptual and methodological framework [p. 20]."

But in constructing such a framework, one's vision need not be restricted to an explanation of the effects of suasory communication. Persuasion has, of course, long been a primary focus for communication theory and research, and the concept of attitude typically figures centrally in explanations of the effects of persuasive messages. But any theory of persuasion depends on a *general* account of human action: Successful persuasive efforts are taken to influence what a person does because they influence the general mechanisms underlying behavior. Thus the kinds of explanations theorists offer of persuasive effects ideally should be integrated with a general theory of why persons act as they do; and in any case, these accounts imply such a general theory.

Of course, the analysis of the attitude–behavior relationship proposed here is explicitly grounded in just such a general theoretical framework, and represents an attempt to extend that theory to a new empirical domain. The present analysis thus might be taken to be an exemplar of the maxim that "maximally productive research involves the systematic extension, elaboration, and defense of a theoretical perspective [D. O'Keefe, 1975, p. 177]." The kinds of individual developmental differences constructivism identifies as important are not ones likely to have been discovered in a statistical dragnet, but flow directly from the theory's claims. The proposed analysis and much of the summarized research are grounded in an explicit general theoretical orientation in which concept, theory, and method are systematically integrated.

None of this is designed to suggest that constructivism is the only viable existing theoretical framework for communication studies generally or for the attitude–behavior problem in particular. The point is simply that to the extent that communication research, whether on the attitude–behavior relationship or some other topic, is not conducted as part of a programmatic effort to refine and extend a given theoretical approach, to that same extent that research is likely to prove less useful than it might have been. Solutions to difficulties like the attitude–behavior problem are most likely to be discovered through systematic research conducted from a given conceptual framework.

ACKNOWLEDGMENTS

Jesse G. Delia and Barbara J. O'Keefe provided helpful commentary on earlier versions of this essay.

REFERENCES

Abelson, R. P., & Rosenberg, M. J. Symbolic psycho-logic: A model of attitudinal cognition. *Behavioral Science*, 1958, *3*, 1–13.

Ajzen, I. Attitudinal versus normative messages: An investigation of the differential effects of persuasive communications on behavior. *Sociometry*, 1971, *34*, 263–280.

Ajzen, I., & Fishbein, M. The prediction of behavioral intentions in a choice situation. *Journal of Experimental Social Psychology*, 1969, *5*, 400–416.

Ajzen, I., & Fishbein, M. The prediction of behavior from attitudinal and normative variables. *Journal of Experimental Social Psychology*, 1970, *6*, 466–487.

Ajzen, I., & Fishbein, M. Attitudes and normative beliefs as factors influencing behavioral intentions. *Journal of Personality and Social Psychology*, 1972, *21*, 1–9.

Ajzen, I., & Fishbein, M. Attitudinal and normative variables as predictors of specific behaviors. *Journal of Personality and Social Psychology*, 1973, *27*, 41–57.

Ajzen, I., & Fishbein, M. Factors influencing intentions and the intention–behavior relation. *Human Relations*, 1974, *27*, 1–15.

Ajzen, I., & Fishbein, M. Attitude–behavior relations: A theoretical analysis and review of empirical research. *Psychological Bulletin*, 1977, *84*, 888–918.

Alwin, D. F. Making inferences from attitude–behavior correlations. *Sociometry*, 1973, *36*, 253–278.

Alwin, D. F. Attitude scales as congeneric tests: A re-examination of an attitude–behavior model. *Sociometry*, 1976, *39*, 377–383.

Applegate, J. L. Four investigations of the relationship between social cognitive development and person-centered regulative and interpersonal communication. Unpublished doctoral dissertation, Department of Speech Communication, University of Illinois at Urbana–Champaign, 1978.

Applegate, J. L., & Delia, J. G. Person-centered speech, psychological development, and the contexts of language usage. In R. St. Clair & H. Giles (Eds.), *The social and psychological contexts of language*. Hillsdale, N.J.: Erlbaum, in press.

Atwood, G. A developmental study of cognitive balancing in hypothetical three-person systems. *Child Development*, 1969, *40*, 73–85.

Bieri, J., Atkins, A. L., Briar, S., Leaman, R. L., Miller, H., & Tripodi, T. *Clinical and social judgment*. New York: Wiley, 1966.

Bigner, J. J. A Wernerian developmental analysis of children's descriptions of siblings. *Child Development*, 1974, *45*, 317–323.

Biskin, D. S., & Crano, W. Structural organization of impressions derived from inconsistent information: A developmental study. *Genetic Psychology Monographs*, 1977, *95*, 331–348.

Blumer, H. *Symbolic interactionism: Perspective and method*. Englewood Cliffs, N.J.: Prentice-Hall, 1969.

Chu, G. C. Prior familiarity, perceived bias, and one-sided versus two-sided communications. *Journal of Experimental Social Psychology*, 1967, *3*, 243–254.

Clark, R. A., & Delia, J. G. The development of functional persuasive skills in childhood and early adolescence. *Child Development*, 1976, *47*, 1008–1014.

Clark, R. A., & Delia, J. G. Cognitive complexity, social perspective-taking, and functional persuasive skills in second- to ninth-grade children. *Human Communication Research*, 1977, *3*, 128–134.

Cohen, A. R. *Attitude change and social influence*. New York: Basic Books, 1964.

Cohen, J., & Cohen, P. *Applied multiple regression/correlation analysis for the behavioral sciences*. Hillsdale, N.J.: Erlbaum, 1975.

Crockett, W. H. Cognitive complexity and impression formation. In B. A. Maher (Ed.), *Progress in experimental personality research* (Vol 2). New York: Academic Press, 1965.

Crockett, W. H., Gonyea, A. H., & Delia, J. G. Cognitive complexity and the formation of impressions from abstract qualities or from concrete behaviors. *Proceedings of the 78th annual convention of the American Psychological Association*, 1970, *5*, 375–376.

Crockett, W. H., Press, A. N., Delia, J. G., & Kenny, C. T. The structural analysis of the organization of written impressions. Unpublished manuscript, Department of Psychology, University of Kansas, 1974.

Cronen, V. E., & Conville, R. L. Fishbein's conception of belief strength: A theoretical, methodological, and experimental critique. *Speech Monographs*, 1975, *42*, 143–150.

Delia, J. G. Dialects and the effects of stereotypes on interpersonal attraction and cognitive processes in impression formation. *Quarterly Journal of Speech*, 1972, *58*, 285–297.

Delia, J. G. A constructivist analysis of the concept of credibility. *Quarterly Journal of Speech*, 1976, *62*, 361–375.

Delia, J. G. Constructivism and the study of human communication. *Quarterly Journal of Speech*, 1977, *63*, 66–83.

Delia, J. G. The research and methodological commitments of a constructivist. Paper presented at the annual convention of the Speech Communication Association, 1978.

Delia, J. G. Cognitive complexity and organizational aspects of interpersonal impressions. Unpublished manuscript, Department of Speech Communication, University of Illinois at Urbana–Champaign, 1979.

Delia, J. G., Burleson, B. R., & Kline, S. L. The organization of impressions in childhood and adolescence. *Journal of Genetic Psychology*, in press.

Delia, J. G., & Clark, R. A. Cognitive complexity, social perception, and the development of listener-adapted communication in six-, eight-, ten-, and twelve-year-old boys. *Communication Monographs*, 1977, *44*, 326–345.

Delia, J. G., Clark, R. A., & Switzer, D. E. Cognitive complexity and impression formation in informal social interaction. *Speech Monographs*, 1974, *41*, 299–308.

Delia, J. G., Clark, R. A., & Switzer, D. E. The content of informal conversations as a function of interactants' cognitive complexity. *Communication Monographs*, 1979, *46*, 274–281.

Delia, J. G., & Crockett, W. H. Social schemas, cognitive complexity, and the learning of social structures. *Journal of Personality*, 1973, *41*, 413–429.

Delia, J. G., Crockett, W. H., Press, A. N., & O'Keefe, D. J. The dependency of interpersonal evaluations on context-relevant beliefs about the other. *Speech Monographs*, 1975, *42*, 10–19.

Delia, J. G., Gonyea, A. H., & Crockett, W. H. The effects of subject-generated and normative constructs upon the formation of impressions. *British Journal of Social and Clinical Psychology*, 1971, *10*, 301–305.

Delia, J. G., Kline, S. L., & Burleson, B. R. The development of persuasive communication strategies in kindergarteners through twelfth-graders. *Communication Monographs*, 1979, *46*, 241–256.

Delia, J. G., & O'Keefe, B. J. The interpersonal constructs of Machiavellians. *British Journal of Social and Clinical Psychology*, 1976, *15*, 435–436.

Delia, J. G., & O'Keefe, B. J. Constructivism: The development of communication in children. In E. Wartella (Ed.), *Children communicating*. Beverly Hills, Calif.: Sage, 1979.

Delia, J. G., & O'Keefe, D. J. The relation of theory and analysis in explanations of belief salience: Conditioning, displacement, and constructivist accounts. *Communication Monographs*, 1977, *44*, 166–169.

Fishbein, M. Attitude and the prediction of behavior. In M. Fishbein (Ed.), *Readings in attitude theory and measurement*. New York: Wiley, 1967. (a)

Fishbein, M. A consideration of beliefs and their role in attitude measurement. In M. Fishbein (Ed.), *Readings in attitude theory and measurement*. New York: Wiley, 1967. (b)

Fishbein, M. The prediction of behaviors from attitudinal variables. In C. D. Mortensen & K. K. Sereno (Eds.), *Advances in communication research*. New York: Harper & Row, 1973.

Fishbein, M., & Ajzen, I. Attitudes and opinions. *Annual Review of Psychology*, 1972, *23*, 487–544.

Fishbein, M., & Ajzen, I. Attitudes toward objects as predictors of single and multiple behavioral criteria. *Psychological Review*, 1974, *81*, 59–74.

Fishbein, M., & Ajzen, I. *Belief, attitude, intention, and Behavior*. Reading, Mass.: Addison–Wesley, 1975.

Fishbein, M., & Raven, B. H. The AB scales: An operational definition of belief and attitude. *Human Relations*, 1962, *15*, 35–44.

Freeman, D. N. Personal construct theory, political perception, and mass communication: The judgmental dimensions employed in the evaluation of political figures based on mass media messages. Unpublished doctoral dissertation, Department of Speech Communication, University of Illinois at Urbana–Champaign, 1976.

Hale, C. L., & Delia, J. G. Cognitive complexity and social perspective-taking. *Communication Monographs*, 1976, *43*, 195–203.

Hass, R. G., & Linder, D. E. Counterargument availability and the effects of message structure on persuasion. *Journal of Personality and Social Psychology*, 1972, *23*, 219–233.

Heider, F. Attitudes and cognitive organization. *Journal of Psychology*, 1946, *21*, 107–112.

Horsfall, R. B. A comparison of two cognitive complexity measures. Unpublished doctoral dissertation, Department of Psychology, The Johns Hopkins University, 1969.

Insko, C. A. *Theories of attitude change*. New York: Appleton–Century–Crofts, 1967.

Jackman, M. R. The relation between verbal attitude and overt behavior: A public opinion application. *Social Forces*, 1976, *54*, 646–668.

Jackson, H. W. Cognitive complexity, vigilance, and anticipated interaction. Unpublished doctoral dissertation, Department of Speech Communication, University of Illinois at Urbana–Champaign, 1978.

Jackson, S. A. A constructivist analysis of the perception of political candidates. Paper presented at the annual convention of the Speech Communication Association, 1977.

Kaplan, B., & Crockett, W. H. Developmental analysis of modes of resolution. In R. P. Abelson, E. Aronson, W. J. McGuire, T. M. Newcomb, M. J. Rosenberg, & P. H. Tannenbaum (Eds.), *Theories of cognitive consistency: A sourcebook.* Chicago: Rand McNally, 1968.

Kelly, G. A. *The psychology of personal constructs* (2 vols.). New York: Norton, 1955.

Klyver, N., Press, A. N., & Crockett, W. H. Cognitive complexity and the sequential integration of inconsistent information. Paper presented at the annual convention of the Eastern Psychological Association, 1972.

Kohlberg, L. Stage and sequence: The cognitive–developmental approach to socialization. In D. A. Goslin (Ed.), *Handbook of socialization theory and research.* Chicago: Rand McNally, 1969.

Kohlberg, L. From is to ought: How to commit the naturalistic fallacy and get away with it in the study of moral development. In T. Mischel (Ed.), *Cognitive development and epistemology.* New York: Academic Press, 1971.

Liska, A. E. Introduction. In A. E. Liska (Ed.), *The consistency controversy.* Cambridge, Mass.: Schenkman, 1974.

Markus, H. Self-schemata and processing information about the self. *Journal of Personality and Social Psychology,* 1977, *35,* 63–78.

Mayo, C. W., & Crockett, W. H. Cognitive complexity and primacy–recency effects in impression formation. *Journal of Abnormal and Social Psychology,* 1964, *68,* 335–338.

McGuire, W. J. The nature of attitudes and attitude change. In G. Lindzey & E. Aronson (Eds.), *The handbook of social psychology* (2nd ed., Vol. 3). Reading, Mass.: Addison–Wesley, 1969.

Meltzer, B., Crockett, W. H., & Rosenkrantz, P. S. Cognitive complexity, value incongruity, and the integration of potentially incompatible information in impressions. *Journal of Personality and Social Psychology,* 1966, *4,* 338–342.

Nidorf, L. J., & Crockett, W. H. Cognitive complexity and the integration of conflicting information in written impressions. *Journal of Social Psychology,* 1965, *66,* 165–169.

Norman, R. Affective–cognitive consistency, attitudes, conformity, and behavior. *Journal of Personality and Social Psychology,* 1975, *32,* 83–91.

O'Keefe, B. J. The theoretical commitments of constructivism. Paper presented at the annual convention of the Speech Communication Association, 1978.

O'Keefe, B. J., & Delia, J. G. Construct comprehensiveness and cognitive complexity. *Perceptual and Motor Skills,* 1978, *46,* 548–550.

O'Keefe, B. J., & Delia, J. G. Construct comprehensiveness and cognitive complexity as predictors of the number and strategic adaptation of arguments and appeals in a persuasive message. *Communication Monographs,* 1979, *46,* 231–240.

O'Keefe, B. J., Delia, J. G., & O'Keefe, D. J. Construct individuality, cognitive complexity, and the formation and remembering of interpersonal impressions. *Social Behavior and Personality,* 1977, *5,* 229–240.

O'Keefe, B. J., Delia, J. G., & O'Keefe, D. J. Interaction analysis and the analysis of interaction. In N. Denzin (Ed.), *Studies in symbolic interaction* (Vol. 3). New York: Johnson Associates, in press.

O'Keefe, D. J. Logical empiricism and the study of human communication. *Speech Monographs,* 1975, *42,* 169–183.

O'Keefe, D. J. Constructivism and its philosophical foundations. Paper presented at the annual convention of the Speech Communication Association, 1978.

O'Keefe, D. J., & Delia, J. G. Cognitive complexity and the relationship of attitudes and behavioral intentions. Unpublished manuscript, Department of Speech Communication, Pennsylvania State University, 1980.

Osgood, C. E., & Tannenbaum, P. H. The principle of congruity in the prediction of attitude change. *Psychological Review,* 1955, *62,* 42–55.

Perry, R. W., Gillespie, D. F., & Lotz, R. E. Attitudinal variables as estimates of behavior: A theoretical examination of the attitude–action controversy. *European Journal of Social Psychology*, 1976, *6*, 227–243.

Petersen, K. K., & Dutton, J. E. Centrality, extremity, intensity: Neglected variables in research on attitude–behavior consistency. *Social Forces*, 1975, *54*, 393–414.

Press, A. N., Crockett, W. H., & Delia, J. G. Effects of cognitive complexity and of perceiver's set upon the organization of impressions. *Journal of Personality and Social Psychology*, 1975, *32*, 865–872.

Press, A. N., Crockett, W. H., & Rosenkrantz, P. S. Cognitive complexity and the learning of balanced and unbalanced social structures. *Journal of Personality*, 1969, *37*, 541–553.

Rosenberg, M. J. Cognitive structure and attitudinal affect. *Journal of Abnormal and Social Psychology*, 1956, *53*, 367–372.

Rosenberg, M. J. A structural theory of attitude dynamics. *Public Opinion Quarterly*, 1960, *24*, 319–341.

Rosenkrantz, P. S., & Crockett, W. H. Some factors influencing the assimilation of disparate information in impression formation. *Journal of Personality and Social Psychology*, 1965, *2*, 397–402.

Saltz, E., & Medow, M. L. Concept conservation in children: The dependence of belief systems on semantic representation. *Child Development*, 1971, *42*, 1533–1542.

Scarlett, H. H., Press, A. N., & Crockett, W. H. Children's descriptions of peers: A Wernerian developmental analysis. *Child Development*, 1971, *42*, 439–453.

Schofield, J. W. Effects of norms, public disclosure, and need for approval on volunteering behavior consistent with attitudes. *Journal of Personality and Social Psychology*, 1975, *31*, 1126–1133.

Seibold, D. R. Communication research and the attitude–verbal report–overt behavior relationship: A critique and a theoretic reformulation. *Human Communication Research*, 1975, *2*, 3–32.

Supnick, J. Unpublished senior honors thesis. Department of Psychology, Clark University, 1964. (Cited in Crockett, 1965.)

Swanson, D. L. Political communication research and the uses and gratification model: A critique. Paper presented at the annual convention of the International Communication Association, 1977.

Swanson, D. L., & Freeman, D. N. Political construct sub-systems as an approach to political communication: A preliminary report. Paper presented at the annual convention of the Central States Speech Association, 1975.

Werner, H. *Comparative psychology of mental development* (Rev. ed.). New York: International Universities Press, 1948.

Werner, H. The concept of development from a comparative and organismic point of view. In D. B. Harris (Ed.), *The concept of development*. Minneapolis: University of Minnesota Press, 1957.

Wicker, A. W. Attitudes versus actions: The relationship of verbal and overt behavioral responses to attitude objects. *Journal of Social Issues*, 1969, *25*, 41–78.

Wicker, A. W. An examination of the "other variables" explanation of attitude–behavior inconsistency. *Journal of Personality and Social Psychology*, 1971, *19*, 18–30.

Wicker, A. W., & Pomazal, R. The relationship between attitudes and behavior as a function of specificity of attitude object and presence of a significant person during assessment conditions. *Representative Research in Social Psychology*, 1971, *2*, 26–31.

5

An Information-Processing Explanation of Attitude–Behavior Inconsistency

JOSEPH N. CAPPELLA
JOSEPH P. FOLGER

The Information-Processing Perspective

The intent of this chapter is ambitious. Its ambitions lie in an attempt to synthesize approaches to human information processing with the study of attitude change. These ambitions are restrained by setting our sights on demonstrating the *utility* of the information-processing approach to attitude and behavior change. One primary goal is to encourage scholars of attitude processes to become attuned to theoretic developments in cognitive science so that synthesis rather than fractionation and differentiation may be encouraged. As Allen Newell (1973) pointed out in a paper entitled, "You Can't Play 20 Questions with Nature and Win," continued "ground breaking" research, continued distinctions, and continued focus on anomaly will not offer long-term payoff in understanding unless the proliferation of questions is accompanied by synthesis and a little perspective. We agree. We hope to show that the perspective of human information-processing (HIP, hereafter) research is one that ultimately must infuse theories of attitude and belief change, especially those giving messages a central role.

149

MESSAGE–ATTITUDE–BEHAVIOR RELATIONSHIP
Theory, Methodology, and Applications

By HIP we mean an *approach* to cognitive processes rather than a *theory* of cognitive processes. HIP approaches are active, feedback-oriented, and hierarchical rather than passive, linear, and branching as are associationism approaches. The recent theory and research done under the auspices of the HIP label is extremely broad and varied, including work in artificial intelligence, cognitive psychology, linguistics and psycholinguistics (for example, Bobrow & Collins, 1975; Kintsch, 1974; Norman & Rummelhart, 1975; Schank & Colby, 1973; Schank & Nash-Webber, 1975; Tulving & Donaldson, 1972; Winograd, 1972). All this work has been carried out with mutual disciplinary awareness rather than (the more common) disciplinary independence. Aside from the work of Abelson (1973) modeling the belief systems of ideologues, the HIP literature has not included approaches to attitude and belief systems. However, this indifference does not imply that attitude–belief structures and processes are irrelevant to HIP concerns. What we will argue here is that issues that have been crucial in HIP research such as the data structure of long-term memory (LTM), types of LTM, and retrieval from LTM, are also central to the functioning of attitude and belief systems.

It is certainly fair to ask why we intend to add all the mental paraphrenalia of information processing to the message–attitude–belief–behavior problem. Certainly other explanations of the relationship between message inputs and behavioral outputs are more parsimonious, more efficient, and assume less complexity on the part of processors. The basis for our choice is quite simple. Ashby (1963, p. 87) noted that the study of any machine can proceed only on the basis of observed inputs and outputs. The set of connections linking inputs and outputs (that is, the explanation) is not in general unique. There are many possible sets of internal (and unobservable) linkages that can explain the observable regularities between inputs and outputs. As long as the same regularities can be explained by multiple sets of black-box connections, and these hypothetical connections do not permit a crucial test because they are unobservable, the simplest explanation is to be preferred.

But any machine can be but a homomorph of the reality being modeled. That is, only a portion of the reality being studied is represented. Attitude- and belief-change models simulate a small part of all message-processing phenomena. Distortion, encoding, comprehension, and retrieval models simulate other aspects of message processing. *To the extent that it is desirable that partial representations of phenomena meet, so that the homomorphisms of model-to-reality become more like an isomorphism, the explanatory connections linking inputs and outputs in one machine must be compatible with the linkages of input and output in some other more complex machine.* If explanations in one machine are incompatible with explanations in the other machine, the machines cannot be linked, for they will fail the criterion of conceptual coherence. This is the heart of the strategy of this chapter.

Since the goal of research into the information-processing capabilities of individuals is a coherent description and explanation of all the separate capabilities, the description and explanation of message–attitude–belief–behavior relationships cannot be excluded. As Herbert Simon (1976) has stated this matter:

> Social choices are choices; attributions of human agency are causal inferences; perceptions of others are perceptions. When the processes underlying these social phenomena are identified . . . they turn out to be the very same information processes we encounter in nonsocial cognition. . . . We neither need nor want separate theories of social thinking and other (antisocial?) thinking. We simply need a theory of thinking [p. 254].

If we are to explain the assortment of message processing phenomena, then message–attitude–belief–behavior relationships must be explained by cognitive processes whose complexity matches the complexity of other message-processing phenomena like encoding, distortion, comprehension, and retrieval. If such explanations can be successfully offered, the ultimate matching of persuasion processes with other message processing becomes a possibility. This chapter takes some humble and hesitating steps toward this goal.

To launch the substance of our discussion, let us for the moment consider the rudiments of a verbal simulation of attitude and belief change in the face of an external message. Assuming that the audience is attending to the message, the first concern from a processing perspective is comprehension. How messages are understood is predicated on an identification of the psychologically meaningful text base units. That is, the message (in text or discourse form) is broken down into a set of meaning units, which can be handled by comprehension processes. Once understood (or misunderstood, as the case may be) the information of the external message needs to be encoded in LTM. This step entails an integration of the now understood text base units into the listener's existing and presumably organized store of knowledge. Such integration allows for systematic retrieval processes to operate when the incorporated information is being accessed. Thus, when a listener is confronted with situations requiring either physical or symbolic action, he or she will respond on the basis of information presently at his or her disposal through retrieval.

If the above outline is even a remotely accurate description of the message–attitude–belief–behavior sequence, four major processing concerns surface, and seem to demand further attention: message structure, comprehension processes, information storage and organization principles, and retrieval processes. This chapter will treat only the last two concerns.

Information storage and organization principles are our first major concern. Given an accurately comprehended message, how is the newly acquired information integrated within existing memory structures? To answer this question, we will review some recent work on the structure and organization of LTM. The reason for this review of storage principles centers on the commonly accepted notion that the ease or difficulty of information *retrieval* is often determined by the nature of information storage.

The second major concern is with retrieval processes per se and the possible insights they may offer into attitude–behavior discrepancies. Here we assume that, when faced with a response situation, an individual's decision is determined by the information at his or her disposal in the situation. Thus we consider in some detail the determinant of information retrieval in behavioral situations. Although we may not be able to offer completely satisfying answers, we do expect to sketch the form these answers must take, and to encourage the adoption of an information processing perspective on the relationship between attitudes and behaviors.

Storage Principles: The Determination of Attitudinal Responses from Informational Beliefs

Our analysis begins by assuming that some persuasive message (in text or discourse form) has already passed through comprehension, distortion and paraphrase stages of processing and exists in memory in some stored form. Of course, the translation of a message from some overt form to some cognitive representation is a significant and a complex question, both for persuasion and for human information processing. For example, one expects that comprehension is a necessary condition for attitude and belief change (McGuire, 1968), that the affective distortion of message intent especially by highly ego-involved audiences is common (Dawes, Singer, & Lemons, 1972; Kiesler, Collins, & Miller, 1969, pp. 264–278), that messages are paraphrased as to their gist even rather quickly after initial exposure (Sacks, 1974), and that message information is multileveled, consisting of at least the storage of surface structure, meaning structure (or gist), and associated concepts activated by message inputs (Ortony, 1978). Unfortunately, these processes must await a future discussion. The present chapter assumes that these processes have already operated, and that a version of the information in the message now resides in memory. Our focus then centers on the retrieval of this information and the implications that such retrieval processes have on attitude–behavior consistency and message design.

Representing Information in Long-Term Memory (LTM)

Currently, cognitive psychologists and those in artificial intelligence are debating the question of which representational system for information in LTM is most desirable.[1] We adopt the network format for representation

---

[1] The debate rages between propositionalists (Pylyshyn, 1973) and analogists (Paivio, 1970, 1974). The propositionalists are divided (Winograd, 1975) among proceduralists and declarativists. Craig (1977) has argued the relative merits of network versus spatial models of information representation. See Anderson (1976) for a review of propositional representations, as those are the focus of this essay.

(Rummelhart, Lindsay, & Norman, 1972) because it is widely used in cognitive psychology and artificial intelligence, and because a simple and direct representation of the linguistic information of a text or discourse is most desirable in the case of attitude change.

The network representation consists of a set of nodes that are the lexical entries (words) of some message, and directed line segments representing grammatical relations between the nodes. The kinds of relations represented in Figure 5.1 are *is*, *isa*, *has*, *agent*, and *object*. More generally, the set of potential relations is not infinite, but is limited to the linguistic relations tying lexical entries together. These relations have been taken almost directly from the case grammar approach to syntax (Fillmore, 1968). Because our focus is on beliefs, we can be primarily interested in *agent*, *object*, *instrument*, *is*, *isa*, and *has* relationships, and not the more complex relations of location, time, quantification, and so on. However, the representational system is quite general and can easily incorporate these other grammatical cases (Kintsch, 1974).[2]

In Figure 5.1, there are two classes of nodes: concept and event nodes. Concept nodes are all those lexical items except event nodes. The event nodes are the verbs of action in each sentence of the message (e.g., STEALS, DECEIVES, etc.) in Figure 5.1 and have a special status. The edges (arrows) in the network link concept and event nodes according to their grammatical relationships in the input message. The number of types of edges is finite and determined by the confines of case grammar (Kintsch, 1974). These special advantages of the network representation make computer programming representations feasible (e.g., Winograd, 1972).

When new information about THE MAN or GIGOLOS is encountered and stored, the network scheme represents the addition quite clearly. The new information is tacked directly on to the focal node. Also the totality of informational beliefs about the focal mode is easily seen in the first- and second-order links in the network. If two networks of information have no common links, information retrieved from one network will not necessarily lead to retrieval from the other.

The relationship between the network representation of information and standard conceptions of belief is quite straightforward. Beliefs about a given focal concept are nothing more than the one-step links to the focal concept (that is the concept–concept links) and the two-step concept–event–concept links.

---

[2] Two important notes about network representations of information must be made: (*a*) The network representation of syntactic word strings is essentially identical to Kintsch's linearized structuring of these strings. We shall use both interchangably; and (*b*) Many network representations do not employ surface structures in representing meaning, but rather decompose such surface structures into elementary conceptual units (Norman & Rummelhart, 1975; Schank & Abelson, 1977). Although there are advantages to decomposition, there is some evidence (Kintsch, 1974) that more complex decompositions do not exhibit greater reaction times as one would suppose. Consequently, we adopt the simpler surface representations. Whichever way this controversy is resolved, our chief arguments will remain intact.

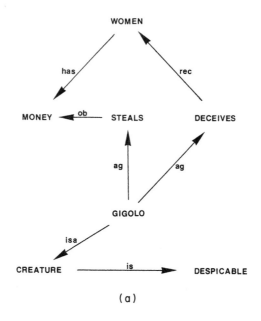

(a)

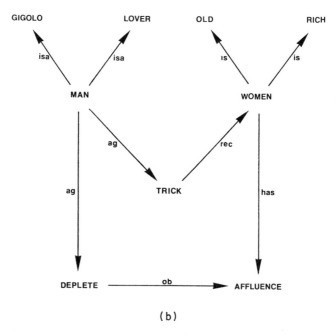

(b)

Figure 5.1. (a) Network representation of a proposition derived from a text or discourse: "Gigolos are despicable creatures. They deceive women and steal their money." (b) Network representation of a proposition derived from a text or discourse: "The man is a lover and a gigolo. He tricks rich, old women and depletes their affluence" (ob, object; ag, agent; rec, recipient).

In Figure 5.1a, beliefs about gigolo fall into both classes. There is a concept–concept belief of the form GIGOLO *isa* CREATURE and the associated descriptor of CREATURE is DESPICABLE. In addition, two concept–event–concept links are encountered: (STEAL, GIGOLO, MONEY), and (DECEIVE, GIGOLO, WOMEN). This representational system for belief information has several advantages. First, the representation is general enough to permit the mapping of text or discourse (Kintsch, 1974). Because the representation of messages in a memory store is a crucial issue in any comprehensive theory of message–attitude–behavior, it is desirable to have a representational scheme for cognitive store, and for messages, which is compatible with both. Second, because event information is given a separate representation (e.g. STEALS in Figure 5.1a), then it is possible to focus on beliefs about events, and not merely on beliefs about concepts. Third, each descriptor of a focal concept is given a separate concept status with its relationship to the focal concept specified. Thus, new information about "suave, Italian gigolos" can be added to the GIGOLO node without requiring the manufacture of a new node, SUAVE ITALIAN GIGOLO. Also, the specified link between descriptors and the concepts they describe will suggest certain combinations of evaluative responses. Fourth, the ability to give a network representation to agent–action–object sequences as beliefs is very efficient. Most other systematic representations of beliefs (Fishbein & Ajzen, 1975; Wyer, 1974) turn agent–action–object sequences into concept–concept beliefs. For example, *The man tricks rich, old women* becomes a concept–concept belief of the form *The man is a tricker of rich, old women*. This transformation can be carried to ridiculous extremes as each addition of an adjectival or adverbial modifier necessitates a new belief to be evaluated. As we shall see in what follows, the network representation permits economies in the display of belief information and in the calculation of an evaluative response associated with a focal concept.

Belief information is only half the story. Every theory of attitude change has given a significant place to affective evaluations either of the focal concepts themselves or of the beliefs associated with those focal concepts. Our view is no different. In order to ultimately assess the likelihood of behavioral action, we find it necessary to determine the individual's affective response to information that the individual deems pertinent to the proposed action. This general supposition lies behind many attempts to link attitude as affective response to behavioral response (Abelson, 1972).

The research literature points to three procedures for calculating the audience's affective response to a focal concept (e.g., GIGOLO in Figure 5.1) when that concept is embedded in a set of beliefs (a) providing an audience with a complete set of beliefs on an issue and obtaining their subjective acceptance of the belief as well as their affective reaction to the belief statement (Fishbein & Ajzen, 1975, pp. 222–228); (b) eliciting a set of beliefs and obtaining the affective evaluations of those elicited statements (Cronen & Conville, 1975a); and (c) treating the inherent affective connotations of words (Osgood, Suci, & Tannenbaum, 1957) used in stating beliefs as indicators of the individual's affective evaluation of the focal concept (Eiser, 1971). Our own view coincides with the last of these three methods.

The first two methods mentioned are essentially research procedural surrogates for the process of "cognitive weighing" that each individual presumably carries out in responding to an evaluative situation. However, these two surrogate procedures are adopted, not because they are believed to simulate the cognitive processes of affective evaluation, but because they are efficient research procedures for tapping this process. It is difficult to believe that individuals proceed to evaluate actions by listing their beliefs to themselves, evaluating the acceptability of each belief, determining the affective value of each, and then taking a weighted sum. Despite the absurdity of this "simulation," it does reveal high correlations to stated attitudes (Fishbein & Ajzen, 1975, pp. 222–228). Thus, it would be wise to preserve the structure of this procedure—namely, elicitation of accepted beliefs that are affectively weighted—but then to substitute procedures that are cognitively more realistic. We hope to achieve this goal by answering two questions: (a) Given a set of elicited beliefs, how are the affective implications of these beliefs cognitively determined in the absence of a researcher demanding such a response; and (b) Based upon the structure and organization of LTM, which sets of beliefs are likely to be elicited in various situations?

The Affective Evaluation of Beliefs

The information we have about a focal concept does not merely describe that concept, but reflects our affective evaluation of the concept. The lexical entries of a network of beliefs each have affective connotations. In choosing to describe our beliefs with lexical items having positive rather than negative affective connotations, we are representing the same set of beliefs in different evaluative lights. Thus the GIGOLO of Figure 5.1a STEALS and DECEIVES, whereas the MAN of Figure 5.1b TRICKS and DEPLETES. The actions undertaken by the GIGOLO are affectively more negative than those undertaken by the MAN and, hence, we would expect the attitude toward GIGOLO to be more negative than that toward MAN. More generally, we maintain that the affective connotations of the lexical items used to represent beliefs inextricably confound attitudes (as evaluations) and beliefs (as lexically described information). When a set of beliefs surrounding a focal concept has been elicited, so have the affective connotations of the terms that constitute those beliefs. If it were possible to calculate the affective impact of a set of beliefs on a focal node from the a priori affective evaluations of the lexical items themselves, it would be possible to *explain* how an attitudinal response arises from the retrieval of informational beliefs without recourse to a separate evaluation process for each elicited belief.

This is the scenario. When faced with the necessity of responding to an issue (e.g. *What did you think of the fellow?*) an individual retrieves information (by processes we hope to explain later) that is already affectively loaded, so that the person not only describes but evaluates. The person "responds" to self or to the questioner *He is a gigolo. He deceives women and steals their money.* It would be ridiculous for the questioner at this point to ask *But do you think well of him?* It is equally ridiculous to suggest that the respondent queries himself with *He's a gigolo which is somewhat negative. He deceives women which is quite bad. He steals their money and that is reprehensible.* Making evaluation a separate process for the purposes of research is a viable procedure, but it should not then be taken as a simulation of the actual cognitive process of evaluation or attitude formation from beliefs.

Rather we suggest that the attitudinal response is intimately intertwined with the structure of cognitively held beliefs and the a priori affective evaluations of the lexical entries making up the belief structure. All that we need to replace the separate explicit procedure of evaluating listed or elicited beliefs is a set of combination rules, based upon the network representation we have described, for transforming a priori affective connotations of words structured as beliefs into an attitude toward a focal concept. Although this sets forth an immense task, which we cannot completely review, we do wish to sketch the form that these combination rules must take.

For the purposes of this chapter, the beliefs of a network representation are of two generic types: concept–concept links and concept–event–concept links (primarily representing agent–action–object relationships). These classes are classes of propositions as stored in memory according to Kintsch (1974). Moreever, these propositional units may be fundamental units for cognitive information processing if Kintsch's research withstands the test of time and replication. Kintsch and his associates have found consistent differences in subject's comprehension, recall, and reaction to messages differing only in the number and structure of propositional units in messages as revealed by analyses such as Figure 5.1. Whereas Kintsch's work has not been concerned with the combination of affective connotations of words in different propositional structures, it does provide a framework within which combination rules can be explored.

There are, however, two bodies of literature relevant to combination rules. One concerns itself with concept–concept links, the other with concept–event–concept links. The study of impression formation was the first literature to investigate combination rules for concept–concept types of beliefs (Asch, 1946). Literally hundreds of studies and several programs of research have been carried out primarily to study how an attitude toward a person (the focal concept) may be obtained by combining the a priori evaluations of adjectives describing the focal concept. The lists have been manipulated to take into account the order of presentation of the adjectives, their evaluative consistency, their redundancy, their context, and so on. Reviews of this literature, its findings, and existing controversies can be found in Anderson (1971), Fishbein and Ajzen (1975),

Slovic and Lichtenstein (1971), and Wyer (1974) will not be repeated here. In spite of the controversies surrounding averaging and adding combination rules, and information integration versus expectancy-value models, one trend consistently emerges: The attitude toward a focal concept is a linear (perhaps weighted) combination of the a priori evaluations of the terms attributed to that concept. Although this trend has been found primarily for lists of adjectives, the same linear effect has been found for adverbs (Cliff, 1959; Howe, 1966a; Lilly, 1968). The finding of linearity and additivity of a priori evaluations may seem imprecise since the regression weights are left indeterminate. However, this must be contrasted to the potential discovery of configurality (i.e., interaction) among the presented concepts (Anderson, 1972). If interaction were present in subject's subsequent attitudes, such interactions would complicate greatly the determination of subject's attitudes from combinations of word lists, since lists longer than three words lead to fourth- and higher-order interactions. The absence of such a finding, despite the imprecision of what we do know, is a great relief.

Based on the these findings, we suggest that an individual's attitude toward a focal concept is a linear combination of the a priori affective evaluation of the concepts linked to the focal concept. The number of entries in the linear combination would equal the number of one-step concepts linked by *is*, *isa*, and *has* relations to the focal concept. For example in Figure 5.2, the number of entries in predicting the person's attitude toward the MAN would be three: CODGER, RICH, and MISERLY. However, the MAN is a particular kind of CODGER, namely an ORNERY and OLD one. Thus, the entry to the prediction equation

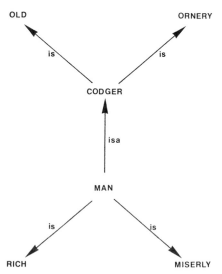

Figure 5.2. Network representation of an embedded "is" relation: "The man is an ornery, old codger who is rich, but miserly."

for the MAN would be based *not* on the a priori evaluation of CODGER but on the affective value of ORNERY, OLD CODGER itself determined as a function of the a priori affective values of the three words separately.

Although little successful research has been aimed at combination rules for adjective–noun pairs[3] (which is an *is* relation), combination rules for adverb–adjective and adverb–verb pairings (Cliff, 1959; Howe, 1963; Howe, 1966b) tends to yield simple multiplicative models with each adverb serving to amplify or to attenuate the a priori affective value of the verb or adjective. Whereas it is probably naive to assume that adjective–noun pairs will follow such simplified combination rules as adverb–adjective and adverb–verb pairs, simplicity of combination rules should be expected, given the evidence against configurality in human judgment (Anderson, 1972). Given an affective evaluation of ORNERY, OLD CODGER, that evaluation becomes the input to the prediction equation for attitude toward the focal concept, MAN. Thus, attitudes toward a focal concept based on concept–concept relations would be a linear combination of the a priori affective evaluation of the one-step concepts linked to the focal concept unless any links have *is* relations with other concepts. In the latter case, the affective evaluation of the terminal concept with its modifiers (e.g. ORNERY, OLD CODGER) is determined first by combination rules (as yet unspecified), and this evaluation is one of the predictors of the attitude toward the focal concept.

Thus far, we have treated concept–concept beliefs. Concept–event–concept beliefs remain to be treated. In terms of Figure 5.1a how do the beliefs that GIGOLO STEAL MONEY and that GIGOLOS DECEIVE WOMEN produce affective impacts on GIGOLO? Work by Heise (1969) has helped to illuminate combination rules for the evaluation of actor–action–object-of-action combinations. In prior research, Heise (1965) obtained semantic differential (evaluation, activity, and potency) ratings of the 1000 most frequently used nouns and verbs in the English language. Subsequently, he drew a stratified random sample of nouns and transitive verbs from the 1000, based on distributions of scores across the semantic differential scales. From this stratified sample, groups of sentences of the form THE MAN DECEIVED THE WOMAN were prepared. A priori evaluation of the subject, verb, and object were obtained in neutral contexts (i.e., not in the sentence itself) and evaluations of the actor, the action, and the object of the action were obtained in the sentence context. Heise then regressed (*a*) the evaluation of the actor in the sentence (ACTOR(S)) on the evaluations of the actor in neutral context (ACTOR(N)), the action in neutral context (ACTION(N)), and the object in neutral context (OBJ(N)); (*b*) the evaluation of the action in the sentence (ACTION(S)) in terms of the three a priori evaluations; and (*c*) the evaluation of the object in the sentence

---

[3] See Osgood, Suci, and Tannenbaum (1957, pp. 275–284) for an initial attempt at combining the affective values of adjective–noun pairs using congruity predictions.

(OBJ(S)) in terms of the three a priori evaluations. Heise (1969) reports the following regression models

$$ACTOR(S) = .37 \times ACTOR(N) + .55 \times ACTION(N) + .07 \times OBJ(N)$$
$$+ .25 \times ACTION(N) \times OBJ(N)$$
$$ACTION(S) = .23 \times ACTOR(N) + .60 \times ACTION(N) + .07 \times OBJ(N)$$
$$+ .25 \times ACTION(N) \times OBJ(N)$$
$$OBJ(S) = .17 \times ACTOR(N) + .40 \times ACTION(N) + .36 \times OBJ(N)$$
$$+ .30 \times ACTION(N) \times OBJ(N)$$

with variances explained of 70, 75, and 67%, respectively. The conduct of the research and its results are most impressive.[4]

As Heise points out, the symmetry of the three regressions suggests a simple underlying combination rule: The evaluation of the action, actor, or object of the linguistic description of an event depends linearly on the evaluations of the action, actor, and object apart from the event plus an interaction involving the kind of action carried out on the object. The interaction term is crucial, since it has the power to qualitatively change (from + to −) the evaluation of the action in THE WOMAN BEAT THE MUGGER and THE MUGGER BEAT THE WOMAN. The two events (i.e., BEATING) described are perceived quite differently in terms of their affective evaluation, are linguistically different, and should be evaluatively different, as indeed they would be in Heise's model. When information about the WOMAN is retrieved, we find that she BEAT the MUGGER; when information about the MUGGER is retrieved, we find that he BEAT the WOMAN. Both beliefs retrieved involve the act of beating, an evaluatively negative one. But if MUGGER is evaluatively negative and WOMAN is evaluatively positive in neutral contexts, then the interaction between BEAT(−) and MUGGER(−) will be positive so that the overall evaluation of the WOMAN who BEAT the MUGGER would be positive, whereas the interaction between BEAT(−) and WOMAN(+) would be negative, so that the overall evaluation of the MUGGER who BEAT the WOMAN would be negative.

We propose then, that the cognitive assessment of attitude toward a focal concept is determined by the affective connotations of the lexical items attached to the focal concept by concept–concept and concept–event–concept links and the associated combination rules. In the analysis presented thus far, we have presumed that beliefs have already been retrieved from LTM so that attitude is determined on the basis of *retrieved* and not simply *stored* information. In the next section, we wish to consider those factors that determine which stored information might be retrieved. Before turning to the retrieval question, we wish to consider three possible difficulties with the account of attitude formation we have just offered.

---

[4] Some research (Anderson & Lopes, 1974; Gragg, Nash, & Touhey, 1974) has called Heise's results into question on methodological grounds.

First, it might be objected that our simulation of the generation of attitudes from beliefs plus affective connotations is too simplistic. After all, there is an extensive literature in impression formation, suggesting that order effects, redundancy, discounting, context effects, inferential beliefs, and other processes greatly complicate the determination of attitudes from beliefs. Whereas this objection is an accurate reading of available research literature, it is an inappropriate objection to the process we are describing. The studies of impression formation using adjective lists usually proceed by providing subjects with lists of adjectives purportedly descriptive of a person or role and then obtaining subsequent evaluations of the person or role and the adjectives in isolation. Such work is irrelevant to the combination of retrieved information; it deals with the combination of *provided* information. The verbal simulation stated earlier insisted that the combination rules operated over *retrieved* informational beliefs. The distinction is an important one (Fishbein and Ajzen, 1975, pp. 250–255).

For example, the question of order effects, although of great significance in list-learning and persuasion situations, is irrelevant when the information is retrieved. The reason is that the observed order effects in impression formation are usually explained in terms of attention decrement or standard serial position curves (Lindsay & Norman, 1977, p. 341). Such explanations suggest that certain information is not entering the system, and hence is irrelevant for processing. If the information has already been retrieved, appeals to its lack of availability are misplaced. Also certain inconsistencies and complexities in impression formation (such as discounting, and context effects or change in meaning) may be explained in terms of inferential beliefs (Fishbein & Ajzen, 1975, pp. 144–156). When a subject in an impression formation task receives a list of adjectives, the person may be led to draw inferences about other attributes of the described person beyond the adjective list and to form overall evaluations of the person in terms of both inferred and provided beliefs. Studies in the impression formation tradition in general focus only upon the provided list to determine subsequent evaluations. Studies reported by Bransford and McCarrell (1974) indicate that when inferences are strongly expected, even though not a part of the initial information, people tend to report that what they inferred was actually stated in the initial information. Thus, when retrieved information is the basis for subsequent evaluations, that information should include inferential beliefs as well as certain provided beliefs (see Van Dijk, 1977 for a discussion of inference-making processes). We would expect the elicited beliefs (which include both inferred and provided beliefs) to be a better predictor of overall evaluation than the provided beliefs alone. Indeed, a study by Jaccard and Fishbein (1975) found exactly this result. Thus, the criticism that the integration of belief information into attitudinal responses is more complex than we have suggested is founded upon a confusion between provided messages and retrieved information.

Second, the reader might object that we have assumed that retrieval of beliefs stops after searching only two steps from a focal node. Does the search process not proceed beyond the two-step network links? The answer to this objection must unfortunately be that we simply do not know how many steps removed from the focal concept belief search will proceed. Studies of semantic LTM (Collins and Quillian, 1969) that have artificially induced hierarchical structures of the *is*, *isa*, and *has* variety suggest that even hierarchically structured LTMs are probably only several steps deep. Studies of reaction time to retrieve stored information suggest that normal LTMs are probably not hierarchical, but more richly interconnected (Conrad, 1972). Thus, it is likely that the depth of search beyond the focal node is relatively shallow.

Third, the whole concept of calculating the attitude at the focal node in terms of the beliefs linked to it might be challenged. Once the attitude toward the MAN or the GIGOLO in Figure 5.1 is established by whatever process, would not the affective value of that node (the attitude) be henceforth determined (in the absence of outside input of course) and associated with that node? Thus, the internal calculation and its associated mental paraphernalia would be avoided. We insist that the internal calculation procedure is necessary in light of arguments now to be made. Briefly, however, we argue that the information an individual retrieves relevant to a focal concept is determined by various cue sets. One set of such cues is the focal node itself and its associated definitional information. The other set includes various situational factors, which elicit different beliefs in differing situational environments. In the latter case, the situational cues will determine which beliefs will be retrieved, and hence the reported attitude will be "recalculated" as a function of the retrieved information that, in turn, is determined by the situational cues. Since the beliefs retrieved from situation to situation must differ, so must the attitude. It cannot be fixed once and for all.

Semantic and Episodic Organization in LTM

Thus far our discussion of LTM has considered only the most basic description of structure and has discussed that structure in terms of attitudes and beliefs. The question to which we must now turn is one of retrieval. If memory is the storehouse of a diversity of information, how and under what conditions is each type of information retrieved? To begin to answer this question, we find it necessary to distinguish two forms for encoding information within the network framework—the semantic form and the episodic form.

In 1972, Tulving proposed the semantic–episodic distinction to differentiate the storage of events or experiences along one's personal time line (episodic memory) from one's event-free knowledge structure (semantic or conceptual memory), "Episodic memory is concerned with storage and retrieval of temporally dated, spatially located, and personally experienced events or episodes and temporal relations among such events. . . . Semantic memory is the system concerned with storage and utilization of knowledge about words and concepts, their properties and inter-relations [Tulving & Thomson, 1973, p. 354]."

The distinction, as Ortony (1975) has noted, points to the different kinds of knowledge in memory. Semantic and episodic memory differ in content but are isomorphic structurally. One stores, for example, a series of historical facts or events chronologically in semantic memory. The circumstances in which those facts were learned (i.e., reading a book, hearing a lecture, etc.) are also stored chronologically, but as events in episodic memory. Temporal structure is common to both memories but what is stored in each differs (Collins, 1975). The role ultimately attributed to semantic memory is "that of a repository of knowledge . . . knowledge, that is, which has been stripped of its autobiographical reference and its source and circumstances of acquisition information too; always the result of inference [Ortony, 1975, p. 67]." Episodic memory, on the other hand, is a record of personal experiences.

The first crucial point about the episodic–semantic distinction is that certain network representations contain information that is freed from its context of acquisition, and that other network representations contain information embedded in the circumstantial or contextual aspects of its acquisition. Episodic memory seems to contain two types of information: that of the encoded message, and that marking the occasion of its receipt.

If the context or circumstances of acquisition (called encoding conditions from now on) are a part of the information of episodic memory, then at least two competing structures are possible: (a) each node–node link has associated with it a set of "tags" indicating each occasion that the node–node link has been experienced; or (b) information is organized on the basis of encoding situations so that identical node–node links may be represented several times, each time under the organization of a different set of encoding conditions. The question can be put as follows: *Is episodic memory organized on the basis of semantic similarity among node–node links with encoding tags attached or on the basis of encoding situations with multiple "locations" for semantically identical (or similar) node–node links?*

There is accumulating evidence suggesting that the latter is the case. The crucial studies that suggest that episodic memory is organized around encoding conditions were carried out by Tulving and Osler (1968) and by Thomson and Tulving (1970). Subjects were asked to learn a list of words and some associated cue words that might help them in later recall. When later given a stimulus word that was semantically similar to the to-be-recalled word from the initial list, only 24% of the subjects who produced the to-be-recalled word as a response *recognized* that it was a part of the initial list. However, when later given the cue word, a much higher percentage was able to *produce* the desired to-be-recalled word. That is, without the encoding condition (the cue word in this case), subjects were unable to recognize that the word they had produced was part of the initial list. With the encoding condition (the cue word), the subjects more readily produced, and hence must have retrieved the desired word. As Kintsch (1974, pp. 78–79) points out, this result is contrary to all accepted conceptions of memory in which recognition is a necessary prerequisite to generation. Clearly, subjects can retrieve and produce the necessary information when given the appropriate encoding conditions, even though recognition of the very same word is quite low.

These data suggest that the structure of episodic memory is by circumstance (or encoding condition) with concepts repeated rather than tagged. If the tagging scheme were the correct organization of episodic memory, in the Thomson and Tulving (1970) study, once the target word was inadvertently generated, it would have been recognized as a target because the encoding tag would have been retrieved as well. Since it was necessary to have the encoding cue to recognize the target word as a target word, it is likely that information "is stored in memory not just in one central place with tags but as several separate copies [Kintsch, 1974, p. 78]," with encoding tags at each copy.

This consistent finding gives rise to the encoding specifity principle:[5] "Specific encoding operations performed on what is perceived determine what is stored and what is stored determines what retrieval cues are effective in providing access to what is stored [Watkins & Tulving, 1975, p. 7]." This principle is crucial to our analysis of the retrieval of information by individuals faced with a behavioral choice situation. At the risk of redundancy, what the principle implies is (a) the different copies of the word or concept are accessed by different retrieval cues; (b) the cues are drawn from the conditions or situations of encoding; and (c) access to one representation of a set of information does not mean that any of the other representations are necessarily accessed. Different cues access different representations.

Since we agree with Kintsch that one must understand the whole structure of memory if memory processes are to be understood, then we must consider the relationship between semantic and episodic memories.

Knowledge held in semantic memory is, of course, frequently derived from experiential encodings. It is through events and autobiographical experiences with information, objects, and activities that our knowledge of the world is generated. In fact, Schank (1975) has argued that the episodic–semantic distinction falters because of the extent to which semantic memory is dependent upon experiences. There seems to be little need for the distinction, according to Schank, if semantic memory is basically episodic in nature. Whether or not Schank's argument warrants a rejection of the distinction is equivocal and need

---

[5] Encoding specificity has been challenged in a study by Santa and Lamwers (1974), and in a reply by Santa and Lamwers (1976). The challenge is not a significant one as we see it. Santa and Lamwers obtain different results with a different instruction set, one that tells subjects to use cue words to aid in recognition. Whereas their results are a testimony to human ability to reorganize retrieval processes around different instruction sets, the results do not invalidate Tulving's work and inferences about encoding specificity with a more "neutral" instruction set.

not concern us here. What is important to note however, is that both Schank and those who have postulated the dichotomy recognize that conceptual knowledge is abstrated from personal experiences to a lesser or greater extent. At one point, Ortony (1975) actually defined semantic memory as "knowledge which has been organized around concepts from knowledge originally encoded around events [p. 67]."

Ortony indicated that one of the key unanswered questions for future theory and research is "how and when does information get into semantic memory [p. 68]?" No obe doubts that information that is initially obtained within episodic context is, in many instances, freed and becomes part of one's general storehouse of conceptual knowledge. But little is known about the general conditions under which this occurs.

In summary, there are at least two networks of information in LTM—an episodic and a semantic one. Episodic memory is organized around events and occurrences rather than semantically similar concepts. It is subject to the encoding specificity principle in retrieval, and is the basis for the information held in semantic memory. Contrary to episodic memory, semantic memory is organized around concepts, holds information that is definitional as well as information treated as if it were definitional, and is capable of reasoning.

We are now in a position to describe what we believe happens when an individual, who has a storehouse of information upon which his or her self-report attitude is based, must act in a behavioral situation.

Attitudinal Reports and Behavioral Actions as Information Retrieval Processes from LTM

Toward an Information-Processing Model of Attitude Reports and Behavioral Actions

The details of the model which we are about to propose rest on an important assumption: When an individual acts either by verbally reporting his or her attitude on an issue or by choosing to act (behaviorally) on an issue in a context, the individual reports or chooses in accordance with the information *at his or her disposal* at the time of action. There are two important parts of this assumption. First, actions are assumed to result from the retrieval of *information* that we have represented as a set of concept–concept and concept–event links. No appeal to affect, drives, or sentiments is made in the assumption. However, the affective character of attitude reports is retained because the lexical entries in LTM networks are themselves affectively loaded. Given these affective loadings, a linear combination rule for concept–concept links, and Heise's combination rules for concept–event links, the reported attitude as an affective value is calculable. Thus we retrieve information to produce affective reports.

Unfortunately, the task of retrieval is not that simple and brings us to the second major point. The phrase *at his or her disposal at the time of action* is a crucial one. If actions are taken on the basis of information, actions are predictable from information that can be retrieved. If information is not retrieved, it cannot be the basis for decision making, no matter how consistent or inconsistent it may be with other available information or with behaviors.

Thus far we have argued that the organizational format of LTM is dependent upon encoding conditions for episodic memory and is independent of encoding conditions for semantic memory. The differing structures carry the implication that the retrievability of information from episodic memory is based upon the encoding specificity principle (that is, the match between current and stored situational cues), and that the retrievability of information from semantic memory is based upon semantic cues. A further point on the retrievability of information needs to be made. Research by Brigham and Cook (1969) (also reviewed by Fishbein & Ajzen, 1975, pp. 139–142) indicates that concept and event information that is inconsistent with a person's reported attitude is neither recalled nor recognized to any lesser degree than information consistent with reported attitudes.

The implications of these conclusions are quite clear. When a person is faced with a behavioral choice, that person will choose on the basis of the information that can be retrieved at the time of decision. If the information that is retrievable is not, in general, biased toward consistency or inconsistency with the person's reported attitude, it is possible for a range of information to be *at the disposal* of the decision maker. Because there is a range which can be retrieved, we should not be surprised to find the decision maker acting on one subset of the information in one situation, and on another subset in a different situation. In other words, inconsistency in behaviors across situations is not incompatible with the assumption that individuals act on information at their disposal.

But what factors place certain subsets of information at the decision maker's disposal? In each behavioral situation, the individual is presented with at least two sets of cues that are important for retrieval: semantic cues and situational (encoding) cues. Semantic cues are those aspects of the situation that point the decision maker toward the definitional knowledge necessary in his or her decision. These cues are probably derived from the decision maker's verbal encoding of the act to be carried out, for example, *to go for a chest X ray or not*. The key terms in this verbalization become the cues for retrieving definitional information (that is, accepted beliefs) from semantic memory. The retrieved beliefs are assumed to have some affective impact based upon the combination rules discussed earlier. The affective impact of these definitional beliefs determines *in part* the direction that the decision will take.

If semantic cues were the only cues for retrieval present to the decision maker, our view would not be appreciably different from standard (and unacceptable) explanations of the attitude–behavior relationship (Abelson, 1972). Essentially, reported attitudes would be the best predictors of associated behaviors. However, the decision-making situation is just that, *a situation*. It is an episode in the decision maker's life and is perceived to have certain characteristic cues of other similar situations. For example, in making a decision about having a chest X ray, the individual might focus on "hospital visits," "medical tests," "anxiety-producing settings," or a multitude of other dimensions of this setting. If the encoding specificity principle is correct, the decision maker will be more likely to retrieve from memory those episodes in which conditions of encoding most closely resemble the conditions perceived in the current situation. In other words, the greater the match between current situational cues and stored episode tags, the more likely will be the retrieval of the information associated with that episode. The way in which situational cues match episodes in memory will be discussed in more detail later.

Granting that situations make a difference in what information is available for retrieval, what importance does that have for explaining attitudes' relationship to behavior? First, we should not expect the same information to be accessed as the decision maker moves across situations. The detailed aspects of the situation as perceived by the decision maker become important determinants of what is likely to be retrieved. Thus, we should not be surprised at behavioral inconsistency as the situations facing the decision maker change. Second, whereas the fully accepted information of semantic memory will always be retrieved, it is not at all impossible that less accepted information will be retrieved from episodic memory. Contrary to Fishbein and Ajzen (1975), semantic cues and situational cues, *not salience of belief*, are the primary determinants of accessibility to belief information. Thus, we should be surprised to find decision makers using only that information that they view as totally acceptable. Hackman and Anderson (1968) (cited in Cronen and Conville (1975a)) found correlations between belief strength and order of elicitation of the belief to range from $-.85$ to $+.95$. Our own view is that individuals act on information at their disposal because of semantic and situational cues. Using a free elicitation situation, Cronen and Conville reported no improvement in predicting attitude scores when a sum of affective values of elicited beliefs was compared to a sum of affective values of elicited beliefs weighted by belief strength. Thus, if semantic and situational cues rather than degree of belief strength determine information at the decision maker's disposal, it is the former set of cues rather than the belief strength that is the key to unlocking a reasonable explanation of the attitude–behavior relationship.

This view of retrieval in attitude–behavior situations is at odds with that of Fishbein and Ajzen (1974, pp. 217–222). They maintain

That only a relatively small number of beliefs serve as determinants of . . . attitude at any given moment. Research on attention span, apprehension, and information processing suggests that an individual is capable of attending to or processing only five to nine items of information at a time. . . . It can therefore be argued that a person's attitude toward an object is primarily determined by no more than five to nine beliefs that are *salient* at a given point in time [p. 218].

We find this view inadequate on several grounds.

1. It ignores evidence on contextual cues that alter what is "salient" as the situation changes.
2. It is an argument about the capacities of *short*-term memory rather than a *long*-term memory which has tremendous capacity (Lindsay and Norman, 1977).
3. Even granting that short-term memory is the correct store to be invoking, Miller (1956) and Simon (1974) both show that storage capacity is in "chunks" of information.
4. The concept of salience is nonexplanatory and is basically tautological.

The first two points are self-evident in light of the discussion of this chapter. The "chunking" criticism would be invalid *if* it could be shown that one belief constituted a chunk of information in the Miller and Simon sense. No such evidence is available and Fishbein and Ajzen offer no reasons as to why a belief should be considered as the chunking unit.

The fourth point marks the major source of divergence between our own explanation and that of Fishbein and Ajzen. Using salience as an explanatory construct to determine which beliefs are retrieved is equivalent to treating salience as a primitive term in the model. What makes information salient is left unexplicated. Just as rewards are those things that produce desired responses, and costs those that produce undesired responses, salient beliefs are those that are retrieved earlier, and less salient beliefs are those that are retrieved later or not at all. Such a view is as tautological as one can expect to find in a developed theory.

Our own view differs in two important respects on the "salience equals elicitation strength" issue. First, we assume that it is situational cues that determine saliency. Salience is not associated with a belief stored in LTM but is associated with a behavioral situation. Second (but implicit in the first comment), our model seeks to directly explain what information is retrieved in a given situation.

The schematic diagram of Figure 5.3 flowcharts the sequence of processes that we have been describing. There are two major lines of flow in the diagram. One describes the process of message receipt from input to storage. The other describes the process of retrieval in a decision-making situation. The two sequences are not completely independent, of course, because they both operate on the same information storehouse (LTM) and the results of a decision, whether to take action or not, are episodes and, therefore, potential inputs to the episodic portion of LTM. Tulving (1972) recognized this point when he considered the consequences of retrieval from episodic memory:

> While retrieval operations can be considered neutral with respect to the contents and structure of semantic memory, . . . the act of retrieval from either system may, and usually is, entered as an episode into episodic memory. Retrieval as feedback into the

episodic system may lead to changes in the contents, and the retrievability of these contents, of episodic memory [pp. 390–391].

We will show this facet of episodic memory to be a crucially important one in explaining certain relationships between attitudes and behaviors. This process is akin to what Tesser (1978) would label as "thinking about attitudes," but is much more specific.

Ignoring for a moment the input of external messages in Figure 5.3, let us ask what happens when an individual makes a decision to act based upon infor-

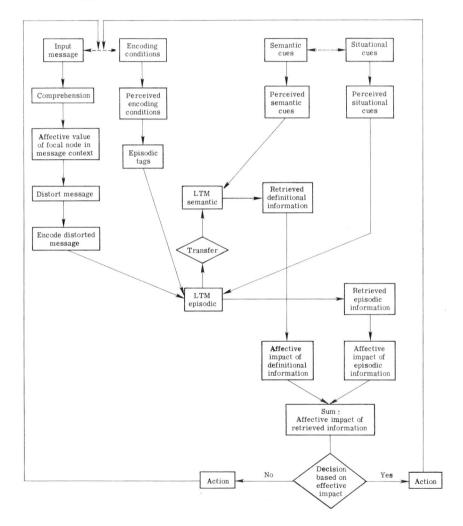

Figure 5.3. A flow chart of subprocesses of information acquisition, storage, retrieval, and behavioral action.

mation retrieved. If Tulving's suggestion and our model of Figure 5.3 are correct, the action taken will be encoded and stored as an episode in episodic memory. When, at a later time, the person is faced with making a decision to act in a highly similar situation, the situational cues in this later decision-making situation will most closely resemble the encoding tags of the recently encoded episode. The information encoded in the stored episode should be more readily retrievable than that stored in other episodes, precisely because the match between situational cues and encoding tags is so complete. If the person acts upon information at his or her disposal, as we have assumed, the very act of retrieval and action has the consequence of enhancing the likelihood of repetition of the same act as long as the situational cues remain relatively constant. If the act *is* repeated, another episode is entered into episodic memory further increasing the chances of retrieval of information whose affective impact spurs the same action. Thus, in the absence of outside messages, and for similar situational cues, our model implies that actions will be consistent over time with the affective implications of stored information, though not necessarily consistent across diverging situations.

Situations, Plans, and Goals

In arguing for an information-processing explanation of the attitude–behavior relationship, we have found it necessary to give a prominent place to situational cues. Such prominence is not new to the concept of situation. Simon (1969) has maintained that the human information processor can be better understood as a highly flexible organism, which adapts to the constraints of its environment. From this view, environmental constraints rather than information-processing laws would constitute the nexus of explanation and prediction. The social psychological literature relevant to group processes has recently been captured by a similar view (see Hackman and Morris, 1976 for a review). Task oriented groups interact and perform on a variety of different tasks. To what extent are the results, relevant to performance and interaction, determined by the task at hand rather than by social psychological laws independent of the task?

In the attitude–behavior area, Seibold (1975) points to a host of empirical evidence favoring the situation as a prominent predictor and an explanatory key to consistency between attitudes and behaviors. His own causal model of the attitude–behavior relationship gives a prominent role to situational factors under the label "locus of control" (McDermott, 1974). Delia, Crockett, Press, and O'Keefe (1975) also give a prominent place to context in their explanation of interpersonal evaluations. Delia *et al.* found that

> The sum of the evaluations of the component beliefs implicitly judged as relevant to a particular context predicted the obtained evaluations of Walt (the hypothetical stimulus person) in that context, but did not predict either his overall evaluation or his evaluation in the other interaction context [p. 16].

Not only were evaluations of the other in one context *not* transferred to the other context but the "predictions were not improved through the addition of component belief strength weightings [p. 16]." Delia *et al.* attribute this failure to replicate Fishbein and Ajzen's predictive formula to the free elicitation task they employ as contrasted to the supplied beliefs commonly used by Fishbein and Ajzen. Cronen and Conville (1975a) replicated this finding also using the free elicitation procedure.

Delia *et al.* carry the implications of their results beyond the interpersonal setting to the attitude–behavior arena (see also O'Keefe, Chapter 4, in this volume). Let us summarize these implications as reported by Delia *et al.* and then indicate points at which our view departs from theirs. First, context relevant beliefs rather than attitudes are the key predictors of individual choice. Second, the predictive validity of Fishbein and Ajzen's multiple act approach (1975, pp. 352–359) to predicting behavior can be explained by noting that the variety of beliefs elicited across a multiplicity of contexts is very likely to be related to the generalized attitude. Third, the free elicitation strategy is a crucial methodological requirement in attitude–behavior studies precisely because "beliefs about an object become differentially relevant (and thus salient) in various contexts [Delia *et al.*, 1975, p. 18]" as a function of "the implicit cognitive judgment of relevance made by the situated social actor [p. 19]."

Our own view is very much in line with these implications. However, with respect to the first implication, we maintain that the affective impact of a belief is inextricably intertwined with the affective connotations of the terms used to encode the belief. Because any verbal proposition has an a priori calculable affective impact, beliefs, stored in verbal form, also have affective impact. We think that Delia *et al.* are objecting to the concept of generalized attitude and not to the affective impact of beliefs, so our point is only one of clarification, and not one of difference (see O'Keefe, Chapter 4, this volume for a updated discussion).

The second implication should be extended. Fishbein and Ajzen (1975) not only consider multiple-act criteria but also single-act and repeated-observation criteria. In their review of studies attempting to predict single-act behaviors or single-act intentions, Fishbein and Ajzen suggest (pp. 333 and 361) that high correspondence is obtained when the level of specificity of the attitudinal measure matches that of the behavior or the intention. We would explain these findings by suggesting that the semantic and contextural cues in a highly specific behavioral situation would make specific episodes and specific semantic information more available to the decision maker. If the experimenter provides beliefs that do not match in specificity the information that would naturally be retrieved using a free elicitation methodology, those provided beliefs are likely to be irrelevant to the behavioral or intentional act which is the object of prediction.

The third implication suggested by Delia *et al.* is consistent with our own view of the dependence of salience upon context, but errs by giving the term "relevance" the same role that Fishbein and Ajzen have given the term "salience." Whereas Fishbein and Ajzen would have the most salient beliefs retrieved regardless of situation, Delia *et al.* would have the most "relevant" beliefs retrieved in each situation. While giving prominence to situational factors, Delia *et al.* fall prey to the same circularity of reasoning with "relevant" beliefs as Fishbein and Ajzen do with "salient" beliefs. The question is: *What is it about a situation that makes certain beliefs relevant and others irrelevant?*

Our model attempts to provide an answer to this question by specifying two sets of cues that determine the relative retrievabilities of various information sets (beliefs) located in semantic and episodic memory. These are the now familiar semantic and situational cues that match the lexical entries of semantic memory and match the encoding conditions of episodic memory respectively. Thus, our explanation of the attitude–behavior relationship is consistent with that of Delia *et al.* in the centrality it attributes to situational factors, but departs from their analysis by insisting that the basis of explanation be more specific than the "cognitive judgment of relevance made by the situated social actor." We agree with Cronen and Conville's (1975b) assessment that "an adequate focus on the cognitive determinants of salience and behavior requires that attention be directed to the *content of cognitive plans* for the retrieval of beliefs as well as to the *content of beliefs* themselves [p. 301]." Without knowing what factors affect the retrieval of information in a given behavioral situation, there is little hope of controlling actions through manipulation of message content.

For the term "situational cues" not to become entrapped in the same circularity as the concepts salience and relevance, the dimensions of social situations need to be unpacked. If such dimensions can be detailed, situations can be categorized and manipulated systematically, and the criteria for matching situational cues with stored episode tags can be specified. Unfortunately, those who have spoken most forcefully for the importance of situational factors have had the least to say about more abstract dimensions of these situations. Delia *et al.* manipulated the situation by considering a *work* setting and a *social* setting. The spokespersons for the encoding specificity principle have nothing to say about encoding tags outside of the list-learning and list-recognition situations standard to studies of memory.[6]

Although little can be said definitively about strategies for conceptualizing situational cues in general, some suggestions can be offered. One plausible answer is that information is relevant or irrelevant to the common *actions* and common *goals* that are routinely associated with the situations being discussed (work and social ones in the Delia *et al.* case). This response is plausible in that individuals are assumed to continuously generate plans and strategies necessary to achieve their ends. The results of Delia *et al.* and Cronen and Conville (1975a) cannot only be explained by appealing to situational factors, but can also be explained by appealing to the actions and goals, which by our common understanding, inhere in social situations.

---

[6] A study of memory for real-world events (Linton, 1975) fails to specify a definition of an event. Such an effort at definition would be a step toward separating social events from variables independent of socially construed events.

The concept of *plan* as central to theories of cognitive processing is certainly not new, having been treated (in different terminology) by Lewin (1951), by Miller, Galanter, and Pribram (1960), by Goldman (1970) in philosophy, and most recently in artificial intelligence under the label "procedures" (Winograd, 1975), and in cognitive science under the name scripts (Schank & Abelson, 1977). Following the terminology of Miller *et al.*, 1960, but not their definitions, a plan consists of a well-defined goal or endstate and a sequence of actions which a person imagines will lead to the goal. A strategy is a particular sequence of actions aimed at a particular goal so that several strategies might be imagined as leading to the same goal. Miller *et al.*'s "image" is roughly equivalent to our semantic and episodic beliefs. Like Miller *et al.* our next purpose is "to explore the relationship between the Image and the Plan [p. 18]."

Our aim is to use the terminology of plans as "goal plus imagined action sequences" to unpack the concepts of semantic cue and situational cue which we have argued are central to information retrieval. A persuasive message advocates a goal by its very definition. It advocates *action* on the part of the audience (for example, obtaining a chest X ray). The advocated action may be quite specific (X ray at the campus clinic during this week) or quite general (X ray for protection against illness sometime in the future). When faced with a behavioral choice, the decision maker sees a goal to be reached (getting a chest X ray) through an imagined strategy of subactions (e.g., Action 1: Call for an appointment; Action 2: Notify secretary of absence; Action 3: Take car, not bus, to office; Action 4: Drive car to clinic; Action 5: Enter waiting room. and so on . . . Action k: Get X ray taken; Action $k + n$: Await results). The goal, as encoded, serves as the set of semantic cues prompting retrieval of definitional information about chest X rays.[7] To the extent that the affective impact of the definitional beliefs of semantic memory are negative, the plan would be aborted before any imagined strategies because the goal itself would not be seen as worthy of pursuit. While this early abortion should not often happen given a persuasive speaker, it is a possibility. For example, *getting X rays* might be believed to *cause injury to reproductive organs* and to *fail to be a useful diagnostic method*. These affectively negative beliefs would christen the goal itself as undesirable. The persuasive message failing to attack these key beliefs in semantic memory would have failed to change the person's attitude. But the reported attitude would be consistent with behavior since the person would *not* get an X ray and would report a negative attitude based solely upon the semantic cues associated with getting an X ray. In this case, particular action sequences would not be imagined, since the goal is never viewed as desirable.

On the other hand, if other beliefs included that X rays *are a useful diagnostic method*, the goal would be equally positive and negative and imagined strategies for achieving the goal would commence. Each action in the sequence leading to the goal would serve as a cue for retrieving information from an

---

[7] Note that semantic information is assumed to be true (that is, is definitional) so that belief strength or acceptability is an irrelevant concern.

episode in LTM that centers around the same action. For example, an imagined action ($k + n$) might cue an episode in which great anxiety, and hence affectively negative information, accompanied the wait for results from important tests. Thus, even though the goal may be viewed positively or neutrally on the basis of semantic memory, the actions imagined to be necessary for its achievement may cue episodic information that outweighs the positive affect associated with the goal itself (Miller *et al.*, 1960, p. 63). In such a case, we would predict a favorable attitude toward the goal (the proposed action) but an unfavorable intention to behave. Inconsistency between general attitude and behavior should reign with the behavior *not* being carried out for reasons to be discussed later (cf. especially Nisbett, Borgida, Crandall, & Reed, 1976).

The notion that a strategy (or imagined sequence of actions) relevant to achieving a goal increases the accessibility of certain episodes over others may be stated differently: An imagined strategy "knits together" the beliefs stored in disjointed episodes. Thus, planning serves to organize the episodes of LTM on a nonpermanent basis. The organization derives from the actions in a strategy cuing associated episodes. As goals differ, so will the episodic cues and the retrieved information; as strategies differ for the same goal, so will the episodic cues and the retrieved information.

We recognize, as did Miller *et al.* (1960, p. 182), that using the terminology of plans and verbal explanations of cognitive processes is not sufficient to make precise statements and not sufficient to draw nonobvious implications about planning and information retrieval. A calculus of plans is needed. There have been several recent attempts to provide such a calculus (Abelson, 1975b; Rieger, 1975, 1976; Schank & Abelson, 1977). Most of these calculi have been explicitly designed to aid in the modeling of human understanding of discourse. Rieger's work has been more directly concerned with problem-solving activity by humans in mundane situations, and is for this reason discussed further here. We are assuming that behavioral action is like decision making when faced with a problem—the problem of acting or not acting.

The aim of Rieger's system is to represent a broad cross section of human purposive activity in terms of a small number of primitive terms and a set of relations among those terms. Based on analyses of verbs of thought (Schank, Goldman, Rieger & Riesback, 1972, cited in Reiger, 1975), Rieger proposes five primitive terms, WANTS, ACTIONS, STATES, STATECHANGES, and TENDENCIES. WANTS are equivalent to goals and must be specified beforehand. ACTIONS, STATES, and STATECHANGES are self-explanatory. A TENDENCY is a "special type of non-purposive action which *must* occur whenever its enabling conditions are satisfied [Rieger, 1975, p. 201]." For example, *growing hungry* is a tendency enabled by the absence of food. Thus, the action *fasting* will cause the state *absence of food* enabling the tendency *growing hungry* to take place. Notice in this example that actions (either purposive or not) cause states and/or statechanges. States, in turn, enable actions. Causality and enablement constitute the two basic classes of relations linking primitives.

Rieger unpacks these two classes into 25 different relations including one-shot, single act, and continuous causality and enablement, "gated" causality requiring preexistent state for the cause to operate, antagonistic states, disenabling actions (including gated and continuous relations) causing states *not* to exist, and only a few others.

The encompassing aim of Rieger's system is to write algorithms for any situation using the five primitive terms and primitive relations from his calculus. A situation can be "characterized as a collection of goal states [Rieger, 1975, p. 204]" and to act in a particular situation is to engage in the algorithms particular to that situation. Notice that Rieger's commonsense algorithms do not give us the substance of the algorithms for various situations, but give only a common and simple set of terms and relations to describe purposive action across situations.

There are several aspects of the Rieger formalism that dovetail with our own analysis and show the limits of its applicability. First, the availability of formalisms like Rieger's makes it possible to model the retrieval of information based upon situations viewed as planning algorithms. Without such a formalism, our analysis must remain speculative, highly theoretical, and verbal. The possibility of formalization through simulation is at least reassuring.

Second, Rieger's system gives a special place to actions in the realization of of goals. Without actions or tendencies, states could not be caused, and goals (which are nothing more than specified states) could not be achieved. Actions differ from tendencies because actions are volitional. They need *not* occur simply because all the enabling conditions are present. Tendencies *must* occur when all the enabling conditions are present. Rieger's ACTIONS would constitute the cues for retrieving information stored in an action-centered episode.

Third, while ACTIONS and WANTS cue information retrieval, *the goal may not be achieved or achievable even if all of the belief information is affectively positive.* As Rieger's system clearly points out, the possibility of an action depends on either (*a*) all enabling states being present; and (*b*) all gating conditions being operative. For example, the action *driving to the clinic* is possible only if one has *access to a vehicle* which is the enabling state. In general, STATES are caused by ACTIONS and TENDENCIES. To the extent that all enabling states are under the direct and immediate control of an individual planner's actions, and all such actions are affectively positive, then behaviors relevant to the goal should be consistent with the affective evaluation of the information retrieved. For example, the action *borrow Charlie's car* would cause a state-change to *access to a vehicle* and, hence, driving to the clinic would be enabled. Notice this enablement does not imply that the person would go the clinic, only that the strategy is operative. Whether the person goes or not depends upon the affective implications of the beliefs stored in *driving to the clinic* episodes. However, to the extent that one or more enabling states are caused by a tendency, or are caused by an affectively negative action, then *intentions to behave* relevant to the goal should be consistent with retrieved information but the actual behavior may not be. The reasoning is that if a person must act to cause an enabling state, and the act is negatively viewed, the act will not be pursued and the enabling state not achieved. On the other hand, when an enabling state is caused by a tendency, which unlike an action, is not under control of the person, the person must be able to take advantage of the tendency rather than being frustrated by the tendency. More simply stated, in order for affective information to be consistent with behaviors, the imagined action sequences must be *seen* by the actor as feasible and natural and social conditions (tendencies) must permit rather than frustrate plans.

More particularly, the feasibility of a strategy depends on the actor's control of enabling conditions. If enabling states can be produced by the actor's actions but are highly negative (for example, when the state *access to a vehicle* is caused by the action *buying a car*, which is financially prohibitive), the strategy for *getting an X ray*, which involves the action *driving to the clinic*, which in turn, is enabled by *access to a vehicle* is not feasible. If enabling states can be caused by TENDENCIES, then the plan is feasible only if those TENDENCIES can be harnessed by the actor to his or her advantage. If the enabling states are disenabled by TENDENCIES, then the plan is feasible only if those tendencies can be overcome by the actor. In cases where the strategy is not feasible for either of those two reasons, and no other strategies present themselves, planning is abandoned, and therefore information retrieval is ended. In such cases, the intention to behave may be consistent with retrieved semantic and episodic information, but behaviors will not necessarily be consistent with those intentions.

Finally, Rieger notes that alternative actions can cause the same state or statechange. He posits an unspecified selection process which chooses among alternative actions. We would argue that such a selection operates on the basis of stored beliefs with affectively more positive information determining the choice among alternatives.

This section has presented arguments for the situational specificity of information retrieval and has tried to explicate terms like salience and situational relevance in the terminology of plans and strategies. From the point of view of the persuasive speaker, the origin of plans is crucial. If plans and strategies are highly individualistic or are difficult to instill through simple instruction, the message maker is at the mercy of individual planners. However, as Schank and Abelson (1977; Abelson, 1976) have argued, much planning is "scripted." That is, many sequences of actions imagined in obtaining various goals are common, broadly shared, and even clichéd. If this were not true, many of the common inferences made in understanding stories would not be shared, and understanding would be flawed. It is obvious that there exist plans and act sequences ranging from highly idiosyncratic to common cultural types. In a persuasive setting, the speaker cannot know the preexistent plans of each audience member which the proposed goal invokes. On the other hand, it is quite feasible to offer plans for action as a part of the persuasion, and to thereby *create* retrieval strategies by defining or structuring the situation in the persuasive message. The possibility of instilling plans suggests a message strategy in achieving behavior change that we shall discuss further in the next section.

Summary

In this section, we have argued that behavioral actions depend upon the affective value of beliefs at the disposal of the decision maker at the time of action. In explicating the phrase *at the disposal of the decision maker*, we have rejected concepts such as salience and relevance as determinates of retrieval. Rather, based upon recent theory that LTM has semantic and episodic organizational schemes, we maintained that two sets of cues, semantic or goal-specific and episodic or action-specific, determine the retrieval of beliefs (and their associated evaluations) from semantic and episodic memory, respectively. The language of goals and action-sequences, that is, plans, replaced salience and situational relevance as explanations of retrieval. Using the formalism of Rieger's (1975, 1976) conception of purposive action, we concluded that feasible plans cue belief information whose affective import should be consistent with both behaviors and intentions to behave. However, nonfeasible plans can only cue information that will be consistent with intentions to behave. Behaviors may not follow due to the actor's perceived inability to cause or control the necessary enabling conditions.

Implications of the Information-Processing Explanation

The implications of the view of the attitude–behavior sequence, which we have been presenting, can only be fully explored when our explanation is tested and formally modeled. However, since that is a future goal, we first must draw more mundane implications of the predictive variety, and second, implications that concern the explanation of these predictions.

Predictions from the Information-Processing View

Three classes of predictions will be discussed: (*a*) general expectations about the consistencies among attitudes, behavioral intentions, and behaviors; (*b*) changes in attitude and belief structure due to individual effort such as thinking and acting; and (*c*) changes in attitudes, beliefs, and consequent behaviors due to message manipulations.

Consistencies

The views espoused thus far identify a person's attitude with an evaluative response to some goal advocated by a message, a behavioral intention with an evaluative response derived from the information at the disposal of the retriever (semantic and episodic), and a behavior as an action undertaken (or not) which is of interest in its own right (thus eliminating *reports* of behaviors as surrogates). These three factors may be consistent or inconsistent with one another depending upon certain specifiable conditions:

1. If advocated goals (semantic cues) lead to the retrieval of affectively positive information, planning begins; the retrieval of affectively negative information aborts further planning, and the possibility of action is short-circuited.

In this case attitudes are consistent with behaviors. Once the goal is viewed as affectively positive, then other situational cues, conceived as action sequences leading to the goal, activate retrieval of episodic information.

2. If the goal is affectively positive, the strategy for goal achievement leads to the retrieval of episodic information, which may be consistent or inconsistent with the evaluation of the goal.

In Proposition 2, the claim is simply that the overall behavioral intention is determined by the combination of semantic information as well as by the more personalized episodic information. In general, we would expect the more personally relevant information of episodic store to weigh more heavily in the person's overall behavioral intention than would the more abstract semantic information (Abelson, 1975a, 1976; Nisbett *et al.*, 1976). Behavioral intention by this proposition is a joint function of semantically held beliefs cued by the imagined (or provided) act sequences leading to the goal, but the different classes of elicited beliefs which make up the behavioral intention need not be consistent. Behaviors can be consistent or inconsistent with behavioral intentions.

3. Given a feasible strategy (as discussed earlier) for the achievement of a goal, behaviors should be consistent with the affective impact of freely elicited beliefs, where elicitation conditions cue not only the goal but action-sequences leading to the goal.

4. Given a nonfeasible strategy for goal achievement, generalized desirability of the goal should be consistent with the affective impact of freely elicited beliefs, but behaviors may not be.

Propositions 3 and 4 merely restate the fundamental assumption of the view that individuals act in accordance with the affective impact of the information at their disposal at the time of action. However, we modify that assumption by taking into account the feasibility of the situation. These predictions are congruent with those of Fishbein and Ajzen (1975, Ch. 8), though not entirely congruent with their explanation. It is more in congruence with Abelson's (1976) notions that "attitude toward an object consists in the ensemble of scripts concerning that object [p. 41]" and that "cognitively mediated social behavior depends on . . . (*a*) the selection of a particular script to represent the given social

situation and (b) the taking of a participant role within that script [p. 42]."
Empirically these predictions are consistent with the findings that high fear
messages tend to be more efficacious in producing behavioral change when
accompanied by detailed plans of action to remove the anxiety-producing
situation than without such plans (Leventhal, 1970).

Our view has given a prominent role to situational cues in information
retrieval and these situations may differ in terms of goals, strategies or both.

5. Under the conditions of Proposition 3, individuals who evaluate the
identical goal equally, but have different strategies for achieving it, may
retrieve affectively different beliefs and behave inconsistently with one
another, but not inconsistently with their beliefs given their plans.

6. Under the conditions of Proposition 3, goals that are semantically
similar but differ in specificity should elicit different strategies, different
affective beliefs, and possibly, inconsistent behaviors. The behaviors
would be inconsistent from the point of view of the similarity of the
goals but not inconsistent with retrieved information.

Proposition 5 suggests: (a) That two individuals may have the same
semantic information about the goal and, hence, evaluate its desirability
equally; but (b) that different strategies aimed at achieving the goal may elicit
different belief information stored in episodic memory. To the extent that the
elicited belief information has affectively different implications for each person,
their behaviors should differ even though they evaluate the goal's desirability
equally. In other words, given different construals of the situation, the definitional information of semantic memory is overriden by the more personalized
beliefs of episodic memory. When there is inconsistency between more abstract,
definitional information and more personally experienced information, the
personal information weights more heavily (Abelson, 1975a, 1976; Nisbett,
et al., 1976; Solvic, Fischoff, & Lichtenstein, 1976). Such weighting of personal
information suggests the importance of accounting for situational cues to
retrieval from episodic memory.

Proposition 6 notes that goals that differ in level of specificity (e.g., *being
more concerned about lung cancer* to *getting a chest X ray on Tuesday next*)
produce very different strategies and, hence, retrieval cues. Even though the
reported consistency among conceptually similar goals should be positive, the
associated strategies for achieving them can produce affectively differential
beliefs and, hence, low correlations among associated behaviors. Of course,
Fishbein and Ajzen (1975, Ch. 8) and Ajzen and Fishbein (1977) make essentially the same specificity argument. They maintain that to adequately predict
behaviors from affective evaluations, the specificity of both must match. We
agree, but we also insist that the *reason* for the predictive success of "specificity-
matching" is found in the differential strategies imagined when conceptually
similar goals differ in specificity.

If our contentions that people act on the basis of information at their disposal, and that access to information depends upon retrieval cues are valid, there is *no reason to expect*, on cognitive grounds, that, when faced with context-specific behaviors, persons will retrieve a base of beliefs across a broad set of episodes. Rather their retrieval will be based upon a narrow set of cues and, hence, or a restricted set of episodes. If correlations between affective responses and behavioral responses are to be high, the cues of the paper and pencil response situation (whether narrow or broad) must be the cues of the behavioral situation.

Individual Effort

A second class of predictions concerns the feedback effects on attitude and belief structure of an individual's behavioral action, thinking about an issue, or role-playing and acting counter-attitudinally. In our view these processes affect the information in episodic memory in certain specifiable ways.

Recent work by Tesser (1978) on thinking and attitude change operates from a set of assumptions about cognition roughly consistent with our own. Tesser and his colleagues typically have found that the opportunity for thought about a particular attitudinal object intensifies the reported attitude more than when there is little opportunity for thought. The reason for this polarization phenomenon is somewhat unclear. Tesser maintains that thinking about an attitude issue is carried out within the confines of a mental schema, which indicates what information is relevant to the stimulus, and describes associations between stimulus and attributes thus permitting inferences about the stimulus (Tesser, 1978, pp. 290–291). Thought carried out within a particular schema should lead to the retrieval of evaluatively consistent (rather than inconsistent) information because

> All of us have schemas concerning evaluation which lead us to expect liked objects to have/be associated with likeable attributes and objects and disliked objects to have/be associated with disliked attributes and objects [Tesser, 1978, p. 310].

Thus, the more time one has to think about and report on an attitude, the more beliefs that are retrieved and the more extreme the reported attitude.

This reasoning is a valid explanation of polarization *only if* a person is working within a particular schema and it is correct to assume that evaluatively consistent beliefs cluster together within these schema. In an ingenious and fascinating set of experiments, Tesser and his colleagues have shown (*a*) that more developed schemas produce greater polarization (Tesser & Leone, 1977); (*b*) that reality constraints (e.g. the presence of the object) reduces polarization effects (Tesser, 1976); (*c*) that polarization need *not* result if two or more competing schemas are "tuned-in" (Tesser & Danheiser, 1978); and (*d*) that polarization results from the generation of additional consistent beliefs rather than from the loss of inconsistent ones (Sadler & Tesser, 1973; Tesser & Cowan,

1975). These results are consistent with our own explanation of the attitude-formation process. That is, when a person is faced with a set of semantic cues, a particular region of semantic memory is activated and, with greater time for thinking, retrieval of a greater number of allied beliefs is made possible. The more knowledge and experience the person has had with the topic, the more richly connected will be the semantic memory region (i.e., schema). Furthermore, in the presence of alternative semantic or episodic cues, beliefs associated with multiple schemas or with multiple episodes which are evaluatively inconsistent can be retrieved.

The chief difference between our view and that of Tesser is that the process of tuning-in alternative schema is given a fuller explication here. Tuning-in involves matching semantic cues to semantic memory features and matching situational cues to the tags of episodic memory. Since retrieval depends upon tuning-in and polarization depends upon retrieval of consistent beliefs, the polarization result is centrally dependent upon the process of cuing various schema and personal episodes.

As suggested earlier the polarization phenomenon is dependent upon the assumption that schema are clusters of evaluatively consistent beliefs. Without this assumption, within-schema retrieval could not lead to polarization. The evidence for this claim is the weakest link in Tesser's argument. However, there is some evidence from the literature on word association and semantic-differential ratings suggesting that semantic-differential ratings between stimulus words and their first associates are positive and sometimes substantial (Pollio, 1964; Staats & Staats, 1959). With continuous association, Pollio (1964) also found that the more highly clustered "rapid sequence" word associations exhibited less within-group semantic-differential distance than the less clustered "slow sequence" word associations. Coupled with the usual assumptions about local balance in cognitions (Abelson & Rosenberg, 1958), the evidence suggests within-schema evaluative consistency although no requirement of between-schema consistency.

Tesser's research on polarization, the centrality of the cueing process for retrieval, and the evidence on within-schema consistency may be summarized in a few propositions.

1. In the presence of specific semantic and/or episodic cues, the more time spent in thinking about the topic, the greater the number of beliefs retrieved and the greater the polarization.
2. In the presence of a broad set of semantic and/or episodic cues, the more time spent in thinking about the topic, the greater the number of beliefs retrieved but the less likely the polarization (as compared to Proposition 1).

Proposition 1 can fail in the case for which the schema or episode evoked is undifferentiated and simplistic so that the number of beliefs available for retrieval is small (Tesser & Leone, 1977). These propositions also suggest certain message strategies. If semantic and episodic cues can guide retrieval, it is important that schemas or episodes with competing evaluative implications not be evoked by the *same* set of cues that evoke supportive beliefs. Also in establishing new schema or episodes, the organization of beliefs pertinent to the schema or episode should be so chunked in the message itself. Other message implications will be noted in the following section.

Let us turn from individual effort of the mental variety to the effects of actual behavior on the storage of information in memory.

3. In the absence of any external persuasive messages relevant to a focal behavior, performance of some behavior in a given situation should enhance the likelihood of performing that behavior in the same situation at a future time.

Whereas this is certainly *not* a startling prediction, its basis is a bit unusual. If the model of episodic memory is correct, to retrieve information relevant to some behavior, and act on that information, is an episode itself. It is therefore available for encoding and storage as an episode whose encoding tags are those of the particular behavioral situation. Thus, when the situation arises again, the cues of the situation have a ready match in the encoding tags of the prior episode. The likelihood of retrieving exactly the same information set as in the first act is increased. There is one important caveat, however. The affective impact of the beliefs gathered in acting must not be appreciably different from the affective impact of the beliefs from the initial information. Such a situation can arise when there is deviation from the expected consequences of the action. In this case, the information encoded as a part of the episode would include the new beliefs and their associated affective implications.

Proposition 3 also offers an information-processing explanation of Bem's view of self-attribution of attitudes (Bem, 1965, 1972). We agree with Bem that a person's attitudes or description of self will change as a result of the person's observation of his or her own behavior. But we disagree with the basis for the change. In our view, the information derived from the episode is stored as an episode in LTM. Given the appropriate cues, the information from the behavioral episode becomes the basis for self-descriptive statements (attitudinal responses). The predictive relationships suggested by our view and Bem's, then, are similar, but the explanatory bases differ significantly.

One of the peculiar characteristics of episodic memory is its self-feeding character. As information is retrieved, the very set of information gathered from semantic LTM and several episodes in episodic LTM itself becomes an episode in LTM. Such an episode can be called an *activated* episode because it is made up from information actively retrieved by a person in acting out a goal or in actively imagining a sequence of actions leading to the goal. The information of an activated episode is all the information the person has concerning a particular goal and particular strategy. Further, it is located in one episode. The above characteristics suggest the following proposition:

4. The more actively an individual is involved in information storage (e.g., role-playing versus observing) or in information retrieval (e.g., counter-attitudinal advocacy with free elicitation versus provided arguments), the more retrievable the activated episode in a similar subsequent situation, and the more behavior change in the direction of the affectively held beliefs.

In reviewing the role-playing literature, Fishbein and Ajzen (1975) conclude "that role-playing will facilitate change only to the extent that the role player is forced to actively search through his own belief system [p. 424]." The basis of this conclusion is found in studies showing (a) that the probability of elicitation of nonsalient beliefs is enhanced once retrieved (Maltzman, 1960) and (b) that recall of self-generated arguments is greater than recall of other-generated arguments (Greenwald & Albert, 1968). Their analysis of key role-playing studies by Clore and Jeffry (1972), Culbertson (1957), and Janis and King (1954, 1956) in terms of the importance of active participation is impressive. However, their perspective once again calls upon salience enhancement as the key to the explanation. We feel that our own view, represented in Proposition 4, avoids the problems of salience as an explanatory construct.

When an activated episode is generated, it is allied with a particular goal and sequence of actions. Because the plan is self-generated, the activated episode has specific encoding tags associated with it. Hence, when faced with a similar subsequent situation, the match between the situational cues and the tags of the activated episode should be quite good. Thus, the retrievability of information in the activated episode should be high. On the other hand, when information is passively absorbed, neither active planning (role-playing) nor imagined planning (counter-attitudinal advocacy) is required. Although there will be encoding tags associated with these passive episodes, they will not be the goal plus action sequence tags pertinent to the more active situations. Hence, the cues of a subsequent behavioral situation will provide less of a match to the encoding tags of the passive situation. The information retrieved in the behavioral situation by those in the passive group will depend upon their strategies for goal achievement but will surely include information from episodes other than the passive one in which they were involved. Because behavioral responses will presumably be consistent with retrieved information, the change in behavior for those in the active group should be more in line with information stored or retrieved from storage in that setting.

Abelson (1976) has recently made a similar point about participating in scripted behaviors. He argues that the decision to participate in a social action depends upon both the selection of a script pertinent to a social situation and the adoption of the role of participant within that script (p. 42). Research by

Langer and Abelson (1972) points to the legitimacy of such an assumption. Whether the person engages in novel social behavior, Abelson notes, depends crucially on first participation in an episode. As participation continues, the likelihood of continued participation is enhanced. However, the *reason* for this enhanced likelihood is unclear in Abelson's comments but follows naturally from our explanation of Propositions 3 and 4.

More directly relevant to the attitude–behavior question is research by Fazio and his colleagues on direct involvement and attitude–behavior consistency (Fazio & Zanna, in press a, b; Regan & Fazio, 1977; Zanna & Fazio, n.d.). This research has shown that individuals who have been directly involved in situations pertinent to the behavior exhibit greater consistency between reported attitudes and exhibited behaviors. In seeking to explain these findings Zanna and Fazio (n.d.) report that direct experience subjects typically report greater confidence in their held attitudes even in the face of false feedback. This increased confidence in personally experienced information is consistent with the findings of Nisbett *et al.* (1976) on the relative strength of personalized (episodic) information in contrast to abstract or semantic information. On our view, Proposition 4 explains the Fazio data by maintaining that direct experience either established "first participation" in an episode and/or established an episode whose tags are matched by the subsequent behavioral situation.

Finally, Fazio, Zanna, and Cooper (1978) report data on information-processing differences when subjects are instructed to observe versus empathize with a videotaped stimulus. Those instructed to empathize exhibited greater attitude–behavior correlation than the control group. The empathy group may be considered to be engaged in more imaginative planning than the more passive controls.

Message Implications

The importance of semantic and situational cues in information retrieval conceptualized as goals and projected act sequences in the achievement of goals points directly to the use of goals and act sequences as a part of a message structure to guide retrieval.

Since situational cues (as goals and strategies for the accomplishment of goals) are a significant determinant of information retrieved, to enhance the retrievability of information consistent with a desired behavior, a goal and plan for action should be part of the persuasive message.

Although the sequence of actions necessary to achieve some goal is often part of an audience's knowledge and experience, messages may impart new plans or restructure existing ones. If plans can be introduced, minimizing actions that might cue information contrary to the advocated behavior (e.g., anxiety production while awaiting results from chest X ray), then plans introduced by speakers would organize episodic recall rather than be controlled by the heterogeneous plans held by individual audience members. Whereas it is never possible to know completely the necessary encoding conditions with an arbitrary audience, in a controlled situation with artificial issues, episodes and their tags may be established in an audience's memory store. Later messages can seek to retrieve this information with appropriately specified plans serving as cues. Furthermore, strategies for satisfying contingencies such as enabling states and gating conditions can enhance the likelihood of behavior change as noted earlier. Attention to the details of strategies for achieving goals and not simply to the desirability of the goals themselves would be required in message design.

This reasoning helps to explain, from a retrieval point of view, why the presence of detailed plans along with high fear messages tend to be more efficacious in producing behavioral change than high fear messages without detailed plans (Leventhal, 1970). If our characterization of episodic memory as organized around events and actions that are unconnected is correct, then the plans of action leading to goals could be the organizational thread knitting together the unwoven episodic information in a given behavioral situation. Messages or instruction sets specifying different plans make different information sets available to the decision maker. For messages or instruction sets to reorganize episodic memory, memory must be very flexible, a proposition to which many scholars of memory processes attest (Fridja, 1972; Santa & Lawmers, 1976; Simon, 1969). Such purported flexibility suggests the persuasive strategy just discussed.

More realistically, few advocated behavioral actions are specific enough in their demands to conjure a single goal and a singular plan of action. Rather many calls to action are sufficiently broad to imply several goals, several plans, and on our reasoning, several lines of information retrieval. If the information retrieved from these several plans is mutually compatible, message makers need not be concerned with down-playing competing goals and plans while making others more prominent. On the other hand, when different goals lead to the retrieval of evaluatively incompatible information, message designers need to be concerned about goal compatibility and goal hierarchy. If certain classes of goals are preeminent in an audience's psychology or are necessary prerequisites for other goals, behavioral change can occur only if prior goals lead to information retrieval consistent with the advocated behavioral change.

The upshot of the worry about goal multiplicity is the orientation of research and message designers to the question of goal priority. If an advocated behavior presumes that prior goals be achieved before the behavior change, then those prior goals will direct retrieval whether or not the goal appears as a message element. Some speculation on goal classes and goal priorities has been carried out by Schank and Abelson (1977, pp. 111–122). They identify five goal classes—satisfaction, enjoyment, achievement, preservation, and crisis—and two subgoal classes—instrumental (necessary in the pursuit of another goal) and delta (planning processes necessary in the achievement of a goal). More importantly, they spend some time discussing goal priority (pp. 117–119). While the empirical validity of their precedence relations is not established, it is important to note that because message consumers will have goal priorities in evaluating advocated change, persuaders must either take advantage of these priorities or minimize their effects on retrieval to assure that the desired information is retrieved at the time of action. The "more research" cliche is appropriate here.

In arguing that behavioral action depends upon information, we have been led to focus attention on the cues that prompt the retrieval of various information, that is, that make it more available to the actor. Thus, one set of message strategies aims at manipulating retrieval cues for information already stored. Persuasive messages also can provide informational beliefs. Given our arguments about retrieval, how can messages provide information that will be more retrievable? A question similar to this is addressed by Tversky and Kahneman (1973, 1974): What biases do information receivers have in judging the frequency and probability of certain events? What makes information about these events more available to decision makers?

Tversky and Kahneman describe three availability biases: retrievability of instances, effectiveness of search set, and imaginability. Each can be used to guide message design in presenting information that will be more likely to be available in subsequent retrieval. The "retrievability of instances" bias points out that personalized and particularized occurrences of events tend to be more readily available to people in making judgments about the likelihood of those events. This observation dovetails with research noted earlier by Nisbett *et al.* (1976) on the relative importance subjects give to concretized and personalized information in contrast to abstract or statistical information. These researches point to the necessity of building "episode-like" information into persuasive messages. Not only will the information be given greater weight than more abstract information, but should in later tests of retrieval be more readily recalled. As Nisbett *et al.* put it: "If people are unmoved by the sorts of dry, statistical data that are dear to the hearts of scientists and policy planners, then social and technological progress must be impeded unless effective, concrete emotionally interesting ways of communicating conclusions are developed [p. 132]."

The "effectiveness of search set" bias maintains that information becomes more available as there are more different contexts of which the information is a part, regardless of its actual, context-free objective frequency. Consequently information that is portrayed as common to many personalized episodes in which the individual sees him or herself embedded should be more available and more readily retrievable in subsequent behavioral settings.

The "imaginability" bias argues that the ability to actively imagine actions leading to, and consequences from, a proposed behavioral action will affect the risks and rewards that accrue as a result of the action. In terms of message design, imaginability is implied in Proposition 1 stated earlier. The well-designed message will seek to guide imagined actions and to take advantage of goal priorities in cueing information retrieval. That is, the persuasive message will help define what is imaginable. The availability biases may be summarized: In order to make information available to subjects in later recall situations, messages should take advantage of availability heuristics that bias audiences' retrieval of information.

It is interesting to note that Tversky and Kahneman's (1973, 1974) availability heuristics are consistent with our own view of retrieval. If information is embedded in multiple episodes, the likelihood of its retrieval is enhanced. Strategies of message design then derive directly from the cognitive biases of information use that audiences' employ. The tactic is as old as persuasion itself—employ the audience's own "psychologic" in message organization, looking *first* to cognitive processes for message design clues.

Explanation in the Information-Processing View

Whereas none of the propositions discussed is particularly startling or "counter-intuitive," each offers predictions consistent with currently available evidence but derived from explanatory premises giving prominence to the information-processing characteristics of the audience. We feel that this is an important step in attitude-change theory and research. Social psychological approaches to attitude change (e.g., dissonance, congruity, balance) have often been "closet" cognitive theories. They have made either implicit or explicit assumptions about the working of the inner sanctum that somehow handles the messages, beliefs, source factors, behavioral constraints, and so on, that constitute the message–attitude–behavior situation. Although social psychologists and communication scholars have been primarily concerned with the predictive validity of observed relationships, it is certainly beyond time that these relationships were explained by mechanisms and processes permitting a meeting of cognitive theories of attitude and behavior change and more general theories of cognitive information processing. Part of our aim has been to take some hesitating but perhaps incautious steps toward this integration.

The target of our efforts has been the message–attitude–behavior relationship. The prevailing view of this relationship is that of Fishbein and Ajzen (1975). We have compared our explanation to theirs, often critically throughout this chapter. This criticism should be viewed as a compliment to the significance, breadth, depth, and scope of their work. Were their theory and research trivial, it would not be worthy of critical review. But it is worthy, and we now summarize its merits and demerits as viewed from our own perspective.

In one very significant and fundamental way, Fishbein and Ajzen's view is consonant with our own: Behaviors are determined by the affective impact of the information viewed as relevant to those behaviors. Fishbein and Ajzen unpack this statement by assuming that "intentions to behave" are highly related to the behaviors themselves (under certain conditions) and that these intentions, in turn, are determined by the evaluative consequences of the act and perceived normative pressure to act weighted by probabilities of belief or applicability.

Whereas our own view does not depart from the essence of Fishbein and Ajzen's, it does alter certain of the significant details of their view.

First, Fishbein and Ajzen maintain that (in predicting attitudes and intentions to behave) the salience of beliefs determines the likelihood of their retrieval and use. Based on the studies of Cronen and Conville (1975a) and Delia *et al.* (1975), and the theoretical work of Tulving (1972) on encoding specificity, we find salience to be a useless and theoretically invalid explanatory construct. It is replaced by semantic and situational cues, the former being the projected goals and plans, the latter being action sequences aimed at achieving those goals. This, then is the crux of our view: Behavioral responses are determined by the affective impact of stored information, which can be retrieved, and retrieval, in turn, depends upon semantic and situational cues. In this way, the explanation of retrieval becomes an important goal, and is not merely taken for granted.

Second, Fishbein and Ajzen determined the affective impact of beliefs by obtaining individual evaluations of the belief statements on favorability scales. One goal of our model, although it is a distant one, is to calculate the affective impact of any elicited belief on the basis of a priori norms for the affective connotations of the terms and rules for combination of syntactic units to yield an overall evaluation. One advantage, if we are successful, is that of parsimony. Fishbein and Ajzen's current model for predicting a single generalized attitude from 15 beliefs requires fixing 30 input parameters. Occam would turn over in his grave. A second advantage permits the tracing of the affective impact of the belief statements in an input message from encoding and storage, to retrieval (through cued, but free, elicitation).

Third, Fishbein and Ajzen hold that prediction of behaviors and intentions to behave from attitudinal and normative beliefs is possible, only if the beliefs are measured at the same level of specificity as the behavior and the intention. We find no fault with this predictively valid statement. The reason for its validity, we maintain, is to be found in the match between the semantic and episodic cues of the behavioral situation and the encoding tags of the episodic store. When very general behaviors or intentions are cued, a large number of different plans are conjured, since many different specific actions are implied. Each plan serves to link episodic memory in slightly different ways and, hence, to make available a vast array of beliefs. As more and more beliefs of increasing heterogeneity are retrieved, it becomes possible to project only generalized sentiments and reactions. By the same token, if a specific behavior or action is cued, a specific plan is invoked. Information is retrieved that projects a particularized action, which may not generalize to other equally particular behaviors or to a more abstract attitude.

Fourth, the concept of planning as goal plus strategy functions as the important link between the cognitive world of beliefs and affective evaluations and the behavioral world of actions. Without such a linkage, the association between cognitive reality and behavioral reality must remain a mystery. Given the advances we have described in the formal calculus of planning, the possibility of describing and comparing situations on the basis of planned activity is inching toward realization.

REFERENCES

Abelson, R. P. Are attitudes necessary? In B. T. King & E. McGinnies (Eds.), *Attitudes, conflict and social change*. New York: Academic Press, 1972.

Abelson, R. P. The structure of belief systems. In R. C. Schank & K. M. Colby (Eds.), *Computer models of thought and language*. San Francisco: Freeman, 1973.

Abelson, R. P. The reasoner and the inferencer don't talk much to each other. In R. Schank & B. L. Nash-Webber (Eds.), *Theoretical issues in natural language processing*. Proceedings of an Interdisciplinary Workshop., Cambridge, Mass., 1975. (a)

Abelson, R. P. Concepts for representing mundane reality in plans. In D. G. Bobrow & A. Collins (Eds.), *Representation and understanding*. New York: Academic Press, 1975. Pp. 273–309. (b)

Abelson, R. P. Script processing in attitude formation and decision making. In J. S. Carroll & J. W. Payne (Eds.), *Cognition and social behavior*. Hillsdale, N.J.: Erlbaum, 1976. Pp. 33–45.

Abelson, R. P., & Rosenberg, M. J. Symbolic psycho-logic: A model of attitudinal cognition. *Behavioral Science*, 1958, *3*, 1–13.

Ajzen, I., & Fishbein, M. Attitude–behavior relations: A theoretical analysis and review of empirical literature. *Psychological Bulletin*, 1977, *84*, 888–918.

Anderson, J. R. *Language, memory, and thought*. Hillsdale, N.J.: Erlbaum, 1976. Pp. 33–45.

Anderson, N. H. Integration theory and attitude change. *Psychological Review*, 1971, *78*, 171–206.

Anderson, N. H. Looking for configurality in clinical judgment. *Psychological Bulletin*, 1972, *78*, 93–102.

Anderson, N. H., & Lopes, L. Some psycholinguistic aspects of person perception. *Memory and Cognition*, 1974, *2*, 67–74.

Asch, S. E. Forming impressions of personality. *Journal of Abnormal Social Psychology*, 1946, *41*, 258–290.

Ashby, W. R. *An introduction to cybernetics*. New York: Wiley, 1963.

Bem, D. An experimental analysis of self-persuasion. *Journal of Experimental Social Psychology*, 1965, *1*, 199–218.

Bem, D. Self-perception theory. In L. Berkowitz (Ed.), *Advances in experimental social psychology* (Vol. 6). New York: Academic Press, 1972. Pp. 1–62.

Bobrow, D. G., & Collins, A. (Eds.) *Representation and understanding*. New York: Academic Press, 1975.

Bransford, J. P., & McCarrell, N. S. A Sketch of a cognitive approach to comprehension: Some thoughts about understanding what it means to comprehend. In W. B. Weimer & D. S. Palermo (Eds.), *Cognition and the symbolic processes*. New York: Halstead, 1974. Pp. 189–229.

Brigham, J., & Cook, S. The influence of attitude on the recall of controversial material: A failure to confirm. *Journal of Experimental and Social Psychology*, 1969, *5*, 240–243.

Cliff, N. Adverbs as multipliers. *Psychological Review*, 1959, *66*, 27–44.

Clore, G. L., & Jeffry, K. M. Emotional role-playing, attitude change, and attraction toward a disabled person. *Journal of Personality and Social Psychology*, 1972, *23*, 105–111.

Collins, A. The trouble with memory distinctions. In R. Schank & B. L. Nash-Webber (Eds.), *Theoretical issues in natural language processing*. Proceedings of an Interdisciplinary Workshop. Cambridge, Mass., 1975. Pp. 56–58.

Collins, A. M., & Quillian, M. R. Retrieval time from semantic memory. *Journal of Verbal Learning and Verbal Behavior*, 1969, *8*, 240–247.

Conrad, C. Cognitive economy in semantic memory. *Journal of Experimental Psychology*, 1972, *92*, 149–154.

Craig, R. C. Limiting the scope of the spacial model of communication effects. *Human Communication Research*, 1977, *3*, 309–325.

Cronen, V. E., & Conville, R. E. Fishbein's conception of belief strength: A theoretical, methodological and experimental critique. *Speech Monographs*, 1975, *42*, 143–150. (a)

Cronen, V. E., & Conville, R. E. Belief salience and interpersonal evaluations: A reply to Delia, et al. *Speech Monographs*, 1975, *42*, 298–301. (b)

Culbertson, R. M. Modification of an emotionally held attitude through role playing. *Journal of Abnormal and Social Psychology*, 1957, *54*, 230–233.

Dawes, R. M., Singer, D., & Lemans, F. An experimental analysis of the contrast effect and its implications for intergroup communication and the assessment of attitudes. *Journal of Personality and Social Psychology*, 1972, *21*, 281–295.

Delia, J., Crockett, W., Press, A., & O'Keefe, D. The dependency of interpersonal evaluations on context-relevant beliefs about others. *Speech Monographs*, 1975, *42*, 10–19.

Eiser, J. R. Attitudes and the use of evaluative language: A two-way process. *Journal for the Theory of Social Behavior*, 1971, *5*, 235–248.

Fazio, R. H., & Zanna, M. P. Attitudinal qualities relating to the strength of the attitude–behavior relationship. *Journal of Experimental Social Psychology*, in press. (a)

Fazio, R. H., & Zanna, M. P. On the predictive validity of attitudes: The roles of direct experience and confidence. *Journal of Personality*, in press. (b)

Fazio, R. H., Zanna, M. P., & Cooper, J. Direct experience and attitude–behavior consistency: An information processing analysis. *Personality and Social Psychology Bulletin*, 1978, *4*, 48–51.

Fillmore, C. J. The case for case. In E. Back & R. G. Harms (Eds.), *Universals in linguistic theory*. New York: Holt, 1968.

Fishbein, M., & Ajzen, I. *Belief, attitudes, intentions and behavior: An introduction to theory and Research*. Reading, Mass.: Addison–Wesley, 1975.

Frijda, N. H. Simulation of human long-term memory. *Psychological Bulletin*, 1972, *77*, 1–31.

Goldman, A. I. *A theory of human action*. Englewood Cliffs, N.J.: Prentice-Hall, 1970.

Gragg, R. L., Nash, J. E., & Touhey, J. C. Individual differences in ratings of words combined in sentences. *Journal of Psycholinguistic Research*, 1974, *3*, 311–318.

Greenwald, A. C., & Albert, B. D. Acceptance and recall of improvised arguments. *Journal of Personality and Social Psychology*, 1968, *8*, 31–34.

Hackman, J. R., & Anderson, L. R. The strength, relevance, and source of beliefs about an object in Fishbein's attitude theory. *Journal of Social Psychology*, 1968, *76*, 55–67.

Hackman, J. R., & Morris, G. G. Group tasks, group interaction process, and group performance effectiveness: A review and proposed integration. In L. Berkowitz (Ed.), *Advances in experimental social psychology* (Vol. 8). New York: Academic Press, 1976. Pp. 45–99.

Heise, D. Semantic differential profiles for 1,000 most frequent English words. *Psychological Monographs*, 1965, *76* (8, Whole No. 601).

Heise, D. Affectual dynamics in simple sentences. *Journal of Personality and Social Psychology*, 1969, *11*, 204–213.

Howe, E. S. Probabilistic adverbial qualifications of adjectives. *Journal of Verbal Learning and Verbal Behavior*, 1963, *1*, 225–242.

Howe, E. S. Probabilistic adverbial qualifications of adjectives. *Journal of Verbal Learning and Verbal Behavior*, 1966, *5*, 147–155. (a)

Howe, E. S. Associative structure of quantifiers. *Journal of Verbal Learning and Verbal Behavior*, 1966, *5*, 156–162. (b)

Jaccard, J. J., & Fishbein, M. A. Inferential beliefs and order effects in personality impression. *Journal of Personality and Social Psychology*, 1975, *31*, 1031–1040.

Janis, I. L., & King, B. T. The influence of role playing on opinion change. *Journal of Abnormal and Social Psychology*, 1954, *49*, 211–218.

Janis, I. L., & King, B. T. Comparison of the effectiveness of improvised versus nonimprovised role playing in producing opinion change. *Human Relations*, 1956, *9*, 177–186.

Keisler, C., Collins, B., & Miller, N. *Attitude change*. New York: Wiley, 1969.

Kintsch, W. *The representation of meaning in memory*. Hillsdale, N.J.: Erlbaum, 1974.

Langer, E., & Abelson, R. P. The semantics of asking a favor: How to succeed in getting help without really dying. *Journal of Personality and Social Psychology*, 1972, *24*, 26–32.

Levanthal, H. Findings and theory in the study of fear communications. In L. Berkowitz (Ed.), *Advances in experimental social psychology* (Vol. 5). New York: Academic Press, 1970. Pp. 119–186.

Lewin, K. Intention, will and need. In D. Rapaport (Ed.), *Organization and pathology of thought*. New York: Columbia University Press, 1951.

Lilly, R. S. Multiplying values of intensive, probabilistic, and frequency adverbs when combined with potency adjectives. *Journal of Verbal Learning and Verbal Behavior*, 1968, *7*, 854–858.

Lindsay, P., & Norman, D. *Human information processing* (2nd ed.). New York: Academic Press, 1977.

Linton, M. Memory for real world events. In D. A. Norman & D. E. Rumelhart (Eds.), *Explorations in cognition*. San Francisco: Freeman, 1975. Pp. 376–404.

Maltzman, I. On the training of originality. *Psychological Review*, 1960, 67, 229–242.

McDermott, V. The development of a functional message variable: The locus of control. Paper presented at the convention of the Speech Communication Association, Chicago, December, 1974.

McGuire, W. J. The nature of attitudes and attitude change. In G. Lindzey & E. Aronson (Eds.), *The handbook of social psychology* (Vol. 3, 2nd ed.). Reading, Mass.: Addison–Wesley, 1968. Pp. 136–314.

Miller, G. The magic number seven plus or minus two: Some limits on our capacity for processing information. *Psychological Review*, 1956, *63*, 81–97.

Miller, G., Galanter, E., & Pribram, K. *Plans and the structure of behavior*. New York: Rinehart & Winston, 1960.

Newell, A. You can't play 20 questions with nature and expect to win. In W. G. Chase (Ed.), *Visual information processing*. New York: Academic Press, 1973. Pp. 283–303.

Nisbett, R. E., Borgida, E., Crandall, R., & Reed, H. Popular induction: Information is not necessarily informative. In J. S. Carroll & J. W. Payne (Eds.), *Cognition and social behavior*. Hillsdale, N.J.: Erlbaum, 1976. Pp. 113–134.

Norman, D., & Rumelhart, D. (Eds.) *Explorations in cognition*. San Francisco: Freeman, 1975.

Ortony, A. How episodic is semantic memory? In R. Schank & B. L. Nash-Webber (Eds.), *Theoretical issues in natural language processing*. Proceedings of an Interdisciplinary Workshop. Cambridge, Mass., 1975. Pp. 65–69.

Ortony, A. Remembering, understanding, and representation. *Cognitive Science*, 1978, *2*, 53–69.

Osgood, C., Suci, G., & Tannenbaum, P. *The measurement of meaning*. Urbana, Ill.: University of Illinois Press, 1957.

Paivio, A. *Imagery and verbal processes*. New York: Holt, Rinehart & Winston, 1970.

Paivio, A. Images, propositions, and knowledge. Unpublished mimeo, Department of Psychology, University of Western Ontario, 1974.

Pollio, H. R. The composition of associative clusters. *Journal of Experimental Psychology*, 1964, *67*, 199–208.

Pylyshyn, Z. What the mind's eye tells the mind's brain: A critique of mental imagery. *Psychological Bulletin*, 1973, *80*, 1–24.

Regan, D. T., & Fazio, R. On the consistency between attitudes and behavior: Look to the method of attitude formation. *Journal of Experimental Social Psychology*, 1977, *13*, 28–45.

Rieger, C. The commonsense algorithm as a basis for computer models of human memory, inference, belief and contextual language comprehension. In R. Schank & B. L. Nash-Webber (Eds.), *Theoretical issues in natural language processing.* Proceedings of an Interdisciplinary Workshop. Cambridge, Mass., 1975. Pp. 199–214.

Rieger, C. An organization of knowledge for problem solving and language comprehension. *Artificial Intelligence,* 1976, *7,* 89–127.

Rumelhart, D., Lindsay, P., & Norman, D. A process model of long-term memory. In E. Tulving & W. Donaldson (Eds.), *Organization of memory.* New York: Academic Press, 1972.

Sacks, J. S. Memory in reading and listening to discourse. *Memory and Cognition,* 1974, *2,* 95–100.

Sadler, O., & Tesser, A. Some effects of salience and time upon interpersonal hostility and attraction during social isolation. *Sociometry,* 1973, *36,* 99–112.

Santa, J. L., & Lawmers, L. L. Encoding specificity: Fact or artifact. *Journal of Verbal Learning and Verbal Behavior,* 1974, *13,* 412–423.

Santa, J. L., & Lawmers, L. L. Where does the confusion lie?: Comments on the Wiseman and Tulving paper. *Journal of Verbal Learning and Verbal Behavior,* 1976, *15,* 53–57.

Schank, R. C. Using knowledge to understand. In R. Schank & B. L. Nash-Webber (Eds.), *Theoretical issues in natural language processing.* Cambridge, Mass.: Proceedings of an Interdisciplinary Workshop 1975, Pp. 131–135.

Schank, R., & Abelson, R. P. *Scripts plans goals and understanding.* Hillsdale, N.J.: Erlbaum, 1977.

Schank, R., & Colby, K. (Eds.). *Computer models of thought and language.* San Francisco: Freeman 1973.

Schank, R., Goldman, N., Rieger, C., & Riesback, C. Primitive concepts underlying verbs of thought. Stanford University AI memo 162, 1972.

Schank, R., & Nash–Webber, B. L. (Eds.), *Theoretical issues in natural language processing.* Proceedings of an Interdisciplinary Workshop. Cambridge, Mass., 1975.

Seibold, D. Communication research and the attitude–verbal report–overt behavior relationship: A critique and theoretical reformulation. *Human Communication Research,* 1975, *2,* 1–32.

Simon, H. A. *The sciences of the artificial.* Cambridge, Mass.: MIT Press, 1969.

Simon, H. A. Discussion: Cognition and social behavior. In J. S. Carroll & J. W. Payne (Eds.), *Cognition and social behavior.* Hillsdale, N.J.: Erlbaum, 1976. Pp. 253–267.

Simon, H. A. How big is a chunk? *Science,* 1974, *183,* 482–488.

Slovic, P., & Lichtenstein, S. Comparison of Bayesian and regression approaches to the study of information processing in judgment. *Organizational behavior and human performance,* 1971, *6,* 649–744.

Slovic, P., Fischhoff, B., and Lichtenstein, L. Cognitive processes and societal risk-taking. In J. S. Carroll & J. W. Payne (Eds.), *Cognition and social behavior.* Hillsdale, N.J.: Erlbaum, 1976. Pp. 165–184.

Staats, A. W., & Staats, C. K. Meaning and m: Correlated but separate. *Psychological Review,* 1959, *66,* 136–144.

Tesser, A. Thought and reality constraints as determinants of attitude polarization. *Journal of Research in Personality,* 1976, *10,* 183–194.

Tesser, A. Self-generated attitude change. In L. Berkowitz (Ed.), *Advances in experimental social psychology* (Vol. 11). New York: Academic Press, 1978. Pp. 289–338.

Tesser, A., & Cowan, C. L. Some effects of thought and number of cognitions on attitude change. *Social Behavior and Personality,* 1975, *3,* 165–173.

Tesser, A., & Dannheiser, P. Anticipated relationship, salience of partner, and attitude change. *Personality and Social Psychology Bulletin,* 1978, *4,* 35–38.

Tesser, A., & Leone, C. Cognitive schemas and thought as determinants of attitude change. *Journal of Experimental Social Psychology,* 1977, *13,* 340–356.

Thomsen, D. M., & Tulving, E. Associative encoding and retrieval: Weak and strong cues. *Journal of Experimental Psychology,* 1970, *86,* 255–262.

Tulving, E. Episodic and semantic memory. In E. Tulving & W. Donaldson (Eds.), *Organization of memory.* New York: Academic Press, 1972.

Tulving, E., and Donaldson, W. (Eds.) *Organization of memory.* New York: Academic Press, 1972.

Tulving, E., & Thomson, D. M. Encoding specificity and retrieval processes in episodic memory. *Psychological Review,* 1973, *80,* 352–372.

Tulving, E., and Olser, S. Effectiveness of retrieval cues in memory for words. *Journal of Experimental Psychology,* 1968, *77,* 593–601.

Tversky, A., & Kahneman, D. Availability: A heuristic for judging frequency and probability. *Cognitive psychology,* 1973, *5,* 207–232.

Tversky, A., & Kahneman, D. Judgment under uncertainty: Heuristics and biases. *Science,* 1974, *185,* 1124–1131.

Van Dijk, T. A. Semantic macrostructures and knowledge frames in discourse comprehension. In M. A. Just & P. A. Carpenter (Eds.), *Cognitive processes in comprehension.* Hillsdale, N.J.: Erlbaum, 1977. Pp. 3–32.

Watkins, M. J., and Tulving, E. Episodic memory: When recognition fails. *Journal of Experimental Psychology. General,* 1975, *104,* 5–29.

Winograd, T. *Understanding natural language.* New York: Academic Press, 1972.

Winograd, T. Frame representations and the declarative procedural controversy. In D. G. Bobrow & A. Collins (Eds.), *Representation and understanding.* New York: Academic Press, 1975. Pp. 185–210.

Wyer, R. S. *Cognitive organization and change: An information processing approach.* New York: Wiley, 1974.

Zanna, M. P., & Fazio, R. H. Direct experience and attitude–behavior consistency. Paper presented to American Psychological Association, San Francisco, 1977.

6

Attitude–Verbal Report–Behavior Relationships as Causal Processes: Formalization, Test, and Communication Implications

DAVID R. SEIBOLD

Overview

To say that interpersonal influence can affect psychological and behavioral change is to utter a commonplace. But the concept "influence" is scopic. It connotes tactics ranging from coercion to altruistic appeals, and it circumscribes responses including moral internalization and mere imitation. Communication theorists traditionally have focused on persuasion as a vehicle for social influence.[1] Persuasion involves reinforcement or change, in the direction and degree advocated, in others' "mental states" (e.g., affective reactions, beliefs, behavioral tendencies) and associated "overt acts" (e.g., statements reflecting concurrence or related nonverbal behavioral compliance). Theorists have therefore assumed that the optimal targets for persuasive messages are listeners' mental states *and* behavioral manifestations if both agreement and accordance are sought.

---

[1] Some reviewers have lamented this emphasis on persuasion as communicative influence. See Simons' (1971) position and a more recent statement by Miller and Burgoon (1978).

MESSAGE–ATTITUDE–BEHAVIOR RELATIONSHIP
Theory, Methodology, and Applications

The interrelationships within and between these influence foci have not received research attention commensurate with their significance, however. Investigations of message factors, source characteristics, receiver traits, and channel considerations have predominated. Effects of these variables rarely have been measured in terms of reinforcement or change in overt actions, for behavioral assessment has proved costly and time consuming (Chaffee & Linder, 1969). Despite admonishments (Cronkhite, 1969; Hewes, 1975; Miller, 1967), investigators simply have relied on verbal reports of affect, beliefs, or planned acts as psychological state indicants and as measures of persuasive impact. Authors reporting persuasion research imply that verbal reports are substitutable for related physical acts. Similarly, postmessage change in verbal reports is presumed to signal behavioral change. This is not surprising, for (a) since attitude is usually conceptualized as a predisposition to respond evaluatively toward some perceived object in a consistent manner (Campbell, 1963); and (b) because researchers have relied on an assumed stability of the construct to explain the consistency of favorable or unfavorable actions toward an object (DeFleur & Westie, 1963); then (c) a "logical expectation" also has developed that verbal reports of attitudes and overt, nonverbal behaviors should be closely related if the same attitude referent is involved (Ajzen & Fishbein, 1977).

Issues

Communication researchers have not fully come to terms with one aspect of verbal report–overt act relationships: Logical expectations withstanding, there are various degrees of empirical correspondence between what persons report they feel, or think, or anticipate doing with regard to someone or something, and how they otherwise act in relation to that person or object. Phrases like "Practice what you preach," Talk is cheap," and "Do as I say, not as I do" evidence popular recognition that deeds are not isomorphic with verbal indications of related mental states. Within academe, research has revealed low to strong associations between political attitudes and voting (Jackman, 1976; Kelly & Mirer, 1974; Kimsey & Atwood, 1979); work attitudes and job-related behaviors (Herman, 1973; Schwab & Cummings, 1970; Smith, 1977); prejudicial attitudes and discriminatory acts (Green, 1972); consumer attitudes and behaviors (Bearden & Woodside, 1977; Bonfield, 1974; Katoma, 1975; Warland, Hermann & Willits, 1975); health attitudes and preventative or compliant acts, (Seibold & Roper, 1979); and verbal report–behavior relationships throughout applied and theoretical social psychology research (cf. reviews by Ajzen & Fishbein, 1977; Eagly & Himmelfarb, 1978; Schuman & Johnson, 1976).[2] Social scientists from many disciplines have successively

---

[2] The studies cited are merely recent examples of theory and research on the "attitude–behavior" relationship. A comprehensive bibliography of scholarly work in this area is provided by Seibold and Roper (1980).

rediscovered the issue of empirical correspondence between attitude indicators and actions, characterizing it as "the attitude–behavior problem" (Deutscher, 1973) and generating a "consistency controversy" (Liska, 1975).

Nor have these fields provided definitive answers for persuasion researchers concerned with the dynamics of communicative influence and appropriate "impact" measures. Theoretical discussions and empirical investigations sometimes have failed to address, or have blurred, fundamental issues and distinctions. To illustrate, the attitude–behavior problem involves two issues that are rarely distinguished: (a) the adequacy of verbal reports for the *prediction* of behaviors (i.e., how confidently can we anticipate action from verbal evidence of presumably related mental states?); and (b) the level of *consistency* between attitudinal reports and actions (i.e., what type of association, literally and in correlational terms, should we expect between some verbal report of attitude and some other measure of overt, nonverbal behavior?) Failure to find evidence for the high predictive value of certain types of attitude reports in relation to certain types of behaviors (Wicker, 1969) has led many to conclude that no relationship (consistency) exists between attitude reports and deeds or, by extension, between underlying attitudes and action. In turn, this has undermined confidence in the utility of the attitude construct (Miller, Afterword to this volume) and may have precipitated movement away from persuasion–attitude research to the current "interpersonal behavior" paradigm in communication research.

The bedrock of a science of communicative influence, whether persuasion or more interpersonal factors, will be answers to the following questions, for these issues form the nexus of message–attitude–behavior relationships. From the standpoint of explaining induced behaviors, is it necessary and/or useful to think of persons as having underlying mental states concerning those behaviors? If so, what psychological constituents should be conceptualized, and how are they theoretically related? What are the verbal report counterparts to these mental state components (stated technically, how may they be operationalized validly and reliably)? Should we expect isomorphism between thought and verbal report? If not, what factors diminish the verisimilitude of verbal reports as representations of mental states? Do the same factors moderating verbal expressions of internal states also affect instantiation of related physical acts, or are the psychological antecedents to action different? What relationships may be theorized among underlying attitudinal states, verbal reports, and overt acts? In particular, how shall the relationship between attitude reports and other behaviors be conceptualized, and how can the relationship be tested? Do the same factors able to vitiate correspondence between underlying attitudes and verbal reports also (a) affect prediction of behaviors from those reports; and (b) diminish report–behavior consistency, or must we identify potentially different groups of "other variables" intervening in the underlying attitude–verbal report–overt behavior relationship? What organizing perspective can be used to develop theory in this area, and what are the methodological considerations attendant to a particular theory form? Ultimately, how do persuasive messages affect the relationships described so far and with what effects? The breadth and complexity of these questions suggest that (*a*) the notion of an attitude–behavior problem is, at least, a simplication and could be erroneous failing recognition of these distinctions; and (*b*) answering these questions is necessary even as we investigate communication effects on attitudes and behaviors.

Definitions

Having raised these questions and distinctions, several preliminary definitions are in order. More precise definitions will emerge from specific discussion of these concepts throughout the chapter. For now, *attitude* shall refer to a construct describing a particular psychological state persons may have with regard to social stimuli. This state involves a predisposition to respond, in an evaluative sense, toward perceived persons and objects. In turn, the basically positive or negative internal evaluation(s) will be reflected in individuals' feelings, beliefs, or behavioral tendencies toward the object of orientation. Hence, an attitude is an underlying, latent psychological state with affective, cognitive, and conative components, though I will ignore for now the nature of these attitudinal constituents and their interrelationships. *Verbal reports* are oral or written responses to attempts to measure attitudes via questionnaires or interviews and associated scaling techniques. Attitudes as "true" states are therefore to be distinguished from manifestations of these underlying states via verbal statements. *Behavior* circumscribes all overt acts not elicited via verbal reports but presumed to be related to the underlying attitude. *Communication* encompasses the processes and behaviors of persons involved in the creation and negotiation of meaning through the use of shared symbols. Messages, manifestations of mental and behavioral symbol manipulation, are vehicles for transacting communication, their purpose and function being to enable interactants to achieve shared meanings. *Persuasion* is a species of communication directed at personal influence through messages designed to demonstrate how some object of coorientation should "mean." Thus, persuasion as influence entails the use of messages designed to reinforce or change others' attitudes, and ultimately their behaviors, through the effects that coincident meanings (with the source) will have on receivers' evaluative feelings, beliefs, or predispositions with regard to the message topic.

A distinction between verbal report–overt behavior "prediction" and "consistency" has been offered, but the notion of *consistency* warrants clarification. Schuman and Johnson (1976) have distinguished "between literal consistency (do people do what they say they will do?) and correlational consistency (are people ordered in the same way on both attitude and behavior measures?) [p. 164]." Literal consistency is important to persuaders, concerned as they are with demonstrating that persons will do something if they say they will (Miller,

1968). Failing isomorphism, the degree to which attitude reports and actions are statistically correlated will be important, in part for predictive reasons but also for what such findings may reveal about potential consistency. Paltry contributions to charity may not correlate perfectly with attitudes toward the act of contributing (Fishbein & Ajzen, 1975) and even less so with attitudes toward charitable contributions in general, but neither correlation should imply meaningful inconsistency. Such may be instances of "pseudoinconsistency," in which literal inconsistency inferences have been confounded with correlational inconsistency produced by "threshold" differences associated with each variable measured (Campbell, 1963) or the mediating effects of "other variables" (Wicker, 1969). *Other variables* are specific factors, other than those theorized to be endemic to the underlying attitude–verbal report–overt behavior process, assumed or shown to affect verbal reports, overt behaviors, or the relationships between them.

Plan

From the communication discipline's standpoint, answers to the questions (pp. 197–198) are theoretically, methodologically, and pragmatically vital. If persuasion theories posit effects of different classes of message variables on psychological and behavioral targets, then explanatory power and predictive utility demand careful specification of the relationships among these potential influence foci. Too, insofar as the questions remain unanswered, and as long as doubts about attitudes as epiphenomena persist, social action generalizations about compliance from previous "attitude studies" remain suspect. Second, since attitudinal measures are so frequently used in the communication field and in laboratory research, delineation of the conditions under which such measures will be associated with related behaviors should delimit the confidence that can be placed in interview and paper–pencil protocols. Finally, and practically speaking, answers to the questions raised may aid in the development of efficacious persuasive communication strategies.

For these reasons, development and test of communication-related theory of attitude–verbal report–behavior relationships is undertaken in this chapter. Elsewhere I have discussed metatheoretical concerns related to message–attitude–behavior relationships (Seibold, 1976); theoretical bases for empirical research in this area (Seibold, 1975a); methodological procedures germane to interpreting attitude–behavior relationships, including approaches to the decomposition of explained variance in multiple regression analyses involving attitudinal predictors (McPhee & Seibold, 1979a; Seibold & McPhee, 1979a) and strategies for testing alternative sources of change in attitudes and behaviors (McPhee & Seibold, 1979a); and empirical issues, such as comparison of specific attitude–behavior models (Seibold & Roper, 1979), longitudinal test of several genres of attitude–behavior models (Seibold & McPhee, 1979b), and test of moderators of attitude–behavior relationships (Seibold, 1979). The present effort is synthetic insofar as many of these papers are tied together here and given greater coherence. But this chapter also represents a retrenchment (in dealing with the more fundamental questions posed to this point), and an extension (in empirically testing the theory proposed, and in discussing communication implications).

The remainder of the chapter is divided into three parts. The bases for interpreting message–attitude–behavior relationships as causal processes are detailed in the following section, and the groundwork is laid for the logical and empirical causal process theory construction that succeeds it. Following a review of empirical research on attitude–action and message–attitude–behavior relationships, I propose a specific causal model and report research results pertinent to its adequacy. Implications of these findings for persuasion are discussed in the final pages.

Causal Process Theories

Significance and Definition of Theory

Clarion calls for the development of communication "theory" are coincident with empirical communication research (Winans, 1915; Woolbert, 1918). The advantages accruing to theory-based research stem from the specific functions that theory performs: (a) description, classification, and analysis of phenomena; (b) specification of meaning domains and rules of inference; (c) identification and interpretation of logical and empirical relationships among phenomena; (d) elimination of inconsistency among theoretical statements; (e) specification of the bases for measurement and testability of the theory; and, (f) indication of alternative explanatory positions. Hage (1972) discusses four criteria for evaluating how well such functions are met: theoretical scope, predictive utility, explanatory accuracy, and parsimony.[3]

Until lately, lack of integrative and predicitive theory has prelimited understanding attitude–report–act relationships (Eagly & Himmelfarb, 1978). Diverse findings regarding report–act consistency were usually explained by recourse to atheoretical accounts (measurement invalidity, methodological flaws in design and sampling, illogical inferences by researchers, and so forth). Recently, cogent explanations for attitude–report–behavior relationships have been supplied by sociological and psychological theorists concerned with cognitive antededents to social behavior (Ajzen & Fishbein, 1977; Fishbein & Ajzen, 1975; Triandis, 1977, 1979) and the contingent consistency postulate

---

[3] See Pepper (1942) for an alternative position on criteria for the adequacy of theory, especially the argument that criteria for structural corroboration are developed in "world hypotheses (pp. 47–82)."

(Warner & DeFleur, 1969). Also theoretical but restricted in scope, less parsimonious, or limited in the directionality of attitude–behavior relationships
discussed have been studies emmanating from dissonance theory (Wicklund &
Brehm, 1976), self-perception theory (Bem, 1968), balance theory (Insko,
Worschel, Folger, & Kutkins, 1975) and the newer response contagion (Nuttin,
1975) and self-monitoring (Snyder & Tanke, 1976) theories. Communication
theorists usually have ignored attitude–behavior relationships, treated the issue
summarily (Cronkhite, 1969), or based discussions on others' theories (cf.
Burhans, 1971; Miller, 1967; Steinfatt & Infante, 1976). A notable exception is
an article by Larson & Sanders (1975), but it is problematic in other respects
(Steinfatt & Infante, 1976).

The discussion thus far begs more basic questions: What is theory?; What
forms may theories take?; How are theories (particularly causal process
theories) formalized and tested? The focus of this chapter limits response to
these questions, and I have treated them in more detail before (Seibold, 1976).
With regard to the first question, however, I shall consider a *theory* to be a set
of statements which (*a*) precisely specify causal relationships among constructs;
(*b*) are nonspatially and nontemporally bound; (*c*) are testable, refutable, and
capable of systemmatic alteration; (*d*) are nontautological; and (*e*) are related
and organized by the presence of some unifying principle(s). Elements of this
definition will receive detailed treatment when I discuss formalization of
attitude–behavior relationships as causal processes. For now, I wish to return
to the second question posed earlier: What forms may theory take?

Theory Types

It has been fashionable to distinguish among three theory types in communication research: "classical" (laws), "systems," and "rules" (Cushman,
1977). This trichotomy is defended by recourse to the types of explanatory
necessity assumed to be inherent in each: nomic necessity for laws, logical
necessity for systems, and practical necessity for rules (Cushman & Pearce,
1977). Within this framework further species-specific structures have emerged.
For example, Monge (1973, 1977) has delineated several variants of system
theory: structural functionalism, cybernetics, and general systems. Cushman
and Pearce (1977) have explicated alternative positions within the rules perspective: linguistic, analytic, and evolutionary. And, within the classical rubric,
McDermott (1975) has identified three subforms: set-of-laws, axiomatic, and
causal process.

By this accounting, the causal process theory to be proposed in this chapter
complements Woelfel's (Chapter 3, this volume) set-of-laws theory and Hewes'
(Chapter 2, this volume) axiomatic formulation as a third type of "laws" formulation. But these chapters may be more compatible by virtue of labels
affixed from the prevailing metatheory trichotomy than by virtue of common

characteristics. The truism that things are never as simple as they appear to be is veridical threefold in this case. First, the trichotomy rests upon an assumed independence of explanatory modes associated with each theory type, a presumption that is tenuous. Cronen and Davis (1978) have shown that, whereas laws approaches inherently assert nomic necessity, systems perspectives are not restricted to logical necessity as an explanatory mode, and rules perspectives may involve logical as well as practical necessity justifications. Moreover, practical necessity accounts may be lodged in factors other than rules. The efforts of Fishbein and Ajzen (1975) and Triandis (1977) to account for the psychological antecedents to conation are illustrative in this regard. Both propose lawlike formulae concerning the relationship between attitudinal and social factors with behavioral intentions, but root these statements about cognitive mechanisms in the practical force of (*a*) normative pressures, on the theoretical level; and (*b*) at the empirical level, variable regression weights associated with each antecedent.

A second problem with casting causal process theories within the meta-theoretical confines of the "laws" prespective is that causal process theories often have features more similar to systems theory, especially cybernetics. For example, Reynolds (1971) at once distinguishes causal process theory from classical theory and underscores a systems theory characteristic (i.e., "process") when he states: "The major difference between causal theory and the axiomatic form is that all statements are considered to be of equal importance, they are not classified into axioms and propositions, and the statements are presented in a different fashion, as a causal process [p. 97]." And, like systems theories, the explanatory power of this mode of theory formalization stems from the greater "understanding" it provides when an entire process of relationships has been time sequenced, and the causal, generative mechanism(s) underlying the process fully explicated.

Finally, comparing causal process theories to either systems or laws perspectives ignores the potential conceptual richness, heuristic utility, and precision attendant to this theory mode. Following Reynolds (1971) and McDermott (1975), the essential features of causal process theories are these:

1. A set of existence statements that delineate "scope conditions" within which the causal process is expected to operate.
2. A set of causal statements that describe one or more causal mechanisms and that identify the effect of one or more exogenous variables.
3. Although different causal mechanisms may have different impact on the dependent variables, all propositions are considered to be of equal importance within the theory.
4. All propositions must reflect causal relationships.
5. Not all propositions in the chain need be tested or directly testable (i.e., in isolation from the rest of the causal process).

Several issues implicit in this scheme are significant for constructing attitude–behavior theories and treating message effects: causal mechanisms, the viability of causal explanations in this area, and how causal process theories may be tested. Consideration of these concerns in the remainder of this section will provide the groundwork for the underlying attitude–verbal report–overt behavior causal process theory to be described in the next section of this chapter. Explication of the metatheoretical bases for the following comments, including treatment of causality and causal inferences, causal statements, and causal explanations may be found in Seibold (1976).

Attitude–Behavior Relationships as Causal Processes

Theory and research on attitude–behavior relationships reflect diversity in differing assumptions about causality, causal explanations, and the nature of attitudes as generative mechanisms. While no attitude–behavior theorist appears to have ruled out the principle of causality, those researchers who have adopted a learning theory perspective (Doob, 1947; Lott, 1955; Staats, 1964) are characteristic of one approach arguing that causality cannot be apprehended or definitively demonstrated (Seibold, 1976). Thus attitude–behavior relationships are best viewed as "associations" in much the same way that both are learned implicit or explicit associations with stimuli. Too, attitudes are not treated as generative mechanisms by these conventionalists (Achinstein, 1971; Cushman, 1977) who rely instead on the nomological force of hierarchical classical conditioning (Staats, 1968), instrumental conditioning (Lott & Lott, 1968), and mediating generalization (Lott, 1955).

In contrast, others have systematically treated attitudes as generative mechanisms for behaviors and have offered commensurate causal accounts of social behaviors. A noteworthy example is the causal process described by social psychologist Martin Fishbein and colleagues. While attitudes (summated, conditioned evaluative responses) are rooted in learned beliefs (Fishbein, 1963), only attitudes toward the behaviors in question are proposed to have a generative force on intention and then only indirectly:

> According to our conceptual framework, a person's intentions, in the final analysis, are a function of certain beliefs. Rather than being beliefs about the object of the behavior however, the relevant beliefs are concerned with the behavior itself. Some of these beliefs influence the person's attitude toward the behavior. Specifically, his attitude toward performing a given behavior is related to his beliefs that performing behavior will lead to certain consequences and his evaluation of those consequences. This attitude is viewed as one major determinant of the person's intention to perform the behavior in question [Fishbein & Ajzen, 1975, p. 16].

Fishbein and Ajzen go on to propose that, in similar cognition–attitude–conation fashion, behavioral intentions may be affected by the practical force of normative beliefs (i.e., the perceived expectations of significant others). Intention to act, in turn, is posited to be causally related to action when volitional, stable, and measured at the same level of specificity as the behavior.

Implicit in these examples, and a basic question for the relevance of causal process formalization to attitude–behavior relationships, is whether or not attitudes can stand in causal relationships to behaviors routinely explained by and predicted from them. There are epistemological, theoretical, axiological, and methodological facets to this issue.

Philosophical Issues

Most fundamental is the philosophical tenableness of attitudinal causality. Some writers argue against mental states as "causes" of action (Anscombe, 1958; Melden, 1961; Taylor, 1964); others contend that such causal relationships are warrantable (Alston, 1967; Audi, 1972; Davidson, 1963; McClelland, 1975; von Wright, 1971). A persuasive defense is supplied by Goldman (1970) in developing a theory of human action. A central tenet of the theory is an analysis of intentional action in terms of want-and-belief causation (a quality Goldman ties to a number of psychological constructs including attitudes). Goldman's position is germane to this discussion (and the theory proposed) insofar as he demonstrates that (a) social action can best be understood as a process; it is (b) both a hierarchy of act types and a generative chain of causal factors; (c) wants and beliefs (read "attitudes") are included as key elements in the process: (d) they are mediators of behaviors to the extent that wants and beliefs are themselves causally generated (by memory, perceptions, communications, other beliefs, and so forth). Furthermore, Goldman argues that the notion of interpersonal causation he proposes: (a) does not imply universalism nor await the discovery of precise universal laws, but is defensible as a common sense notion and for its nomological force (owing to practical inference, purposeful explanation, and potential probablistic laws); (b) can accord both agent- and event-causation; (c) may place attitudes into logical relationship with behaviors while not precluding the existence of a contingent causal relationship; and (d) is sufficiently general as to apply to most behavioral science theories of social action.

Theoretical Issues

If causal process interpretations of attitude–behavior relationships are philosophically defensible, do theory and research in the area admit causal explanation? That they do is evident from several perspectives. First, even when causality is not explicitly discussed, theorists *imply* a causal attitude–behavior link when they embed attitudes in a larger causal process involving both antecedents to cognition and behavioral outcomes (see Fishbein & Ajzen,

1975; Ch. 2 for a review of these positions). Second, arguments about the "directionality" of attitude–behavior relationships presuppose causality but evidence differences concerning which element is causal: Attitudes influence behaviors (Schuman & Johnson, 1976); behaviors affect attitudes (Festinger, 1957); they are reciprocally causal (Kelman, 1974); attitude–behavior consistency may be constrained by other variables which affect attitudes and behaviors simultaneously (Wicker, 1969), or upon which both are "contingent" (Andrews & Kandel, 1979). Finally, treatments of general versus specific (Heberlein & Black, 1976, p. 479) and underlying versus measured attitudes (Schuman & Johnson, 1976, p. 198) have explicitly invoked the notion of "cause" in theoretically depicting attitudinal effects on behaviors. Like many social scientists who "extrapolate" (McClelland, 1975) the notion of causality from instances where it is easily inferred to other situations involving "hidden variables" (Cohen & Nagel, 1934), theorists concerned with attitude–behavior relationships frequently treat attitudes as latent, causal, *generative* mechanisms (Harré, 1970). Rarely met, however, are the two conditions for causal accounts suggesting the operation of generative mechanisms: (*a*) explication of the scope conditions for the cause–effect relationships proposed; and (*b*) description of the mechanism and process by which the effect is generated from the cause. The theory proposed will be explicit in both regards.

Axiological Issues

All this is not to say that causal accounts can be given with equanimity. Viewing attitudes as causal forces is axiologically troublesome to the humane scientist. Causal accounts of human behaviors seem overly mechanistic, positivistic, and deterministic—qualities that do not jibe with many observers' values (Dunnette, 1966; O'Keefe, 1975; Ring, 1972; Walsh, 1972). None of this discussion should imply that causal explanations of attitude–behavior relationships entail assertion of such "strong" causality. Rather, the notions of causality and process can be used heuristically and analogically to vitiate traditional arguments and to accrue the following advantages. First, theorizing about attitude–behavior relationships in causal terms is consistent with commonsense notions, for routinely we attribute the "causes" of others' behavior to their attitudes. Second, discomfort with the application of causal accounts to attitude–behavior relationships has resulted from discussions of them as solely predetermining, rather than as explanations of and contingent with social behaviors. Third, causal process theories in this area need not entail the operation of universal laws as if deterministic. As Goldman (1970) remarks, "Knowledge of precise laws is not necessary to justify the statement that wants and beliefs *cause* acts (since) most of our knowledge of singular causal propositions is not based on knowledge of precise causal laws [p. 72]." Instead, theories in this area may depict the causal force of attitudes (and other generative mechanisms) in nondeterministic and contingent causal process formulations.

Methodological Issues

The methodological facet of causal process formalization of attitude–behavior relationships turns on the empirics underlying causal inferences, how causal relationships can be specified so as to be testable, and the requirements for causal modeling.

Tests of causal process theories hinge on causal inferences. As I have suggested before (Seibold, 1976), these inferences rest on careful a priori conceptualizations and on empirical bases related to variability, covariation, directionality, temporal ordering, and control. First, cause and effect variables must vary sufficiently to permit inference of conjunction. Second, we must theoretically expect and observe covariation among all variables presumed to be related in the causal process system. How these variables are causally related must also be specified beforehand, and will be discussed in the following pages. Third, the direction of causality in the relationship must be ascertainable theoretically and empirically. Even in instances of reciprocal causation (nonrecursive systems) it is vital, fourth, to identify the time ordering of variables, for causal inferences are premised on the assumption that "events are not caused by other events that occur later in time [Heise, 1969, p. 52]." Finally, other variables, which could affect and account for observed covariation, must be controlled. By these criteria, if it can be assumed and demonstrated that cause and effect variables covary and occur in the order theorized, and that confounding factors have been physically or statistically controlled, a strong causal inference is possible.

Experimental methods elevate the certainty with which Mill's canons of causality (agreement, differences, and concommitant variation) can be used to infer the existence of causality. Even in these instances, however, "constant conjunction is only *prima facie* evidence for asserting that there is a causal relation between event-pairs, and, at best, can be a necessary condition for causality [Harré, 1970; p. 105]" if complete description of the generative process remains unconfirmed. In nonexperimental research, causal inference is more difficult. Pelz and Andrews (1964) and Duncan (1969) developed cross-lagged correlational techniques for detecting causal priority in nonexperimental panel data, but these have been criticized and supplanted by Heise's (1970) path analytic procedure. Path analysis, as a type of causal analysis permitting test of models that propose causal relationships (or paths) among variables in a system based on their intercorrelations and time ordering, is a methodology concordant with the causal process mode of theory formalization set forth in this chapter.[4] Path analysis also is particularly applicable for testing attitude–behavior processes to the extent that there is usually strong *a priori* theory about the causal patterning among a multiplicity of endogenous variables (affect, belief,

---

[4] The literature on path analysis is now widespread, and informative treatments are supplied in Blalock (1971), Cappella (1975b), Duncan (1975), and Goldberger and Duncan (1973).

intentions, perceived norms, perceived situational constraints, behaviors)—including unmeasured variables such as underlying attitudes. Finally, path analysis facilitates causal inferences in several respects. First, causal modeling demands a priori consideration of temporal ordering among variables found to covary. Since the timing of variables has not been experimentally controlled, this theoretical rationale is vital. Without it, correlational data reflecting interrelationships in a system would be insufficient to justify causal inferences about particular relationships, especially in the face of the many possible causal structures that could be drawn from the correlations. Second, careful consideration is given to the model's residuals (reflecting disturbances, or errors of measurement and errors in equations due to misspecifications in the model). The correlations among these residuals provide a key control over causal inference to the extent that high correlations among residuals may point to a specious relationship caused by unmeasured influences from outside the system. Hence, if covariation exists between two variables occurring in theoretically dictated order of cause-then-effect, and if their residuals can be assumed or shown to be uncorrelated, a strong causal inference can be made. The magnitude of the causal impact is represented by the size of the path coefficient, representing the effect of a causal variable on a dependent variable in unit changes with all remaining variables in the model held (statistically) constant. The remainder of this discussion emphasizes causal inference in nonexperimental research, since most causal modeling (including that reported in the following section is performed with nonexperimental data.

To say there is a causal relationship between attitudes and behaviors does not exhaust what can and must be said in fully specifying the theoretical relationship between them. For the directionality, probableness, time ordering, sufficiency, and necessity of their relationship must be explicated if the theory is to be precise and testable. It may be, for example, that there are forces competing with or intervening between attitudinal effects on behaviors (and vice versa), and it may be that attitudes stand in some substitutable, or contingent, or sequential relationship to those elements of the causal process. Some procedure must be employed for specifying these dimensions of variable relationships (and their "paths" in derived causal models). Zetterberg's (1965) scheme facilitates specification of both logical and empirical linkages, and aids in bridging them to causal modeling methods.[5] Zetterberg proposes that relational propositions (including causal statements) may be depicted as:

1. *Reversible* (if X then Y; and if Y then X) or *irreversible* (if X then Y; but if Y then no conclusion about X)
2. *Deterministic* (if X then always Y) or *stochastic* (if X then probably Y)
3. *Sequential* (if X then later Y); *coextensive* (if X then also Y)

---

[5] Different views on formalizing propositions adequate for causal modeling are offered by Bailey (1970), Blalock (1969), and Costner and Leik (1964).

4. *Sufficient* (if X then Y regardless of anything else) or *contingent* (if X then Y but only if Z)
5. *Necessary* (if X, and only if X, then Y) or *substitutable* (if X then Y, but if Z then also Y)

The utility of this scheme for transforming assumptions about attitude–behavior processes into propositions capable of being modeled and tested will be demonstrated with the theory proposed.

Finally, the requirements for modeling causal process systems are germane to specification of attitude–behavior theories. As summarized by Cappella (1975b), the logical assumptions for recursive and nonrecursive systems are these:

1. Cause and effect relations are linear
2. Undebatable temporal priority among variables
3. Structure of the system does not change over time
4. Exogenous (independent) and disturbance (residual) variables are uncorrelated. For recursive systems it is also assumed that residuals are uncorrelated with each other and that mutual causal linkages among endogenous variables are ruled out
5. There is no measurement error

The *empirical* assumptions for recursive and nonrecursive systems are these:

1. Interval or ratio level data for the endogenous (dependent) variables
2. The assumptions of multivariate linear regression hold (e.g. homogeneity of variance, no multicolinearity, no autocorrelation)

To the extent that these assumptions are met, causal modeling can proceed. Of course serious violation of any assumption, especially violations of level of measurement, theoretical time ordering, and system instability, are damaging to path analyses (Cappella, 1975b). When appropriately performed, path analysis yields causal inferences about particular relationships and, via goodness-of-fit tests, information about the extent to which the entire hypothesized causal structure "fits" the data.

Causal Process Formalization

Perhaps the best way to conclude this prefatory discussion is to review the steps that a causal process theorist follows in constructing and testing causal models. The starting point is one's "theory" identifying the causal patterning among relevant exogenous and all endogenous variables. As Cappella (1975b) has observed, "If there is one characteristic which this review has emphasized as characteristic of causal modeling, it is that causal modeling cannot be undertaken without sound theory to guide it [p. 369]." Presumably intuition, extant theory, and previous research have guided one through the inventional steps of theory construction: (a) the reasonableness of causal accounts in this problem area; (b) explication of the generative mechanism(s) underlying the causal process and identification of all variables within the system; (c) delineation of the scope conditions for application of the theory; and (d) complete specification of all relationships in the causal process in the form of testable propositions. The theorist then makes operational the theoretical structure reflected in these propositions. This may first involve pictorial simulation of the process (e.g., a path analysis diagram), but ultimately involves simulating the system with a set of equations that fully represent the theory's assumptions, relationships, and paths of influence. The model then is tested against empirical data by means of certain logical and statistical tests. Such tests permit inferences of whether the constraints imposed by the theory on the data are invalid or permissible. If permissible, there still may be considerable latitude in the correctness of the model, and revision may range from slight modification of particular causal paths in the model to more complete model-fitting. In short, statistical support for the model only implies that the model has not been falsified; there may be other models which suitably explain patterns in the data. Finally, the theorist works at expanding the scope of the successful model to account for larger causal processes in the hierarchy of natural events (macroanalysis) and at detailing more specifically the nature of the generative mechanism underlying the causal process (microanalysis). As suggestive of these procedures, I turn now to formalization and test of a communication related attitude–verbal report–behavior causal model.

A Causal Process Theory of Attitude–Verbal Report–Behavior Relationships

Review

Empirical findings provide equivocal support for a twofold presumption of persuasion theory: If attitudes are related to behaviors, then induced attitude change should also produce behavioral change (Burhans, 1971). Relevant studies may be divided into (a) traditional research on the relationship between verbal reports and behaviors, studies which involve no message variables; and (b) research assessing message effects on attitude reports and behaviors.

Verbal Report–Behavior Studies

Many writers since LaPiere (1934) have rejected the natural necessity of attitude–behavior consistency, primarily on account of studies reporting weak prediction from verbal reports to behaviors. Wicker (1969) reviewed 46 studies and concluded:

> These studies suggest that it is considerably more likely that attitudes will be unrelated or only slightly related to overt behaviors than that attitudes will be closely related to actions. Product–moment correlation coefficients relating the two kinds of responses are rarely above .30 and often are near zero. Only rarely can as much as 10 percent of the variance in behavioral measures be accounted for by attitudinal data [p. 65].

Vroom's (1964) survey of 15 studies revealed that job attitudes had only a slight relationship with behavioral criteria such as productivity and absenteeism. Ethnic attitudes were poor predictors of overt discrimination in 14 studies reviewed by Ehrlich (1969). DeFleur and Westie (1963) proposed that researchers assuming consistency between verbal reports and overt acts demonstrated the "fallacy of expected correspondence." Greenwald (1965) concluded, "Our safest hypothesis as to the relationship between belief and behavior is that there is, in fact, no relationship; rather belief and behavior may be independently determined by the environment [p. 600]." Deutscher (1966) documented inconsistencies between attitudes and behaviors in widely disparate areas. He opined that "no matter what one's theoretical orientation may be, he has no reason to expect to find congruence between attitudes and actions and every reason to expect to find discrepancy between them [p. 247]." Three arguments implicit in these reviews have been distilled by Alwin (1973): (*a*) underlying attitudes are not stable; (*b*) verbal reports are not necessarily valid measures of underlying attitudes; and (*c*) neither underlying nor verbalized attitudes are sufficient determinants of behavior, thereby weakening their explanatory power and predictive utility as well as the logical necessity of verbal report–overt behavior consistency. Despite flaws in the conclusions drawn by some of these reviewers (cf. analyses by Dillehay, 1973; Fishbein & Ajzen, 1975, pp. 339–361; and Schuman & Johnson, 1976, pp. 162, 183), "theoretical despond" prevailed, and the utility of the general attitude construct became suspect (Abelson, 1972).

Not all reviews in the area have been so despondent. Campbell (1963) assured that the exact nature of the relationship between attitudes and behaviors had not been discovered. Ehrlich (1969) tendered that research in the area was equivocal, and that there were no valid conceptual or methodological grounds to argue for no relationship between attitudes and acts. Even Deutscher (1973) relaxed his stance:

> It would be a serious selective distortion of the existing evidence to suggest all of it indicates an incongruence between what people say and what they do. . . . The empirical evidence can best be summarized as reflecting wide variations in the relationships between sentiments and acts [pp. 59–60].

Positive reviews by Calder and Ross (1973), Kelman (1974), Liska (1974b), Schuman and Johnson (1976) and Ajzen and Fishbein (1977) have enlivened debate on attitude–behavior correspondence. For example, after reviewing the several early and classic studies indicating no attitude–behavior relationship, Schuman and Johnson stated:

> Recent reviews have tended to merge these few and special—which is not to say unimportant—negative results with those that show reliable associations, leaving the impression that there is frequently virtually no relationship between attitude and behavior. In light of the research available through 1975, that is clearly not the case. Moreover, the typical associations reported are small or moderate only in terms of expectations that they be very large; they are not particularly small in comparison with magnitudes reported in social research generally.

Most recently, Eagly and Himmelfarb (1978) have proposed that there has been a resurgence in the attitude area which "can probably be attributed to a more promising outlook for the attitude–behavior relationship . . . [p. 295]."

Renewed optimism about attitude–behavior correspondence stems from research specifying conditions under which strong relationships should obtain and accounting for instances in which correspondence has not been high. Writers purveying this optimism have focused upon (a) attitude measurement; (b) the behaviors predicted; (c) contextual and moderating variables; and (d) how "consistency" between verbal reports and behaviors should be viewed.

In the first area, attitude measures are more predictive of and consistent with behaviors: (a) if cast at the same level of specificity as the criterion behavior (Heberlein & Black, 1976; Weigel, Vernon & Tognacci, 1974; Wicker & Pomazal, 1971) than if global measures are used to predict specific acts (Fishbein & Ajzen, 1974; Schwartz, 1978); (b) if attitude toward the act—in relation to an attitude "target"—is used (Fishbein & Ajzen, 1975), although act- or situation-specific measures with attitude toward the object may improve prediction (Petersen & Dutton, 1975; Rokeach & Kliejunas, 1972); (c) if multiple-item attitude scales are used (Tittle & Hill, 1967b), though single-item measures have served well in certain instances, and multiple-item measures may even have reduced verbal report–behavior correlations if the resultant "index" lost the specificity commensurate with the predicted behavior (Schuman & Johnson, 1976); and (d) if measurement error or real change occuring between measurement of attitudes and behavior are accounted for so that "true" attitude–behavior correlations are not underestimated (Alwin, 1973; McPhee & Seibold, 1979a) and, if congeneric tests are employed, "when unreliability and instability (attitude change) are taken into account, attitudes account for more variability in behavior than when they are not (Alwin, 1976; p. 380)."

Second, attitude–behavior correspondence improves with more careful conceptualization of behaviors (Fishbein & Ajzen, 1974), refined measurement of behaviors (Rosen & Komorita, 1971; Weigel & Newman, 1976), and when there is clear conceptual and operational correspondence between the "entities" associated with each (Ajzen & Fishbein, 1977). In particular, results indicate: (a) global attitudes are better suited for prediction of multiple-act behavioral criteria, although they do not result in report–behavior correlations as strong as when specific attitude measures (especially toward the act itself) are used to predict single-act criteria (Fishbein & Ajzen, 1974); (b) even a general attitude index measuring attitude toward object (rather than specific acts) "will make strong predictions of behavioral variation when the behavior is sought in the context of patterned sets of actions rather than a single act [Weigel & Newman, 1976; p. 801];" (c) persons' attitudes will bear a strong relationship with behaviors when the attitude target is highly correspondent with the attitude action, whereas low or inconsistent relationships in 103 of 142 relevant studies reviewed resulted from low or partial conceptual correspondence between attitudes and behaviors (Ajzen & Fishbein, 1977); (d) attitude measures appear to be more predictive of "symbolic" behaviors (e.g., petition signing, commitments, etc.) than behaviors involving direct experience with the attitude object (Schuman & Johnson, 1976; pp. 197–198); (e) attitude–behavior correspondence is higher when the behaviors are highly institutionalized, routinized, and familiar (Crespi, 1971; Tittle & Hill, 1967a) or, more generally, when persons know or can imagine how they will act (Schuman & Johnson, 1976) and are willing to disclose their behavioral tendencies (Ehrlich, 1969); and (f) attitude–behavior correspondence can diminish as the time interval between measurement of attitudes and behaviors increases (Fishbein, 1973).

    That researchers have identified how certain factors moderate (increase, decrease, or obviate) attitude–behavior correspondence is a third source of optimism about attitude–behavior consistency. The review by Schuman and Johnson (1976; pp. 185–199) indicates that (a) attitude–behavior associations may vary considerably across attitude objects and situations (Bem & Allen, 1974 Davey, 1976); (b) although there is an independent effect of attitudes on behaviors even when there are perceived reference group pressures, normative beliefs can affect behavior independently of, and conjointly with, attitudes (Andrews & Kandel, 1979); (c) attitude–behavior correspondence can be enhanced or depressed through immediate social pressures to behave in a manner similar to or different from formerly assessed attitudes (Fields & Schuman, 1977; Norman, 1975) (d) attitude–behavior correspondence may be a function of certain personal traits (Snyder & Tanke, 1976); (e) attitude–behavior consistency can be diminished if privately expressed attitudes must be publicly enacted (Green, 1972); (f) attitude–behavior correspondence increases with increased attitudinal certainty (Sample & Warland, 1973), confidence (Fazio & Zanna, 1978), salience (Brown, 1974), intensity (Petersen & Dutton, 1975), internal consistency (Norman, 1975), and stability (Schwartz, 1978); (g) inconsistency between personal and perceived reference-group attitudes will decrease personal attitude–behavior consistency (Frideres, Warner, & Albrecht, 1971); and (h) attitudes formed on the basis of direct experience are more consistent with subsequent related behaviors than attitudes borne of indirect experience with the attitude object (Regan & Fazio, 1977).

    Finally, optimism about attitude–behavior correspondence must be viewed against how "consistency" has been conceptualized. Schuman and Johnson's (1976) distinction between "literal consistency" (is there isomorphism between verbal report and action?) and "correlational consistency" (how similarly are people ordered on both measures?) is useful. Much of the disenchantment with the attitude construct stemmed from the seemingly literal inconsistency between attitudes and behaviors in early studies (e.g., Himmelstein & Moore, 1963; Kutner, Wilkins & Yarrow, 1952; LaPiere, 1934; Minard, 1952; Zunich, 1962). However, as Dillehay, (1973) and Ajzen and Fishbein (1977) have shown, inconsistencies in conceptualization and measurement produced empirical inconsistencies among measures that should never have been expected to be consistent in the first place. Today, even the staunchest defenders of potential attitude–behavior correspondence do not presume literal consistency, and acknowledge that consistency may be mediated by factors extrinsic to attitude–behavior relationships such as those already identified.

Given the multitude of factors moderating attitude–behavior consistency and the fruitlessness of seeking literal isomorphism, the real issue of attitude–behavior consistency is correlational consistency: "Are people ordered in the same way on both attitude and behavior measures [Schuman & Johnson, 1976, p. 164]?" Wicker's (1969) summary analysis that "product–moment correlation coefficients are rarely above 0.30 [p. 65]" offered a resounding "No" to the question of correlational consistency. But there are several reasons why Wicker's answer to the question of correlational consistency is not definitive. First, because many of the studies serving as warrants of Wicker's claim have been shown to be "of literal relevance" (Fishbein & Ajzen, 1975; p. 360) or "irrelevant" (Dillehay, 1973) to attitude–behavior theory per se, much of the previous evidence for low correlational consistency is eroded as well. Second, when methodological problems such as measurement unreliability (Alwin, 1973), statistics utilized (Schuman & Johnson, 1976), behavior measure distributions (Mervielde, 1977) and threshold levels (Raden, 1977) have been treated in some of the remaining studies in Wicker's review, the low correlations originally reported are found to be underestimates of attitude–behavior consistency. Finally, following theoretical and research refinements of attitudes, behaviors, and moderating factors of the kinds just discussed, results from studies more recent than those reviewed by Wicker usually indicate moderate, and in some cases strong, correlational consistency (cf. Acock & DeFleur, 1972, $r = .53$; Albrecht, DeFleur & Warner, 1972, gamma $= .71$; Brannon, et al., 1973, phi $= .46$ as computed in Schuman & Johnson, 1976; Fishbein & Ajzen, 1974, mean $r = .66$ as computed in Weigel & Newman, 1976; Fazio & Zanna, 1978, $r_s = .524$ and $.593$ for two studies; Frideres, 1971, gamma $= .94$ and tau–$b = .46$; Heberlein & Black, 1976, $r = .634$; Kothandapani, 1971, mean point biserial, transformation to Fisher's $Z = .69$ as computed in Ajzen & Fishbein, 1978; Norman, 1975, r's $= .50$; Regan & Fazio, 1977, $r_s = .544$; Rokeach & Kliejunas, 1972, mean $r = .61$; Sample & Warland, 1973, $r =$

.437; Veevers, 1971, gamma = .72; Weigel & Newman, 1976, r = .62; Weigel *et al.*, 1974, r = .68; Weinstein, 1972, point biserial = .69).[6] Ten other recent studies reporting moderate to strong attitude–behavior consistency are discussed in Ajzen and Fishbein (1977, pp. 900–901). Hence, there is substantial evidence that the (correlational) consistency between attitudes and behaviors will be moderate, even strong, under specifiable conditions.

Message–Verbal Report–Behavior Studies

In the second area (communication–attitude–behavior literature), findings have been less detailed and more equivocal, but nonetheless suggestive. Comprehensive reviews have been provided by Festinger (1964), Seibold (1975a), and Cook and Flay (1978); more limited surveys are offered by Rokeach (1967) and Calder and Ross (1973, pp. 25–27). With regard to the efficacy of persuasion, results of each review call into question the adequacy of traditional persuasive messages alone for producing (*a*) persistent, experimentally induced attitude change (Cook & Flay, 1978); (*b*) both attitude change and behavior change from the same persuasive message (Festinger, 1964; Rokeach, 1967); and (*c*) necessary, high correspondence between attitude reports and behaviors following persuasive communications producing change in one or the other (Calder & Ross, 1973; Seibold, 1975a). Although these detrimental findings are interpretable in light of deficiencies in experimenters' message construction and controls (Seibold, 1975a), they are not in contradistinction to critiques of previous laboratory persuasion studies arguing that obtained changes in attitudes were really temporal "elastic shifts" (Cialdini, Levy, Herman, Kozlowski, & Petty, 1976) affected by demand characteristics of the experiment and subjects' anticipatory belief changes (Hass & Mann, 1976).

From the standpoint of attitude–behavior consistency, even these equivocal persuasion results have proved informative. Festinger (1964) found that none of only three relevant studies conducted to that time provided evidence that changes in attitude reports corresponded with overt acts. However, Seibold (1975a) examined 16 studies published during the decade after Festinger's survey and permitting inference of the effects of messages on verbal reports and behaviors. Of these, half revealed moderate or high report–action associations and half indicated low correspondence following communicative interventions. Calder and Ross (1973), reviewing a subset of the studies Seibold reviewed, came to a similar conclusion: "This brief survey of studies incorporating measures of both attitude and behavior change reveals apparently contradictory results [p. 25]." Finally, in the broadest and most recent survey of relevant research, Cook and Flay (1978, p. 49) found that cognitive and behavioral

---

[6] In some cases, the coefficients depicted are the highest from that study, but because they involve the theoretical or empirical advancement being tested, they are consistent with my argument that strong correlational consistency is obtainable under specifiable conditions.

measures were "nearly always" correspondent. Their findings do not permit inference about the degree of literal or correlational consistency and are limited to studies of experimentally induced changes in attitudes and behaviors. However, in addition to their finding of correspondence, Cook and Flay found no cases of reported literal inconsistency between cognitions and behaviors across the many experimental attitude changes approaches studied.

Theory

Contemporary writers frequently rely only upon early reviewers' conclusions that attitude–behavior relationships are "problematic" on account of low correlations between measures of each (cf. O'Keefe, Chapter 4, this volume). The preceding review suggests that, in many of the early studies used as warrants for concluding low correlational consistency exists between attitudes and behaviors, stronger correlations could not theoretically have been expected. Too, reanalysis of the data in other studies has revealed moderate correspondence between measures of attitudes and behaviors when methodological flaws have been controlled. Finally, meaningful inconsistencies between attitudes and behaviors are virtually nonexistent in research of the 1970s; on the contrary, moderate correlational consistency is often in evidence under theoretically delineated conditions.

The real issue rests not in explaining "problematic" relationships between attitudes and behaviors, but in answering more basic theoretical questions:

1. What gives attitudes generative force when they do affect behaviors?
2. Under which circumstances will attitudes be causally related to action; under which conditions will behaviors be the result of other factors, and how consistent with behaviors will attitudes be when they are not the primary determinants?
3. What are the scope conditions for the operation of the processes theorized, and how do the relationships specified operate over time?

Viewed within the context of these questions, correlational consistency between attitudes and behaviors is only a special case of the larger causal analysis of action. Too, it will be unproductive to probe attitude–behavior consistency without recourse to the broader set of relationships implied by the theoretical framework and overtime processual analysis of these relationships. That this is so can be demonstrated through the following formalization and analysis of a widespread conception of attitude–behavior relationships.

Latent Process Conception of Attitude–Behavior Relations

Researchers have been less than uniform on the nature of attitudes (McGuire, 1969), and space limitations preclude discussion of their substantive differences. Instead, I shall assert what seem to be widespread assumptions about the characteristics of attitudes. First, attitudes are personal psychological configurations which are socially derived. Stated differently, attitudes may be developed uniquely depending on an individual's attention, information processing, and memory processes, but the grist for this learning mill are data from the individual's social reality as apprehended through personal experience or others' communications. The role of communications in this regard will be discussed more fully later. Second, these psychosocial configurations may be quite global and enduring, depending upon (*a*) the breadth and complexity of their information base; (*b*) the individual's ability to differentiate and organize this perceptual data (and to accommodate new information); and (*c*) the degree to which a particular attitude may hierarchically subsume a number of more restricted psychological evaluations. Third, both global and specific attitudes evidence an evaluative nature: Attitudes represent individuals' evaluations, judgments, and affinities for social objects and actions. Fourth, attitudes inherently assert an anticipatory quality—a state of readiness to respond to stimuli, an action potential. It is the combination of attitudes' evaluative and kinetic qualities that *may* influence the direction and intensity of their physical manifestations (e.g., verbal reports) and other attitude–relevant behaviors. Finally, other factors controlled, these underlying "true" states are assumed to mediate consistent responses over time plus consistent responses between verbal reports and behaviors related to them.

These statements are the bedrock of a "latent process" conception of attitudes (DeFleur & Westie, 1963), the central tenet of which is that an unobserved state is assumed to influence persons' verbal and nonverbal responses toward attitude objects. As I have demonstrated elsewhere, the linkages among the variables identified thus far (underlying attitudes, verbal reports, and overt

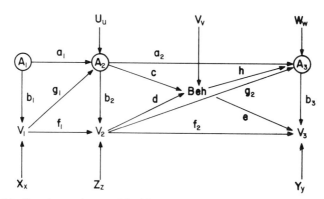

Figure 6.1. Causal, overtime model of latent process conception of attitude–behavior relationships (where A_i = underlying attitude; V_i = unidimensional report of attitude; *Beh* = overt behavior; $U, \ldots, Z$ = disturbance terms; $a, \ldots, h$ = path coefficients; i = each point in time at which the variables are assessed). [From Seibold (1975a). Reproduced with permission of International Communication Association.]

behaviors) are only implicit in these statements, but may be made explicit using Zetterberg's (1965) propositional logic scheme (Seibold, 1975a, pp. 5–6). The logic in the resultant formalization of the latent process conception may be presented diagrammatically in an over-time model (see Figure 6.1), an extension of a model proposed by Alwin (1973) by virtue of its propositional formalization and over-time characteristics.

Given certain simplifying assumptions that make the model overidentified, estimates for parameters a, b, c, d, and a behavioral effect $(bh + e)$ can be derived from the following structural equations for the model (see Table 6.1).[7] The solutions to these theoretical parameter equations, presented in the second half of Table 6.1, render testable some of the theoretic propositions about underlying attitude–report–behavior relationships indicated by the limited latent process conception (e.g., a = stability of underlying attitude, b = validity of verbal report as a measure of underlying attitude, c = influence of underlying attitude on overt behavior).

The model makes it clear that the prevailing latent process conception of attitudes and the attendant conception of attitude–behavior relationships are extremely limited, given the definition and criteria for "theory" outlined earlier, p. 201. First, the model is a closed system of only three endogenous factors whose scope and existence conditions are not well delineated (especially the nature of the verbal reports depicted and the types of behaviors involved). Second, the causal nature of the central component—underlying attitudes—is

TABLE 6.1
Structural Equations and Solutions for Unidimensional Attitude Latent Process Model

Structural equations

(1) $V_3 = bA_3 + eBeh + fV_2 + yY$
(2) $A_3 = hBeh + gV_2 + aA_2 + wW$
(3) $Beh = dV_2 + cA_2 + vV$
(4) $V_2 = bA_2 + fV_1 + zZ$
(5) $A_2 = gV_1 + aA_1 + uU$
(6) $V_1 = bA_1 + xX$

Solutions for theoretical parameters

(7) $bh + e = r_{BehV_3} - r_{V_1Beh}$ [Let $bh + e = X$, a known value $= r_{BehV_3} - r_{V_1Beh}$]
(8) $a = (r_{V_1V_3} - Xr_{V_1Beh})/r_{V_1V_2}$
(9) $b = r_{V_1V_2}/a$
(10) $c = (ab^2r_{V_2Beh} - r_{V_1Beh})/(ab^3 - ab)$
(11) $d = (r_{V_1Beh} - ar_{V_2Beh})/(ab^2 - a)$

---

[7] The mathematical solutions given in Table 6.1 were printed incorrectly in Seibold (1975a). See "Errata," *Human Communication Research*, 1976, *2*, 398. Table 6.1 is reprinted with permission of the International Communication Association.

not clearly specified within the latent process framework. Third, without regard to other determinants of behavior or variables moderating the attitude–behavior relationship, underlying attitudes are depicted as the primary determinants of verbal reports and nonverbal acts (although I have utilized the overtime features of the model to incorporate the empirically substantiated notions that personal expressions of attitudes may exert some independent effect on subsequent behavior [d], and that both verbal reports and overt acts may causally affect underlying attitudes [g,h] at a later time).

In view of these limitations in latent process attitudes as a sole basis for a theory of attitude–behavior relationships, I next wish to focus on the composition and causal nature of attitudes (p. 218), and then to embed this conception in a broader theoretic perspective treating other determinants of action (p. 221). I shall later offer scope conditions specifying when we might expect verbal report–overt behavior consistency to be high. I hope to strike an analytic midpoint between the logical derivations of philosophers from commonsense impressions of attitudes (Audi, 1972), versus the operationalism of psychologists concerned with more technical aspects of attitude assessment (Fishbein, 1967). I will cast a wide conceptual net, and while the analysis will be sufficiently precise to be testable (p. 224), I hope it will prove hueristic by virtue of its compatibility with other theoretical frameworks and suggestive for communication theorists.

Attitudes as Generative Mechanisms

Attitudes intervene between more basic motivational forces and action, and their causal forces on behaviors are the purveyance of these more fundamental mechanisms. To say, for example, that a person acted because he "believed" action was warranted asserts that the act was appropriate *in relation* to something considered worthwhile. Values, drives, traits, pressures, and needs for consistency, novelty, achievement, and equity have all been foci in motivational accounts of behavior. The position taken here is that action derives from persons' attempts to *control* salient aspects of their phenomenal world. Control is not used in a pejorative sense. Rather, I wish to underscore persons' propensities to proactively structure their realities and to choose behavioral options accruing outcomes that they deem personally satisfying (Miller & Steinberg, 1975; Parks, 1977). The need for some semblance of personal control is evident even in social perception processes: Persons seek to comprehend veridically the causes underlying events in order to achieve stability in a world where future events can be understood, anticipated, and controlled (Seibold, 1975b; Wortman, 1976). In mediating fashion, attitudes may facilitate feelings of personal control insofar as they yield psychological assessments of the attitude referents among which control-related behavioral choices must be made. Sometimes control may inhere in the attitude held, as when an attitude object is sufficiently global (religion or patriotism) that feelings or beliefs about it may yield an individual personal complacency without need of concern for specific behaviors related to the attitude. Usually, however, when attitudes do prompt or constrain specific action, it is because they crystallize and channelize personal evaluations of the extent to which such acts stand in relation to personally meaningful outcomes. This distinction between attitude objects and attitude actions will be especially germane when considering conditions for attitude–behavior consistency.

The structure of attitudes, more precisely, channelizes control options into behavioral choices. Attitudes reflect persons' valuations, judgements, and affinities for social objects and relevant actions. These evaluative assessments find expression in affective reactions, beliefs, and/or action potential, a tricomponential view commonly held and possessing empirical support (Kothandapani, 1971; Ostrom, 1969), although others have espoused the predictive utility of unidimensional attitudes (Bem, 1968; Fishbein & Ajzen, 1975; Thurstone, 1931). The and/or conjunction is significant, for these components may be coextensive or substitutable in their relationship to behavior. Behavioral choices, for example, may stem from strong affect in the absence of salient beliefs; or individuals may believe in the appropriateness of action and be predisposed to act, but be affectively indifferent; or individuals may feel and believe strongly but not intend to act because of competing factors (e.g., when persons derive a sense of personal control from prejudicial attitudes, yet would not overtly discriminate). Attitudes may therefore take shape in different evaluative configurations ranging from strong manifestations of all three components to single component predominance. Finally, no claim is made herein for an invariant sequential relationship among these components. The logical possibility that but a single component could generate action precludes the necessity inherent in arguments about belief-then attitude-then intention chains (Fishbein & Ajzen, 1975) or the "two sequence model" of attitude dynamics (Rosenberg, 1960, p. 52). More generally, it is proposed that even when all three attitude components are strongly developed and are coextensively representative of a salient underlying attitude, each of these components may exert different causal forces on action. This is not the result of internal sequencing nor of their effects on each other, but a function of the extent to which each attitude component alone, or in a specific joint effect (Seibold & McPhee, 1979a), is germane to channelizing an individual's control needs into a particular behavioral choice. That attitudinal affect, cognition, and conation may coexist, yet differentially (even substitutably) affect behavior, should not be taken as an indication of fundamentally different variables. For it is their coextensive relationship to underlying "true" attitudes that give these components coherence as tridimensional evaluative manifestations.

Finally, the nature of each of these potentially causative components requires specification, for these components have been variously conceived and operationalized. The affect component has been discussed in terms of continua bordered on the positive pole by supportiveness (Ostrom, 1969), positiveness (Rosenberg & Abelson, 1960), favorableness (Osgood, 1965) and affinity (Bem,

1968). When tied to the previous notion (i.e., attitudes are the application of evaluations concerning the extent to which holding that attitude or action in a particular way will accrue feelings of personal control), the affective component asserts the *desirability* of the attitude target. Attitudinal affect thus reflects what an individual wants or desires in connection with some object or action. The cognitive component of attitude manifests an evaluative judgement of the general *likelihood* that some action or object is linked to a control-related preference, an evaluative response which is more embracing than perceptual responses (Ostrom, 1969), cognitive categorizations (Triandis, 1971), or probability estimates (Fishbein & Ajzen, 1975). Finally, the conative component reflects the *intentionality* of personal attitudes, or propensity to act in accordance with underlying attitudinal evaluations. This behavioral intention is similar to Fishbein's (Fishbein & Ajzen, 1975) conception of intention-to-act, except (*a*) it is not viewed here as distinct from attitude or as necessarily determined by other attitude components (though they will usually be interrelated); and (*b*) intention is not a sufficient mediator of normative influences, as I shall explain next.

In summary, underlying attitudes are more or less global and enduring evaluations of social objects and actions. These "true" psychological assessments may moderate related behaviors through the causal force of particular, socially derived attitude components: evaluations of an action's desirability, judgements of the likelihood that acting will accrue consequences deemed satisfying, or intentional disposition to act. They may be intercorrelated by virtue of the latent state they manifest, but these attitude components have no necessary causal force on each other. These theoretical propositions may be formalized in the following extension upon and departure from the strict latent process conception depicted in Figure 6.1.

1. There is a coextensive causal relationship from underlying attitude to attitude components which is irreversible, deterministic, sufficient, and necessary.

2. There is a coextensive causal relationship between attitude components and corresponding tricomponent verbal reports of attitude which is irreversible, stochastic, contingent (upon physical, social, and environmental factors also affecting reporting and measurement of attitudes), and substitutable.

3. There is a sequential causal relationship from attitude components to overt behavior which is irreversible (at a given point in time), stochastic, contingent (upon physical, social, and environmental factors also affecting action and measurement of behaviors), and substitutable.

4. Over time there may be a sequential causal relationship from verbal reports and overt behaviors to underlying attitudes and attitude components which is irreversible, stochastic, contingent, and necessary.

5. Over time each element of the theory will stand in sequential causal

relationship to itself at time $n + 1$ and this relationship could be irreversible, deterministic, contingent (on other factors affecting the entire system state at the later point in time), and substitutable.

Other Determinants of Behaviors

Behaviors are a consequence of personal, social, and environmental influences, and attitudes are but one of the factors affecting action. If the conception of attitudes delineated so far is to have explanatory and predictive utility, it must be tied to a theoretic framework that treats situated actions in terms of specific configurations of those influences (Acock & DeFleur, 1972; Kelman, 1974). I have proposed such a theoretical framework elsewhere (Seibold, 1975a), but offer several modifications in the following synopsis.

The *locus of control* for action (conceived as the criteria most salient for an individual's choice among alternative behaviors in a given instance) may rest in three areas: personal control, perceived social pressures, and situational constraints.[8] Personal control may be entirely a function of personal attitudes in some instances (i.e., actional desirability, likelihood, or intention). In other instances, personal control may reside in the force of an individual's norms, reflecting personal obligations and responsibilities to act (Schwartz, 1973). Alternatively, the locus of control for action may be more "social" (perceptions of general norms, specific social pressures, spontaneous actions, etc.), especially as purveyed by significant others (Charters & Newcomb, 1958; Woelfel & Haller, 1971). Finally, perceived situational contingencies (task difficulty, alternative commitments, physical obstacles, etc.) may dictate the nature of behavior enacted (Dannick, 1969; Price & Bouffard, 1974).

This conceptualization coheres with the control-oriented account of action supplied in the previous section, but provides for the fact that "control" of personal action may stem from perceived loci other than purely personal ones. Indeed, perceived social and situational forces may be sufficiently strong as to influence not merely overt acts but also verbal reports of attitude states, thereby moderating attitude report–behavior consistency just as underlying attitudes might (Schuman & Johnson, 1976). Too, the locus of control construct admits the possibility that, even when the locus of control is more personal, persons may act more on the basis of what they feel they should do rather than what they might attitudinally prefer to do.

If attitudes *and* other loci of control may be generative forces for action, under which conditions will one or another be causal? The preceding review of previous research (pp. 209–215) indicates that these factors can simultaneously

---

[8] The term "locus of control" should not be interpreted in the more restricted sense associated with Rotter's (1966) research. Rather, its use here represents an extension of the work of McDermott (1974), who has synthesized the writings of Heider, Rotter, and DeCharms and provided empirical support for the more global reconceptualization.

affect behaviors in situations where the different loci are consistent. So their potential coextensive causal relationship to action presents no conceptual difficulty, and the particular configuration of their unique and common effects on action will be an empirical and statistical question in these instances (McPhee & Seibold, 1979a; Seibold & McPhee, 1979a). Given the presumed primacy of an individual's desire for personal control, we should theoretically expect the predominance of attitudinal forces toward action when the perceived loci of control are consistent, insofar as attitudes are the most personal and volitional locus, whereas the other loci of control are more reactive (Allport, 1935) and provide less sense of personal choice in acting. On the other hand, perceived loci of control may be incongruent in certain instances, so that perceived social pressures to act may not jibe with attitudinal evaluations, for example. Even under these circumstances, the present theory proposes that individual behaviors will be a function of the locus of control (or loci) which affords the greatest sense of personal control over the action chosen, as for example when an individual conforms to peer pressures to act in a nonpreferred manner because that appears to be the greatest face saving means of personal control available. Of course, under these threats to freedom of choice and diminished personal control we can also expect other dynamics, such as various means of dissonance reduction (Wicklund & Brehm, 1976), reactance to sources of pressure (Worchel & Brehm, 1971), and/or devaluation of personal preferences (Janis & Mann, 1977). Most important for the present analysis, under these conditions attitudes will bear a different relationship to behavior than when all loci of control are consistent. I shall discuss this in the following section.

In sum, the scope conditions for the operation of these generative mechanisms are these:

If an individual finds the consequences associated with some course of action to be desirable, or likely, or if the individual intends to act toward these preferred consequences, and if the action and its consequences facilitate or do not counteract a sense of personal freedom and control in acting then (a) one or all of these attitudinal loci will be the immediate cause of action, even if other consistent loci of control (personal norms, social pressures, and situational influences) are salient and may have some incremental effect on behavior: (b) but if the perceived loci of control for action are inconsistent, then an individual will act on the basis of the locus or loci of control which enables the actor to retain the greatest sense of personal control within the constraints of that situation.

Verbal Report–Behavior Consistency

Two separate circumstances for assessing verbal report–behavior correlational consistency emerge from the preceding analysis: (a) Under conditions where attitudinal effects on behaviors are primary and are not attenuated by other loci of control, what will be the degree of verbal report–behavior consistency?; (b) under conditions where the perceived loci of control for action rest in factors other than attitude components, how consistent with behaviors will attitude reports be?

When attitudinal components are the sole or principal forces for action, one might expect very strong correlational consistency (assuming that measurement errors and time lag between measurements are minimal). But the review of previous research (pp. 209–215) suggests even this assumption is unfounded, for there are additional factors influencing report–behavior consistency even under conditions in which attitudinal effects on behavior may be strong. These additional factors are inherent in the attitudes and behaviors involved. Many have been revealed by previous research, but there are six factors affecting consistency which may be derived from the theory proposed. First, if attitude development is a function of an individual's informational base (direct experience or communications), the larger that informational base, the greater the individual's attitudinal certainty (see Seibold, 1975a, pp. 18–19). Verbal report–behavior consistency should be high in these instances. Conversely, low report–behavior consistency may be in evidence—even when attitudes causally affect behaviors—if attitudinal certainty is low. A second attitudinal factor affecting report–behavior correlational consistency is the salience of the attitude, or the degree to which an attitude channelizes preferred control to the behavior in question. When attitudes are salient in this sense, we may expect their force on behaviors to be great and reports of those attitudinal evaluations to be more consistent with behaviors than when attitudes are not as instrumentally salient. Third, to the extent that the behaviors causally affected by attitudes are easily controlled acts (i.e. customary and low effort), the greater the correspondence there should be between those actions and equally controllable reports of attitudes. When attitudes do serve as primary generative mechanisms, fourth, if there is consistency among the attitude components their causal force on action should also be stronger than when they are not as internally uniform. As a result, verbal reports should also be more highly correspondent with behaviors when the attitude reports are consistent than when they are less consistent. Fifth, when attitudes are primarily causal, if an individual's attitude is temporally unstable (as a function of competing messages or new experiences that change attitude evaluations, or as a consequence of shifts in the perceived locus of control for acting), verbal reports also will be less consistent with behaviors over time. Finally, because attitudes may vary in complexity, specificity, and hierarchical structure, verbal reports of global attitudes should be most correspondent with global attitude targets (classes of objects, general concepts, and *sets* of behaviors), whereas specific attitudes should be most correspondent with specific targets (particular objects, concepts, or acts).

When the locus of control for action does not rest in attitudinal components, we may expect nihil to low report–behavior consistency compared to conditions in which attitudes are primarily causal. However, the relationship between the attitude in question and the causal locus of control for that action may affect the degree of attitude report–behavior consistency within this range. For example, attitude reports should bear no relationship with action (i.e., appear literally inconsistent) only when the locus of control is social or situational *and* when the attitude in question is inconsistent with or unrelated to that particular causal locus. On the other hand, when personal norms are causally efficacious, *and* if attitudinal evaluations are both salient and consistent with the generative norms, attitude reports will bear some correspondence with the normatively determined action; this correspondence will be greater than (*a*) when other, less personal loci of control are causal; (*b*) when attitudes and norms are inconsistent; or (*c*) when attitudes simply are not salient for that action.

Process Analysis

With the exception of identifying attitudinal stability as a potential moderator of verbal report–overt behavior consistency, the analysis thus far, like most investigations of attitude–behavior relationships, has focused on report–behavior consistency at a single point in time. More process-oriented research on the determinants of action and on attitude–behavior consistency is vital to continued analysis in this area for several reasons. First, since many of the theories reviewed assume or explicate causal process accounts involving attitudes and behaviors, important theoretical underpinnings (e.g. attitudinal stability, validity of verbal reports as measures of underlying attitudes, etc.) remain untested if process analyses are not performed. Second, the major types of inferences drawn from bivariate correlation of report–behavior relationships cannot be verified without overtime analysis (or the inclusion of more theoretically relevant variables at a single time) because the implicit model for this research inference is underidentified (Alwin, 1973). Third, threats to external validity can be reduced and predictive scope broadened when attitude–report–behavior relationships are tracked over time. Stated differently, investigators may be less prone to err in their conclusions about general attitude–behavior correspondence if particular relationships observed are couched within overtime analyses. The following section reports a direct test of portions of the causal process theory by means of analysis of relationships within a three wave model.

Test of Theory

The theory outlined in the preceding pages yields research questions and hypotheses concerning: (*a*) the nature of attitudes; (*b*) other variables as generative mechanisms for behavior; and (*c*) factors affecting verbal report–behavior consistency. Research findings pertinent to the theory's predictions in these areas are reviewed in turn next. Given the emphases of this volume, the first and third areas receive principal consideration. "Test" of the theory rests on data which were collected to analyze portions of the model directly, but data from other research reports are also discussed as indirect warrants for the conceptual adequacy of the theory. Hence each following section adduces *direct* and *indirect* evidence.

All direct tests of the theory's predictions rest upon data collected in a 3-wave, nonexperimental design following an initial wave pilot study. Participants were local chapter members of a national women's community service volunteer organization. All three monthly questionnaires and behavior reports were completed by 98 adult women. Pilot test procedures, final questions, study methods, participant characteristics, sampling techniques, and index construction are fully described in Seibold (1975c) and are summarized in McPhee and Seibold (1979a). It should be noted that the findings reported often entail major reanalyses of the data reported in Seibold (1975c), as well as those reanalyses reported in Seibold (1979), Seibold and McPhee (1979b), and McPhee and Seibold (1979a, 1979b). Finally, even the direct "tests" provided must be viewed circumspectly. Although the data analyzed permit assessment of the theory's adequacy, the causal inferences and conclusions drawn in this field study are necessarily more tenuous than if control groups, comparative analyses, and experimental procedures had been used.

Nature of Attitudes

The proposed theory rests on an elaborated model of the latent process conception of attitudes. Unlike the unidimensional conception depicted in Figure 6.1, the present theory proposes a tricomponent attitude structure moderated by an underlying "true" attitude. In turn, the affective (desirability), cognitive (likelihood), and conative (intention) components may be inferred through measured verbal reports and may causally influence behaviors. This modified latent process model, cast within the context of a 3-wave design, is represented in Figure 6.2.

Evidence for Tricomponent Attitudes. Data collected from the female community volunteer participants during an initial pilot test month were used to assess the viability of a tricomponent conception of attitudes. The women's attitudes toward their own volunteer behaviors were measured with semantic differential scales, Likert-type scales, and an overall rating scale. Scores on these measures were used to construct a multitrait–multimethod correlation matrix (Campbell & Fiske, 1959). Although strongly intercorrelated, none of the scales for a given component was much more correlated with similar scales for other components than with alternative measures of that component. Principal components factor analysis with varimax rotation produced a solution in which the first three conation, affect, and cognition factors (with eigenvalues of 8.29, 4.10, and 3.11, and all loadings except two over .60) respectively ac-

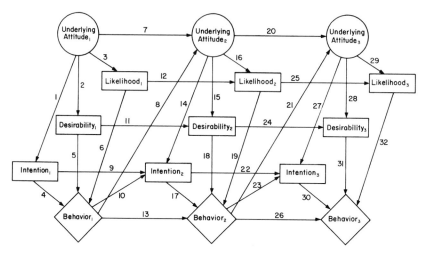

Figure 6.2. Overtime model for path analytic test of attitude–verbal report–behavior portion of causal process theory.

counted for 32, 16, and 12% of the variance in attitudinal responses. These results are consistent with the theorizing of Rosenberg and Hovland (1960) and the findings of Ostrom (1969) and Kothandapani (1971) that the affective, cognitive, and conative measures of underlying attitudes may be treated as distinct and tricomponential. Furthermore, whereas the Ostrom and Kothandapani investigations concerned general attitudes and specific attitudes toward objects respectively, these findings extend the tricomponent position to attitudes toward acts despite Fishbein and Ajzen's theoretical arguments to the contrary (1975, pp. 340–343). As detailed in Seibold (1979), internal consistency reliability coefficients (Cronbach's alpha) for attitude components in the pilot data ranged from .73 to .91.

Evidence for Modified Latent Process Model. Since the theory's predictions about verbal report–behavior consistency stem from an elaborated latent process conception of tricomponent attitudes, the verisimilitude of this reconceptualization must be assessed before further test of the theory can proceed. Of primary concern is the viability of incorporating underlying "true" attitudes into formal tests of attitude–behavior theories, especially in comparison with more parsimonious models that do not rely on latent, unmeasured constructs. Hence, from the standpoint of the causal model depicted in Figure 6.2, we must ascertain whether the attitude *structure* represented (i.e., only the relationships among underlying attitude and the three attitude report components across three points in time) fits overtime attitudinal response data better than alternative conceptions of attitude organization and dynamics.

Direct test of this issue was undertaken by Seibold and McPhee (1979b). Six models of overtime attitude structure were formulated. The models represented formalizations of the elaborated latent process conceptualization discussed, a reinforcement principle formulation, both segments of Rosenberg's (1960) 2-sequence model, a contiguity model (stipulating that either affect or cognition may influence conation), and Fishbein and Ajzen's (1975) cognition-then-attitude-then-conation perspective. All six models were tested for goodness of fit to data reflecting women's attitudes toward their own volunteer activities at three monthly intervals.

The mode of statistical analysis employed should be noted, particularly because it undergirds tests of several attitude–verbal report–behavior relationships reported in what follows. Consistent with the path analytic procedures already outlined in connection with causal process theory construction (pp. 206–209), parameter estimates for all models and the fit of each to the 3-wave data were derived using LISREL–III (Jöreskog & Sörbom, 1976). Werts, Jöreskog and Linn (1973) have demonstrated the applicability of Jöreskog's (1969, 1970) general model and maximum likelihood estimation approach to path analytic models involving multiple indicators of underlying constructs. The utility of LISREL–III for the present research rests in these considerations: (a) the program permits analysis of multiple indicators of latent variables (Werts & Linn, 1970) and provides estimates of "paths" of causal influence from these unmeasured variables (Goldberger, 1973); (b) estimates of residuals are output, thus aiding inferences concerning causality, and all estimates evidence minimum asymptotic sampling variability (Hauser & Goldberger, 1971); (c) the program simultaneously estimates parameters for the system of linear structural equations modeled (Jöreskog, 1970); and (d) the program reports a χ^2 test of the goodness of fit to the data of each model tested. The associated probability value of the test statistic indicates the probability that, if the model were true, the observed correlational values (or a correlation matrix not fitting the model as well) could have resulted from chance fluctuations. Thus low probabilities indicate that variations in the data cannot be explained on the basis of constraints dictated by the specified model.

Results of the path analyses reported in Seibold and McPhee (1979b) indicate strong support for the modified latent process model, especially in comparison to the failure of the other models tested. Indeed, the modified latent process model proved to be the only one not rejected as a hypothetical fit to the data ($\chi^2 = 12.91$; df = 16; $p > .80$). The probabilities for the other models' test statistics never exceeded .000. While several restrictions were needed to achieve identification, examination of parameter value estimates and residuals revealed the qualitative superiority of the latent process conception. Relationships among the attitude components seem most accurately described by the elaborated latent process in which consistency among tricomponent attitudes is induced by a general, latent construct representing "true" attitude. The causal processes in those models proposing within-time, intercomponent relations could not satisfactorily explain patterns of attitude organization in the data as well as the less parsimonious latent process modification.

Finally, the results of the Seibold and McPhee investigation attest to the importance of processual analyses as claimed (p. 224). When data for the three attitude components were assessed at a single point in time, it was clear that several of the simpler models did not hold, but clearcut comparative distinctions did not emerge. When examined in a temporal process context, however, those models which posit no causal, consistency-producing processes over time failed most to fit the attitudinal data (which research by Seibold, 1979 had revealed to be highly stable: there were no significant changes in aggregate means and variances over time, and $Time_1-Time_3$ correlations for the three attitude components, corrected for attenuation, ranged from .80 to .99). In turn, those models positing causal processes over time fared better but not as well as the more general, less parsimonious latent process conception. It does not assign a special role to either affect or belief, but reserves the moderating effect for underlying attitudes. Taken together, these findings suggest that the tricomponent and modified latent process conceptions central to this theory are plausible and may even be more efficacious than alternative conceptions, pending further research. At the least, these findings vouchsafe meaningful test of the attitude–behavior relationships proposed in what follows.

Other Loci of Control for Behavior

Evidence for Alternative Generative Mechanisms. The present theory proposes that the locus of control for behavior may rest in factors other than attitudes, especially personal norms, social expectations, and/or situational constraints. That factors other than attitudes may exert principal influence on action is not only intuitively obvious but is one of the strongest claims to emerge from research on attitude–behavior relationships (Davey, 1976; Ehrlich, 1969; Schuman & Johnson, 1976; Triandis, 1980; Wicker, 1971). Evidence that these alternative loci may be personal normative obligations is supplied by Schwartz (1973).[9] That social pressures and perceived others' expectations may affect action (and even make it correspond better or worse with attitudes) is evident from the experimental research of Frideres, Warner and Albrecht (1971) and Norman (1975), as well as from investigations by Charters and Newcomb (1958) and Woelfel and Haller (1971) and the literature on perceived reference group support for action reviewed by Schuman and Johnson (1976, pp. 186–189). Finally, research by McPhee (1975), Price and Bouffard (1974), Dannick (1969), Raden (1974), and Snyder and Swann (1976) underscore both the independent

---

[9] Schwartz's (1973) finding, that the interaction of personal norms and the personality variable "ascription of responsibility" proved to be a better and more stable predictor of behavior than behavioral intention, may have implications for the present analysis. It is possible that persons' relative needs for a sense of personal control over their actions interact with their attitudes and predict behavior better than the individual attitude components.

effects of situational factors and their potential to moderate verbal report–behavior relationships.[10]

Attitudes versus Other Loci of Control for Behavior. The theory predicts that, when attitudes are consistent (or not inconsistent) with other relevant personal, social, or situational loci for action, attitudes will be primarily causative. In contrast, the locus or loci which afford(s) the greatest measure of personal control will be the principal cause(s) of action when tricomponent attitudes are inconsistent with these other loci. In both cases, tricomponent attitudes and tridimensional loci of control can be expected to make incremental contributions to the prediction of behavior (which should vary inversely with the importance of the principal factor).

Results reported in Seibold (1979) permit evaluation of the first and third propositions. Across the three successive months that the 98 women's volunteerism was assessed, tricomponent attitudes either were positively correlated with the three locus of control variables ($r = .09$ to $r = .72$; median $r = .35$) or exhibited negative coefficients not significantly different from zero ($r = -.06$). Given these instances of no meaningful inconsistencies among attitudes and loci of control, and in line with theoretical predictions, tricomponent attitudes were the principal predictors of the participants' rates of volunteerism (number of hours worked) during the week after questionnaires were completed. At each point in time, at least one attitude component bore a significant regression weight, and together the three components (with likelihood and desirability weighted by certainty; Seibold, 1975c) produced multiple correlations (R) with behavior of .85, .79, and .76. At the same time, the loci of control measures were usually negatively related to behavior; they produced but two of a possible nine significant regression weights; jointly they accounted for 7, 1, and 6% of the variance in behavior across the three months (in contrast to $R^2 = .72, .62$, and .57 for three attitudinal predictions); and they generally produced nonsignificant increments in explained variance when entered into regression equations after attitude components.

Secondary analysis revealed an interesting effect for the incremental, supplementary predictive role of these loci of control variables. Consistent with the third theoretical proposition, among those individual respondents for whom attitudes were not as strongly predictive of behavior (i.e., low-certainty and low-triadic consistency participants as will be discussed), the loci of control measures jointly produced the greatest increment in explained variance in

---

[10] McDermott's (1974) study represents the most systematic investigation of the tridimensional locus of control construct discussed in footnote 8. Items hypothesized to capture each locus of control did factor along three dimensions, and the two factors whose composition most closely reflected the theorized personal and situational loci evidenced strong correlation with the dependent variable. These factors remained stable across the two phases of the experiment.

action. Whereas this was usually about a 4% of explained variance increase, when attitudes were least predictive in general at time 3 the increments were 14 and 22% ($p < .05$) for the low-certainty and low-consistency subgroups, respectively (see Seibold, 1979, Table 4). These results extend others' findings that "other variables" may serve as generative mechanisms for behavior and they lend support to the theory's predictions about (a) the relative importance of attitudinal factors in the prediction of behavior when other loci of control are consistent and cannot be assumed to afford greater personal control for action; and (b) the increasing importance of other loci of control as attitudinal impact on action declines under instances where attitudes are still consistent with these loci.

Verbal Report–Behavior Consistency

Adequacy of Attitude–Verbal Report–Behavior Model. Meaningful test of specific verbal report–behavior consistency predictions requires some verification of the underlying theory which spawned them. While the Seibold and McPhee (1979b) research just discussed bespeaks the adequacy of the attitudinal portion of the model, the relationship of these attitudinal dynamics *to behavior* remains at issue. Path analysis undertaken in Seibold (1979) addressed the issue directly. The model depicted in Figure 6.2 was tested for adequacy of fit to the overtime volunteer attitude and behavior data previously described. The following restrictions were imposed (a) consistent with the present theory, paths 10 and 23 were deleted; (b) the variance of the residual of underlying attitude at Time$_1$ was set to 1.0 to achieve identification; and (c) although cross-time paths were left free to vary, only Time$_1$ within-time paths were set free (T$_2$–T$_3$ within-time paths were set equal to simulate the theoretic condition that, unless other loci of control affect attitudes as well as behaviors, attitude components are assumed to be stable and consistent over time). Results of the LISREL–III path analysis are reported in Table 6.2.

The general adequacy of the structural relationships proposed over time is indicated by the overall chi-square goodness of fit test ($\chi^2 = 50.19$; df $= 39$; $p > .1080$). Examination of the residuals between predicted and actual values also suggests adequate fit of the model to data. Finally, the standardized path coefficients suggest a consistent pattern of attitude component effects on behavior. This pattern of conation, affect, and cognition as the most to least important individual attitudinal predictors at each time is consistent with the secondary R^2 decomposition analyses of these data discussed in McPhee and Seibold (1979a). In the commonality analyses reported, intention consistently bore the strongest relationship to action at each point in time, whereas desirability accounted for smaller independent portions of the explained variance in behavior, and likelihood functioned as a suppressor variable.

These results lend support to the theory underlying the structural model. They also support the theoretic presumption that these attitudinal factors have no necessary causal force on each other (as also evidenced by the attitude structure comparative modeling results already reported), but may have independent causal influences on behavior (cf. the unique effect estimates reported in McPhee & Seibold, 1979a, pp. 374–376). On the other hand, it would be injudicious to say support for the model is unequivocal. The standardized path

TABLE 6.2

Standardized Path Coefficients, Autocorrelations, Residuals, and Test Statistics for Path Model (Figure 6.2)

Standardized path coefficients[a]

1.	.508	9.	1.132	17.	1.453	25.	.230
2.	.964	10.	—	18.	−.190	26.	−.233
3.	1.007	11.	.241	19.	−.132	27.	.018
4.	1.461	12.	.184	20.	.089	28.	.283
5.	−.437	13.	−.316	21.	.032	29.	.318
6.	−.006	14.	.018	22.	.836	30.	1.453
7.	2.554	15.	.283	23.	—	31.	−.188
8.	−.027	16.	.318	24.	.313	32.	−.128

Autocorrelations

	$(T) \times (T + 1)$	$(T_1) \times (T_3)$
Underlying attitude	−.833	1.859
Intention	−.145	−.073
Desirability	.106	.060
Likelihood	.189	.099
Behavior	.322	.501

Residuals between predicted and actual correlation values

T_1

Intention	.057			
Desirability	−.028	.030		
Likelihood	−.072	.037	.013	
Behavior	−.081	−.017	.034	.008

T_2

Intention	−.235	.084	.102	−.048	.223			
Desirability	−.003	.010	.031	−.072	−.033	−.001		
Likelihood	−.032	.009	.034	.001	−.039	−.007	.015	
Behavior	−.182	.028	.036	.023	.059	−.036	.007	.070

T_3

Intention	−.125	−.014	.038	.031	−.098	.049	.054	.076	.121			
Desirability	−.005	.025	.064	−.056	.017	.011	.026	−.015	.026	.010		
Likelihood	−.020	.023	.029	.052	−.020	.008	.015	.016	−.005	.042	.018	
Behavior	−.069	.009	.001	.005	−.008	−.011	.014	.015	.039	−.003	−.006	−.020

Test statistics

$$\chi^2 = 50.198; \ df = 39; \ p > .1080$$

[a] Numbers to left of each coefficient refer to appropriate causal path in Figure 6.2. $n = 98$.

coefficients larger than 1.0, the large autocorrelations and modifications involving underlying attitudes over time, and the barely satisfactory test-statistic probability suggest that the causal inferences permitted by the results are not strong and that certain aspects of the general model results are not theoretically meaningful. Indeed, modifications to the model (e.g., leaving all paths free to vary) produced a somewhat better and more interpretable fit to the data (Seibold, 1979), but these alterations do not inform the theory proposed and tested here.

Factors Affecting Consistency. As discussed (pp. 211–214) renewed optimism about attitude–behavior consistency has been the result of research pointing to factors that influence report–behavior correspondence. In particular, perceived reference group pressures (Andrews & Kandel, 1979), social expectations (Norman, 1975), situational differences (Bem & Allen, 1974), personal traits (Snyder & Tanke, 1976), public commitment (Green, 1972), and attitudinal confidence (Fazio & Zanna, 1978), certainty (Sample & Warland, 1973), salience (Brown, 1974), stability (Schwartz, 1978), and intensity have been shown to moderate verbal report–behavior correspondence. These findings are consistent with the present theory's identification of certainty, salience, behavioral effort, triadic consistency, attitudinal stability, measurement correspondence, and other loci of control as moderators of verbal report–behavior relationships. The nonexperimental nature of the volunteerism data reported thus far, however, obviates its usefulness for direct test of these predictions. Seibold (1979) reports results of secondary analyses of these data involving partitioning respondents into high versus low attitudinal certainty and triadic consistency groups. Comparative analyses of these groups suggested some support for attitudinal certainty and consistency as moderators of report–behavior consistency. Furthermore, reinterpretation of the findings discussed, demonstrating strong prediction of behavior from attitudinal predictors over time ($R = .85, .79$, and $.76$), was consistent with theoretic propositions about the nature of the behavior involved as a factor influencing report–behavior correspondence.

Summary

Following review of recent research suggesting four bases for optimism about explaining and predicting attitude–behavior consistency, a theory of attitudinally relevant social behavior was proposed. The theory embeds a tricomponent and elaborated latent process model of attitude–behavior relations into a larger theoretic framework involving alternative loci of control for behavior. The theory and its scope conditions identify when and which of these alternative causes of action should be primary, as well as factors affecting verbal report–behavior consistency. Whereas the specific predictions offered are quite consistent with previous research findings, their theoretic genesis is somewhat unique and differ from the paradigmatic behavioral intention theory (Fishbein and Ajzen, 1975). Analysis of over-time data revealed preliminary support for the underlying model of attitude organization; the structural modeling of attitude–behavior relationships proposed; the primacy of attitudinal effects on action under conditions where alternative potential loci of control are not inconsistent; the independent effect on behavior of specific attitudinal components; and several of the predictions about moderators of verbal report–behavior consistency. In the absence of replication, without more controlled study, and until comparative test against alternative theoretic predictions is undertaken, these findings are tentative.

Communication Implications

Support for the theory of attitudinally relevant social behavior proposed is qualified but suggestive. Further tests and refinements in the theory may proceed most profitably if they are tied to analysis and test of the theory's communication implications. For, short of personal experiences, information received in communicative interactions with others is a principal mechanism for the formation and development of attitudes and perceptions of salient loci of control, as well as for changing these generative mechanisms (cf. Fazio, Zanna, & Cooper, 1978; Regan & Fazio, 1977). Unlike other theories (Hewes, Chapter 2, this volume) in which adoption of a particular metatheoretical framework may preclude the development of content-specific messages, the present analysis offers a fertile ground for the development of persuasive strategies.

In particular, the theory identifies specific foci for intrapersonal influence (tricomponent attitudes and personal, social, and situational loci of control) and challenges the persuader to negotiate with others the relevance and significance of certain of those factors in particular action contexts. Change in individual factors may make them salient enough to have initial and complementary effects on behavior (or more powerful effects if they are already significantly related to behavior). Alternately, messages may diminish the salience of specific attitude components or loci of control factors by shifting individuals' perceptions of the relevance of alternative, noncomplementary generative mechanisms.

Elsewhere (Seibold, 1975a), I have discussed three message strategies educed from this perspective. Briefly, they include the increased probability of attitude–behavior consistency as a function of communications that are attitudinally consistent and that bolster an individual's certainty along particular attitudinal dimensions. Second, messages may alter an actor's perceptions of the loci of control for behavior so that decision choices are seen in terms of specific personal rules, social expectations, or situational exigencies. Third, messages linking appeals to desired goals, demonstrating the truth or likelihood of this connection, or reinforcing intention to act in accord with the appeal may affect behavior through the moderating effect of change in the individual attitude component influenced. To these potential direct effects, we may add predictions that messages demonstrating inconsistencies between past actions and personal control consequences (or that cast the proposed new action in the context of individuals' motivations for a sense of personal freedom and control) may be more efficacious for behavior than those that do not; and messages which increase consistency among tricomponent attitudes may produce greater attitudinal effects on action. Messages that resolve inconsistencies between personal attitudes and perceived loci of control (especially social expectations) will in turn increase the primacy of attitudes for action (Norman, 1978).

The theory proposed also has implications for potential indirect or "fall-out" effects of persuasive messages. Consider, for example, instances in which more than one attitudinal component may be predictive of behavior. Decomposition of the variance in behavior explained by tricomponent attitudes can identify unique effects of each, first-order "common effects" of pairs of variables, and second-order commonalities representing the variance explained in behavior by all three (McPhee & Seibold, 1979a). As I have argued elsewhere (Seibold & McPhee, 1979a), because the share of variance explained by the first-order pairs or second-order group of all three components can be explained by any single component in that common effect, communications designed to influence behaviors through effects on specific components may have an additional effect on behavior through the joint effect which that component shares with one or both other attitudinal constituents. Conversely, in instances in which one of the attitude components acts as a "suppressor variable" (Nunnally, 1967, p. 162), a message, which produces change in another component identified as causally related to behavior, may have its subsequent persuasive effect on behavior vitiated because a portion of the component's effect is diminished through its shared effect on behavior with the suppressor component. By implication, primary targets for persuasive messages in these instances would need to be the components with the highest total unique and common effects on action. Stated differently, both unique and shared explained variance with behavior may be a better potential influence indicator than attitude components with only large, individual effects on action, if those effects are substantially reduced by negative common effects. Furthermore, in these cases, messages would have to be "purified" of relevance for the suppressor variable (i.e., designed to produce no impact on the variable acting as suppressor). These propositions are highly speculative and warrant careful experimental test to determine whether they have empirical efficacy or are merely mathematical artifacts.

Finally, the theory proposed entails dissonace-related consequences. Dissonance effects occur principally when attitude discrepant behaviors lead to unwanted or aversive consequences (Eagly & Himmelfarb, 1978). However, research by Reiss and Schlenker (1977) suggests that dissonance effects may be reversible when actors are able to utilize others' feedback about low-decision freedom to deny personal responsibility for the counterattitudinal act. Within the context of the present model, behaviors may be counterattitudinally affected by other loci of control and may be discrepant with subsequent underlying attitudes (paths 8 and 21 in Figure 6.2). From a communication standpoint, messages that help instantiate counterattitudinal behaviors (that the change agent views as prosocial), through appeals to significant social pressures, may facilitate compliance and internalization (Kelman, 1961) by following up with reinforcing messages which do not merely make the newly acquired behavior more attitudinally palatable but also reduce individual dissonance through locating the pressures that forced action in perceived external loci of control. In the alternate case, antisocial behaviors produced by social pressures, resistance to persuasion via concept boosting (Tannenbaum, Macaulay, & Norris, 1966) may be possible through messages that support existing attitudes that are threatened by discrepant social expectations.

Conclusion

This chapter has yielded an optimistic review of attitude–behavior issues, optimism that has been closely tied to arguments for the utility of viewing these issues in causal process terms. A causal process theory, causal modeling tests, and potential causal effects of communication on attitudes and behaviors have been mainstays of the content-specific ideas proposed. Like other writers in this volume who have advocated particular metatheoretical frameworks, I must return to questions concerning the fundamental utility of this superstructure. Does the causal process perspective and causal modeling constrain research on attitude–behavior issues? Probably not. Within the context of the variable-analytic, positivistic, laboratory investigations that have engendered most of the "knowledge" in this area, I have tried to point out (p. 204) that it is doubtful that causal process formalization and tests will occasion serious philosophical, theoretical, axiological, or methodological difficulties. Does a causal process perspective have special advantages for theory construction and knowledge generation in this area? Decidedly so. If anything emerges from the work discussed (pp. 209–232), it is that issues like attitude–behavior correlational consistency become special cases of larger causal analyses of social behavior. That these causal analyses may be at once descriptive, yet invoke and depend upon precise underlying theories, makes the approach both empirically heuristic and conceptually vigorous. Finally, wedding causal process analyses to over-time (developmental and sequential) research questions and procedures about attitude–behavior relationships signals another major potential of this approach. The particular theory, test, and communication implications proffered are merely specific examples of the promise of this metatheoretical perspective.

Even if they prove to be incorrect, the causal process approach they embody will have continued utility for attitude–behavior research. As Schuman and Johnson (1976) conclude:

> Our review has shown that most A–B studies yield positive results. The correlations that do occur are large enough to suggest that important causal forces are involved, whatever one's model of the underlying causal process may be [p. 199].

ACKNOWLEDGMENT

I wish to thank Robert McPhee and David Sanford for their helpful comments and assistance during the preparation of this chapter.

REFERENCES

Abelson, R. Are attitudes necessary? In B. King & E. McGinnies (Eds.), *Attitudes, conflict, and social change*. New York: Academic Press, 1972. Pp. 19–32.

Achinstein, P. *Law and explanation*. Oxford: Clarendon Press, 1971.

Acock, A. C., & DeFleur, M. L. A configurational approach to contingent consistency in the attitude–behavior relationship. *American Sociological Review*, 1972, *37*, 714–726.

Ajzen, I., & Fishbein, M. Attitude–behavior relations: A theoretical analysis and review of empirical research. *Psychological Bulletin*, 1977, *84*, 888–918.

Albrecht, S. L., DeFleur, M. L., & Warner, L. G. Attitude–behavior relationships: A reexamination of the postulate of contingent consistency. *Pacific Sociological Review*, 1972, *15*, 149–168.

Allport, G. Attitudes. In C. Murchinson (Ed.), *A handbook of social psychology*. Worchester, Mass.: Clark University Press, 1935. Pp. 798–844.

Alston, W. P. Wants, actions and causal explanation. In H. Castañeda (Ed.), *Intentionality, minds, and perception*. Detroit: Wayne State University Press, 1966. Pp. 301–341.

Alwin, D. F. Making inferences from attitude–behavior correlations. *Sociometry*. 1973, *36*, 253–278.

Alwin, D. F. Attitude scales as congeneric tests: A reexamination of an attitude–behavior model. *Sociometry*, 1976, *39*, 377–383.

Andrews, K. H., & Kandel, D. B. Attitude and behavior: A specification of the contingent consistency hypothesis. *American Sociological Review*, 1979, *44*, 298–310.

Anscombe, G. E. M. *Intention*. Oxford: Basil Blackwell & Mott, 1958.

Audi, R. On the conception and measurement of attitudes in contemporary Anglo-American psychology. *Journal of Theory and Social Behavior*, 1972, *2*, 179–203.

Bailey, K. Evaluating axiomatic theories. In E. Borgatta & G. Bohrnstedt (Eds.), *Sociological methodology*, 1970. San Francisco: Jossey–Bass, 1970. Pp. 48–71.

Bearden, W., & Woodside, A. The effect of attitudes and previous behavior on consumer choice. *Journal of Social Psychology*, 1977, *103*, 129–138.

Bem, D. J. Attitudes as self-descriptions: Another look at the attitude–behavior link. In A. G. Greenwald, T. C. Brock, & T. M. Ostrom (Eds.), *Psychological foundations of attitudes*. New York: Academic Press, 1968. Pp. 197–215.

Bem, D. M., & Allen, A. On predicting some of the people some of the time: The search for cross-situational consistencies in behavior. *Psychological Review*, 1974, *81*, 506–520.

Blalock, H. *Theory construction: From verbal to mathematical formulations.* Englewood Cliffs, N.J.: Prentice–Hall, 1969.

Blalock, H. *Causal models in the social sciences.* Chicago: Aldine, 1971.

Bonfield, E. Attitude, social influence, personal norm, and intention interactions as related to branch purchase behavior. *Journal of Marketing Research*, 1974, *11*, 379–389.

Brannon, R. Attitudes and the prediction of behavior. In B. Seidenberg & A. Snadowsky (Eds.), *Social psychology: An introduction.* New York: Free Press, 1976.

Brinberg, D. *An examination of the determinants of intention and behavior: A comparison of two models.* Unpublished manuscript, Department of Textiles and Consumer Economics, University of Maryland, 1979.

Brown, D. Adolescent attitudes and lawful behavior. *Public Opinion Quarterly*, 1974, *38*, 98–106.

Burhans, D. The attitude–behavior discrepancy problem: Revisited. *Quarterly Journal of Speech*, 1971, *57*, 418–428.

Calder, B. J., & Ross, M. *Attitudes and behavior.* Morristown, N.J.: General Learning Press, 1973.

Campbell, D. T. Social attitudes and other acquired behavioral dispositions. In S. Koch (Ed.), *Psychology: A study of a science* (Vol. 6). New York: McGraw–Hill, 1963. Pp. 94–172.

Campbell, D. T., & Fiske, D. W. Convergent and discriminant validation by the multitrait–multimethod matrix. *Psychological Bulletin*, 1959, *56*, 81–105.

Cappella, J. Detecting causal priority among variables in a nonexperimental design. Paper presented at the annual convention of the International Communication Association, Chicago, 1975. (a)

Cappella, J. An introduction to the literature of causal modeling. *Human Communication Research*, 1975, *1*, 362–377. (b)

Chaffee, S., & Lindner, J. Three processes of value change without behavior change. *Journal of Communication*, 1969, *19*, 30–40.

Charters, W., Jr., & Newcomb, T. Some attitudinal effects of experimentally increased salience of a membership group. In E. Maccoby, T. Newcomb, & E. Hartley (Eds.), *Readings in social psychology.* New York: Holt, 1958. Pp. 276–281.

Cialdini, R. B., Levy, A., Herman, C. P., Kozlowski, L. T., & Petty, R. Elastic shifts: Determinants of direction and durability. *Journal of Personality and Social Psychology*, 1976, *34*, 663–672.

Cohen, M., & Nagel, E. *An introduction to logic and scientific method.* New York: Harcourt, Brace, 1934.

Cook, T. D., & Flay, B. R. The persistence of experimentally induced attitude change. In L. Berkowitz (Ed.), *Advances in experimental social psychology* (Vol. 11). New York: Academic Press, 1978. Pp. 1–57.

Costner, H. L., & Leik, R. K. Deductions from axiomatic theory. *American Sociological Review*, 1964, *29*, 819–835.

Costner, H., & Schoenberg, R. Diagnosing indicator ills in multiple indicator models. In A. Goldberger & O. Duncan (Eds.), *Structural equation models in the social sciences.* New York: Seminar Press, 1973. Pp. 167–199.

Crespi, I. What kinds of attitude measures are predictive of behavior? *Public Opinion Quarterly*, 1971, *35*, 327–334.

Cronen, V. E., & Davis, L. K. Alternative approaches for the communication theorist: Problems in the laws–rules–systems trichotomy. *Human Communication Research*, 1978, *4*, 120–128.

Cronkhite, G. *Persuasion: Speech and behavioral change.* Indianapolis: Bobbs–Merrill, 1969.

Cushman, D. The rules perspective as a theoretical basis for the study of human communication. *Communication Quarterly*, 1977, *25*, 30–45.

Cushman, D., & Pearce, B. Generality and necessity in three types of theory, with special attention to rules theory. *Human Communication Research*, 1977, *3*, 344–353.

Danes, J. E. Communication models of the message–belief change process. In B. Ruben (Ed.), *Communication Yearbook 2.* New Brunswick, N.J.: Transaction Press, 1978. Pp. 110–124.

Danes, J. E. Designing persuasive communication campaigns: A multimessage communication model. Unpublished manuscript, Communication Research Program, University of Connecticut, 1979.

Dannick, L. The relationship between overt behaviors and verbal expressions as influenced by immediate situational determinants. Unpublished doctoral dissertation, Department of Sociology, Syracuse University, 1969.

Davey, A. Attitudes and the prediction of social conduct. *British Journal of Social and Clinical Psychology*, 1976, *15*, 11–22.

Davidson, D. Actions, reasons and causes. *Journal of Philosophy*, 1963, *60*, 685–700.

DeFleur, M. L., & Westie, F. R. Attitude as a scientific concept. *Social Forces*, 1963, *42*, 17–31.

Deutscher, I. Words and deeds: Social science and social policy. *Social Problems*, 1966, *13*, 235–254.

Deutscher, I. *What we say / What we do: Sentiments and acts*. Glenview, Ill.: Scott, Foresman, 1973.

Dillehay, R. C. On the irrelevance of the classical negative evidence concerning the effects of attitudes on behavior. *American Psychologist*, 1973, *28*, 887–891.

Doob, L. The behavior of attitudes. *Psychological Review*, 1947, *54*, 135–156.

Duncan, O. Some linear models for two-wave, two-variable path analysis. *Psychological Bulletin*, 1969, *72*, 177–182.

Duncan, O. Unmeasured variables in linear models for panel analysis. In H. Costner (Ed.), *Sociological methodology, 1972*. San Francisco: Jossey–Bass, 1972. Pp. 36–82.

Duncan, O. *Introduction to structural equation models*. New York: Academic Press, 1975.

Dunnette, M. D. Fads, fashions, and folderol in psychology. *American Psychologist*, 1966, *21*, 333–342.

Eagly, A. H., & Himmelfarb, S. Attitudes and opinions. *Annual Review of Psychology*, 1978, *29*, 517–554.

Ehrlich, H. J. Attitudes, behavior, and the intervening variables. *American Sociologist*, 1969, *4*, 35–41.

Fazio, R. H., & Zanna, M. P. Attitudinal qualities relating to the strength of the attitude–behavior relationship. *Journal of Experimental Social Psychology*, 1978, *14*, 398–408.

Fazio, R. H., Zanna, M. P., & Cooper, J. Direct experience and attitude–behavior consistency: An information processing analysis. *Personality and Social Psychology Bulletin*, 1978, *4*, 48–51.

Festinger, L. *A theory of cognitive dissonance*. Evanston, Ill.: Row & Peterson, 1957.

Festinger, L. Behavioral support for opinion change. *Public Opinion Quarterly*, 1964, *28*, 404–417.

Fields, J., & Schuman, H. Public beliefs about the beliefs of the public. *Public Opinion Quarterly*, 1977, *40*, 427–448.

Fink, E. L. Structural equation modeling: Unobserved variables. In P. R. Monge & J. N. Cappella (Eds.), *Multivariate techniques in communication research*. New York: Academic Press, 1980.

Fishbein, M. An investigation of the relationships between beliefs about an object and the attitude toward that object. *Human Relations*, 1963, *16*, 233–240.

Fishbein, M. The prediction of behavior from attitudinal variables. In C. D. Mortensen & K. K. Sereno (Eds.), *Advances in communication research*. New York: Harper & Row, 1973. Pp. 3–31.

Fishbein, M., & Ajzen, I. Attitudes towards objects as predictors of single and multiple behavioral criteria. *Psychological Review*, 1974, *81*, 59–74.

Fishbein, M., & Ajzen, I. *Belief, attitude, intention, and behavior: An introduction to theory and research*. Reading, Mass.: Addison–Wesley, 1975.

Frideres, J. Situational and personality variables as influencing the relationship between attitudes and overt behavior. *Canadian Review of Sociology and Anthropology*, 1971, *8*, 91–105.

Frideres, J., Warner, L., & Albrecht, L. The impact of constraints on the relationship between attitude and behavior. *Social Forces*, 1971, *50*, 102–112.

Genthner, R. W., & Taylor, S. P. Physical aggression as a function of racial prejudice and the race of the target. *Journal of Personality and Social Psychology*, 1973, *27*, 13–18.

Goldberger, A. S. Structural equation models: An overview. In A. S. Goldberger & O. D. Duncan

(Eds.), *Structural equation models in the social sciences*. New York: Seminar Press, 1973. Pp. 1–18.

Goldberger, A., & Duncan, O. *Structural equation models in the social sciences*. New York: Seminar Press, 1973.

Goldman, A. I. *A theory of human action*. Englewood Cliffs, N.J.: Prentice-Hall, 1970.

Green, J. A. Attitudinal and situational determinants of intended behavior toward blacks. *Journal of Personality and Social Psychology*, 1972, *22*, 13–17.

Greenwald, A. Effects of prior commitment on behavior change after a persuasive communication. *Public Opinion Quarterly*, 1965, *29*, 595–601.

Hage, J. *Techniques and problems of theory construction in sociology*. New York: Wiley, 1972.

Harré, R. *The principles of scientific thinking*. Chicago: University of Chicago Press, 1970.

Harré, R., & Madden, E. *Causal powers*. Totowa, N.J.: Rowman & Littlefield, 1975.

Hass, R. G., & Mann, R. W. Anticipatory belief change: Persuasion or impression management? *Journal of Personality and Social Psychology*, 1976, *34*, 680–693.

Hauser, R., & Goldberger, A. The treatment of unobservable variables in path analysis. In H. Costner (Ed.), *Sociological methodology, 1971*. San Francisco: Jossey–Bass, 1971. Pp. 81–117.

Heberlein, T. A., & Black, J. S. Attitudinal specificity and the prediction of behavior in a field setting. *Journal of Personality and Social Psychology*, 1976, *33*, 474–479.

Heise, D. Problems in path analysis and causal inference. In E. Borgatta (Ed.), *Sociological methodology, 1969*. San Francisco: Jossey–Bass, 1969. Pp. 38–73. (a)

Heise, D. Separating reliability and stability in test–retest correlation. *American Sociological Review*, 1969, *34*, 93–101. (b)

Heise, D. Causal inference from panel data. In E. Borgatta & G. Bohrnstedt (Eds.), *Sociological methodology, 1970*. San Francisco: Jossey–Bass, 1970. Pp. 3–27.

Heise, D. *Causal analysis*. New York: Wiley–Interscience, 1975.

Herman, J. B. Are situational contingencies limiting job attitude–job performance relationships? *Organizational Behavior and Human Performance*, 1973, *10*, 208–224.

Hewes, D. A stochastic model of the relationship between attitudes and behaviors. Paper presented at the annual convention of the International Communication Association, Chicago, 1975.

Himmelstein, P., & Moore, J. C. Racial attitudes and the action of negro- and white-background figures as factors in petition signing. *Journal of Social Psychology*, 1963, *61*, 267–272.

Insko, C. A., Worchel, S., Folger, R., Kutkus, A. A balance theory interpretation of dissonance. *Psychological Review*, 1975, *82*, 169–183.

Insko, C. A., & Schopler, J. Triadic consistency: A statement of affective–cognitive–conative consistency. *Psychological Review*, 1967, *74*, 361–376.

Jackman, M. R. The relation between verbal attitude and overt behavior: A public opinion application. *Social Forces*, 1976, *54*, 646–668.

Janis, I. L., & Mann, L. *Decision making: A psychological analysis of conflict, choice, and commitment*. New York: Free Press, 1977.

Jöreskog, K. A general approach to confirmatory maximum likelihood factor analysis. *Psychometrika*, 1969, *34*, 184–202.

Jöreskog, K. A general method for the analysis of covariance structures. *Biometrika*, 1970, *57*, 239–251.

Jöreskog, K. Analyzing psychological data by structural analysis of covariance matrices. In D. H. Krantz, R. C. Atkinson, R. D. Luce, & P. Suppes (Eds.), *Contemporary developments in mathematical psychology, measurement, psychophysics and neural information processing* (Vol. 3). San Francisco: Freeman, 1974.

Jöreskog, K., & Van Thillo, M. *LISREL: A general computer program for estimating a linear structural equation system involving multiple indicators of unmeasured variables*. Princeton, N.J.: Educational Testing Service, 1972.

Jöreskog, K., & Sörbom, D. *LISREL III*. Chicago: National Education Resources, 1976.

Kelly, S., & Mirer, T. The simple act of voting. *American Political Science Review*, 1974, *68*, 572–591.

Kelman, H. C. Processes of opinion change. *Public Opinion Quarterly*, 1961, *25*, 57–78.

Kelman, H. Attitudes are alive and well and gainfully employed in the sphere of action. *American Psychologist*, 1974, *29*, 310–324.

Kerlinger, F., & Pedhazur, E. *Multiple regression in the behavioral sciences*. New York: Holt, Rinehart & Winston, 1973.

Kimsey, W. D., & Atwood, L. E. A path model of political cognitions and attitudes, communication and voting behavior in a congressional election. *Communication Monographs*, 1979, *46*, 219–230.

Kothandapani, V. Validation of feeling, belief, and intention to act as three components of attitude and their contribution to prediction of contraceptive behavior. *Journal of Personality and Social Psychology*, 1971, *19*, 321–333.

Kutner, B., Wilkins, C., & Yarrow, P. R. Verbal attitudes and overt behavior involving racial prejudice. *Journal of Abnormal and Social Psychology*, 1952, *47*, 649–652.

Land, K. C. Principles of path analysis. In E. F. Borgatta (Ed.), *Sociological methodology, 1969*. San Francisco: Jossey–Bass, 1969. Pp. 3–37.

LaPiere, R. T. Attitudes vs. actions. *Social Forces*, 1934, *13*, 230–237.

Larson, C., & Sanders, R. Faith, mystery, and data: An analysis of 'scientific' studies of persuasion. *Quarterly Journal of Speech*, 1975, *61*, 178–194.

Liska, A. E. Emergent issues in the attitude–behavior consistency controversy. *American Sociological Review*, 1974, *39*, 261–272.

Liska, A. E. (Ed.), *The consistency controversy: Readings on the impact of attitude on behavior*. New York: Halsted Press, 1975.

Lott, B. E. Attitude formation: The development of a color-preference response through mediated generalization. *Journal of Abnormal and Social Psychology*, 1955, *50*, 321–326.

Lott, A. J., & Lott, B. E. A learning theory approach to interpersonal attitudes. In A. G. Greenwald, T. C. Brock, & T. M. Ostrom (Eds.), *Psychological foundations of attitudes*. New York: Academic Press, 1968. Pp. 67–88.

Mayer, L., & Younger, M. Multiple indicators and the relationship between abstract variables. In D. Heise (Ed.), *Sociological methodology, 1975*. San Francisco: Jossey–Bass, 1975. Pp. 191–211.

McClelland, P. *Causal explanation and model building in history, economics, and the new economic history*. Ithaca, N.Y.: Cornell University Press, 1975.

McDermott, V. The development of a functional message variable: The locus of control. Paper presented at the annual convention of the Speech Communication Association, Chicago, 1974.

McDermott, V. The literature on classical theory construction. *Human Communication Research*, 1975, *2*, 83–103.

McGuire, W. The nature of attitudes and attitude change. In G. Lindzey & E. Aronson (Eds.), *The handbook of social psychology* (Vol. 3). Reading, MA: Addison–Wesley, 1969, 139–314.

McPhee, R. Derivation and test of a new model of message–attitude–behavior relations. Paper presented at the annual convention of the International Communication Association, Chicago, 1975.

McPhee, R. D., & Seibold, D. R. Rationale, procedures, and applications for decomposition of explained variance in multiple regression analyses. *Communication Research*, 1979, *6*, 345–384. (a)

McPhee, R. D., & Seibold, D. R. Testing alternative sources of change in attitudes and behaviors. Paper presented at the annual convention of the International Communication Association, Philadelphia, 1979. (b)

Melden, A. I. *Free action*. London: Routledge & Kegan Paul, 1961.

Mervielde, I. Methodological problems of research about attitude–behavior consistency. *Quantity and Quality*, 1977, *2*, 157–280.

Miller, G. R. A crucial problem in attitude research. *Quarterly Journal of Speech*, 1967, *53*, 235–240.

Miller, G. R. Communication and persuasion research: Current problems and prospects. *Quarterly Journal of Speech*, 1968, *54*, 268–276.

Miller, G. R., & Burgoon, M. Persuasion research: Review and commentary. In B. D. Ruben (Ed.), *Communication Yearbook 2*. New Brunswick, N.J.: Transaction Books, 1978. Pp. 29–47.

Miller, G. R., & Simons, H. W. (Eds.). *Perspectives on communication in social conflict*. Englewood Cliffs, N.J.: Prentice-Hall, 1974.

Miller, G. R., & Steinberg, M. *Between people: A new analysis of interpersonal communication*. Palo Alto, Calif.: SRA, 1975.

Minard, R. Race relations in the Pochahontas coal field. *Journal of Social Issues*, 1952, *8*, 29–44.

Monge, P. Theory construction in the study of communication: The systems paradigm. *Journal of Communication*, 1973, *23*, 5–16.

Monge, P. The systems perspective as a theoretical basis for the study of human communication. *Communication Quarterly*, 1977, *25*, 19–29.

Norman, R. Affective–cognitive consistency, attitudes, conformity, and behavior. *Journal of Personality and Social Psychology*, 1975, *32*, 83–91.

Nunnally, J. C. *Psychometric theory*. New York: McGraw-Hill, 1967.

Nuttin, J. M. *The illusion of attitude change: Toward a response contagion theory of persuasion*. London: Academic Press, 1975.

O'Keefe, D. Logical empiricism and the study of human communication. *Speech Monographs*, 1975, *42*, 169–183.

Osgood, C. E. Cross-cultural comparability in attitude-measurement via multilingual semantic differentials. In I. D. Steiner & M. Fishbein (Eds.), *Current studies in social psychology*. New York: Holt, Rinehart & Winston, 1965.

Ostrom, T. M. The relationship between the affective, behavioral, and cognitive components of attitude. *Journal of Experimental Social Psychology*, 1969, *5*, 12–30.

Parks, M. R. Issues in the explication of communication competency. Paper presented at the annual convention of the Western Speech Communication Association, 1977.

Pelz, D., & Andrews, F. Detecting causal priority in panel study data. *American Sociological Review*, 1964, *29*, 836–848.

Pepper, S. *World hypotheses: A study in evidence*. Berkeley: University of California Press, 1942.

Petersen, K., & Dutton, J. E. Centrality, extremity, intensity: Neglected variables in research on attitude–behavior consistency. *Social Forces*, 1975, *54*, 393–414.

Price, P., & Bouffard, D. Behavioral appropriateness and situational constraint as dimensions of social behavior. *Journal of Personality and Social Psychology*, 1974, *30*, 579–586.

Raden, D. Situational thresholds and attitude–behavior consistency. *Sociometry*, 1977, *40*, 123–129.

Regan, D. T., & Fazio, R. On the consistency between attitudes and behavior: Look to the method of attitude formation. *Journal of Experimental Social Psychology*, 1977, *13*, 28–45.

Reynolds, P. *A primer in theory construction*. Indianapolis: Bobbs-Merrill, 1971.

Reiss, M., & Schlenker, B. R. Attitude change and responsibility avoidance as modes of dilemma resolution in forced compliance situations. *Journal of Personality and Social Psychology*, 1977, *35*, 21–30.

Ring, K. Experimental social psychology: Some sobering questions about some frivolous values. In A. G. Miller (Ed.), *The social psychology of psychological research*. New York: Free Press, 1972. Pp. 48–57.

Rockwell, R. C. Assessment of multicolinearity: The Haitovsky test of the determinant. *Sociological Methods and Research*, 1975, *3*, 308–320.

Rokeach, M. Attitude change and behavior change. *Public Opinion Quarterly*, 1967, *30*, 529–550.

Rokeach, M., & Kliejunas, P. Behavior as a function of attitude-toward-object and attitude-toward-situation. *Journal of Personality and Social Psychology*, 1972, *22*, 194–201.

Rosen, B., & Komorita, S. S. Attitudes and action: The effects of behavioral intent and perceived effectiveness of acts. *Journal of Personality*, 1971, *39*, 189–203.

Rosenberg, M. J. An analysis of affective–cognitive consistency. In C. I. Hovland & M. J. Rosenberg (Eds.), *Attitude organization and change: An analysis of consistency among attitude components*. New Haven: Yale University Press, 1960. Pp. 15–64.

Rosenberg, M. J., & Abelson, R. P. An analysis of cognitive balancing. In C. I. Hovland & M. J. Rosenberg (Eds.), *Attitude organization and change: An analysis of consistency among attitude components*. New Haven: Yale University Press, 1960. Pp. 112–163.

Rosenberg, M. J., & Hovland, C. I. Cognitive, affective, and behavioral components of attitudes. In C. I. Hovland & M. J. Rosenberg (Eds.), *Attitude organization and change*. New Haven: Yale University Press, 1960, Pp. 1–14.

Rotter, J. Generalized expectancies for internal versus external control of reinforcement. *Psychological Monographs*, 1966, *80*, 1–28.

Sample, J., & Warland, R. Attitude and the prediction of behavior. *Social Forces*, 1973, *51*, 292–304.

Schoenberg, R. Strategies for meaningful comparison. In H. L. Costner (Ed.), *Sociological methodology, 1972*. San Francisco: Jossey–Bass, 1972. Pp. 1–35.

Schuman, H., & Johnson, M. P. Attitudes and behavior. *Annual Review of Sociology*, 1976, *2*, 161–207.

Schwab, D., & Cummings, L. Theories of performance and satisfaction: A review. *Industrial Relations*, 1970, *9*, 408–430.

Schwartz, S. H. Normative explanations of helping behavior: A critique, proposal and empirical test. *Journal of Experimental Social Psychology*, 1973, *9*, 349–364.

Schwartz, S. Temporal instability as a moderator of the attitude–behavior relationship. *Journal of Personality and Social Psychology*, 1978, *36*, 715–724.

Schwartz, S. H., & Tessler, R. C. A test of a model for reducing measured attitude–behavior discrepancies. *Journal of Personality and Social Psychology*, 1972, *24*, 225–236.

Seibold, D. R. Communication research and the attitude–verbal report–overt behavior relationship: A critique and theoretical reformulation. *Human Communication Research*, 1975, *2*, 3–32. (a)

Seibold, D. R. A formalization of attribution theory: Critique and implications for communication. Paper presented at the annual convention of the Central States Speech Association, Kansas City, 1975. (b)

Seibold, D. A complex model of multidimensional attitude and overt behavior relationships: The mediating effects of certainty and locus of control. Unpublished doctoral dissertation, Department of Communication, Michigan State University, 1975. (c)

Seibold, D. R. Causal modeling in communication: On the logical and empirical bases for causal inference and formalization of causal process theory. Paper presented at the annual convention of the Speech Communication Association, San Francisco, 1976.

Seibold, D. R. Antecedents to attitude–behavior consistency and implications for persuasive communication. Unpublished manuscript, University of Illinois, 1979.

Seibold, D. R., & McPhee, R. D. Commonality analysis: A method for decomposing explained variance in multiple regression analyses. *Human Communication Research*, 1979, *5*, 355–365. (a)

Seibold, D. R., & McPhee, R. D. Attitude–behavior processes: Test of alternative longitudinal models. Paper presented at the annual convention of the Eastern Communication Association, Philadelphia, 1979. (b)

Seibold, D. R., & Roper, R. E. Psychosocial determinants of health care intentions: Test of the Triandis and Fishbein models. In D. Nimmo (Ed.), *Communication Yearbook 3*. New Brunswick, N.J.: Transaction Books, 1979. Pp. 625–643.

Seibold, D. R., & Roper, R. E. A selected (and expanded) bibliography of attitude–behavior research. Unpublished manuscript, University of Illinois, 1980.

Simons, H. Psychological theories of persuasion: An auditor's report. *Quarterly Journal of Speech*, 1971, *42*, 383–392.

Smith, F. J. Work attitudes as predictors of attendance on a specific day. *Journal of Applied Psychology*, 1977, *62*, 16–19.

Snyder, M., & Tanke, E. D. Behavior and attitude: Some people are more consistent than others. *Journal of Personality*, 1976, *44*, 501–517.

Staats, A. W. Conditional stimuli, conditioned reinforcers, and word meaning. In A. W. Staats (Ed.), *Human learning*. New York: Holt, 1964.

Staats, A. W. Social behaviorism and human motivation: Principles of the attitude–reinforcer–discriminative system. In A. G. Greenwald, T. C. Brock, & T. M. Ostrom (Eds.), *Psychological foundations of attitudes*, New York: Academic Press, 1968. Pp. 33–66.

Stein, C. A. A simple user's guide to LISREL. Unpublished manuscript, Department of Communication Studies, University of Massachusetts, 1976.

Steinfatt, T., & Infante, D. Attitude–behavior relationships in communication research. *Quarterly Journal of Speech*, 1976, *62*, 267–278.

Tannenbaum, P. H., Macaulay, J. R., & Norris, E. L. Principle of congruity and reduction of persuasion. *Journal of Personality and Social Psychology*, 1966, *3*, 233–238.

Taylor, C. *The explanation of behaviour*. London: Routledge & Kegan Paul, 1964.

Thurstone, L. L. The measurement of attitudes. *Journal of Abnormal and Social Psychology*, 1931, *26*, 249–269.

Tittle, C. R., & Hill, R. J. Attitude measurement and prediction of behavior: An evaluation of conditions and measurement techniques. *Sociometry*, 1967, *30*, 199–213. (a)

Tittle, C. R., & Hill, R. J. The accuracy of self-reported data and prediction of political activity. *Public Opinion Quarterly*, 1967, *31*, 103–106. (b)

Tosi, H., Hunter, J., Chesser, R., Tarter, J. R., & Carroll, S. How real are changes induced by management by objectives. *Administrative Science Quarterly*, 1976, *21*, 276–306.

Triandis, H. C. *Attitude and attitude change*. New York: Wiley, 1971.

Triandis, H. C. *Interpersonal behavior*. Monterey, California: Brooks–Cole Publishing, 1977.

Triandis, H. C. Values, attitudes, and interpersonal behavior. In H. E. Howe & M. Page (Eds.), *Nebraska symposium on motivation, 1979*. Lincoln: University of Nebraska Press, 1980.

Van de Geer, J. *Introduction to multivariate analysis for the social sciences*. San Francisco: Freeman, 1971.

Veevers, J. E. Drinking attitudes and drinking behavior: An exploratory study. *Journal of Social Psychology*, 1971, *85*, 103–109.

von Wright, G. *Explanation and understanding*. Ithaca, N.Y.: Cornell University Press, 1971.

Vroom, V. H. *Work and motivation*. New York: Wiley, 1964.

Walsh, D. Varieties of positivism. In P. Filmer, M. Phillipson, D. Silverman, & D. Walsh (Eds.), *New directions in sociological theory*. Cambridge, Mass.: MIT Press, 1972. Pp. 37–55.

Warland, R., Herrmann, R., & Willits, J. Dissatisfied consumers: Who gets upset and who takes action? *Journal of Consumer Affairs*, 1975, *9*, 148–163.

Warner, L. G., & DeFleur, M. L. Attitude as an interactional concept: Social constraint and social distance as intervening variables between attitudes and action. *American Sociological Review*, 1969, *34*, 153–169.

Weigel, R. H., & Newman, L. S. Increasing attitude–behavior correspondence by broadening the scope of the behavioral measure. *Journal of Personality and Social Psychology*, 1976, *33*, 793–802.

Weigel, R. H., Vernon, T. A., & Tognacci, L. N. The specificity of the attitude as a determinant of attitude–behavior congruence. *Journal of Personality and Social Psychology*, 1974, *30*, 724–728.

Weinstein, A. G. Predicting behavior from attitudes. *Public Opinion Quarterly*, 1972, *36*, 355–360.

Werts, C. E., & Linn, R. L. Path analysis: Psychological examples. *Psychological Bulletin*, 1970, *74*, 193–212.

Werts, C., Jöreskog, K., & Linn, R. Identification and estimation in path analysis with unmeasured variables. *American Journal of Sociology*, 1973, *78*, 1469–1484.

Wheaton, B., Muthen, B., Alwin, D. F., & Summer, G. F. Assessing reliability and stability in panel models. In D. H. Heise (Ed.), *Sociological methodology, 1977*. San Francisco: Jossey–Bass, 1977. Pp. 84–136.

Wicker, A. Attitudes versus actions: The relationship of verbal and overt behavioral responses to attitude objects. *Journal of Social Issues*, 1969, *25*, 41–78.

Wicker, A. W., & Pomazal, R. J. The relationship between attitudes and behavior as a function of specificity of attitude object and presence of significant person during assessment condition. *Representative Research in Social Psychology*, 1971, *2*, 26–31.

Wicklund, R. A., & Brehm, J. W. *Perspectives on cognitive dissonance*. Hillsdale, N.J.: Erlbaum, 1976.

Winans, J. The need for research. *Quarterly Journal of Public Speaking*, 1915, *1*, 17–23.

Woelfel, J., & Haller, A. Significant others, the self-reflexive act and the attitude formation process. *American Sociological Review*, 1971, *36*, 74–87.

Woolbert, C. The place of logic in a system of persuasion. *Quarterly Journal of Speech Education*, 1918, *4*, 19–39.

Worchel, S., & Brehm, J. W. Direct and implied restoration of freedom. *Journal of Personality and Social Psychology*, 1971, *18*, 294–304.

Wortman, C. B. Causal attributions and personal control. In J. H. Harvey, W. I. Ickes, & R. F. Kidd (Eds.), *New directions in attribution research* (Vol. 1). Hillsdale, N.J.: Erlbaum, 1976. Pp. 23–52.

Zetterberg, H. *On theory and verification in sociology* (3rd ed.). Totowa, N.J.: Bedminster Press, 1965.

Zunich, M. Relationship between maternal behavior and attitudes toward children. *Journal of Genetic Psychology*, 1962, *100*, 155–165.

7

Behavior and Hierarchies of Attitudes: A Deterministic Model

MARSHALL SCOTT POOLE
JOHN E. HUNTER

"Attitude" is a basic concept in our everyday accounts of our own and others' behavior. The idea that our feelings and beliefs influence our behavior is so intuitively appealing that the fairly consistent early findings of relatively low attitude–behavior relationships were surprising and somewhat shocking. However, that there is not a simple attitude–causes–behavior relationship should come as no surprise if we reflect on the enormous complexity of human cognitive processes. Attitudes and beliefs are not isolated entities swimming happily about in our heads. They are influenced by other attitudes and beliefs and by incoming information. Cognitive organization is the medium for translation of thought and emotion into action and, as such, is responsible for many of the twists and turns attitude–behavior research has experienced. Our cognitive structures are subject to reorganization due to internal and external factors, and this reorganization plays a key mediatory role in the message–attitude–behavior relationship. Although improving measures of attitudes and behavioral criteria will undoubtedly strike at some of the problems of past research (Ajzen and Fishbein, 1978), knowing what to measure is not a substitute for understanding the mechanisms governing the message–attitude–

245

MESSAGE–ATTITUDE–BEHAVIOR RELATIONSHIP
Theory, Methodology, and Applications

behavior relationship. The purpose of this chapter is twofold (*a*) to present a mathematical model of change in hierarchies of attitudes as one possible mechanism mediating the message–attitude–behavior relationships; and (*b*) to demonstrate the uses of deterministic mathematical modeling in this area. We will turn to the second concern first.

Usefulness of Deterministic Modeling

The process of theory construction and testing may be conceived of as occurring at three levels. First there is the *theoretical* level, the exposition of general assumptions and a global picture of a phenomenon. Statements at this level are quite general and aim at establishing laws or general rules concerning the phenomenon. Second, there is the intermediate, more specific *model* level. Here we find specific instantiations of the general assumptions made at the theoretical level in various models. Each model embodies different combinations of assumptions and different descriptions of how they fit together and serves to qualify the more general formulation. The lowest level is the *operational* level, where model–theoretical concepts are defined for testing and measurement. At this level, the researcher is concerned primarily with the specific situation where the model is being tested. A model provides the link between theory and "the world": it considers general assumptions and conceptions as they would fit together in practice. For this reason, building a model is a recommended heuristic device in theory construction. It allows researchers to eliminate inconsistencies in assumptions and to consider the implications of various combinations of assumptions. As results at the model level are reflected back to the theoretical level, they in turn shape theory, just as theory initially shapes the model.

Building a mathematical model forces researchers to consider the interrelations within a given set of assumptions and to attempt to specify these relations as rigorously as possible. Rather than testing a series of discrete hypotheses, researchers examine combinations of assumptions from the outset. By relaxing or varying one assumption from the ensemble at a time, weaknesses in the framework of the theory can be found. Building a model also encourages researchers to iron out inconsistencies among assumptions and to consider the interactions among them, aiding in the research design process. Several types of models can be used, including deterministic models, stochastic models, and stochastic versions of deterministic models such as path models or regression models. It is the purpose of this section to point out the advantages of using deterministic models in particular, in the study of human behavior.

Before beginning, it is important to note that no form of modeling has inherent decisive advantages over any other. The great flexibility and range of mathematical and statistical methods allows any form of modeling to duplicate or approximate the moves of other forms. Differences between forms of modeling must be couched instead in terms of the relative ease of application or of the influences they may have on the way the researcher looks at things: Although the different approaches to modeling can ultimately yield the same results, they require different mind sets and induce different tendencies in the investigator. Comparative analysis must weight the advantages and disadvantages of tendencies and complexities. From this type of comparative analysis, four advantages of deterministic modeling emerge:

1. Vis à vis stochastic models (especially Markov models), deterministic models have the advantage of being more easily adaptable to most of the current theories of human behavior. Most contemporary theories take as their underlying approach the explication and testing of causal relationships: They define variables that in turn act on other variables in a specified manner. These causal hypotheses are usually tested against empirical conditions by (a) manipulating a causal factor; or (b) inferring causality from survey data using techniques such as path analysis. These theories are, in essence, deterministic in form, since they look for definite determinant relationships among variables. As a result, deterministic mathematical modeling is better-suited to the idiom of these theories than is stochastic modeling, which operates in terms of probability distributions of behaviors and can incorporate causal notions only with difficulty (see Coleman, 1973; Spilerman, 1972, for some examples of stochastic modeling of causal processes). For this reason deterministic modeling provides easier access to a wider range of theoretical formulations than does stochastic modeling. This is not to say that all theories of human behavior must be causal or deterministic. Hewes (1975) points to several noncausal theories and argues for their advantages. Rather, the advantage discussed here is due to the fact that most current formulations are causal in nature, and thus are more amenable to deterministic modeling than to necessarily more complex stochastic formulations.

2. Deterministic modeling also is a more flexible approach than structural equation or standard stochastic techniques. In deterministic models, the range of functional forms that can be utilized is exceedingly wide and diverse. In structural equation modeling (Blalock, 1972; Duncan, 1975), especially path analysis, the range of functional forms considered generally is restricted by the form of regression equation. Almost all structural models are additive with occasional multiplicative terms. Stochastic formulations such as Markov modeling also tend to restrict the flexibility of the modeler. With more complicated functions such as quadratic or cubic forms, the mathematics of deriving a new density distribution from the original distribution become so difficult that modelers are discouraged from trying these forms (see Coleman, 1964, pp. 626–628). Since deterministic models do not require the modeler to be concerned with distributions, they allow much simpler expression of complex relationships than either of the other two methods. As a result, deterministic modeling encourages the modeler to try a wide range of functional representations, and thus increases the modeler's flexibility (see Cappella, 1974, and Hunter &

Cohen, 1974, for examples of the complex functional forms the deterministic approach allows).

3. Deterministic modeling is also more flexible than traditional path analysis because it allows expression of theories in terms of change equations, rather than confining the modeler to state equations. Path analysis is grounded in state equations: The state of variable X determines the state of variable Y. Over time, the state of X at Time 1 predicts the state of X at Time 2. Mathematically this is:

$$x_2 = px_1 + u$$

If there is a change in X from Time 1 to Time 2 it is reflected in a change in state from X_1 to X_2. Deterministic mathematical modeling allows the researcher to mathematize change in a variable *directly* from theory. For our variable X this would be expressed as follows:

$$\Delta x = \alpha x_1$$

where Δx symbolizes the change in x from Time 1 to Time 2 ($\Delta x = x_2 - x_1$). We could use the above expression to solve for the state x_2 as follows:

$$x_2 - x_1 = \alpha x_1$$
$$x_2 = (1 + \alpha)x_1$$

Thus deterministic modeling gives us the option of "thinking" mathematically in terms of change equations or state equations, whereas path analysis (as well as other structural equation techniques) confine us to state equations. Deterministic modeling allows a more direct theory-to-mathematics translation of theories that deal with change.

4. A final advantage of deterministic mathematical models is that they force the experimenter to come to grips with *error* in tests of the model. Since data are stochastic due to measurement or sampling error, a deterministic model will never fit the data exactly. Because the researcher knows beforehand that errors in the data will keep the model from fitting, he or she is encouraged to investigate the nature and sources of the errors. With some consideration of possible errors, the experimenter is in a better position than before to decide which deviations from the predictions of the model are serious and which are due to errors in the data. In stochastic models or stochastic versions of deterministic models, there is usually an assumption of some randomness in the world. The researcher is encouraged by this assumption to "live with" error, to take it as a given in any study. On the other hand, a deterministic mathematical model recommends that the researcher try to understand error and trace its sources. An example of one such analysis and its implications for a particular test of a deterministic model is presented in this chapter. It is important to note here that consideration of error is possible in both stochastic modeling (see Coleman, 1973) and in stochastic versions of deterministic models (see Blalock,

1971). However, it is our contention that deterministic models encourage this consideration more readily than the other two sorts of models. With a deterministic model the researcher is forced to decide when he or she should be satisfied with the fit of the model (given that it will never fit perfectly); such a decision inevitably involves analysis of sources of error and forces him or her to become intimately familiar with the data.

In the remainder, of this chapter we will attempt to illustrate these advantages of deterministic modeling. Whereas we will not expressly return to metamethodological considerations, the points made in this section hopefully will be reflected and amplified in the substantive work that follows.

A Hierarchical Model of Attitude Organization and Change

The Model

People can respond to psychological objects or concepts at three different levels: belief, attitude (i.e., emotion or affect), and behavior. Researchers long have suspected that if two concepts are related logically, the corresponding beliefs, attitudes, and behaviors also will be related. The vast literature on this topic was reviewed and synthesized by Hunter, Levine, and Sayers (1976) in the form of a mathematical model of attitude change in a hierarchy of concepts.

Hunter *et al.* argued that most logical relations can be cast in the form of inclusion relations between concepts defined at different orders of abstraction. Consider for example, the seven concepts shown in Figure 7.1. The six other concepts all are included in the concept *Federal Government Bureaucracy*, while the *Federal Communications Commission* is included in *Regulatory Commissions* but not in the *Justice Department*. Hunter *et al.* (1976) noted that logical inference in such a hierarchy operates from top down. Thus the proposition *Bureaucracies are inefficient* implies the proposition *Regulatory commissions are inefficient.* On the other hand, the proposition *The bureau of prisons capitalizes on economies of scale* has no such implication for federal bureaucracies in

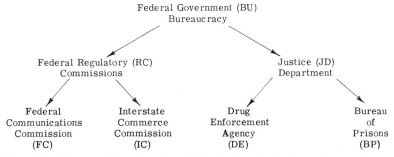

Figure 7.1. Hierarchy of attitude objects. Abbreviations of attitudes are in parentheses.

general. Hunter *et al.* found considerable evidence verifying a top-down-only causal ordering for belief change.

Hunter *et al.* reasoned that the organization of change in an individual's attitudes about the concepts would parallel the process of logical inference among beliefs. The idea that attitudes were arranged in logical hierarchies is suggested by two bodies of work. First, several social psychologists have proposed that attitudes are hierrarchically arranged. Allport (1937) posited an attitudinal continuum with opinions, attitudes, interests, and values as successive points along the continuum. More recently, Rokeach (1969) has suggested that beliefs, attitudes, and values are arranged hierarchically; beliefs being specific and least central, and values being general and most central. Indeed, there is impressive evidence in the area of persuasion immunization (Holt, 1970; Nelson, 1968) and in the general attitude change literature (Rokeach, 1971; Stotland, Katz, & Patchen, 1959; Stotland & Patchen, 1961) that more general attitudinal concepts serve to organize and exert an influence on less general attitudes.

A second source of support for a hierarchical model can be found in research on semantic memory by investigators of human information processing. Although not all cognitive structures are hierarchical in nature, there is evidence supporting the hierarchical nature of some storage networks in semantic long-term memory (Collins & Loftus, 1975; Collins & Quillian, 1972; Linsay & Norman, 1972; Wood, 1972). Given (*a*) that memory often contains hierarchical structures and (*b*) that feelings and emotions about concepts or experiences are often part of a memory trace, it is not surprising that attitudes may be organized in the same fashion as concepts are stored in memory.

Hunter *et al.* could find no evidence one way or the other in the attitude change literature for the assumption that change in attitudinal hierarchies operates only from the top down. However, the consistent findings of downward-only influence from more to less general beliefs, along with the assumption of paralellism of attitude and belief organizations, led them to posit that more general attitudes influenced less general ones, but not vice versa. The model they developed on these assumptions was motivated as follows:

If influence operates only from top down, the analysis of a hierarchy can be broken into the analysis of strings of concepts running from the top down. That is, if X is the top of the hierarchy, Y is one of the second-rung concepts, and Z is one of the third-rung concepts that is included in Y; then the set of corresponding attitudes x, y, z can be analyzed without reference to the other attitudes. For example, BU, RC, IC form such a set in Figure 7.1.

Hunter *et al.* (1976) first considered a situation in which there was no external message. They assumed that if a person thinks of one concept in the hierarchy, the entire hierarchy will be reviewed. In the course of this review, attitude z will be influenced by attitude y, attitude y will be influenced by attitude x, and attitude x will have no superordinate attitude to be influenced by. The model of attitude change adopted by Hunter *et al.* is the "information-processing model" (Hunter & Cohen, 1974), which assumes the linear discrepancy equation of Hovland and Pritzger (1957) as reviewed by Insko (1967). This assumption, paired with the top down assumption, produces the *internal influence model*:

$$\Delta x = 0 \tag{1}$$

$$\Delta y = \beta(x - y) \tag{2}$$

$$\Delta z = \beta(y - z) \tag{3}$$

where Δ is the symbol for "change," and β is a parameter measuring the amount of change or influence of one attitude on another. (Hunter *et al.* assert that individual differences in the parameter β would be due to differences in dogmatism).

If there is an external message, then Hunter *et al.* (1976) assumed that change would be a simultaneous combination of two processes: change in the particular attitude addressed by the message, and change produced by internal processes generated by thinking about the hierarchy. For example, if the message were directed at RC, then the *external change model* would be

$$\Delta x = 0 \tag{4}$$

$$\Delta y = \alpha(M - y) + \beta(x - y) \qquad \text{for } RC \tag{5}$$

$$\Delta y = \beta(x - y) \qquad \text{for } JD \tag{6}$$

$$\Delta z = \beta(y - z) \tag{7}$$

where M is the message value and α is the proportionality factor for the information-processing model applied to the external message. (Hunter *et al.* assume that individual differences in the parameter α, if any, would be due to differences in persuasability).

These models are the two components of the more general Hunter *et al.* model for a three-tiered hierarchy in which messages are directed at all three levels of the hierarchy:

$$\Delta\alpha(M_x - x) \tag{8}$$

$$\Delta\alpha(M_y - y) + \beta(x - y) \tag{9}$$

$$\Delta\alpha(M_z - z) + \beta(y - z) \tag{10}$$

where M_x, M_y, and M_z are messages directed at concepts X, Y, and Z, respectively. If no message pertaining to a given attitude is received, then the term containing the message variable is set to zero. The internal influence model above results when no messages at all are received, and the first term of each equation is set to zero. For the particular external change model considered in the previous paragraph, a message was directed only at attitude RC in the second tier of the hierarchy. Hence the terms $\alpha(M_x - x)$ and $\alpha(M_z - z)$ were set to zero, as was the term $\alpha(M_y - y)$ for attitude JC, which was in the other strand of the hierarchy of Figure 7.1.

In light of this discussion, the Hunter *et al.* model can be considered an instantiation of a more general theory of affective–cognitive organization. A logical hierarchy, as Poole and Hunter (1979) note, is one of several possible cognitive organizations, each of which could give rise to different models of influence between attitudes. The Hunter *et al.* model represents one possible specification of the underlying assumption that the paths of influence among attitudes are determined by the individual's cognitive structure.

A Test of the Hierarchical Model

Poole and Hunter (1979) subjected the Hunter *et al.* model to empirical test and found that only slight modifications were, required. In the remainder of this section, we will (*a*) review the results of the Poole and Hunter study; and (*b*) use the data from this study to directly test the internal process assumptions of the hierarchical model.

The Hunter *et al.* model was tested by measuring the changes that occurred in a hierarchy of attitudes over four time periods. The hierarchy used is the one pictured in Figure 7.1, which was chosen after extensive preliminary testing. The design utilized two groups, whose attitudes were measured at four points in time. The experimental design was:

1. Pretest 1 week in advance.
2. Immediate pretest message.
3. Immediate post-test.
4. Post-test 1 week later.

Different experimental messages were used for the two groups. For one group, a message was directed at the attitude at the top of the hierarchy (BU) in order to determine whether changes in this attitude would filter down the hierarchy. For the other group, a message was directed at an attitude at the bottom of the hierarchy (IC). If the Hunter *et al.* model holds, changing an attitude at the bottom of the hierarchy should have no effect on other attitudes, and the change in IC should decay in the post-tests. The messages were balanced in terms of number of arguments and amount of evidence used. Message valence was estimated by asking subjects to estimate the attitude of the message. Subjects consisted of 130 students from two midwestern universities: 76 of them were in the group receiving the message aimed at BU, while 54 were in the group receiving the IC message. The experimental design and results are summarized at greater length in Poole (1976) and Poole and Hunter (1979).

Poole and Hunter verified the top-down influence assumption of Hunter *et al.* for attitudes. In one group, a message changed attitudes toward the top concept (i.e., BU), and this change filtered down subsequently to all attitudes in the hierarchy. On the other hand, in the group that received a message directed at an attitude at the bottom of the hierarchy (*IC*), there was only change in the attitude toward the *Interstate Commerce Commission*, and that change decayed in subsequent time intervals.

Poole and Hunter did *not* verify the external change model of Eqs. (4)–(7), which posited a simultaneous combination of external and internal change processes as the result of receiving a message. They tested several different versions of the external-change model, based on different assumptions about the sequence of attitude-change processes (external and internal change occurring simultaneously or in two different phases), and about the nature of the hierarchy (independent or embedded in a larger hierarchy). They found that the external message tended to dominate the person's thought while change in the attitude the message was directed at was occurring. Thus the data fit a two-phase model. In the first phase, there is only change in the attitude directly addressed in the message. The second phase is then an internal consideration of the hierarchy that produces the change indicated by the internal-influence model. Only after the external message has been consolidated does the internal-influence process occur. If only attitude *x* receives a message, this yields the following model of message integration, which Poole and Hunter termed the *consolidation* model:

PHASE 1

$$\Delta x = \alpha(Mx - x) \tag{11}$$

$$\Delta y = 0 \tag{12}$$

$$\Delta z = 0 \tag{13}$$

PHASE 2

$$\Delta x = 0 \tag{14}$$

$$\Delta y = \beta(x^* - y) \tag{15}$$

$$\Delta z = \beta(y - z) \tag{16}$$

where x^* is the new value of x after the message effect of PHASE 1.

Complications in the Hierarchical Model

Causal influences are normally described in the language of functions and are naturally modeled in a deterministic model such as that above. However in real empirical situations, there are usually many other processes taking place that are outside the scope of the deterministic model. Some of these are under experimental control and can be added as other deterministic elements, but many are not controlled and hence must enter as probabilistic terms. Some of the complications in the model are listed and considered.

Hunter *et al.* (1976) assumed that the entire hierarchy is observed, though they noted a test to see if this is true in a given empirical situation. The recommended test was to direct a message at the top concept in the empirical hierarchy. If the empirical hierarchy is not embedded in a larger hierarchy, any change produced by the message will be maintained in subsequent follow up measurements. On the other hand, if the empirical hierarchy is a subhierarchy of some larger system, there will be a concept Q which is superordinate to X and hence Eq. (1) of the internal influence model will be replaced by

$$\Delta x = \beta(q - x) \tag{17}$$

where q is the value of the attitude x toward Q.

Poole and Hunter (1979) derived a statistical test from this equation which is suitable for empirical work in which q would be an unknown variable which varies from one person to the next. They used the pretest score on x as a proxy for q in a multiple regression of follow up on post-test and pretest. If X is the top of the hierarchy, then the regression of x_3 onto x_2 and x_1 should show a zero beta weight for x_1 (assuming that corrections for error of measurement have been made). Both tests failed for their data, and hence the system in Figure 7.1 must be regarded as a subhierarchy of some larger system, and Eq. (17) will replace Eq. (1) in the internal-influence model to be tested.

Poole and Hunter (1979) also noted that between observations, some people might hear a message related to the hierarchy while others do not. For example, suppose that half the people heard a message about Y, whereas the other half heard no message at all. Then the deterministic equation of Eq. (2) would be replaced by the probabilistic regression equation

$$\Delta y = \tfrac{1}{2}\alpha(m - y) + \beta(x - y) + \mu \tag{18}$$

where μ is an error term which is $+\tfrac{1}{2}\alpha$ for those who heard a message with value M and $-\tfrac{1}{2}\alpha(m - y)$ for those who heard no message, and where m is the average value of M. In particular, Poole and Hunter noted in this new equation, the weights for x and y are no longer the same, and the term $\tfrac{1}{2}\alpha m$ occurs as an additive constant in a regression equation which would otherwise be without one.

Idiosyncratic events need not be external. Hunter *et al.* (1976) assumed that if the person thinks about one concept in the hierarchy, the person reviews the whole system. But this process could be interrupted, in which case those attitudes not reached would go unchanged. Also, the review of concepts might not be even in terms of time spent. A person might just gloss over Y while dwelling on Z, in which case the change in y would be minimal, whereas the change in z would be larger than predicted by the deterministic internal-influence model.

The upshot of the preceding considerations is that the internal-influence model to be tested with the Poole and Hunter data should be a stochastic model (i.e., structural equation or path model) in which the regression weights are estimated using constant terms even though these do not appear in Eqs. (1)–(3).

A Test of the Internal-Influence Model

The Model to be Tested

Imperfect measurement requires that correlations be corrected for attenuation before they can be submitted to regression analysis (cf. Hunter & Cohen, 1974b). As a result, it is usually easier to test a model in the form of predictive equations rather than change equations. For example, if Eq. (2) is used to generate predictions about Time 2 from the data of Time 1, then it would become

$$y_2 = y_1 + \Delta y = y_1 + \beta(x_1 - y_1) = (1 - \beta)y_1 + \beta x_1 \qquad (19)$$

Furthermore, most of the computations in the model can be greatly simplified by using matrices. Let the variables in the model be stacked into a vector $\mathbf{X}$ such as

$$\mathbf{X} = \begin{bmatrix} x \\ y \\ z \end{bmatrix} \qquad (20)$$

Then the predictive equations corresponding to the change Eqs. (1)–(3) can be written

$$\begin{bmatrix} x_2 \\ y_2 \\ z_2 \end{bmatrix} = \begin{bmatrix} 0 & 0 & 0 \\ \beta & -\beta & 0 \\ 0 & \beta & -\beta \end{bmatrix} \begin{bmatrix} x_1 \\ y_1 \\ z_1 \end{bmatrix} + \begin{bmatrix} 1 & 0 & 0 \\ 0 & 1 & 0 \\ 0 & 0 & 1 \end{bmatrix} \begin{bmatrix} x_1 \\ y_1 \\ z_1 \end{bmatrix}$$

$$= \begin{bmatrix} 1 & 0 & 0 \\ \beta & 1-\beta & 0 \\ 0 & \beta & 1-\beta \end{bmatrix} \begin{bmatrix} x_1 \\ y_1 \\ z_1 \end{bmatrix} \qquad (21)$$

or

$$\mathbf{X}_2 = \mathbf{B}\mathbf{X}_1 \qquad (22)$$

where $\mathbf{B}$ is called the *transition matrix*.

This result is generalizable. If we wish to generate the vector of variables at Time $n + 1$ from the vector at Time n, we take

$$\mathbf{X}_{n+1} = \mathbf{B}\mathbf{X}_n \qquad (23)$$

To generate the vector at Time $n + 2$ from that at Time n, we take

$$\mathbf{X}_{n+2} = \mathbf{B}\mathbf{X}_{n+1} = \mathbf{B}^2\mathbf{X}_n \qquad (24)$$

In general, to generate $\mathbf{X}_{n+k}$ from $\mathbf{X}_n$, take

$$\mathbf{X}_{n+k} = \mathbf{B}^n\mathbf{X}_n \qquad (25)$$

Now we will extend this model to the seven-attitude hierarchy. The extension involves adding one additional equation for the second level of the hierarchy, and three equations for the lowest level. The attitudes will be symbolized by the initials in Figure 7.1. For the seven-attitude hierarchy with no messages we have

$$\Delta BU = \beta(q - BU)$$

$$\Delta RC = \beta(BU - RC)$$

$$\Delta FC = \beta(RC - FC)$$

$$\Delta IC = \beta(RC - IC) \tag{26}$$

$$\Delta JD = \beta(BU - JD)$$

$$\Delta DE = \beta(JD - DE)$$

$$\Delta BP = \beta(JD - BP)$$

This results in the following transition matrix **B**:

$$\begin{bmatrix} BU_2 \\ RC_2 \\ FC_2 \\ IC_2 \\ JD_2 \\ DE_2 \\ BP_2 \end{bmatrix} = \begin{bmatrix} 1-\beta & 0 & 0 & 0 & 0 & 0 & 0 \\ \beta & 1-\beta & 0 & 0 & 0 & 0 & 0 \\ 0 & \beta & 1-\beta & 0 & 0 & 0 & 0 \\ 0 & \beta & 0 & 1-\beta & 0 & 0 & 0 \\ \beta & 0 & 0 & 0 & 1-\beta & 0 & 0 \\ 0 & 0 & 0 & 0 & \beta & 1-\beta & 0 \\ 0 & 0 & 0 & 0 & \beta & 0 & 1-\beta \end{bmatrix} \begin{bmatrix} BU_1 \\ RC_1 \\ FC_1 \\ IC_1 \\ JD_1 \\ DE_1 \\ BP_1 \end{bmatrix} \tag{27}$$

Where the term BQ is absorbed into the error term in the stochastic model, that is,

$$\mathbf{X}_2 = \mathbf{B}\mathbf{X}_1 \tag{28}$$

As before, if we wish to generate $\mathbf{X}_3$ from $\mathbf{X}_1$, we multiply $\mathbf{X}_1$ twice by $\mathbf{B}$. To generate $\mathbf{X}_k$ we take

$$\mathbf{B}^{k-1}\mathbf{X}_1 = \mathbf{X}_k \tag{29}$$

The transition matrix **B** has certain properties that will dictate the form of transition matrices used to test the model. First, all nonzero coefficients below the diagonal are equal. This reflects the assumption that the strength of influence in the hierarchy does not depend upon how far up or down the hierarchy a given superordinate–subordinate pair of attitudes are. Second, a large number of the nondiagonal entries in the matrix are zero. This is because influence in the hierarchy is assumed to move downward only and along specific paths from more to less general attitudes. A zero indicates that there is no direct path of influence from one attitude to another. Third, coefficients in any row sum to one.

Fourth, if BU were the top attitude in the hierarchy, coefficients in the first row of the matrix would be a one and six zeros. However, since BU is not the top of the hierarchy, but has a superordinate attitude q, we would expect change in BU:

$$\Delta BU = \beta(q - BU) \tag{30}$$

So the transition matrix will have a coefficient $1 - \beta$ in its upper left corner instead of one.

Estimation of the Matrix **B**

The nonzero entries of the transition matrix are either β or $1 - \beta$. This suggests that regression weights be separately estimated from the prediction equations over nonmessage time intervals and then averaged. However there are two caveats here. First, the equation for BU is of different character because of the unknown nature of q. Therefore, only regression equations for the other six attitudes were used. Second, the impact of sources of error on regression equations is to reduce the size of regression weights, especially that for the variable onto itself at the previous time. Thus it is unlikely that the regression weights will add to 1.0.

In the experimental design of Poole and Hunter (1979, no experimental messages were given between the first pretest (Time 1) and the immediate pretest (Time 2) or between the immediate post-test (Time 3) and the second post-test (Time 4). Thus, only internal processes should have been operating during the Time 1–Time 2 interval and the Time 3–Time 4 interval. The parameter β thus appears in 12 independent regression equations each based on data from 130 persons. That is, for each of the attitudes except BU, there are two predictive equations of the form

$$y_{n+1} = (1 - \beta)y_n + \beta x_n \tag{31}$$

where the role of x_n is played by the attitude immediately superordinate to the attitude y_{n+1} being predicted. After the correlations were corrected for attenuation, the corresponding beta weights were computed for each of the 12 equations. The average of 12 estimates of β was .09 and the average estimate of $1 - \beta$ was .75. In each case, a chi-square test was run to see if the estimates were statistically homogeneous, and in both cases the chi-square statistic was nonsignificant. The sum of these numbers is $.75 + .09 = .84$, which is less than 1.0, as expected. Thus each was adjusted upward in subsequent analysis of the data, as noted, to .85 and .10, respectively.

Reproducing the Observed Correlation Matrices

The usual method of testing a structural equation or path model is to see if the model correctly reproduces the observed correlation matrix. In the present case, the full correlation matrix is 28×28, corresponding to 7 variables measured at 4 times. However, it is much more convenient to break this matrix up into 16 blocks, each 7×7, corresponding to the correlations between 7 measurements at one time with 7 measurements at a second time. Denote each such matrix of correlations $\mathbf{R}_{ij}$ where i is the time for the row variables and j is the time for the column correlations. $\mathbf{R}_{ii}$ would be the correlations between the 7 variables at Time i.

From the regression equation

$$\mathbf{X}_{n+1} = \mathbf{BX}_n \tag{32}$$

we can derive the predicted values of the nondiagonal blocks of the correlation matrix to be

$$\mathbf{R}_{21} = \mathbf{BR}_{11} \tag{33}$$

$$\mathbf{R}_{31} = \mathbf{B}^2\mathbf{R}_{11} \tag{34}$$

$$\mathbf{R}_{41} = \mathbf{B}^3\mathbf{R}_{11} \tag{35}$$

$$\mathbf{R}_{32} = \mathbf{BR}_{22} \tag{36}$$

$$\mathbf{R}_{42} = \mathbf{B}^2\mathbf{R}_{22} \tag{37}$$

$$\mathbf{R}_{43} = \mathbf{BR}_{33} \tag{38}$$

In the deterministic model, these equations could be further reduced to predictions entirely based on $\mathbf{R}_{11}$ by the following

$$\mathbf{R}_{22} = \mathbf{BR}_{11}\mathbf{B}' \quad \text{if deterministic} \tag{39}$$

$$\mathbf{R}_{33} = \mathbf{B}^2\mathbf{R}_{11}\mathbf{B}^{2'} \quad \text{if deterministic} \tag{40}$$

$$\mathbf{R}_{44} = \mathbf{B}^3\mathbf{R}_{11}\mathbf{B}^{3'} \quad \text{if deterministic} \tag{41}$$

However these equations do not hold in the probabilistic case because of the variance of the error terms. The alternate form is

$$\mathbf{R}_{22} = \mathbf{BR}_{11}\mathbf{B}' + \mathbf{D} \tag{42}$$

where $\mathbf{D}$ is a diagonal matrix of error variances. Predictions for the model were thus tested only for Eqs. (33)–(38).

Even though the reliabilities of single measurements in the Poole and Hunter (1979) data were in the .90s, all correlations were corrected for attenuation to avoid the steady cumulation of errors for long time intervals, which would be quite severe in this case.

A second problem arises in connection with Eqs. (33)–(35). The matrix $\mathbf{R}_{11}$ in these equations plays the role of the correlations among exogenous variables in a path or structural equation model. Usually these are few in number and much more stably estimated than the path coefficients in the model, and hence are estimated by using just the simple observed correlations. However both of these premises are false in the present data. Therefore an alternate method of estimating $\mathbf{R}_{11}$ (and similarly $\mathbf{R}_{22}$ and $\mathbf{R}_{33}$) was derived for this purpose.

The initial correlation matrices σ_{ii} for the estimation were derived by taking a weighted average of the first three observed correlation matrices in the series (R_{11}, R_{12}, and R_{22}, for example). If we conceive of R_{11} as composed of the true correlation matrix σ_{ii} and E_1 a matrix of error terms, the three observed matrices may be defined as follows:

$$R_{11} = \sigma_{11} + E_1 \tag{43}$$

$$R_{21} = B\sigma_{11} + E_2 \tag{44}$$

$$R_{22} = B\sigma_{11}B' + D + E \tag{45}$$

where D is a diagonal matrix of estimated errors. If we solve for σ_{11} we get

$$\hat{\sigma}_{11} = \tfrac{1}{3}[R_{11} + B^{-1}R_{12} + B^{-1}(R_{22} - D)B^{-t}] \tag{46}$$

σ_{11} is then used as the start value and as an estimate of R_{11}. This procedure has the effect of averaging out errors present in any one of the first three correlation matrices. The other initial correlation matrices, σ_{11} and σ_{33} were estimated using the same procedure.

Results and Discussion

The estimated transition matrix is shown in Table 7.1. This is the matrix B which appears in the prediction equations (33)–(42). Using this transition matrix, predicted correlation matrices were generated and compared to observed matrices. Three sets of matrices were generated for each group:

1. Using R_{11}, R_{12}, and R_{22} to determine start matrix $\hat{\sigma}$, $\hat{R}_{11}$, $\hat{R}_{12}$, $\hat{R}_{13}$, R_{14}, and R_{22} were generated.
2. Using R_{22}, R_{23}, and R_{33} to determine the start matrix $\hat{\sigma}$, $\hat{R}_{22}$, $\hat{R}_{23}$, $\hat{R}_{24}$ and R_{33} were generated.
3. Using R_{33}, R_{34}, and R_{44} to determine the start matrix $\hat{\sigma}$, $\hat{R}_{33}$, $\hat{R}_{34}$ and $\hat{R}_{44}$ were generated.

Fit of the model was determined in terms of the proportion of predicted correlations that deviated significantly from observed correlations using a 95% confidence interval (Hays & Winkler, 1971). Sampling error would make this

TABLE 7.1
Transition Matrix B Used in the Test of the Internal Influence Model

.85	0	0	0	0	0	0
.10	.85	0	0	0	0	0
0	.10	.85	0	0	0	0
0	.10	0	.85	0	0	0
.10	0	0	0	.85	0	0
0	0	0	0	.10	.85	0
0	0	0	0	.10	0	.85

TABLE 7.2
**Proportion of Deviations Significantly Greater than Zero for all
Correlation Matrices Predicted**[a]

	Number	Proportion
BU group	17/420	.040
IC group	23/420	.054

[a] Diagonal values for symmetric matrices are not included in the totals.

proportion about .05 even if the model was a perfect description of the population. The number and proportion of significant deviations out of 420 distinct predicted correlations are reported for both groups in Table 7.2. The proportion of significant errors for the *BU* group was .040 while the proportion for the *IC* group was .054 (i.e., chance level in both groups). For both groups, about half of the significant deviations occurred in correlations involving the attitude that was changed by the message at Times 3 and 4. Since the internal-influence model does not allow for effects of messages, taking the messages into account would probably improve prediction.

A second test of the adequacy of the internal model was conducted using an averaged pretest score (Time 1 and Time 2), and an averaged post-test score (Time 3 and Time 4), which were calculated for purposes of looking at mean attitude change. This time, out of 91 correlations, there were no significant deviations for the *BU* group and five for the *IC* group, for a probability level of .055. Both tests, then, seem to support the validity of the internal-influence model with parameter $\beta = .10$.

The present direct test of the internal-influence model supports the Hunter *et al.* (1976) equations very nicely. This was also the conclusion of the Poole and Hunter (1979) analysis of the message-produced change data, since the internal-influence model is contained in the message equations for PHASE 2.

Behaviors and Attitudes in Hierarchical Systems

From a number of reviews, it is evident that attitudes are related very strongly to behaviors under certain conditions (Ajzen & Fishbein, 1978; Schuman & Johnson, 1976). Various factors other than attitudes or attitudinal properties, including situational constraints and societal expectations or norms, have been shown to influence behavior. When these are operating, they can introduce "error" into attitude–behavior relationships by acting counter to or overriding the effect of attitudes. But these are not the only factors that can mask attitude–behavior relations: The complexities of our cognitive organization can foil even the most discerning researchers. For example, if one concept lies between another concept and an individual's conception of a behavior in a logical hierarchy, it will mediate the effect of the attitude toward the second concept on the behavior in question. Even if he or she is correct in assuming that a person's attitudes influence behavior, the researchers may not be measuring the attitude toward the correct concept or taking intervening attitudes into account. The result of these omissions may be a relatively low attitude–behavior correlation and an incorrect acceptance of the null hypothesis.

Fishbein (1973) has noted that attitude toward *general* objects is often a poor predictor when behavior is measured by single acts, but a good predictor when multiple acts are used as the criterion of behavior (Tittle & Hill, 1967). Weigel and Newman (1976) found that, although subjects' general attitudes toward environmental issues exhibited only moderate correlations to single behaviors relating to environmental improvement, its correlation with a set of several such behaviors was .62. Fishbein and Ajzen (1974) found that attitude toward objects (which are general) exhibited a mean correlation of .14 with single behaviors and a mean correlation of .66 with multiple behavioral criteria. On the other hand, Fishbein (1973) presents evidence that attitude toward a *specific* act is a good predictor of intention to act for a single behavior when the situational and normative factors discussed are taken into account. These findings are understandable if we note that a large number of specific behaviors are likely to be associated with general attitudes, whereas for more specific attitudes, there will be fewer associations with specific behaviors. For a question asking the respondent's attitude toward a specific act at a specific time and place, there will probably only be *one* behavior associated with the attitude. We should expect a higher correlation between attitude and behavior when only one behavior is associated with an attitude than when there are several options and our instruments can only tap one or two. The limitation in our instruments artificially attenuates the attitude–behavior relationship in the latter case (i.e., for general attitudes) since some behaviors associated with the attitude will not be counted by the experimenter.

The more general an attitude is, the more behaviors the investigator must consider in order to gauge the full impact of the attitude on subjects' behavior. A general attitude will be connected to a large number of behaviors through the strands of the hierarchy leading from it to more specific attitudes and thence to behaviors. The influence of the general attitude on an individual's behavioral choice comes through the effect it has on more specific attitudes that directly pertain to the behavior. Having a favorable general attitude will influence the individual to undertake any of a large set of behaviors. The specific behavior chosen from this set depends not only on specific attitudes as influenced by the general attitude, but also on additional situational factors such as norms, other's expectations, or recently received messages that temporarily draw one specific attitude out of line with the others and give a more favorable valence to its associated behavior. However, as important as these other factors are, over the long run the general attitude plays the dominant role in determining behavioral choice. The general attitude sets the stage for the effects of situational factors through its influence on lower-order attitudes. If the general attitude is favorable, subordinate attitudes will also be favorable and the balance is tipped toward the behaviors referred to by the specific attitudes. However, if the general attitude is negative, lower attitudes are also likely to be negative, and the scales are weighted against undertaking the behaviors. The general attitude will also diminish the effects of external messages on specific attitudes. An external message may temporarily change a specific attitude so that it is favorable toward a behavior the individual did not previously favor or vice versa. Over the long run, however, the message effect will decay, as the higher-order attitude draws the specific attitude back into line in the internal-influence process. These temporary changes in specific attitudes can lower the correlation between the general attitude and behavior, as can the other sources of error for the hierarchical model discussed earlier. Nevertheless, if we consider the long run and look at relatively stable situations, general attitudes will be found to exert an influence on behavior through their effects on specific attitudes. Although a general attitude has a large impact on behavior, a low attitude–behavior correlation may result if (a) only a subset of the total set of behaviors the general attitude effects is measured; and (b) short-run changes in lower-order attitudes due to external messages or other sources of error are not considered.

General attitudes also serve another important function in the motivation of behavior. Does an individual actually have a preexisting attitude toward a specific act at a specific time and place (e.g., going to a party at 7:30 on Friday night at Joe's house)? Most subjects probably have no such attitude in their cognitive organization, but instead *construct* an attitude on the basis of more general attitudes (i.e., on the basis of their attitudes toward parties and toward Joe). Schwartz (1978) recently has made a similar argument. What we have then is the mediating constructed attitude "going to a party," between attitude toward "parties" and the intention to go to the party. This specific attitude can be regarded as a downward extension of the attitudinal hierarchy of which "parties" is a member. There might be several other specific attitudes involving parties associated with "parties," which, in turn, might be only one of a number of subordinate attitudes to the next higher concept (e.g., recreation). Let us assume that (a) every specific attitude at the lowest level of the hierarchy has a single behavior associated with it; (b) behaviors are associated *only* with these lowest-level attitudes; and (c) the other assumptions of the hierarchical model of attitude organization hold. As we move up the hierarchy, we will find more and more behaviors associated with each more general attitude (see Figure 7.2). They would, however, be associated only indirectly. More general attitudes would only exert influence on behaviors through their influence on the specific attitudes associated with the behaviors. Given a high level of consistency (e.g., $r = .70$) among attitudes in the hierarchy, the general attitude toward recreation could best be predicted by considering all behaviors associated with the hier-

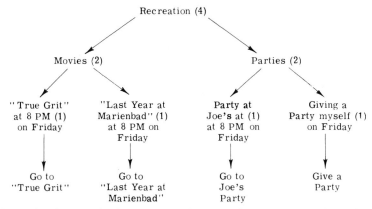

Figure 7.2. Hierarchy of attitudes and associated behaviors. The number of behaviors directly or indirectly associated with the attitude is in parentheses. Behaviors are on the bottom line.

archy since the correlation between recreation and any one specific behavior should be attenuated by the two mediating causal paths.

What evidence is available bearing on the ideas advanced in the preceding paragraphs? Most studies of the attitude–behavior relationships have not attempted to measure attitudes at several levels of generality. The predictions made by the hierarchical model for cases where several levels of attitudes are measured are quite clear. In studies such as Ajzen and Fishbein (1969), DeFleur and Westie (1958), and Green (1968), where sizable relationships were found between general attitudes and behaviors, we should also find a fairly large amount of consistency between more and less general attitudes. Moreover, specific attitudes toward the behavior should mediate the effect of the general attitudes on behavioral intention. In studies such as LaPiere (1934), Bray (1950), or Berg (1966), where little relation between general attitudes and behaviors is found, we should find no hierarchical relationship between the general attitude and more specific attitudes. Indeed, we should find that the specific attitude toward the behavior is part of a different hierarchy entirely than the one belonging to the general attitude. For example, in the LaPiere (1934) study, the behavior consisted of willingness to serve a specific well-dressed Chinese couple, usually accompanied by LaPiere himself. The attitude measured referred to willingness to serve "members of the Chinese race." Whereas the hierarchy containing "members of the Chinese race" is one that could cover the attitude toward serving LaPiere and the Chinese couple, there are also others, such as "well-dressed and pleasant customers." If our hierarchical formulation were correct, we would expect to find that the attitude toward the behavior is subsumed under a different general attitude than the one measured. The studies just discussed are not offered as evidence for our formulations; instead they are mentioned as illustrations of the types of findings we would expect if the data suitable to testing the hierarchical assumption had been collected by these investigators. Luckily, several studies have reported findings that allow a preliminary assessment of the model's viability.

Liska (1974) compared attitude–behavior consistency across five levels of attitudinal generality and two levels of behavioral generality for eight academic "coping behaviors." He found significant correlations between the lowest three levels of attitudes and the more specific behavior. However, where the five attitudinal levels were entered into a multiple regression equation predicting the specific behavior, the partial regression coefficients for the higher level attitudes went to zero, whereas those for the most specific attitude remained significant and about the same as the zero-order correlations. This is consistent with the argument that specific attitudes mediate the relationship between more general attitudes and behaviors. Weigel *et al.* (1974) measured low, moderate, and high specificity attitudes toward the Sierra Club and environmental issues and correlated these measures with level of participation in the Sierra Club. The most specific attitude had the highest correlation with participation ($r = .60$), middle-level attitudes exhibited moderate correlations ($r = .38$), and the least specific attitude had a low correlation ($r = .16$). Partial correlations between the moderate specificity attitudes and behavior controlling for the most specific attitude are approximately zero, as is the second-order partial correlation between the low specificity attitude and behavior when high and moderate specificity attitudes are controlled. If we assume that low, moderate, and high specificity attitudes make up a three-tiered hierarchy with the low specificity attitude corresponding to the highest level of the hierarchy, these results support the assumptions just discussed, where lower-level attitudes mediate the relationship between higher-level attitudes and behavior. Ajzen and Fishbein (1970) and Heberlein and Black (1976) report findings that also support the hierarchical model, in terms of both the relative sizes of attitude–behavior correlations for general and specific attitudes and the effects of partialling more specific attitudes from the correlation of general attitudes and behavior.

Schwartz and Tessler (1972) and Ajzen and Fishbein (1969) also found that more general attitude toward the object shows a lower correlation with behavior than specific attitude toward the act. However, partialling the more specific attitude toward the act from the correlation of attitude toward the object with behavior does not reduce this correlation to zero, although it does reduce ti. Part of the reason for this may lie in the fact that measures of specific attitudes were not corrected for unreliability by Schwartz and Tessler or by Ajzen and Fishbein. Partialling out an unreliable measure of specific attitude from the correlation of the general attitude and the behavior might leave part of the mediating influence of the specific attitude uncontrolled: A significant partial correlation could thus result even if there is no direct influence of the general attitude on the behavior.

For the most part, evidence garnered from past research favors the hierarchical formulation. Several scope conditions and extensions of the basic model suggest themselves. First, the relationships posited will hold only for subjects who have thought about the attitudes in a given hierarchy in relation to one another. Otherwise the consistency-producing internal-influence process will not occur, and causal paths for internal influence will not be well defined. Since existence of the hierarchy depends on amount of thinking subjects have done, in any given sample we are likely to find some subjects with relatively undeveloped hierarchies and some with extremely well-established hierarchies. Only for those subjects with well-established hierarchies, will the relationships elaborated in this section hold. Schwartz (1978) reports evidence germane to this point. In a study of volunteering behavior, he found that temporal stability of general attitudes was a moderator of attitude–behavior relationships. Only for stable general attitudes, such as would be expected in a well-established hierarchy, were correlations between specific attitudes and behaviors significant.

Second, the behavior must be linked with the attitudinal hierarchy for a particular attitude to influence it. A consideration of the various motives that people give for thier behaviors indicates the extremely diverse range of attitude objects a given behavior can be associated with. A person may go to a party primarily for recreation, to make business contacts, or in search of sexual conquests. People may participate in a demonstration because they enjoy open air events, believe in a political party, seek excitement, hate government, or support the cause behind the demonstration. Hence, one or another of any number of possible attitudes may have the primary role in governing a behavior for different people. For some acts and situations, the dominant general attitude will be the same for most subjects, whereas for others, there will be a number of dominant general attitudes in any sample. Insofar as the wrong general attitude (or only one of a number of appropriate general attitudes) is selected, the correlation between general attitude and behavior will be attenuated. Which attitudes a person associates with a behavior will be largely a product of the messages he or she has received about the behavior and the attitude. Depending on experience and messages received, a person may place different behaviors under different classes of attitude objects. Thus one person may attribute going to church or participating in church activities to his liking for his church, whereas another may relate these activities to his religious attitudes or his love for God or for his family. A pretest eliciting attitudes associated with a given behavior could help resolve this issue. Rather than merely assuming that the behavior corresponds to an attitude object, the experimenter could determine beforehand which attitudes are actually relevant to the behavior. In considering the relationship of attitudes to behavior, the researcher must realize that different subjects may relate the behavior to different general attitudes—that is, for different subjects the specific attitude toward the behavior may be subsumed by different general hierarchies. Thus, depending on what messages subjects have received in the past, there may be subgroups in any sample for which different superordinate attitudes are relevant.

The preceding discussion assumes that a behavior is attached to only one

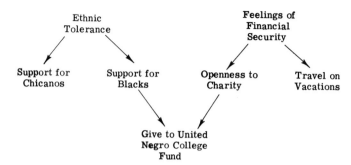

Figure 7.3. A behavior that is attached to two hierarchies of attitudes.

hierarchy; but this need not be so. Figure 7.3 shows a behavior, *Give to the United Negro College Fund*, which is attached to two hierarchies, a hierarchy of ethnic attitudes, and a hierarchy of financial attitudes. In such a case, the correlation between the act and either hierarchy would be low, but the multiple correlation using both hierarchies would be substantial.

In summary, we have considered the message–attitude–behavior question in light of the hierarchical theory of attitude change. We have developed and reviewed evidence relevant to several propositions:

1. Attitudes are hierarchically arranged and internal influence goes down only along hierarchical channels.
2. Behaviors are associated only with attitudes at the bottom of the hierarchy.
3. Influence of higher-order attitudes on behaviors is indirect and mediated by more specific attitudes.
4. There are individual differences in which hierarchy a given behavior is associated with.

Implications of the Hierarchical Model for Message Design

. It is appropriate that we should end on the subject of message design. This is, after all, is a volume on the message–attitude–behavior relationship. We have spent a great deal of space on attitude–attitude and attitude–behavior relations and have generally left ideas concerning message–attitude–behavior relations implicit. In this final section we will attempt to alleviate this lack by making the implicit explicit.

1. Individual differences in attitudinal structure make predicting the specific effect of a message on an individual at best difficult, and at worst quixotic. Different people will have different hierarchies. Differences in the number and type of superordinate attitudes will result in differences in decay of

messages aimed at specific attitudes (Hunter *et al.*, 1976) and in the extent to which message effects on higher-level attitudes filter down to specific attitudes. Differences in the extent to which individual hierarchies are integrated and established will result in differences in the influence general attitudes have over specific attitudes (and thus, over behavior). The nature of the concepts in a hierarchy is an important factor in determining predictability across individuals. For concepts that are an important part of a culture, there will probably be a great deal of consistency across individuals, since people have been exposed to many similar messages about these concepts and have had to think about them in relation to one another. At this time, energy issues are probably a good example of the type of cultural commonplaces that would yield a similar hierarchy for many individuals. For concepts that are not regularly dealt with in a culture, such as attitudes toward novels and novelists, there may be great individual differences in hierarchies for most people (although certain subcultures, such as critical schools, may have similar hierarchies).

2. The higher up in a hierarchy a message can strike, the more wide-ranging its effect on behavior will be. Since higher-order attitudes will bring lower-order attitudes into line, they will tend to counter message effects on lower-order attitudes. However, the effect of a message on an attitude at the top of the hierarchy will not decay. Further, even though attitude change relatively high or in the middle of a hierarchy will decay, it will also filter downward through the hierarchy and have a relatively long-term delayed effect on more specific attitudes. In addition, attitudes higher in a hierarchy are linked to more behaviors than less general attitudes are, and, as a result, changing general attitudes will effect a wider range of behaviors than will changing specific attitudes. In general, the higher up a hierarchy an attitude is, the broader the effect of a message directed at that attitude will be. There is, however, a counter-balancing consideration. A person will probably have been exposed to more information about general concepts than about specific ones. As Salteil and Woelfel (1975), among others, have shown, the impact of a single message on a concept is inversely related to the amount of information associated with the concept. Whereas we may be able to have a more profound effect on people's behavior by addressing messages to general rather than to specific attitudes, single messages are likely to have much less effect on general attitudes than they would on specific ones.

3. A lag will generally occur between reception of a message directed at a general attitude and the indirect impact of the message of behavioral choice, because the filtration of message effects through the hierarchy is gradual. Since thinking about the concepts in a hierarchy triggers the internal influence process, the filtering down of message effects can be speeded if people can be made to review the hierarchy soon after receiving the initial message. A particularly effective stimulus for review can be provided through follow-up messages. If possible, these messages should mention all levels of concepts in the particular strand of the hierarchy the behavior belongs to, to ensure that people do not truncate their reflection on the hierarchy. To the extent that a message can help

people organize their thinking about a hierarchy of concepts, it will favor the influence of more general attitudes on behavior.

4. Messages do not necessarily have to change attitudes to influence behavior. They can also rearrange hierarchies of concepts and create linkages between concepts that were previously unrelated or only weakly related. There are at least two ways of doing this. First, as we have noted, specific attitudes are often constructed from more general ones. If we knew which of an individual's attitudes were somewhat relevant to a behavior were favorable, we could design a message to encourage the individual to construct an attitude toward the behavior from only favorable attitudes. For example, if we knew that a certain man liked giving to charities, and we wanted him to donate blood, we could provide evidence that blood donation was a type of charitable activity, thus associating the constructed attitude toward blood donation with the more general attitude toward charitable giving. A second alternative would be to take a concept that presently falls in one hierarchy and attempt to convince people to reclassify it. Once the concept has been logically reclassified, the internal-influence process should change the attitude toward the concept so that it is more in line with its new superordinate attitudes. Some recent discussions of homosexuality have taken this tack. People are encouraged to reclassify homo-sexuality: Rather than thinking of it as a perversion, they are asked to consider it as a different, but normal sexual preference, common through the ages and harmless.

Amount of exposure to information about the concepts in a hierarchy will moderate how effective external messages are in rearranging concepts. In areas where subjects have little information about the concepts and the behavior, a potent message is likely to encounter little difficulty in effecting a rearrangement. However, where subjects have a large amount of information about the concepts or the behavior, or where hierarchies are well established, messages may run afoul of existing logical structures. A message will be most effective in rear-ranging a hierarchy if it does not have to compete with past classificatory messages. If a person has received a number of messages about the relationships among a set of concepts, reclassification will be difficult, because the new message will have to counteract past information.

Conclusion

It is paradoxical that general attitudes, with their wide-ranging effects, often seem to be less important determinants of behavior than specific attitudes. Over the long run, general attitudes exert a much more profound influence over behavioral choice than do specific attitudes. However, because specific attitude toward the act is a more immediate cause than the general attitudes that set the stage for behavioral choice, it usually shows a higher correlation with behavior. If we are interested only in the prediction of behavior, attitude toward the act is as far as we need to go, since it is the most reliable attitudinal indicator of whether a behavior will occur (subject to scope conditions, of course). However, if we want to understand or explain how behavioral choice occurs, we must investigate cognitive processes, and general attitudes and beliefs become more important concerns.

The model developed in this chapter is an attempt to specify one cognitive process that may mediate the message–attitude–behavior relationship. It is immediately apparent that hierarchies may not be the only cognitive structures that enter into behavioral choice. Research on the organization of memory indicates the logical hierarchy is only one of a number of structural arrangements encountered in mapping memory. It is possible that patterns of internal influence based on different organizational principles could also condition behavioral choice (Poole & Hunter, 1979). Unravelling the complexities of these processes demands the use of rigorous methods for specifying and testing hypotheses about cognitive organization. The techniques of deterministic modeling illustrated in this chapter offer a powerful means of setting out relatively unambiguous alternatives. If we want to understand complexity, we must use methods that take complexity into account.

REFERENCES

Ajzen, I., & Fishbein, M. The prediction of behavioral intentions in a choice situation. *Journal of Experimental Social Psychology*, 1969, *5*, 400–416.

Ajzen, I., & Fishbein, M. The prediction of behavior from attitudinal and normative variables. *Journal of Experimental Social Psychology*, 1970, *6*, 466–487.

Ajzen, I., & Fishbein, M. Attitude–behavior relations: A theoretical analysis and review of empirical research. *Psychological Bulletin*, 1977, *84*, 888–918.

Allport, G. W. *Personality: A psychological interpretation.* New York: Holt, 1937.

Berg, K. E. Ethnic attitudes and agreement with a Negro person. *Journal of Personality and Social Psychology*, 1966, *4*, 215–220.

Blalock, H. *Causal models in the social sciences.* Chicago: Aldine, 1971.

Bray, D. W. The prediction of behavior from two attitude scales. *Journal of Abnormal and Social Psychology*, 1950, *45*, 64–84.

Cappella, J. N. Dynamic mathematical models of dyadic interactions: An information processing *approach*. Unpublished doctoral dissertation Michigan State University, 1974.

Coleman, James *Introduction to mathematical sociology.* Glencoe, Ill.: Free Press, 1964.

Coleman, James. The mathematical study of change. In H. M. Blalock (Ed.). *Methodology in social research*, New York: McGraw–Hill, 1973.

Collins, A., & Loftus, E. A spreading activation theory of semantic processing. *Psychological Review*, 1975, *82*, 407–428.

Collins, A., & Quillian, R. How to make a language user. In E. Tulving & W. Donaldson (Eds.), *Organization of memory.* New York: Academic Press, 1972.

DeFleur, M. L., & Westie, F. R. Verbal attitudes and overt acts: An experiment on the salience of attitudes. *American Sociological Review*, 1958, *23*, 667–673.

Duncan, O. D. *Introduction to structural equation models.* New York: Academic Press, 1975.

Fishbein, M. Introduction: The prediction of behaviors from attitudinal variables. In C. D.

Mortensen & K. K. Sereno (Eds.), *Advances in communication research*. New York: Harper & Row, 1973.

Fishbein, M., & Ajzen, I. Attitudes toward objects as predictors of single and multiple behavioral criteria. *Psychological Review*, 1974, *81*, 59–74.

Green, J. A. Attitudinal and situational determinants of intended behavior toward Negroes. Doctoral dissertation, University of Colorado. Ann Arbor: University Microfilms, 1968.

Hays, W., & Winkler, R. L. *Statistics: Probability, inference, and decision*. New York: Holt, Rinehart & Winston, 1971.

Heberlein, T. A., & Black, J. S. Attitudinal specificity and the prediction of behavior in a field setting. *Journal of Personality and Social Psychology*, 1976, *33*, 474–479.

Hewes, D. E. Finite stochastic modeling of communication processes: An introduction and some basic readings. *Human Communication Research*, 1975, *1*, 271–282.

Holt, L. E. Resistance to persuasion in explicit beliefs as a function of commitment to and desirability of logically related beliefs. *Journal of Personality and Social Psychology*, 1970, *16*, 583–591.

Hovland, C. I., & Pritzker, H. A. Extent of opinion change as a function of amount of change advocated. *Journal of Abnormal and Social Psychology*, 1957, *54*, 257–261.

Hunter, J. E., & Cohen, S. Mathematical models of attitude change in the passive communication context, Psychology Department, Michigan State University, East Lansing, 1974. (a)

Hunter, J. E., & Cohen, S. H. Correcting for unreliability in nonlinear models of attitude change. *Psychometrika*, 1974, *39*, 445–468. (b)

Hunter, J. E., Levine, R., & Sayers, S. Attitude change in hierarchical belief systems and its relationship to persuasibility, dogmatism, and rigidity. *Human Communication Research*, 1976, *3*, 3–28.

Insko, C. A. *Theories of attitude change*. New York: Appleton–Century–Crofts, 1967.

LaPiere, R. T. Attitudes versus actions. *Social Forces*, 1934. *13*, 230–237.

Lindsay, P., & Norman, D. *Human information processing: An introduction to psychology*. New York: Academic Press, 1972.

Liska, A. Attitude–behavior consistency as a function of generality equivalence between attitude and behavior objects. *Journal of Psychology*, 1974, *86*, 217–28.

Nelson, C. E. Anchoring to accepted values as a technique for immunizing beliefs against persuasion. *Journal of Personality and Social Psychology*, 1968, *9*, 329–334.

Poole, M. S. An experimental test of some mathematical models of change in heirarchies of attitudes. Master's thesis, Michigan State University, 1976.

Poole, M. S., & Hunter, J. E. Change in hierarchical systems of attitudes. In D. Nimmo (Ed.), *Communication Yearbook III*. New Brunswick, N.J.: Transaction, ICA, 1979.

Rokeach, M. *Beliefs, attitudes, and values*. San Francisco: Jossey–Bass, 1969.

Rokeach, M. Long-range experimental modification of values, attitudes, and behavior. In W. Hunt (Ed.), *Human behavior and its control*. Cambridge, Mass.': MIT Press, 1971.

Saltiel, J., & Woelfel, J. Inertia in cognitive processes: the role of accumulated information in attitude change. *Human Communication Research*, 1975, *1*, 333–344.

Schuman, H., & Johnson, M. P. Attitudes and behavior. *Annual Review of Sociology*, 1976, *2*, 161–207.

Schwartz, S. Temporal instability as a moderator of the attitude–behavior relationship. *Journal of Personality and Social Psychology*, 1978, *37*, 715–724.

Schwartz, S., & Tessler, R. C. A test of a model for reducing measured attitude–behavior discrepancies. *Journal of Personality and Social Psychology*, 1972, *24*, 225–236.

Spilerman, S. The analysis of mobility processes by the introduction of independent variables into a Markov chain. *American Sociological Review*, 1972, *37*, 277–294.

Stotland, E., & Patchen, M. Identification and changes in prejudice and authoritarianism. *Journal of Abnormal and Social Psychology*, 1961, *62*, 265–274.

Stotland, E., Katz, D., & Patchen, M. The reduction of prejudice through the arousal of self-insight. *Journal of Personality*, 1959, *27*, 507–531.

Tittle, C. R., & Hill, R. J. Attitude measurement and prediction of behavior: An evaluation of conditions and measurement techniques. *Sociometry*, 1967, *30*, 299–213.

Weigel, R., & Newman, L. S. Increasing attitudinal–behavior correspondence by broadening the scope of the behavioral measure. *Journal of Personality and Social Psychology*, 1976, *33*, 793–802.

Weigel, R., Vernon, O. T., & Tognacci, L. N. Specificity of attitude as a determinant of attitude–behavior congruence. *Journal of Personality and Social Psychology*, 1974, *30*, 724–728.

Wood, G. Organization processes and free recall. In E. Tulring & W. Donaldson (Eds.), *The organization of memory*. New York: Academic Press, 1972.

8

The Message–Attitude–Behavior Relationship from the Point of View of the Actor

ROBERT T. CRAIG

This chapter attempts to draw attention to an often ignored but crucially important aspect of the message–attitude–behavior relation. The problem, assuming that *some* behavior correlates with a particular verbal attitude, is that the question of *what* behavior ought to so correlate is not trivial. Researchers usually assume that the consistency relations between attitudes and behaviors are obvious, but the point of view of the actor or subject being studied may be quite different from that of the researcher. This difference of perspectives may account for some failures to predict behavior from attitude. The chapter does not propose a comprehensive model of message–attitude–behavior processes. The intent is only to clarify the issue posed, and to suggest where some solutions may lie. Thus, we will touch the following points: (*a*) That, theoretically, an attitude ought to correlate with *some* behavior, so it is problematic that attitudes often do not correlate with behaviors as expected; (*b*) that the frequent failure of attempts to predict behavior from attitudes is perfectly natural in view of the ignorance that may underlie the hypotheses tested; (*c*) that no technique currently used in attitude research is sufficient to solve the problem; and (*d*) that investigating the actor's point of view, for example by

273

eliciting what are called accounts, might provide a stronger empirical basis for hypotheses about message–attitude–behavior relationships; but (e) that certain inherent limitations of such techniques must be kept in mind. Most of the discussion focuses on the attitude–behavior relationship, placing the message in the background. Such a focus simplifies our task but puts us in danger of distorting the communication process. As will be shown, however, taking the point of view of the actor may relate attitudes to behaviors in a way that naturally and productively integrates the message with the other components of communication.

The Attitude Concept

Attitude has been defined in many ways; tracing the history of the concept, although interesting, would not yield conceptual clarity quickly. Suffice it to say that the concept seems to have originated in the center of the science of *behavior*. Attitude is viewed as a state of readiness to respond, on a positive–negative, approach–avoid dimension, to a particular class of objects. Thus Scott (1968) refers to "the conventional assumption that the mere presence of the relevant object is enough to trigger the prepared response, which does not require additional motivation." This state of readiness to respond, moreover, is "a conscious state that can be expressed verbally . . . [p. 205]."

In this light, it seems odd to wonder whether there is any relation between attitudes, messages, and behaviors. Attitude usually is conceived in terms of both verbalization (thus tied to the realm of messages) and response (thus tied to the realm of behavior). To question that relation is to question the existence of attitudes as usually conceived. There are, to be sure, other ways of defining the concept. Fishbein (1975) has defined attitude as "the amount of affect for or against some object [p. 11]," rejecting the traditional definition as too ambiguous. This, however, is not just a new definition but rather a new concept; to discard the traditional definition in terms of predisposition to respond to an object would be, in effect, to discard the concept of attitude (that is not, of course, an unthinkable act).

Were we to discard the traditional attitude concept, we would still have to content with such things as the fact that *I like the Democratic party and tend to vote for Democratic candidates*—just the sort of human experience that the concept of attitude was meant to encompass. Here I "like" the object (Democratic party) and (consequently?) perform actions (voting) that "approach" the object. My attitudes and behaviors with respect to peanut butter, Ingmar Bergman's movies, and baroque music could be similarly described.

There is considerable evidence that most people at least sometimes behave consistently with their verbalized attitudes. A classic political study, *The American Voter* (Campbell, Converse, Miller, & Stokes, 1964) found, for example, multiple correlations of greater than .7 between attitudes and voting behavior

(p. 36). In another classic political study covering several decades, V. O. Key, Jr. (1968), marshaled a mass of evidence that American voting behavior was consistent with opinions on relevant issues. A widely cited laboratory study by DeFleur and Westie (1958) found that willingness of white college students to commit themselves to be photographed with "a Negro person of the opposite sex" was strongly consistent with racial prejudice as measured by a paper and pencil instrument. Literature reviews by Seibold (1975) and Ajzen and Fishbein (1977) cite many other studies that have found strong attitude–behavior correlations.

In sum, the theoretical definition of attitude requires that attitudes be associated with behaviors, and the association is borne out by both common-sense reflection and a considerable body of scientific data.

That, of course, is not the end of the story. The fact is that the assumption of attitude–behavior correlation often has been found false. Reviewing 46 studies prior to 1969, Wicker (1969) concluded:

> These studies suggest that it is considerably more likely that attitudes will be unrelated or only slightly related to overt behavior than that attitudes will be closely related to action. Product–moment correlation coefficients relating the two kinds of responses are rarely above .30 and often are near zero. Only rarely can as much as 10 percent of the variance in overt behavioral measures be accounted for by attitudinal data [p. 65, cited in Seibold, 1974].

Wicker questions whether there exist stable, underlying attitudes in the person. Other studies and literature reviews that draw similar conclusions are cited in Seibold (1975) and Ajzen and Fishbein (1977).

Attitude, Behavior, and Intuition

Perhaps a brief analysis of hypothetical examples will shed light on the question of attitude–behavior inconsistency.

Certain academics might have very positive attitudes toward scholarly productivity; they might not, however, be productive. Whereas the idea of productivity is attractive, the act of writing is not. Perhaps they are not very talented; or perhaps they are anxious, fearful of evaluation. Note that in this case we have an attitude–behavior inconsistency which the individuals perceive as such. Consistency theories would predict that, in the long run, if their behavior does not change, their attitudes will. They might, for example, strongly disavow the "publish or perish" aspect of academic life.

Let us now imagine a religion in which members normally profess to hold the reading of Holy Scripture in very high regard. Examining their behavior, however, we find that few ever read Holy Scripture; indeed, most seem appalled by the suggestion. It turns out that, in this religion, Holy Scripture is held in such high regard that the reading of it is restricted to a priestly elite.

Thus, there is no inconsistency between attitude and behavior from the point of view of the church members. What we originally thought to be an inconsistency turns out to have been an artifact of our ignorance. Is it implausible that we could be so ignorant?

Consider one final example, a voter who has a negative attitude toward Republicans but votes for a Republican for president of the United States. Political researchers in the tradition of *The American Voter* would try to explain the obvious inconsistency in terms of social "cross-pressures" or the salience of short-term issues or candidate personalities. These attempts at explanation, even if they were fairly successful statistically, would ignore an important possibility: There might be *no* inconsistency. The voter might, after all, hold some sophisticated political opinion, such as the belief that the president operates independently of the political party, or that the president should be of a different party from the congressional majority to ensure a balance of power.

Thus, among our hypothetical examples, we have one genuine inconsistency, perceived as such (uncomfortably so) by the subject, and two states that appear only to the uninformed outsider to be attitude–behavior inconsistency. The question is whether behavioral researchers are not often in the position of ignorant outsider.

That the apparent rationality of humans is often mere rationalization is a truism in the behavioral sciences. Rationality and rationalization, however, both reflect a strong need for *consistency*, also a much-studied subject. The consistency principle suggests that genuine attitude–behavior inconsistency is a rare and transient bird. Much of it may prove illusory as soon as the investigator discovers what is really going on in the subject's head, just as Henle (1962) found that many of her subjects' apparent errors in syllogistic reasoning proved not to be errors when she discovered how the task or the premises of the syllogism were *interpreted* by the subjects.

A prominent example from the attitude literature further illustrates the point. LaPiere (1934) found that hotel managers who had avowed beforehand that they would not admit Chinese people, in fact, did admit a traveling Chinese couple who entered each hotel to request a room. LaPiere stated: "In the end I was forced to conclude that those factors which most influenced the behavior of others toward the Chinese had nothing to do with race [p. 232]." He goes on to mention factors such as quality of clothing, appearance of baggage, and cleanliness. This has been interpreted as evidence for lack of attitude–behavior correlation. It seems to me equally likely that the relevant attitude has been misinterpreted. The *attitude* may have had nothing directly to do with race. The hotel managers simply may have been under the unfortunate impression that most Chinese were dirty, carried beat-up luggage, and so forth—people like *that*, surely, were not to be accommodated.

Kiesler, Collins, and Miller (1969) clearly recognize the problem that I have been discussing:

> In summary, our notion that a *particular* attitude correlates with a *particular* behavior may be incorrect, not because of a general failure of attitudes to have any relationship to behavior, but because our intuitive notions about which attitudinal factors are correlated with which behavioral factors are incorrect. While our theoretical analysis of attitudes definitely commits us to a position that attitude factors should, in general, be correlated to *some* behavioral factor, it does not commit us to a position that each attitude factor should be correlated to *all* behavioral factors. It does not commit us to the position that a particular attitude factor should be correlated to a particular behavioral factor—even if the logical and intuitive arguments that a particular attitude and behavior belong in the same factor are very compelling [pp. 36–37].

In their recent review article, Ajzen and Fishbein (1977) even more pointedly indicate the undesirable consequences of intuitive attitude–behavior matching by researchers:

> In the absence of an explicit and unambiguous definition of attitude–behavior consistency, therefore, many tests of the attitude–behavior relation reduce to little more than tests of the investigator's intuition. From a theoretical point of view, such tests of the relation between arbitrarily selected measures of attitude or behavior are of rather limited value [p. 889].

As I will show, no one has yet proposed an adequate way of dealing with this problem, and most investigators still appear oblivious to the problem itself. The seemingly uncontroversial principle that the investigator cannot depend on intuition to designate a priori which attitudes "go with" which behaviors has been ignored in most attitude research. For example, Schwartz and Tessler (1972) write simply of "the discrepency between attitudes people profess and their overt behavior [p. 225]." Seibold (1975) defines the message–attitude–behavior problem as "the effects of communication on attitude statements and related behaviors (i.e., on manifest acts which *ought to be consistent* with verbal reports [p. 3, emphasis altered]." Werner (1978) concludes that there may be "differences in the extent to which the attitudes of pro-abortion men and women *parallel their attitudes* [p. 1383, emphasis added]." These quotations are typical in that they beg the question of whether a given behavior corresponds with a given attitude.

The Problem of Attitude–Behavior Matching

Some investigators have attempted to treat attitude–behavior matching systematically, although no one has developed a fully satisfactory solution to the problem.

One line of approach has been to reconceptualize attitude. Rokeach (1967) argued that behavioral prediction must be based on the interaction of two attitudes, called attitude toward the object (A_o) and attitude toward the situation (A_s). Rokeach is vague as to the nature of A_s. His research does, however, show that a change in the behavioral situation can change the relevance of an attitude to predicting behavior.

Fishbein (1967) reconceptualized attitude, for purposes of behavioral prediction, as attitude toward a behavior in a situation. This move indeed permits better behavioral prediction. It entails, however, throwing out the baby with the bath water, the baby being the seminal proposition that behavior toward an object is a function of attitude toward that object. Fishbein himself admits that his behavioral prediction model "fails to specify the conditions under which specific behaviors can be predicted from traditional attitudes toward an object or class of objects [1974, p. 80]." More recently, Fishbein has integrated the concept of attitude-toward-the-act within a broader theory of attitude–behavior relationships that has helped greatly to clarify the problem. This more recent theory is discussed later.

Seibold (1975) proposed a model postulating that behavior is a joint function of several cognitive structures. These include the tripartite division of attitudes into desirability, likelihood, and intention, and the extraattitudinal factors of certainty and locus of control. The concept of attitude in this model corresponds quite closely to Fishbein's "attitude toward the act." Consequently, the model tends toward the same disadvantage as Fishbein's earlier model, that of discarding the proposition that behavior toward an object is a function of attitude toward that *object*.

Since Seibold's model seems to be the most developed of its type, let us see how well it might account for the examples introduced earlier. The model surely accommodates academics who like academic productivity, but whose locus of control for writing is situational. In the case of the religious group, the researcher just has to catch a distinction between the reading of Scripture (good) and the *lay* reading of Scripture (inappropriate). Nothing in the model itself suggests such a cognitive structure. In the case of the Democrat who votes for the Republican presidential candidate, the belief that the president is independent of party fits nicely under the concept of likelihood (voting for the Republican likely will not lead to the evils of Republicanism); whereas the belief that the president and the members of Congress should be of different parties entails a distinction that the researcher just has to know about: Voting Democratic in general (good) is not the same as voting for a Democratic president when the Congress is also Democratic. Finally, the model does not seem to suggest a way in which we could determine whether it was *dirty* people, rather than *Chinese* people, that LaPiere's hotel managers would refuse to admit. The problem seems to be that models of this type, by forcing the attitude concept into certain cognitive structures, tend to foreclose other structures that may be important in the particular case. This is not to invalidate the model, but is to suggest that the model does not solve the problem of attitude–behavior matching.

A review of the literature has uncovered some structured methods that do seem to speak directly to the issue of attitude–behavior matching. One is the factor analysis of attitudes and behavioral syndromes. Another is the use of multiple behavioral criteria (Ajzen & Fishbein, 1977; Fishbein & Ajzen, 1974, 1975). The rationale for these approaches derives from measurement theory. A single behavior ought to be considered as a single item measuring an underlying construct that we might call "behavior in relation to Attitude A." Single item measures tend to be relatively unreliable because they are easily affected by random factors, and invalid because they confound item variance with true score variance (no single item is likely to correspond perfectly to a theoretical construct). This, in essence, is the argument made by Scott (1968, p. 252), as well as by Fishbein and Ajzen (1974).

Triandis' (1964) approach was to construct a "behavioral differential" along the lines of the semantic differential. Many behaviors toward a variety of types of people were rated by a sample of students on bipolar "would–would not" scales, and those sets of scales were factor analyzed. The output of such an analysis is hoped to compose a set of pure, underlying behavioral factors. Thus we can discover what goes with what in the thinking about behaviors typical of a population. The factors could be used to construct behavioral scales that could be correlated with attitude scales. As Kiesler, Collins, and Miller (1969) point out, the behavioral differential has the potential to correct our intuitions about behavioral syndromes:

> We might feel that admiring the character of, falling in love with, being partners with, allowing favors to be done for us by, and treating as a subordinate, should form a single consistent pattern of behavior; but Triandis (1964) found that these five behaviors were parts of relatively separate and distinct clusters [p. 36].

Behaviors that are uncorrelated with one another cannot all be expected to correlate highly with the same verbal expression of attitude; yet that, in effect, is what intuition sometimes leads us to assume.

A study by Insko, Blake, Cialdini, and Mulaik (1970) illustrates a different application of factor analysis to the attitude–behavior problem. Those investigators measured attitudes toward 48 objects that might be related to birth control usage and also measured 48 corresponding beliefs concerning the effects of birth control on those objects. Principle components analysis of the 96 items yielded 23 factors, which then were related to birth control behavior in a multivariate analysis of variance. Nine of the 23 factors showed significant univariate relationships with use of birth control. Given a population of attitudes, this sort of analysis can help to determine which members of that population are most relevant to a particular behavior.

Fishbein and Ajzen (1974) applied Thurstone, Likert, and Guttman scaling techniques to self-reports of 100 behaviors and behavioral intentions selected as indicative of the attitude of religiosity. Several standard religiosity attitude scales then were correlated with the behavioral scales. The mean correlation with single behaviors ranged from .13 to .20, while the correlations with multiple-behavior scales ranged from .45 to .73, with the majority of correlations greater than .60. Thus, Fishbein and Ajzen demonstrated that multiple-act scales are superior to single-act scales as behavioral indicators of attitude. They went on, however, to argue another important point concerning the *selection* of single-act criteria in studies using attitude to predict a single behavior. They argue that only behaviors that meet the criteria of Likert scaling can be expected to have a linear relationship to attitude; they propose validity and linearity indices that permit assessment of single behaviors without recourse to the usual Likert scaling procedure; and they show that these indices discriminate between behaviors having high or low correlations with verbal attitude measures. Fishbein and Ajzen (1974) conclude:

> Clearly, if there is no theoretical basis for assuming that a given behavior (with respect to some object) will be related to attitude (towards that object), the failure to find a relationship between the attitude and the single-act criterion *cannot* be taken as evidence that attitudes are unrelated to behaviors. Even more important, unless there is some high *a priori* likelihood that a given criterion will be affected by attitude under at least some circumstances, it is pointless to conduct research investigating the ways in which other variables moderate or influence the attitude–behavior relationship [pp. 71–72].

This extremely important argument should condition the interpretation of all past research and the design of all future research.

The methods discussed in this section provide means of evaluating the degree to which a given behavior is tied to a given attitude in the minds of the population being studied. The methods might be viewed as alternatives to be used where most convenient. On the whole, the factor-analysis approach is better suited for exploration of the structure of a set of behaviors, whereas Fishbein's scaling approach is a more direct and sophisticated way of evaluating particular behavioral items.

Ajzen and Fishbein (1977) have set forth a general position on the attitude–behavior issue and have reviewed the literature from the point of view of that position. As was mentioned earlier, they explicitly acknowledge the problem of intuitive attitude–behavior matching. Their solution is to match the "entities" to which attitude and behavior measures refer by matching the action, target, context, and time aspects of the entities. In particular, attitude and behavior measures must be matched in the degree to which they *generalize* one or more of the four aspects of the entity. For example, an attitude toward a general class of targets (Chinese) generalizes both the action and target aspects; an attitude toward a specific act toward a class of targets (admitting Chinese to a specific hotel) generalizes the target but not the action; an attitude toward a specific act directed toward a specific target (admitting a specific Chinese couple to a specific hotel) generalizes neither aspect. The traditional attitude toward an object, which generalizes the action aspect of the entity, would be matched with a multiple-act criterion, which also generalizes the action aspect. A single behavior usually must be predicted from attitude toward the act, which is behavior-specific.

This seems to be a reasonable approach to the problem. An examination of Ajzen and Fishbein's (1977) review of the literature, however, makes it clear that their approach still leaves a great deal of room for researchers to make intuitive, possibly erroneous, judgments about attitude–behavior correspondence. It is still the *researcher* who decides "what goes with what" in matching attitudes and behaviors. Ajzen and Fishbein frequently use the phrase "It can be seen that. . ." to introduce a summary judgment as to whether the attitude and behavior measures correspond properly in a particular study. The reader often wonders what empirical basis those judgments might have. Ajzen and Fishbein (1977) in making the judgments, presumably draw upon their general knowledge of the social world. Sometimes the information used is explicit, as in the following:

> For example, in Great Britain voting for the most preferred candidate may contribute to the formation of a government by the least preferred party under the leadership of a disliked prime minister. Voting for a given candidate in Great Britain may thus be an indication of a person's attitude toward the party rather than toward the candidate. This implies that in Great Britain, the attitude toward voting for a particular candidate would correlate more highly with actual voting for that candidate than would the attitude toward the candidate [p. 908].

This passage reads much like the hypothetical examples introduced earlier. Even if all of Ajzen and Fishbein's judgments about attitude–behavior correspondence were entirely correct, the ad hoc and intuitive character of those judgments would still make them scientifically questionable. And, as the authors freely acknowledge, "The reader may occasionally have disagreed with our interpretation of correspondence in the studies reviewed [p. 911]."

In summary of this section, a review of the literature yields several techniques that can be extremely helpful in determining attitude–behavior correspondence. Those techniques include factor analysis, the behavioral differential, scaling analysis of behavioral items, and matching the action and target aspects of the entities referred to by attitude and behavior measures. The limitations, as well as the usefulness, of these techniques should be evident, however. The techniques fail to resolve entirely the problems associated with the matching of attitudes and behaviors. Several aspects of matching still depend upon arbitrary decisions of the investigator. First, the selection of attitude and behavior items for study still is unsystematic. Second, the interpretation of factors still depends upon the investigator's (perhaps erroneous) intuitions about the meaning of behaviors. Consider a fine distinction such as that in the hypothetical example in which *lay* people were not expected to read Scripture. Such a distinction would not be captured by a factor analysis, barring sheer chance, unless the behaviors to be analyzed were quite judiciously selected. Might not such a subtle distinction underlie what Werner (1978) interprets as a lack of

attitude–behavior correspondence among proabortion males? Systematic uncovering of such distinctions might provide information needed to explain
many of the low correlations in the literature. Third, the scientific explanations
derived from techniques based on quantitative scaling theory are weak, failing
to satisfy our curiosity about *why* clusters of behaviors and attitudes go together. The investigator is free to speculate, of course, but such speculations
are difficult to ground empirically.

The Point of View of the Actor

A radical analysis of the problem of attitude–behavior matching might be
derived from the premises of contemporary movements in the social sciences,
such as ethnomethodology, espousing phenomenological–descriptive, rather
than behavioral–experimental modes of inquiry. Those movements have
attacked "behaviorism" (a name broadly applied to the behavioral–experimental modes) for its overblown assertions of scientific status and practical
failure to account for human action. The two grounds for attack are interrelated,
for behaviorism's pretentiousness results from (and masks) the *uncritical* and
unconscious operation of commonsense cultural assumptions, and behaviorism's practical failures might be lessened by the very methods developed to
raise the investigators' own consciousness of assumptions, since those assumptions affect the conduct of ordinary mortals (the subjects of behavioral research)
as well. The critics of behaviorism emphasize the phenomenological underpinnings of scientific data. Cicourel's (1974) view may be taken as representative:

> The sociologist relies on his implicit knowledge of his own society's language and
> non-oral meanings to describe the outputs of human communication relevant to his
> interests in substantive research. The substantive terms used to describe the language
> outputs of social interaction presuppose that the recipient understands the society
> from the 'inside' as a native speaker–hearer. Hence the researcher relies on his
> unexplicated native competence to describe observations and verbal outputs, and the
> reader must presume or simulate this competence to interpret the results presented
> [p. 74].

This line of argument is quite consistent with the main point of this chapter,
that predictions about attitude–behavior correspondence should not be, as
they have been, based on unacknowledged intuitive judgments. I believe that
the argument must be taken seriously, and that the proper response to it on the
part of social scientists is to be more systematic in dealing with their assumptions
and interpretations. According to some theories of the effects of behavior on
attitudes, this change in practice also may be expected, over time, to lessen our
scientific pretentiousness. In any case, what this chapter calls for is not the
abandonment of systematic, quantitative methods, but rather their extension
into new areas.

One line of attack would be to devise methods for obtaining data on the cognitive relations between attitudes and behaviors from the point of view of the persons whose behavior is to be predicted. Such data could provide a stronger empirical basis for attitude–behavior matching. The problem is that no such procedure now exists in a well-developed form. One approach to the development of the needed methods might be found in Harré and Secord's (1973) proposal of the systematic investigation of accounts.

The term *account* refers to the verbal explanation offered by an actor whose behavior is challenged. The term was introduced by Scott and Lyman (1968), who built on a considerable sociological tradition (for example, Mills, 1940), and has been expanded and elaborated by Harré and Secord (1973) into a fundamental methodological theory for the social sciences.

Harré and Secord are a good deal weaker in their treatment of specific methods than in their treatment of general principles; however, they do provide the rudiments of a technique that could be adapted to the attitude–behavior problem. Let us outline the method before discussing its rationale and implications. The description draws heavily on Harré and Secord (1973, pp. 309–313).

The technique may be summarized in the following points:

1. The paradigmatic setting is a face-to-face interview between subject and investigator.
2. The subject must be placed in a *justificatory context*. That is, the subject must feel a genuine commitment to account for his or her behavior. Research on the social psychology of the psychological experiment suggests that the investigator, an authority figure, will not have great difficulty in creating such a context. (See Adair, 1973.)
3. The investigator calls into question an attitude or behavior of the subject.
4. "If the response to challenge is an account in justification of the attitude, this account must be collected and analyzed [Harré & Secord, 1973, p. 311]." The accounts provided are then further challenged.
5. "The upshot . . . would then be a set of accounts, falling into two stages: (a) the items which were partitioned between the logically simple in which simple emotional response is expressed, and (b) the logically complex, which are themselves open to further challenge. The skilled ethogenic investigator will break off the challenging at the point where further steps might be felt to be the opening moves of an attempt to change or modify the simple attitudes and basic beliefs [Harré & Secord, 1973, p. 312]."
6. Finally, the accounts are content analyzed. "The final content analysis of accounts will yield internal structures of varying degrees of strength and connectedness. It is presumed that it may be possible to discover what are the possible cognitive structures associated with attitudes [Harré & Secord, 1973, p. 312]."

Harré and Secord go on to talk about the need for subsequent behavioral testing as a check on the "authenticity" of the verbal accounts. Of course, the whole point of introducing the method here is to advance towards methods of measuring attitudes that will be "authentic" in that regard. Ironically, Harré and Secord, at this point, fall into the same trap as the behaviorists, assuming that the behavioral criteria that will authenticate an account are intuitively obvious. I am suggesting that the method of investigating accounts may be applied to that very problem of attitude–behavior correspondence.

The systematic investigation of accounts, considered as an approach to the problem of attitude–behavior matching, although the method admittedly is sketchy as of yet, seems to attack each of the problems listed at the end of the last section. The three problems of the scaling approach to attitude–behavior matching were (a) the arbitrary selection of behaviors for study; (b) the intuitive interpretation of factors; and (c) the weakness of resulting scientific explanations. The first problem would be solved by asking the respondent to connect attitudes and behaviors verbally; thus, the conceptual association would be made by the subject rather than by the investigator. The second problem would be solved to the extent that accounts would give the investigator insight into the cognitive structures in which the relevant attitudes were embedded; thus, the investigator would have more to go on than his or her intuition in interpreting the results of structured scaling methods. The third problem should be solved because the availability of accounts would permit the investigator to report not only *that* certain attitude–behavior syndromes are typical of a population, but also *why* those syndromes exist.

The investigation of accounts as an integral part of attitude–behavior research might offer a significant further advantage in that it would lead directly to the study of *message strategies*. This discussion has largely ignored the message part of the message–attitude–behavior transaction, and it was acknowledged at the outset that there is some danger in doing so; but here we find at least a hint that what is good for understanding the attitude–behavior relationship will also prove helpful for understanding the whole transaction. The concept of account implies a verbalization of attitude *in relation to* behavior. The cognitive structure by which attitude *accounts for* behavior directly attaches a verbal handle to the relationship. The job of a persuasive message is to grasp that handle and move it. The job is facilitated by knowledge of what Harré and Secord call the *logical status* of the attitude—whether it is simple or is further accounted for by, and therefore anchored in, a deeper cognitive structure.

That we should study cognitive structures is not, of course, a new idea. What is shown here is that available scaling procedures do not encompass the whole field of potentially relevant cognitive structures. The addition of cognitive variables such as locus of control to attitude models (McDermott, 1974; Seibold, 1975) is a definite advance, but is insufficient because such variables force upon the set of recognized structures a degree of closure for which we are not yet, and perhaps never will be, ready. The investigation of accounts, a more open-ended procedure, would force us to confront whatever cognitive structures exist in a particular population for a particular attitude domain. General models of cognitive structure doubtless both would contribute to and benefit from this policy.

Limitations of the Actor's Point of View

Although a method such as the investigation of accounts seems to offer some advantages, those advantages have yet to be demonstrated empirically. Further development of the method in application to the message–attitude–behavior problem obviously is required. My initial attempts to use the Harré–Secord interview format suggest that the selection of behaviors to be accounted for, the process of unpacking the subject's cognitive structure, the recording of the data, and the content analysis of the accounts are some of the areas that require further specification.

More importantly, there seem to be some limitations inherent in *any* methodology that might be developed along these lines. One problem is that the actor's own self-understanding is limited, thus the extent to which the actor's point of view will provide a full account of attitude–behavior relationships is limited. Nisbett and Wilson (1977) have reviewed a mass of empirical evidence that persons are incapable of describing their own mental processes and often are unaware of the causes of their own behavior. A response to Nisbett and Wilson by Smith and Miller (1978) questions the conclusion that subjects are *never* aware of their mental processes, but does not question that such awareness is quite limited. This suggests that actors' accounts of their own behavior are not a complete or infallible source of data for explaining attitude–behavior relationships.

A second limitation is inherent in any scientific investigation that seeks to generalize across individuals. If the point of view of the actor determines the correspondence between attitude and behavior, and if different actors have different points of view, then the correspondence between any particular attitude and behavior will vary across individuals. The whole thrust of scaling methods, after all, is to obtain a set of items that represent a typical dimension of thinking in a statistical population. This is accomplished at the cost of ignoring idiosyncratic meanings (Scott, 1968, pp. 232–233), a choice that the investigator should make in full awareness. One *could* construct a scale for a single person (given a suitable variable); the scale would be valid only for that individual. If we choose to ignore idiosyncratic meanings for the sake of generalizability, we must refrain from accusing individuals or subpopulations of inconsistency because they fail to conform to statistical norms. For example, Werner (1978) correlated attitude toward abortion with a multiple-act behavioral scale. Finding differences in attitude–behavior correlations when the sample was broken down by sex and direction of attitude, Werner (1978) concluded that the differences among subgroups in the attitude–behavior correlations might have resulted from differences in "the extent to which the activism of pro-abortion men and women parallel their attitudes [p. 1383]." The problem with such a conclusion is that the very definition of "parallel" may vary among subgroups, rendering the conclusion either erroneous or meaningless.

A third limitation of the actor's point of view is that all research ultimately is done from the researcher's point of view and reflects the researcher's intuitive understanding of methods, procedures, and results. Not all assumptions can be made explicit. Polanyi (1964) has shown the profound sense in which all knowledge, even the most precise theories of the hardest physical and mathematical sciences, finally rests upon intuition or what he calls tacit knowledge. Behavioral science hardly can hope to avoid this limitation. The investigation of accounts may reinforce the empirical basis for attitude–behavior matching, but large areas necessarily will remain in the realm of intuition. For example, the researcher must reason from the accounts to the selection of items for scale construction and to the explanation of attitude–behavior relationships. The reasoning might be supported by formal procedures such as the formulation and testing of topic-specific multivariate models, but certain conceptual leaps will remain unavoidable.

In closing, it should be emphasized that the proposal that researchers take the actor's point of view by investigating accounts is not intended as a radical departure from current practice, but as a supplement to the usual scaling and experimental techniques. Advocates of such causes as ethnomethodology and ethogeny often proclaim the new order and the demise of pseudoscience. But behavioral science seldom entirely ignores its phenomenological roots in the actor's point of view. For example, the initial generation of items for scale construction often is done by some procedure intended to produce items reflecting a distribution of cognitions representative of the population. What is proposed here, in effect, is that more careful attention be given to the methodology of this early stage of scaling, whether of attitudes, of behaviors, or of attitude–behavior syndromes. A method like the systematic investigation of accounts would force us to attend to the cognitive structures that generate message–attitude–behavior connections. The point is not to banish intuition; indeed, the myth that intuition can be banished from behavioral science is a source of those pseudoscientific pretensions that are under attack. The point is to make sympathetic understanding of the actor's point of view an explicit and elaborated component of methodology.

REFERENCES

Adair, J. G. *The human subject: The social psychology of the psychological experiment.* Boston: Little, Brown, 1973.

Ajzen, I., & Fishbein, M. Attitude–behavior relations: A theoretical analysis and review of empirical research. *Psychological Bulletin*, 1977, *84*, 888–918.

Campbell, A., Converse, P., Miller, W., & Stokes, D. *The American voter*. New York: Wiley, 1964.

Cicourel, A. *Cognitive sociology: Language and meaning in social interaction*. New York: Free Press, 1974.

DeFleur, M., & Westie, F. Verbal attitudes and overt acts. *American Sociological Review*, 1958, *23*, 667–673.

Fishbein, M. Attitude and the prediction of behavior. In M. Fishbein (Ed.), *Readings in attitude theory and measurement*. New York: Wiley, 1967.

Fishbein, M., & Ajzen, I. Attitudes towards objects as predictors of single and multiple behavioral criteria. *Psychological Review*, 1974, *81*, 59–74.

Fishbein, M., & Ajzen, I. *Belief, attitude, intention and behavior: An introduction to theory and research*. Reading, Mass.: Addison–Wesley, 1975.

Harré, R., & Secord, P. F. *The explanation of behavior*. Totowa, N.J.: Littlefield, Adams, 1973.

Henle, M. On the relation between logic and thinking. *Psychological Review*, 1962, *69*, 366–378.

Insko, C. A., Blake, R. R., Cialdini, R. B., & Mulaik, S. A. Attitude toward birth control and cognitive consistency: Theoretical and practical implications of survey data. *Journal of Personality and Social Psychology*, 1970, *16*, 228–237.

Key, V. O., Jr. *The responsible electorate: Rationality in presidential voting 1936–1960*. New York: Vintage, 1968.

Kiesler, C. A., Collins, B., & Miller, N. *Attitude change: A critical analysis of theoretical approaches*. New York: Wiley, 1969.

LaPiere, R. T. Attitudes vs. actions. *Social Forces*, 1934, *13*, 230–237.

McDermott, V. The development of a functional message variable: The locus of control. Doctoral dissertation, Michigan State University, 1974.

Mills, C. W. Situated actions and vocabularies of motive. *American Sociological Review*, 1940, *5*, 904–913.

Nisbett, R. E., & Wilson, T. D. Telling more than we can know: Verbal reports on mental processes. *Psychological Review*, 1977, *84*, 231–259.

Polanyi, M. *Personal knowledge*. New York: Harper Torchbooks, 1964.

Rokeach, M. Attitude change and behavioral change. *Public Opinion Quarterly*, 1966–1967, *30*, 529–550.

Schwartz, S., & Tessler, R. A test of a model for reducing measured attitude–behavior discrepancies. *Journal of Personality and Social Psychology*, 1972, *24*, 225–236.

Scott, M. B., & Lyman, S. M. Accounts. *American Sociological Review*, 1968, *33*, 46–62.

Scott, W. A. Attitude measurement. In G. Lindsay & E. Aronson (Eds.), *The handbook of social psychology* (Vol. 2) Reading, Mass.: Addison–Wesley, 1968. Pp. 204–273.

Seibold, D. R. Communication research and the attitude–verbal report–overt behavior relationship: A critique and theoretic reformulation. Paper presented at the annual convention of the Speech Communication Association. Chicago, Illinois, December 27–30, 1974.

Seibold, D. R. Communication research and the attitude–verbal report–overt behavior relation: A critique and theoretic reformulation. *Human Communication Research*, 1975, *2*, 3–32.

Smith, E. R., & Miller, F. D. Limits on perception of cognitive processes: A reply to Nisbett and Wilson. *Psychological Review*, 1978, *85*, 355–362.

Triandis, H. C. Exploratory factor analyses of the behavioral component of social attitudes. *Journal of Abnormal and Social Psychology*, 1964, *68*, 420–430.

Werner, P. D. Personality and attitude–activism correspondence. *Journal of Personality and Social Psychology*, 1978, *36*, 1375–1390.

Wicker, A. Attitudes vs. actions: The relationship of verbal and overt behavioral responses to attitude objects. *Journal of Social Issues*, 1969, *25*, 41–78.

9

Wittgenstein's *Philosophical Investigations* and The Relationship between Mental States and Social Action

THOMAS J. LARKIN

The goals of science may be said to include prediction, control, and understanding. This chapter will focus almost entirely on understanding. What is to be understood is the relationship between internal mental states (i.e., meanings, intentions, attitudes) and external social action. The philosophical perspective chosen for this examination is the work of Ludwig Wittgenstein and more specifically his book, first published in 1953, entitled, *Philosophical Investigations.*[1]

Being able to predict something does not add up to being able to explain or understand the thing in question. Prediction involves covariance, that two things do or do not vary together; it is understanding, however, that provides the conceptual link between the two things that vary. It is understanding that supplies and enunciates the principle that governs or regulates the relationship between the variables. To find a correlation of .99 between mother's weight and the number of hours an individual watches television is, by itself, completely

---

[1] Roman numerals in parentheses refer to remarks in Parts I and II, respectively, of Wittgenstein (1958a), *Philosophical Investigations.* The numbers for Part I refer to the paragraph and the numbers for Part II, preceded by a "p," refer to the page.

289

MESSAGE–ATTITUDE–BEHAVIOR RELATIONSHIP
Theory, Methodology, and Applications

meaningless. What this empirical finding stands in need of is a principle that explains the relationship. It is precisely the principle, however, which does not emerge out of the data, but is added to the data by the investigator. The principle is supplied by the investigator and is valid to the extend that the investigator *understands* the phenomenon in question.

Winch (1958) provides a hypothetical example of an individual who, after years of studying the Chinese language, is able to provide probability estimates of the likelihood of one particular Chinese character being followed by a second particular character. Despite the accuracy of these predictions, we do not say that the individual understands Chinese. "a man who understands Chinese is not a man who has a firm grasp of the statistical probabilities for the occurrence of various words in the Chinese language. Indeed, he could have that without knowing that he was dealing with a language at all . . . 'Understanding' in situations like this is grasping the point or meaning of what is being said or done [p. 115]."

Max Weber argues that explanations of social action must be adequate on two levels. First, the explanation must be adequate on "the level of meaning." By this, Weber means that the investigator must be able to make sense of the relationship between the variables; and this is done, according to Weber, by understanding the subjective meanings of intentions motivating an individual's action. In addition, Weber argues that explanations must be "causally adequate," meaning that the investigator must be able to determine the likelihood of a given observable event being followed or accompanied by another event. Weber is suggesting that an adequate explanation of a social action must include both understanding and prediction. It is in this sense that this chapter, or one like it, is necessary but not sufficient for a social scientific explanation of the relationship between mental states and social action.

Wittgenstein was interested in understanding.[2] Specifically, he was interested in understanding what it is that makes our language meaningful. How does it occur that we are able to communicate symbols to one another in a meaningful fashion. More accurately, Wittgenstein was interested in the place or source from which our language is endowed with meaning (I, 218). Wittgenstein suggests that our language is meaningful not because of its association with mental states and psychological phenomena, but because of its role and function in social life (I, 491). Even if a patient groans in pain, this groan is taken not so much as an expression of an internal state, but is rather received as a signal that the patient needs to be moved, or given water, or a dressing change, or more analgesic (II, p. 179). The meaning of a word or

---

[2] Although Wittgenstein was interested in understanding, he did not frequently claim to have obtained it. In the preface to the *Philosophical Investigations* he writes, "I should have liked to produce a good book. This has not come about, but the time is passed in which I could improve it." Norman Malcolm (1958) also writes of Wittgenstein, "He was constantly depressed, I think, by the impossibility of arriving at understanding in philosophy."

message, according to Wittgenstein, is determined by the function or purpose that word or message fulfills in some social context. That "meanings are in people" is a thesis that Wittgenstein repeatedly argues against (I, p. 639).

Any difficulties which social scientists might experience while trying to establish a relationship between self-reports of attitudes and subsequent behavior would probably not surprise Wittgenstein at all.[3] Social action, including verbal behavior, is not to be explained, according to Wittgenstein, by reference to preceding mental states. Behaviors derive their meaning and significance from the role or function they perform in some situation. We can, for example, think of a community of people where orders, in the sense of commands, are never obeyed (I, 345). In this community, the verb, to order, would be meaningless, and no matter how intently one tried to order these people, it would be impossible to do so. To order has some meaning for us because it has a place or function in our social life; *and* the *meaning* of a particular order derives from our response to it, not from some particular frame of mind or mental image called up by the orderer (I, 199, 503).

It is not attitudes that breathe life into behaviors; it is "usefulness" which gives behaviors their significance. To understand people's behavior does not require getting into their heads to see what they think; but instead, requires getting into their social environment, to see what these behaviors mean, that is, what response they elicit from others.

This chapter will attempt to examine three relationships; the relationship between meanings and messages, the relationship between intentions and behaviors, and the relationship between attitudes and social action. In each case, the argument, taken from Wittgenstein, is the same: The behavioral components of the relationships (i.e., messages, behaviors, social actions) are not explained or given significance by the mental components of the relationships (i.e., meanings, intentions, attitudes). Understanding the behavioral components, according to Wittgenstein, requires understanding their use or function in a particular social situation. "The very fact that we should so much like to say: 'This is the important thing'—while we point privately to the sensation—is enough to shew how much we are inclined to say something which gives no information [I, 298]."

Meanings and Messages

A significant portion of Wittgenstein's *Philosophical Investigations* examines the question; how is it possible that we can communicate in a meaningful way (I, 90). Messages, which we symbolically transfer to one another, do

---

[3] The reader is referred to the Chapter 6 in this volume by David R. Seibold, "Attitude–Verbal Report–Behavior Relationships as Causal Processes: Formalization, Test, and Communication Implications."

convey meaning. It is possible for us to say things that are meaningful to others. Wittgenstein suggests that our ability to communicate in this way stems from our desire or need to coordinate behaviors with others in social situations. Throughout the *Investigations*, Wittgenstein is encouraging his reader to see that we hold many unexamined assumptions about the way messages are capable of being meaningful. Wittgenstein argues that we have a particular idea, or picture, of how we give meaning to our messages, and that this picture has escaped critical investigation and, therefore, frequently causes us to make errors in our analysis of meaning (I, 54, 115, II, p. 184).

Specifically, the erroneous picture that Wittgenstein warns us about is that meaning is something that we privately give to our messages in our minds (I, 693). Within this picture, to say "it's cold in here" and mean it, involves conjuring up some psychological feeling, or conviction, and in some sense attaching this to the words. In this view, the meanings are in the mind, and our messages are a mere reflection or representation of the deeper mental meaning. When in the grip of this picture, one feels that one means something first, and then searches for the appropriate word to represent this nonlinguistic meaning. In this picture, meaning is something essentially private, inaccessible to others, and something that may or may not be given to the messages we utter (I, 333).

The picture, that individuals privately attach meanings to their messages in the mind, is a view subscribed to by both philosophers and social scientists. To some extent, philosophers like Plato (Guthrie, 1975), Husserl (Schmitt, 1967) and Schutz (Walsh & Lehnert, 1976), explain that the location of meaning is in the mind, and that the meaningful quality of symbols is essentially psychological in nature. Social Scientists like Max Weber (1964) claim that it is the job of a sociologist to determine the "subjective meanings" which individuals give to their behavior. Wundt, a psychologist working in the early 1900s attempted to found an experimental psychology based on the introspective reports of subjects (Mischel, 1969). The picture, which Wittgenstein refers to, has held a prominent position in both philosophy and social science.

Say out loud, "It's cold in here," and mean it. Now say it again, but don't mean it. Now, mean it in your mind, but don't say it (not even silently to yourself). Say out loud, "It's cold in here" but mean "It's warm in here" only don't mean, its "warm in here" in words, just silently mean it in feeling or intuition. If the picture drawn above is correct, that is, if meaning is internal and independent of messages, this little exercise should produce no confusion or difficulty at all (I, 510, 692, II, pp. 175, 181, 215, 217). If meanings are something that we voluntarily wrap around our messages, we ought to be able to wrap and unwrap these messages quite easily.

Wittgenstein's point is that whether or not you wrap your messages with some psychological qualities is superfluous. What matters, and what makes messages meaningful, is the purpose or function they serve in a particular situation (I, 43, 180, II, p. 219). "It's cold in here," spoken in the appropriate circumstances, is meaningful because it usually is followed by turning up the thermostat, getting a sweater, fixing a hot drink, or perhaps rubbing one's hands together. Imagine a man who, after saying "It's cold in here" usually took off his sweater, turned on a fan, put a cold towel on his forehead, and so on. Eventually, when this man would say "It's cold in here," others around him would say, "Sure, he said it, but he doesn't mean it." When they say, "He doesn't mean it" they are not implying that his messages have inappropriate psychological wrapping (how could anyone ever know this in the first place, since in its essence, a mental state is private and inaccessible to others); instead they are implying that he does not "use" these words, "It's cold in here," in the usual way. Wittgenstein says that learning a language is learning a technique. By this he means that there are certain things you must do when you say certain things; and if you fail to do these things, we will say of you that you do not mean what you say (I, 199, 569, 692, II, p. 209). Psychological wrappings need not enter the issue at all.

We can ask of someone, "Did you recognize your desk when you entered your room this morning?" and the individual might well respond, "I certainly did [I, 602]." We might now direct our attention to what this message, "I certainly did," means. Would it not be misleading, as Wittgenstein tells us, "to say that an act of recognition has taken place?" When you return to your home or apartment in the evening, do you perform an act of recognition on all your furniture and belongings? When you respond, "I certainly did recognize my desk," this is not a report of an internal mental act (because it would be misleading to say one took place); rather, this response means that there was nothing in your behavior to indicate that there was anything new or unusual about the desk.

I might ask you, "When you sat down in that chair, did you believe it would support you?" and you might respond, "I surely believed that it would support me [I, 575]." It is accurate, however, in this case, to say that your mind was actively assessing the supporting capabilities of the chair as you sat in it? Does your response not really mean that you did not behave in the way people usually do when they are uncertain if something will support them? Does your response not mean something about behavior, and not something about what went on in your mind (II, p. 219)? Does your response not make sense, not in light of what you thought, but in light of what you did? "We don't say that the man who tells us he feels the visual image two inches behind the bridge of his nose is telling a lie or talking nonsense. But we say that we don't understand the meaning of such a phrase. It combines well-known words but combines them in a way we don't yet understand. The grammar of (such phrases) has yet to be explained to us [1958b, p. 10]."

In saying, "The grammar of (such phrases) has yet to be explained to us," I interpret Wittgenstein to mean that the phrase has no place or use in our language (I, 496). If the one says, "he feels the visual image two inches behind the bridge of his nose," we are left wondering about the next step. What does one usually do after a statement like this? How does someone respond to this statement? What further messages or utterences are likely to follow on this one? If one says, "It's cold in here," we have some idea of what can be expected from the speaker and others present, and what is done determines the meaning of what is said. When one says, "he feels the visual image two inches behind the bridge of his nose," the message serves no purpose or function, and it is this absence that results in its being meaningless.

The point Wittgenstein is making here is an important one. The meaning of a word or a message is not to be located in the privacy of the speaker's mind. The meaning is here interpreted as the normal or regular use the message performs among a community of language users (Kenny, 1973). This transforms the "meaning of message" from an essentially private phenomenon to an essentially public one. It changes the focus of the investigator from introspective reports from subjects, to observable social practices and customs (I, 337, 454). Wittgenstein is not saying simply that personal meanings can be operationalized into external social practices, but that the external practices are themselves the place or location of meaning. When one investigates the uses and reactions to messages in a particular language community, one is investigating the meanings themselves. Wittgenstein characterizes the meanings of our messages so that they are observable, regular, and specific to groups of people participating in the same language (Phillips, 1977).

Intentions and Behaviors

What philosophical position best describes the behavior of a jury when they are considering a case of first-degree murder? Certainly they are not Cartesian. Descartes held that thinking is performed by an incorporeal mind, that thoughts are private to one and inaccessible to others.[4] This will not do for our jury, for the question of first degree murder is inherently a question of intentionality, did the accused *intentionally* ("with malice aforethought") commit the violent act. If one holds that thoughts are private and inaccessible to others, if I am the sole or most authoritative arbiter of what I may have thought, then a decision of my intentionality could come only from me, and never from others. The jury may be able to decide whether or not a murder was committed, but would be unable to determine its degree, even a decision involving manslaughter would be beyond its powers. Quite obviously, our jury could not be following a position of strict behaviorism either. Central to the determination of guilt in first degree murder is that the accused acted with certain malicious thoughts or intentions. If we must restrict our judgments solely to physical

---

[4] The manner in which one defines a human has important implications for later descriptions of human behavior. Descartes (1955) defines man as a thinking being, whereas Wittgenstein (like Durkheim) would be more likely to define man as a social being.

behavior, we will be unable to make a decision between guilt and innocence in this case.[5]

But, of course, juries do make these kinds of decisions all the time. In 1976, juries found 18,800 people guilty of murder and nonnegligent manslaughter.[6] Some philosophers and social scientists may ascribe to the view that mental states, like intentionality, are private and not susceptible to investigation by external observers, but in actual practice, we make these investigations all the time, and we hold to our conclusions with almost frightening certainty. You can stand up and say you are the sole authority on whether certain thoughts did or did not go through your mind, and that on a certain date you did not think certain things. Twelve people can disagree with you, they can say: Despite what you claim, you really did think certain things at certain times, and on the basis of their decision you can be killed.

There are grounds for intentionality. There are certain actions, which if performed, will count as acting intentionally. If you have just "adjusted" the brakes on your boss's car, invited him or her to visit you at a mountain cabin, and on the same day bought a plane ticket to South America, we are likely to say that you have attempted a murder and what is more, that you have done it intentionally. We do not need to look into your mind; we do not need you to perform an introspective investigation while connected to a polygraph machine. These actions, adjusting the brakes, and so on, add up to, in our culture, intentional behavior. In our culture, these actions count as "intentional behavior." You are *not* the sole authority in deciding whether you have acted intentionally (II, pp. 215, 217, 223).

Wittgenstein tells us that "an intention is embedded in its situation (I, 337)." By this, I believe Wittgenstein to be saying that it is the situation, not the mental states, which must be examined when determining questions of intentionality. At 11:00 A.M. in my office in Albany, I cannot intend to have lunch at the Savoy Grill in London. If I tell my colleagues I intend to have lunch at the Savoy, they will tell me I am wrong, I cannot intend this. Given the present means of transportation available in our society, one cannot intend the above message. In this situation, that intention will not be granted to you. And if you insist: "But wait, I have called up all the correct mental images, I am in an intending frame of mind, I have attached meaning and conviction to my expression of intention;" then we are left with two possible responses; to again affirm that you cannot really intend this, or to assume you are crazy. And to be "crazy" here means that you do not *use* your words the way the rest of us do (Toulmin, 1967).

---

[5] Even "modified" interpretations of behaviorism that posit algorithms that parallel or perform the same function as human thought will be inappropriate here. The operation or result of the thought is not in question. The question involves whether or not a particular thought occurred in a particular individual in a particular span of time (see Suppes, 1975).

[6] See Bureau of the Census, 1968.

What you say or do permits us to make certain inferences about what you mean or intend. Cavell (1969) provides an example: "If a person asks you whether you dress the way you do voluntarily, you will not understand him to be curious merely about your psychological processes (whether your wearing them 'proceeds from free choice' . . .); you will understand him to be implying or suggesting that your manner of dress is in some way peculiar [p. 9]."

This question, whether you dress the way you do voluntarily, when asked of a prisoner of war while visiting a foreign country will mean something completely different than when it is asked of a colleague at work. If you ask this question of a colleague, he or she will interpret you as meaning that there is something strange about their appearance. You can deny this interpretation, you can say, "I am the sole arbiter of what I mean, and what I meant was the dictionary definition of these words and nothing more." To make this denial, however, is to say one of two things, either, "I am a liar," or, "I am not a proficient speaker of the language." For among this community people, these words count as meaning a particular thing. Cavell continues,

> What needs to be argued now is that something does follow from the fact that a term is used in its usual way: it entitled you (or, using the term, you entitle others) to make certain inferences, draw certain conclusions. (This is part of what you say when you say that you are talking about the logic of ordinary language.) Learning what these implications are is part of learning the language; no less a part than learning its syntax, or learning what it is to which terms apply: they are an essential part of what we communicate when we talk [p. 11].

Just as certain messages will count as meaning certain things, certain behaviors will count as intending certain things. You are not in a privileged position always to know what you have intended (this is a picture that Wittgenstein wants us to be able to remove ourselves from). Those people with whom you share a social environment can and will assume that certain behaviors in certain situations will add up to certain intentions, and those assumptions will frequently be made with certainty.[7] " 'But, if you are *certain*, isn't it that you are shutting your eyes in face of doubt?'—They are shut [II, p. 224]."

Wittgenstein may here be interpreted as striking a middle ground between a radical phenomenology and a radical behaviorism.[8] Phenomenology places the important operators of human behavior in the mind (i.e., meanings, intentions, attitudes), and thus they are private and inaccessible to a scientific methodology requiring observable (or at least measurable) phenomena. When

---

[7] Anscombe (1976) provides an additional example of a situation that demands that the actor acted intentionally. If someone went through their house, found all their green books and carefully placed them on the roof, we might well ask "why" this was done. In this situation, the actor cannot respond "No particular reason; I just thought I would." In our culture, an observer of an action like this has a right to assume an intention.

[8] Much of this argument is borrowed from Stephen Toulmin in his article quoted, see especially pp. 89–99.

phenomenology is used as a foundation for scientific inquiry, it frequently relies on "accounts."[9] In these accounts, the actor reports to the investigator what was going on in the mind (i.e., meanings, intentions, attitudes) while the action was being performed (or perhaps prior to the action).[10] Wittgenstein's point is that we do not need people to tell us what was going on in their minds; we can tell them. If you are a member of our language community and you say this message, it means the following, _____. If you are a member of our culture and you perform the following behaviors, we will say that you intended the following, _____. These messages and these behaviors are grounds for assuming these meanings and these intentions. And as long as you are a member of our culture, a proficient speaker of the language, and not insane, our inferences are applicable to you.

It is important to note that Wittgenstein is not denying that we have internal mental states (I, 305). Instead, what I interpret him to be saying is that if you are interested in investigating mental states, do not begin by looking in the mind; instead focus your attentions on what particular messages, behaviors, or social actions add up to (or serve as the ground for) inferences about mental states in this community of people.

Wittgenstein is not denying that we have mental states, but is changing the place in which we should look for an investigation of them. Wittgenstein has not done, however, what a radical behaviorist would do. Wittgenstein is not saying that we are unable to make judgments about other people's meanings, intentions, or attitudes; he is saying that, on the basis of behavior, we can make judgments about mental states, and what is more, we can make them with certainty. The problem with a radical behaviorism is that, by the time human behavior has been stripped of meanings, intentions, and attitudes, we no longer even recognize it as human. Wittgenstein permits us to make evaluations and judgments about mental states, but has posited a ground for these evaluations that is external to the actor and accessible to those who understand the respective language community in which the action is performed.

Attitudes and Social Action

To ask the question, "What is an attitude?" is to show a misunderstanding of the phenomenon being investigated (I, 24).[11] The question, "What is an

---

[9] The reader is directed to Chapter 8 in this volume by Robert T. Craig, "The Message–Attitude–Behavior Relationship from the Point of View of the Actor."

[10] Alfred Schutz (1976) argues that meanings and intentions occur prior to the action itself, and more specifically that these mental states operate in a future perfect time. See, *The Phenomenology of the Social World*, p. 61.

[11] Wittgenstein's work is more focused on meaning and intention than on attitudes. However, this section of the chapter will take Wittgenstein's position on mental states in general and apply it to attitudes. What is written in this section hopefully will be consistent with Wittgenstein's overall views about the relationship between mental states and social action.

attitude?" is a request for an essence. It asks for the primary quality that would distinguish attitudes from other mental states such as beliefs, idelolgy, values, opinions, and faith (Rokeach, 1968). This question asks for the essential variable which can be found in all those things we refer to as "attitudes" (Fishbein & Ajzen, 1975).

Wittgenstein, as I understand him, would prefer to replace the essentialist question, "What is an attitude?", with a more functional question, "How is the word attitude used [I, 29, 43, 340, 370, 371, II, p. 212]?" When the question asks for an essence, it directs our attention into the mind of the actor; when the question asks for a function, it directs our attention toward a role or purpose *between* actors. Wittgenstein would not want us to think of attitudes as things that exist in the mind, and would prefer the concept that attitudes were instruments that performed some social function (I, 569).[12] Wittgenstein would have little sympathy for the view that people carry around with them a mental bag of attitudes; that upon request they can reach into the bag and pull out particular attitudes about race, politics, or religion. The picture, that people carry attitudes around with them and can show these attitudes to investigators whenever asked, follows naturally from the idea that an attitude is an essence. However, when attitudes are thought of as functions, then an attitude becomes, not something that a person has, but something that a person does; and the investigation does not look at mental processes within the mind, but at social processes within a community of language users.

Expressions of attitudes may have a number of uses within a particular community of people. A few of the uses that attitudes might have can be listed:

1. Attitudes may be used to portray an ideal self-concept. My expressions of attitudes may serve to communicate to others an image of the kind of person I would like to be.[13]
2. Attitudes may be used as accounts. My expressions of attitudes may assist me in explaining an action of mine to another person.
3. Attitudes may be used to manipulate the behavior of others. Expressions of attitudes may serve to elicit certain responses from others. When attempting to sell my car, I may express attitudes about safe driving and about obeying the law.

---

[12] There is at least one important point of agreement between this chapter and the afterword in this volume written by G. R. Miller. Miller argues that the picture of attitudes causing behavior has not been empirically productive, in the sense of useful research findings and predictions. This chapter is arguing that the same picture has not been philosophically productive, in that it leaves us with an image that obscures our understanding. Perhaps this partial agreement about private conceptions of attitudes is best expressed in the following quotation by Wittgenstein. "The conclusion was only that a nothing would serve just as well as a something about which nothing could be said [I, 304]."

[13] The notion of an "ideal self-concept" can be found in Cushman, Valentinsen, and Whiting (1979).

4. Attitudes may be used as a reference to a generalized other. Expressions of attitudes may not refer to one's own personal behavior, but to the behavior of a social collective. A woman might express very positive attitudes about the legalization of abortion, but be violently opposed to an abortion involving herself.
5. Attitudes may be used to facilitate conversation. Expressions of attitudes may create topics that are interesting and entertaining to talk about.

When seen in this light, attitudes are viewed as having a variety of uses. Attitudes may well be capable of serving many social functions, and an experienced language user is one who knows how to use expressions of attitudes in a variety of situations.

Should someone ask me, "What is your attitude?" I might find it a little difficult to respond. Attitudes are usually expressed in the performance of certain social activities, and the exact characterization of the attitude will depend on the use to which the expression will be put, and the particular response desired from others. Asking someone for their attitudes is like asking for their meanings. Meanings are not something that I have. Meanings are something that occur because of the response given by others to one's behavior.[14]

When asked for a self-report of my attitudes, what I must do is imagine a possible use for my response. If asked for my attitude, I may respond as if the researcher were going to draw up some personality profile of me; or perhaps I will report the attitudes I usually express when explaining the performance of some past behavior; perhaps the attitudes I express are designed to increase the chances of my being called back for a second paid interview; perhaps the attitudes I provide are the ones I feel an average United States citizen should hold; or perhaps the attitudes I give are the ones I usually express in conversation.

I do not carry around with me an attitude about Blacks or Orientals. You cannot realistically come up to me and say, "Pull out your attitude and show it to me." My attitude about racial minorities, and the expression of my attitude—which Wittgenstein would argue are the same thing—will depend on the reaction I expect from the receiver, and the purpose which the utterance is meant to accomplish (I, 452, 504). When viewed in this light, it is not surprising that the attitude expressed by a hotel manager on a questionnaire about racial minorities might differ from the attitude inferred from his behavior when confronted with an actual minority person at his business (Kutner, Wilkins, & Yarrow, 1952). These are radically different social situations, and the attitudes

---

[14] There is an interesting similarity between the views of meaning held by Wittgenstein and George Herbert Mead. Mead locates the meaning of a social action in the situation of its occurence. For Mead, the meaning emerges out of the initial gesture, the response of the other, and the resultant of the social act. Mead, like Wittgenstein has pulled "meaning" out of the mind of the actor and into the external world. Wittgenstein, however, locates meaning in the regular practices of social collectives, and not merely in particular situations (see Mead, 1964).

expressed in each instance were obviously meant to accomplish different purposes. Our expressions of attitudes are not more or less honest representations of the "real" attitudes kept deep within our minds; expressions of attitudes are social performances meant to accomplish particular things.

It is perhaps tempting to say that one is not interested merely in the attitudes that people express in a variety of social situations; that our actual interest is the "real" attitude that exists within the person; to make this comment, however, is to miss the entire point of this chapter. What one means by a particular message is not something that is completely within one's determination. Within our language community, certain messages, when spoken, carry with them particular meanings ("Do you dress the way you do voluntarily?"), and to speak that message is grounds for our attributing a meaning to the speaker. Within our social collective, the performance of certain behaviors allows us to say that one has acted intentionally. A person can deny the intention, but that probably will not matter; in this community, these behaviors count as intentional. It makes little sense to say, we can never know a person's attitudes, but only the expressions of their attitudes and the outer behavioral manifestations of the attitudes. The expressions of attitudes and the social actions individuals perform count as their attitudes. Attitudes are social performances that people do, not mental entities that people have.

If you express culturally conservative attitudes in your conversation, if you are a member of conservative causes, we will say of you, that you are a conservative (hold conservative attitudes). You might respond, "Well, I have fooled you, really I am an extreme liberal and have simply led you off the track with all this outer conservative behavior." You might respond that down deep, your real attitudes are extremely liberal. These comments of yours might cause us to undertake a more thorough examination of your behavior. We may try to ascertain whether you have secretly expressed liberal attitudes to other people, whether you have joined liberal groups under a different name, whether you have liberal magazines sent to you at a different address, whether other people have witnessed your performance of actions considered liberal in our culture. If we cannot find conflicting evidence, that is, expressions and actions considered liberal in our culture, we will say that you are a conservative, and your disclaimers will not matter. If you persist in making them, and can provide no evidence to the contrary, we will assume that you do not understand what it means to be a conservative (that is, you do not know what social actions count as having particular attitudes in our culture), or that you are crazy.

It does not make any sense to say that your "real" attitudes are politically liberal, it is just that all your utterances and actions are politically conservative. I does not make any sense because attitudes are not something that you have, but something that you do. Breaking down the single concept "attitude" into further psychological components (i.e., conative, cognitive, behavioral intention, affect, certainty, etc.), does not solve the problem at all. This merely transfers the concept "attitude" from one private psychological component, to numerous private psychological components. To redefine attitudes as pre-depositions to behave is a step in the right direction, but it does not go far enough. A "predisposition" is an inclination, habit, or tendency, and a private psychological inclination, habit, or tendency, is not a great deal different than a private psychological attitude. Both cf these approaches hold to the original picture that an attitude is a private mental state that exists in the mind of the actor.

It is Wittgenstein's insight that we attribute mental states to actors all the time, and what is more, we do so with certainty. In particular cultures, certain messages carry with them certain meanings. If you say the following _____ in this culture, it means _____. What you intend by particular behaviors is as accessible to you as to other members of the culture. In particular communities of people, the performance of certain behaviors carries with it the implication of certain intentions. Any member of the culture who observes you performing this cultural set of behaviors is in a position to know what you intend. In a similar manner, particular social actions performed in a specific culture will count as a particular attitude.

It is interesting to note that social scientists define mental states so that they are private, incorporeal, inaccessible, and known with certainty only by the subject; and that a philosopher posits a conception of mental states so that they are public, observable, regular, and accessible with certainty to all of those who understand the culture in which the subject is located. Wittgenstein argues that we are trapped by a picture. A picture of "real" meanings, intentions, and attitudes mysteriously held within the confines of the mind. As an alternative, Wittgenstein suggests that mental states are better thought of as social performances. That meanings, intentions, and attitudes are things that people do while interacting with one another. In this view, an attitude is considered a publically observable social activity that performs some function among a community of people.

REFERENCES

Anscombe, G. E. M. *Intention*. Oxford: Basil Blackwell, 1976. P. 26.

Bureau of the Census, Department of Commerce, *The U.S. Fact Yearbook*. New York: Grosset & Dunlap, 1968.

Cavell, S. *Must we mean what we say?* London: Cambridge University Press, 1969.

Cushman, D. P., & Valentinsen, B. The self concept as a generative mechanism. Paper presented at the 1980 International Communication Association Convention, Acapulco, Mexico, 1979.

Descartes, R. Meditations on first philosophy. In R. M. Eaton (Ed.), *Descartes selections*. New York: Scribner's, 1955.

Fishbein, M., & Hyzen, I. *Belief, attitude, intention and behavior: An introduction to theory and research*. Reading, Mass.: Addison–Wesley, 1975.

Guthrie, W. K. C. *The Greek philosophers*. New York: Hayer, 1975.

Kenny, A. *Wittgenstein*. Harmondsworth, England: Penguin, 1973.

Kutner, B., Wilkins, C., & Yarrow, P. Verbal attitudes and overt behavior involving racial prejudice. *Journal of Abnormal and Social Psychology*, 1952, *47*, 649–652.

Malcolm, N. *Ludwig Wittgenstein: A memoir*. London: Oxford University Press, 1958.

Mead, G. H. *On social psychology*. Chicago: University of Chicago Press, 1964.

Mischel, T. (Ed.). *Human action*. New York: Academic Press, 1969. Pp. 21–26.

Phillips, D. *Wittgenstein and scientific knowledge*. Totowa, N.J.: Rowman & Littlefield, 1977.

Rokeach, M. Attitudes. In *The international encyclopedia of the social sciences*. New York: Free Press, 1968. P. 454.

Schmitt, R. Husserl. In P. Edwards (Ed.), *The encyclopedia of philosophy* (Vols. 3–4). New York: Macmillan, 1967. Pp. 96–99.

Schutz, A. *The phenomenology of the social world* (G. Walsh & F. Lehnert, trans.). London: Heinemann, 1976.

Suppes, P. From behaviorism to neobehaviorism. *Theory and Decision*, 1975, *6*, 269–285.

Toulmin, S. Concepts and explanations of human behavior. In T. Mischel (Ed.), *Human action*. New York: Academic Press, 1967. P. 98.

Weber, M. *The theory of social and economic organization* (A. M. Henderson & T. Parsons, trans.). New York: Free Press, 1964.

Winch, P. *The idea of a social science and its relation to philosophy*. London: Routledge and Keegan Paul, 1958.

Wittgenstein, L. *Philosophical investigations* (3rd ed. English text) (G. E. M. Anscombe, trans.). New York: Macmillan, 1958. (a)

Wittgenstein, L. *The blue and brown books*. Oxford: Basil Blackwell and Mott, 1958. (b)

10

A Structural–Functional Model of the Message–Attitude–Behavior Relationship

NORMAN E. FONTES
JENNIFER L. SHELBY
BARBARA O'CONNOR

This chapter examines the relationship between messages and behaviors from a structural–functional perspective. Whereas traditional persuasion paradigms have focused upon the relationship between source, receiver, and message variables with respect to the "attitude-change" process, the focus of this chapter centers upon the manipulation of various message strategies and their effect upon the maintenance of specific behaviors. The utilization of a structural–functional perspective implies that the goal state for any system is the maintenance of some specific behavior or state. Thus, although the focus of this approach is limited, it does provide a viable approach for examining the impact of persuasive strategies aimed at behavioral maintenance as opposed to change. The authors feel that this area is one which merits further attention by communication scholars interested in the persuasion process.

Communication plays a central role in all of our lives. Our ability to successfully interact with others in our respective environments is dependent upon our communication skills. Each of us exists in a dynamic web of communicative exchanges in which sometimes we assume the role of source, and sometimes

MESSAGE–ATTITUDE–BEHAVIOR RELATIONSHIP
Theory, Methodology, and Applications

the role of receiver. That is, sometimes we generate messages to impact upon others, whereas, at other times messages are impacted upon us.

In addition to taking on the role of source and receiver, we also emit and respond to multiple *types* of messages, which serve different behavioral functions. It is incumbent upon each of us to determine what types of messages are being directed at us. Determination of various message types allows us to identify the intent of the external message source who has sent us a particular message. Some of the many message types are informative, interpersonal, and persuasive. Our ability to discriminate among message types allows us to communicate effectively with others in our environment and to predict how others will respond to our communicative efforts. Additionally, effective communication will enable us to maximize our environmental rewards and minimize environmental costs.

Communicative behavior can be viewed conceptually as an intentional and goal-directed behavior. Specifically, it can function as a means of achieving specific goals (i.e., it can be used to influence the behavior of those in our environment). Such influence, we would consider neither inherently bad or good. At times, the source may induce the receiver to engage in behavior that is only of benefit to him or herself. At other times, the source may solicit behavior that is of benefit to both parties. Those communication interactions that benefit only the source pose a potential threat to receivers in that they may often imply malevolent manipulative intent. The dangers of malevolent manipulation at a societal level are all too apparent in this post-Watergate era. At an interpersonal level, malevolent manipulation can prohibit relational growth. We are not suggesting that all communication is intended to influence others' behavior. However, we are going to restrict ourselves to the domain of intentional and influence-oriented communication in this chapter. A few comments concerning the typical persuasion paradigm and the use of the attitude construct as a predictor of behavior will be offered. Moreover, structural–functionalism as one means of developing theory concerning communication and behavioral maintenance will be explored by providing an explanation of the method and a brief example of its application.

Most traditional views of persuasion include a persuader who impacts a message upon a persuadee with the intent of influencing the persuadee in some manner. As Burgoon, Jones, and Stewart (1975) note, the most frequently used criterion for assessing the effectiveness of various persuasive strategies has been the attitude construct: "The typical paradigm has been the manipulation or control of some source, situation, or receiver variable, the presentation of an uncontrolled but constant message and the measurement of attitude change [p. 240]." This narrow view of persuasion ignores those situations in which a source attempts to reinforce a receiver's existing commitments and/or behavioral patterns. For example, during the 1976 presidential election, Jimmy Carter used different political rhetoric in his appeals to different segments of the population. For those groups that supported him, President Carter encoded messages designed to reinforce existing voting commitments. Individuals who expressed no voting commitment to either candidate received messages intended to establish a pro-Carter voting commitment. Finally, messages designed to alter pro-Ford commitments were directed at that segment of the populace that was committed to vote for Ford.

Obviously, it is important for a source not only to identify the nature of a receiver's existing commitments and behavioral patterns, but the reasons for them as well. This information is necessary for the development or selection of effective persuasive strategies. There are a number of factors which may be considered by a receiver during the development of behavioral commitments or behavioral patterns. These include: personal information relevant to the object or situation of concern; the influence or means control exerted by significant others in the individual's environment; and information disseminated by mass media sources.

Traditional persuasion paradigms place excessive reliance upon the *attitude construct* as the criterion for assessing the effectiveness of persuasive strategies. The utility of this construct is predicated to some extent upon an implicit assumption that a relationship exists between attitudes expressed by individuals and their behavior. Although we are somewhat tempted to address this assumption in some detail, it is necessary to restrict ourselves in this chapter to a brief discussion of the issue. Our concern about the use of this construct stems from the meager success achieved by behavioral scientists in using the construct to predict behavior.

If, as communication scholars, we are interested in the relationship between information provided by sources, and receivers' subsequent behavior, perhaps we should focus our attention more directly upon the relationship between information and behavior. Specifically, more consideration should be given to the information an individual possesses or is given, germane to a particular behavior, and the consequences of that behavior. This alternative may have more utility for predicting behavior than the attitude construct. It is not being suggested that there is no relationship between information, attitudes, and behaviors. We are simply questioning whether the attitude construct is a more useful predictor of behavior than is the "raw" information an individual possesses concerning any given situation.

Certainly one can construct a cogent argument concerning how attitudes reflect the information an individual possesses about any given situation or object. Whereas an argument of this nature may have merit, we would like to raise one final point before proceeding with the main thesis of this chapter. If attitudes do represent a composite of information, the question still remains whether an individual's attitude toward a given object or situation reflects how the individual would *like* to behave; feels he or she *should* behave; or *how* the individual will, in fact, behave.

Without becoming embroiled in the attitude–behavior controversy, we are attempting merely to suggest another approach for scholars investigating the relationship between communication and behavior. Specifically, we should look at the relationship between information already possessed by receivers, messages (reinforcing, or new information) and behavioral outcomes. The information already possessed by an individual should facilitate identification of not only the initial conditions that would have to exist before an individual would engage in a specific behavior, but also the types of messages that would have to be generated to establish (or reinforce the existence of) those initial conditions.

In our quest for understanding the relationship between communication and behavior, regardless of whether we use the attitude construct or some other type of information construct, we must strive to develop theories to guide our research. It has been argued elsewhere that theory construction is a central concern in communication research (Burgoon, Jones, & Stewart, 1975; Fontes & Guardalabene, 1975). Without theories to guide our research in problematic areas of social significance, we are at a loss in identifying what we should observe, how we should measure it, and how our findings should be interpreted. One of the problems that exists within our field is that whereas numerous theories applicable to communication have been generated, there have been few clearly developed methods that will guide us in our efforts to construct theory.

Some researchers would disagree with the position that we need methods for the construction of theory. They would argue that if we continue to test hypothesis after hypothesis, a theory will emerge. Dubin (1969) makes the following observation concerning this point:

> Starting with an ad hoc hypothesis represents a characteristic fiddling around that may be encountered in social research. For example, a researcher finds a measuring instrument, proceeds to use it, discovers some relationship between the values measured on several units, and then asks the question, "Into what kind of theoretical model can I refer this observed relationship between these two units?" Mindless fiddling around of this sort may turn out, therefore, to have scientific value, providing the researcher is willing to build back to the theoretical model from the empirical uniformity he accidentally uncovered [p. 220].

Certainly this is one approach to theory construction, although it may not be the most efficient. On the other hand, the claims of some scholars engaged in the formulation of methods for the construction of theory have undoubtedly exceeded the number of theories they have produced. Until it can be demonstrated through research, rather than through enthusiastic rhetoric, that these methods are superior to more traditional approaches to research, we should avoid developing unrealistic expectations. Unfilled expectations might result in a premature abandonment of potentially useful methods of theory construction.

As has been argued elsewhere (Fontes & Guardalabene, 1975), no foolproof, finite method of theory construction has emerged in our field (and probably none ever will) to correct this *potential* impediment to the growth of theory. However, it is incumbent upon us to examine and reexamine all methodologies that have the potential of assisting in the development of theories. Structural–functionalism is one form of theory construction that may be applied to a limited area of persuasion, namely, those situations in which a message source's goal is to influence a message recipient to continue to engage in a specific set of behaviors. The message source must determine what types of influence must be exerted upon the receiver to ensure continued exhibition of the behavior. It is not our intent to defend this method or advocate its use indiscriminately for exploration of this area of human behavior. The methodology has definite limitations, which have been discussed by Fontes and Guardalabene (1975).

The relationship between communication and behavior may be researched utilizing structural–functionalism since the variables can be viewed conceptually as functional in nature. Communication (or messages) designed to influence behavior will be conceptualized for the purpose of this chapter as the transfer of symbolic information between a source and a receiver in which the source intentionally attempts to affect the receiver's behavior. Communication serves the function of providing a means to an end—the receiver's enactment of a behavior deemed desirable by the source.

Structural–functionalism is one form of systems analysis. According to Meehan (1968), a system may be defined in the following manner:

> A system is not defined by its capacity to predict or explain but by its internal logical structure; no system is necessarily useful in explanation though all explanations make use of systems. Any set of two or more variables and one or more rules of interaction is a system. Given two variables (A and B) and one rule of interaction (A is the inverse of B), the system is complete and there are two entailments: if the value of A does not change, the value of B will not change; if the value of A is stipulated, the value of B is the inverse of the value of A [pp. 53–54].

A source (or researcher) interested in communication and behavioral maintenance would be concerned with the effects of a system of message strategy variables upon the behaviors exhibited by message recipients.

Structural–functional analyses facilitate identification of means to maintain the existing state of affairs or the status quo. This type of analysis can be approached from multiple perspectives including (a) the quasi-teleological approach; and (b) the teleological approach (von Wright, 1971). The quasi-teleological form of analysis is dependent upon laws or lawlike statements for its explanatory power. It is most suited for analyzing systems that already exist and determining what conditions are sufficient to account for a system's extant state. Teleological analysis is dependent upon rules for its explanatory power and is best suited for those types of analyses in which a researcher is attempting to determine what initial conditions are sufficient for bringing a system into existence. We will focus our attention upon teleological structural–functional analysis.

In the ensuing discussion, "causality" *will not* be used either implicitly or explicitly when referring to universal invariant relationships. Rather, it *will be* used in the sense that A causes B in the presence of the antecedent conditions that are sufficient to trigger a relationship. In a teleological explanation, it is possible to have multiple sets of sufficient conditions functioning as antecedents for A causing B. This suggests that a given teleological theory concerning the relationship between communication and behavior admits the possibility of multiple explanations.

Multiple sets of sufficient conditions also admit the existence of choice of behaviors for both sources and receivers involved in communicative transactions. The issue of choice has been addressed by others during the discussion of an actor's locus of control. When we talk about choice, we mean that an individual can choose from multiple sets of sufficient conditions to bring about desired effects. Simply stated, teleological explanations focus upon those situations in which individuals wish to maintain an existing state of affairs and can choose from a set of alternative courses of action to do so. If a message source wanted to influence a receiver in a manner designed to reinforce existing behavior, there are undoubtedly various message strategies to choose from that are sufficient to bring about the desired effect.

Since teleological explanations take into consideration the intentions of a source and acknowledge a source's ability to choose from alternative courses of action, the practical syllogism rather than the demonstrative syllogism is used (von wright, 1971). An example of a practical syllogism should help clarify this point:

INTENTIONAL MAJOR PREMISE: *A source intends to reinforce a specific behavior exhibited by his or her receivers.*

NOMIC MINOR PREMISE: *Reinforcement can be achieved through the use of positively reinforcing messages or negatively reinforcing messages of varying intensities.*

INSTANTATION: *The source chooses to use highly intense positively reinforcing messages.*

Note that the major premise in the syllogism identifies the source's intention. The minor premise, which contains a nomic relationship, identifies a multiple set of conditions that are logically (though not necessarily empirically) sufficient to facilitate the achievement of the source's goal. The instantiation or conclusion identifies the plan of action the source chose in order to satisfy his or her intention.

Explanation and prediction are the core of science, and they in turn are dependent upon the discovery of recurrent patterns of behavior. When one employs a teleological analysis, the locus of pattern is determined by individual

The development of an explanation presupposes a closed system of relationships among the variables included in the analysis. von Wright (1971)
makes the following observation concerning this issue:

> There are several senses in which a system, when it is instantiated, can be said to be
> closed to causal influences from outside the system. One sense is that no state (or
> feature of a state) at any stage in the system has an antecedent sufficient condition
> occurring outside the system. Since the word "cause" is quite commonly used to
> refer to something else, I think that this sense of closedness to causal influences is
> what we very often contemplate when we speak of certain chains of successive states
> as forming a closed system [p. 54].

The issue of "closed systems," given this perspective, can be dealt with by
ifferentiating between empirically closed systems and logically closed systems.
n empirically closed system will be defined here as a "self-contained set of
riables, nothing moves into or out of the system and the notion of an 'external'
fluence is a contradiction in terms since the system would then be open
eehan, 1968, p. 54]." The system could not be considered "closed" if there
re any external causal influences acting upon the system. A logically closed
tem will be defined as an arbitrarily constructed set of variables with the rela-
ships among the variables specified. The system is considered to be closed
n those variables exerting major influence on the investigator's research
stions have been included in the system. The system may be subject to exter-
causal influences that are not relevant to the investigator's research questions.
In practice, the researcher picks out those variables that are felt to be
ssary and sufficient for bringing the system into existence. The researcher
defines the system as closed given what is believed to be the necessary and
ient conditions and measures the empirical interactions among the var-
s included in the analysis. If a variable that is central to the analysis has
excluded, either there will be no empirical entailment where one was
lly predicted or measurement error will load heavily on the residuals
amount of variance explained will be statistically insignificant.
eleological analysis, then, attempts to locate the sufficient conditions that
ring a system into existence. The logical conceptualizations of systems
this approach are arbitrary, given some set of questions or problems that
ing to be investigated. A logical pattern based upon sufficient conditions
nging a system into existence is established when this form of analysis
. The logical pattern is then overlaid on the empirical world. If the
pattern fits the empirical world, it serves as an explanation of the
al events subsumed under the pattern (Meehan, 1968, p. 102). If, how-
e empirical observations do not conform to the patterns constructed
gical level, the empirical observations can be used as a guide to correct
cal entailments predicted. It is for this reason that in the structural–
al paradigm, the logical and empirical requirements are separated.
ision enables us to correct logical errors that we have committed in the

and social norms. In our example, identification of what receivers wi᷾
as rewarding is accomplished through an assessment of the personal
norms subscribed to by the receivers. This facilitates identificatior
premises specifying relationships capable of producing the effect i᷾
a message source.

There are three different types of impediments that may negate
and empirical sufficiency. These must be considered by a source w᷾
ing to identify valid nomic premises that will facilitate influencing
of a receiver: (a) physical impediments; (b) psychological impe᷾
(c) social impediments. An impediment is any belief, value, o᷾
possessed by a receiver that mitigates against the behavioral
advocated by the source. A physical impediment exists when the
material resources necessary to continue engaging in a specif
psychological impediment exists when the message recipient be
tinued exhibition of a behavior conflicts with his or her values.
impediment exists when the receiver has reason to believe valu
with others will be adversely affected if engagement in a beha᷾

It is important for a source to identify the impediments th᷾
against a receiver's behavioral maintenance. Through an a
impediments, a source will gain insight into the conditior
receiver will or will not continue the desired behavior, which
prediction and explanation of behavioral outcomes. This kn᷾
is important when making a decision (instantiation in the ᷾
about the type of communication strategy to employ, and t
formation that should be incorporated into messages ᷾
message recipient. Knowledge of these impediments in the
functionalism reduces the number of plausibly valid nomic
be both logically and empirically sufficient to influence a᷾

A researcher using structural–functionalism to inves᷾
of various reinforcing message strategies employed by s᷾
number of other issues in addition to the identification o᷾
According to Meehan (1968), "a phenomenon being
imbedded in a set of relationships . . . so that observ᷾
of interactions leads to justified expectations about ᷾
This will allow for control, at least in principle. Cont᷾
achieved by manipulation of the relations specified i
explanatory principle along which the system varies i᷾
structural–functional analysis, the explanatory princi᷾
varies is the goal state, and the strength of the explan
scope of control facilitated through the explanation
1971). The goal state is defined in terms of the mair
affairs.

construction of our theory. Specifically, this separation of requirements allows for the evaluation of the logical and empirical aspects of our theory to be carried out separately.

It is extremely important to identify the necessary and sufficient conditions when we execute a teleological structural–functional analysis. Our ability to determine how to bring a system into existence is dependent upon the identification of those conditions. The necessary and sufficient conditions are defined in terms of the goal state, and must be present for the system to exist. The goal state is used as the organizing principle to determine what the necessary and sufficient conditions are for maintaining the goal state in its equilibrium range. Furthermore, the traits and functions are conceptually defined and operationalized in terms of the goal state. It is important to note that the necessary and sufficient conditions are the functions, since several traits may be available to produce the same function.

Certain tasks must be completed by a researcher prior to specifying the relationships among the set of variables contained within a system when executing a teleological analysis. The approach requires that the researcher (a) identify the system state with which the research is going to be done; (b) identify the goal state of the system and its respective range; (c) identify the functions in the system and their respective ranges (Brown, 1963; Martindale, 1960; Merton, 1957; Radcliffe-Brown, 1952); and (d) identify the traits that produce the functions and their respective ranges. The following symbols are used as a matter of convention for the execution of these tasks. S stands for the system being analyzed. G represents the goal state of the system. The goal state can have a range from a to n with G_a representing minimal survival and G_n, maximal survival of the system. The symbol f represents the functions having a range from a to n. The functions once again are the necessary and sufficient conditions for the maintenance of S in the state G_{a-n}. An uppercase T represents a dominant trait in the system, whereas a lowercase t represents a subordinate trait in the system. Both types of traits have ranges of output of a to n. A dominant trait must be both logically and empirically independent. That is, it must not interact with other traits. If one subordinate trait, for example, fails to produce its respective function, another subordinate trait, if it has an output range great enough, could fill the void and produce its respective function as well as the dysfunctional trait's function. This could not occur with dominant traits (between dominant traits). This distinction is extremely helpful in generating logical entailments as well as in interpreting empirical data. It is also essential in determining the conditions under which a system will fail, thus suggesting means of intervention to control against failure or inducing failure (e.g., propaganda efforts designed to cause the fall of a governmental system).

A simplified example of how these conceptual distinctions are related should prove helpful (see Figure 10.1). The theory consists of a specification of the relationships among the traits and functions necessary to keep the system

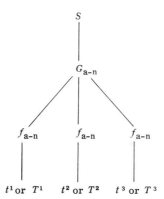

Figure 10.1. Diagram showing relationships among various conceptual distinctions.

within the specified goal state. For example, an increased output from t^1 will lead to a decreased output from t^2 and t^3. A decreased output from t^3 will lead to an increased output from t^1 and t^2, and so forth. If these hypotheses (and any others posited) were validated, they would constitute the propositions for the theory being constructed.

Given the previous discussion and example, the logical (Merton, 1957) and empirical requirements of teleological analysis can now be specified. The logical requirements are as follows:

1. Identify the system under consideration.
2. Identify the goal state of the system and its theoretic equilibrium range. It is crucial to do this so that a measuring instrument that will facilitate measurement of the range can be chosen.
3. Identify the traits that would contribute to the maintenance of the goal state.
4. Identify the normative criteria for choice (either personal or social) among alternatives capable of yielding the desired goal state (for which a nomic premise exists that is sufficient to bring into being the desired goal state.
5. Specify how the traits are functionally related to the goal state.
6. Specify which of the traits are subordinate and which are dominant.
7. Specify the theoretic range of output of each trait. Again it is important to do this because it will help to identify an appropriate instrument for measuring the output of each trait. (It should be pointed out that multiple instruments may be needed to measure the respective ranges of the traits, functions, and goal state.)
8. Specify the theoretic ranges of the functions. Again, the same argument concerning measuring instruments holds. In addition, it is a necessary act, because it might take two subordinate traits interacting to produce enough output to meet the requirements of one function.

9. Using a logical calculus (or ordinary language), predict the logical entailments within the system.

The empirical requirements are as follows:

1. Identify the measuring instruments to be used to measure the goal state, respective functions, and respective traits.
2. Translate the logical predictive calculus into empirical calculus (e.g., regression equations).
3. Measure the system and determine if the entailments predicted at the logical level have been supported.
4. Use the empirical findings to correct the entailments predicted at the logical level that were not supported.
5. After the correction at the logical level, if possible, repeat the measurements to determine whether or not the empirical observations now follow from the logical entailments.

Given this framework, let us examine a communication phenomenon in which a message source attempts to reinforce the behavior of a message recipient and briefly delineate at least the initial steps in a structural–functional analysis. We will assume that a source intends to reinforce the positive relational social behavior exhibited by a receiver with whom he or she maintains an interpersonal relationship. Specifically, the source wants the receiver to continue engaging in relational behaviors with the source, such as going out for dinner together, attending concerts, going to the theater, and so forth, two to four times a week.

The system being considered is the interpersonal relationship between a message source and receiver involving behavioral maintenance. The goal state, from the source's perspective, is the continued exhibition by the receiver of positive relational social behaviors two to four times per week. The traits that would contribute to achievement of this goal are different message variables including types of messages, the intensity of language used in the messages, and the frequency with which messages are impacted upon a receiver. The source must then consider the impediments that might militate against the receiver's continued exhibition of the behavior including financial and time constraints (physical impediments); the value the receiver places upon these types of behavior (psychological impediment); and the value the receiver places upon the relationship with the source (social impediment). If any of these impediments existed, the source would need to consider these issues when attempting to identify and select a valid nomic premise(s) that would facilitate establishment and manipulation of a reinforcing system of communication variables that will facilitate achievement of the goal.

For our purposes here, let us assume that no physical impediments existed that would militate against the receiver's continued enactment of the specified behavior. Let us also assume that the source knows the receiver does not place much value on the social behaviors, suggesting the existence of a psychological impediment, although the receiver does value the relationship with the source.

Armed with this information, the source decides to positively reinforce the receiver for the continued behavior, even though negatively reinforcing the receiver for deviations from the desired behavior is another option. Positive reinforcement is selected because the use of negative reinforcement increases the probability of relational conflict. The source decides to frequently impact intense positively reinforcing messages upon the source. Whether or not this is an effective strategy, of course, is an empirical question.

The strategy encompasses two variables at a minimum—the frequency of positively reinforcing messages, and the intensity of the language used in the messages. These two variables constitute the traits in the behavioral maintenance system and are functionally related to the goal state in terms of the amount of reinforcement each provides to the receiver for the continued behavior or behavioral consistency.

The traits are subordinate to one another because they are interrelated (i.e., not logically and empirically independent of one another). The theoretic range of output of each trait can be specified. The intensity of language can range from moderately intense to extremely intense, and the frequency with which messages are directed to the receiver can range from infrequent to very frequent.

The functions in the analysis are the necessary and sufficient conditions for the achievement of the source's goal. The traits function to reinforce the receiver's behavior. If the message traits fail to produce any reinforcement for the message recipient, the goal state will not be achieved, and the system will fail. The theoretic range for each of the functions is *no* reinforcement to *maximum* reinforcement. The system is presented graphically in Figure 10.2.

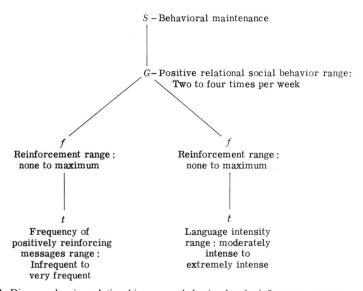

Figure 10.2. Diagram showing relationships among behavioral and reinforcement ranges.

Having now satisfied these logical requirements, the entailments for the system can be specified. For our purposes, we will provide only a few examples:

H_1: *Highly intense positively reinforcing messages will produce greater behavioral consistency in message recipients than positively reinforcing messages of low intensity.*

H_2: *The greater the frequency of highly intense positively reinforcing messages, the more behavioral consistency exhibited by a message source.*

With the empirical requirements in mind, these hypotheses would then be tested. If validated, they would become the propositions in the theory being developed concerning the effects of various message variables upon behavioral reinforcement and consistency.

One of the more problematic issues that must be dealt with when executing teleological structural–functional analyses is the identification of valid nomic premises. We would like to make a few observations concerning this problem prior to concluding. There are many types of nomic premises that may be used to predict and explain the effects of communication upon behavior. One category of nomic premises that may prove particularly useful is that containing premises that focus upon the interdependence between message sources and receivers. If a receiver is dependent upon a source, the probability is enhanced that the source can influence the receiver's behavior. The greater the dependence, the greater the probability the receiver's behavior can be influenced. This may be attributable to means control in some situations and to interdependence between the transactants in others. The existence of interdependence between transactants has the potential of transcending discrepant value systems, while not altering them. We are becoming increasingly aware of the fact that we live in an age in which a pluralism of values exists. Concomitantly, we have become intensely aware that it is becoming increasingly difficult to engage in behavior without affecting others in our environment.

The continuing energy shortage bears testimony to this. The relatively recent Arab oil embargo unleashed a chain of events that had international, national, and individual repercussions. Americans, for the first time in a period of "peace," were confronted with a fuel shortage of serious magnitude. We were deluged with messages from government leaders (and the oil companies) that elucidated the interdependence among ourselves, and the necessity of cooperation to ensure that the crisis was dealt with effectively. Whereas there were differences among our value and belief systems, we were able to transcend our differences, modify our fuel consumption behavior, and weather the storm. Other factors such as access to, and the high cost of, fuel undoubtedly contributed to the reduction in our fuel consumption. Unfortunately, we did not maintain the desired behavior. Nevertheless, this incident focuses attention upon *interdependence*, a construct that may prove useful in predicting behavioral outcomes. This construct is certainly congruent with the transactional nature of human communication because of its focus on the *relationship* between message source, receiver, and a given situation or object.

Interdependence can be conceptually defined as the perceived need for mutual coordination to achieve a common goal. For example, if a receiver is in a position of relying on a source for economic, social, or psychological resources, the probability that the source can influence the receiver's behavior through communication is enhanced. We are assuming, of course, that the source needs the cooperation and assistance of the receiver to achieve the goal. The use of the interdependence construct in research focusing upon the relationship between messages and behavioral outcomes has several theoretical implications. One implication that we have already noted is that the requirements for action have the potential of transcending discrepant value systems while not altering the respective value systems of a source and a receiver. A second implication is the awareness that we live in an age in which a pluralism of value systems exist among individuals, groups, societies, and nations. In short, we are not a homogeneous world populace, and yet we have become increasingly more interdependent. We have come to understand that it is difficult to pursue independent courses of action without affecting others in our environment and without them affecting us. Indeed, our age may be described as the age of interdependence and diversity (McKeon, 1957).

It is through communicative interaction that we identify our interdependencies and these interdependencies can in turn be used to establish consistent patterns of behavior that are mutually beneficial to the concerned transactants. Inherent in that process is the identification of the specific communication rules that will have to be observed during message exchanges between individuals with discrepant value systems. Rules governing communicative transactions may be culturally or socially determined, or generated by the individual communicators themselves. Usually, both types of rules are operative simultaneously. This implies the need for both a source and a receiver to understand each other's rules, if effective communication is to be established and maintained. An understanding of the rules governing our communicative transactions will contribute to our ability to predict the responses of others, in that it will suggest methods for structuring messages to circumvent impediments and impose order on our environment (Heider, 1958).

There are, at a minimum, three different types of information that we should consider when constructing messages (*a*) cultural information; (*b*) sociological information; and (*c*) psychological information (Miller & Steinberg, 1975). Cultural information includes the beliefs, habits, norms, values, and language shared in general by a group of people. Sociological information emanates from membership in various social groups. Psychological information entails knowledge of an individual's unique learning experiences.

The degree of success in reinforcing extant behavior by a message is a specific product of the type of information that the message incorporates. If a message source desires to influence culturally related behavior, the requisite cultural information needed to avoid violating cultural communication rules must be available. If a source's goal is influencing a specific group's behavior, applicable sociological data, as well as relevant cultural information during communicative transactions with the group in question, must be considered. It logically follows that if a source desires to influence an individual's unique behavior, cultural, sociological, and psychological information specific to the receiver to be influenced must be given consideration. Two implications follow from this: (a) As a source moves from the cultural to the psychological level, the complexity of messages necessarily increases; and (b) there is a greater probability of successful behavioral influence at the individual level, assuming that the source has access to all three types of information. This will enable the source to construct messages that either counteract or avoid potential impediments that may militate against the receiver continuing to exhibit a desired behavior. Stated somewhat differently, attempts to influence behavior will be more successful when a source is able to capitalize on cultural, sociological, and psychological information during the construction of messages. In short, the more a source can tailor messages to avoid an individual receiver's specific physical, psychological, or social impediments to the behavior advocated, the greater the probability that the messages will have the intended effect.

The relationships among different message variables and behavioral influence are important and merit further exploration. Research focusing upon communication strategies for inducing behavioral maintenance has been retarded by the pervasiveness of persuasion paradigms that have focused attention upon message variables and attitude change. We have attempted to delineate a methodology in this chapter and demonstrate its applicability to communication and behavioral maintenance. The structural–functional approach discussed in this chapter, which is applicable to a limited range of communicative behaviors, may prove useful in the generation and testing of theories that will enhance our own understanding of human behavior.

References

Brown, R. *Explanation in social science.* Chicago: Aldine, 1963.
Burgoon, M., Jones, S., & Stewart, D. Toward a message-centered theory of persuasion: Three empirical investigations of language intensity. *Human Communication Research*, 1975, *1*, 240–256.
Dubin, R. *Theory building.* New York: Free Press, 1969.
Fontes, N., & Guardalabene, N. Structural–functionalism: An introduction to the literature. *Human Communication Research*, 1976, *3*, 299–310.
Heider, F. *The psychology of interpersonal relations.* New York: Wiley, 1958.
Martindale, D. *The nature and types of sociological theory.* Boston: Houghton Mifflin, 1960.
McKeon, R. Communication, truth and society. *Ethics.* 1957, *67*, 89–99.
Meehan, E. *Explanation in social science: A system paradigm.* Homewood, Ill.: The Dorsey Press, 1968.
Merton, R. *Social theory and social structure.* Glencoe, Ill.: Free Press, 1957.
Miller, G., & Steinberg, M. *Between people.* Palo Alto, Cal.: Science Research Associates, 1975.
Radcliffe-Brown, A. *Structure and function in primitive society.* New York: Free Press, 1952.
Reynolds, P. *A primer in theory construction.* Indianapolis: Bobbs–Merrill, 1971.
von Wright, G. *Explanation and understanding.* Ithaca, N.Y.: Cornell University Press, 1971.

Afterword

GERALD R. MILLER

Ever since Gordon Allport (1935) confidently pronounced *attitude* to be *the* single most important concept in social psychology, scores of social psychologists, sociologists, and communication researchers have filled thousands of pages with theoretical, methodological, and empirical undertakings aimed at establishing the truth of his pronouncement. Many communication researchers, including myself, have found the clarion call of attitude-change research impossible to resist, the skeptics' warnings notwithstanding. How vividly I recall sitting by the side of a motel swimming pool in Iowa City, Iowa, some 20 years ago, drinking gin and tonics with a group including my friend and mentor, Professor Milton Rosenbaum, himself a committed social learning theorist with a strong Skinnerian bent. Turning to a new arrival, Professor Rosenbaum introduced me as follows: "This is Gerry Miller. I consider him one of the best students I've ever had in class, and I really thought he would make a solid contribution to the field until he got sidelined by that infernal attitude-change research!"

Twenty years later, I am not engaged in any attitude-change research, and

319

MESSAGE–ATTITUDE–BEHAVIOR RELATIONSHIP
Theory, Methodology, and Applications

perhaps the kind invitation of the editors to contribute this Afterword once again underscores the truth of the assertion that those who conduct research in an area write theoretical papers and research articles whereas those who do not are relegated to the mundane chore of composing forewords, afterwords, and state-of-the-art papers. Be that as it may, I take the task seriously, and in the next few pages, I want to share some of my impressions of this volume and to identify what I view as some of the major issues raised by these chapters. Hopefully, my remarks also will establish the fact that my present research inactivity in attitude change stems from something more than professional sloth or professional menopause.

Let me begin by stating unequivocally that this is a useful, well-executed volume for precisely the reasons emphasized by Cushman and McPhee in Chapter 1. As with a picture, I have always considered one good example to be worth a thousand words, and each of the contributors, whether commencing from a causal or from an action perspective, has created an excellent example of how inquiry can be grounded in rigorously derived theory. Although there has been a surplus of papers exhorting the importance of theory-grounded communication research, attempts to explicate the logical and empirical requirements for constructing various genres of theory and to demonstrate the derivation and testing of logically implied hypotheses have been relatively infrequent. Because each of the authors has achieved one or both of these ends, the book provides a model for both practicing communication researchers and students enrolled in classes on theory construction in communication.

Moreover, as Cushman and McPhee stress, various powerful methodologies are illustrated in the chapters. An important feature of the volume is the congruence, or "goodness of fit," between the varying theoretical postures and the differing methodologies that are employed. Rather than permitting methodology to dictate the point of theoretical embarkation—or even more counterproductively, forcing theory and hypothesis to fit the tools contained in a relatively small methodological tool kit—the contributors seemingly have begun with a particular theoretical perspective regarding the message–attitude–behavior relationship and have then selected, or in some cases created, methodologies permitting powerful and appropriate tests of their theories. Granted, such methodological freedom and diversity owes much to the rapid strides made during the past decade in developing new analytical tools, but the important points are that these advances permit a logical and empirical sophistication in theory construction not found in earlier crude approximations and allow the theorists to construct their theories and choose the appropriate method(s) for testing them, rather than proceeding in the reverse, "cart before the horse" manner.

Having praised these strengths of the volume, however, I must confess that I finished reading it still harboring some doubts about the total of scientific knowledge that the various theories are likely to yield about communication behavior. Lest I am misunderstood, these doubts do not stem from any theoretical or methodological inadequacies of the contributors; without exception, their chapters are crisp and thoughtful. Rather, my skepticism derives from my serious reservations about the scientific utility of the attitude link in the message–attitude–behavior triad. In other words, I am increasingly convinced that decades of persuasion researchers have been plunging down an Allportian blind alley, and even theoretical and methodological advances of the kind reflected by this volume are unlikely to yield high payoffs if the basic conceptual thrust is in error. Since my position will probably strike the reader as heretical at best, and naive at worst, some background elaboration is necessary before considering how my doubts relate to the chapters found in this volume.

Certainly I agree with the proposition that all students of persuasion worth their salt should manifest a lively curiosity about the ways that messages affect behavior. Whether postulating an intervening construct such as attitude— particularly as it is typically conceptualized—offers the best way of gaining such insights is decidedly open to question. Indeed, a somewhat dispassionate appraisal of the history of research utilizing the attitude construct does not yield an optimistic prognosis. For despite the fact that attitude and attitude change have probably received more hours of attention than any other topic in social psychology or communication, we are far from achieving a science of persuasion that yields useful advice regarding prediction and control in everyday persuasive transactions. In fact, were it not for one persistent bias of most persuasion researchers, the attitude construct would probably long since have been abandoned.

What is this bias to which I refer? Quite simply, I believe persuasion researchers have continued to subscribe to the idea that it is somehow more important to construct hypothetical maps of changes in people's cognitive structures than to identify specific patterns of behavioral response engendered by varying message stimuli. Of course, the typical response to this charge is that success in the former provides a *means* for predicting the latter (i.e., if attitude change can be reliably measured, prediction of other behavioral changes becomes possible). Although this argument has a convincing ring, an uncharitable observer could label it little more than a red herring; for by and large, persuasion researchers typically have remained unconcerned as to whether or not their measures of attitude and attitude change permit accurate prediction of other behaviors. After all, if predicting other behaviors were the primary goal of the research, the inclusion of such measures, along with the inevitable "attitude scales," would constitute standard operational procedures. Instead, writers such as Festinger (1964) remind us of what we already know: Out of the hundreds of persuasion studies conducted, only a handful have obtained a second behavioral measure to correlate with the attitude index; and even when such measures occasionally have been obtained, they have usually been nothing more than a second verbal report of anticipated future actions or ostensible after-the-fact behaviors. Thus, unless one assumes pervasive laziness or remarkable naivete, the inescapable conclusion seems to be that most persuasion researchers do not care about other behaviors, preferring instead to treat attitude as the focal point of inquiry.

Preoccupation with evaluative predispositions, or attitudes, is also illustrated by the persistent reification of the paper-and-pencil, verbal reports traditionally used as inferential measures of the attitude construct. Though lacking any rational justification for doing so, persuasion researchers have continued to equate responses to these scales with the intervening variable of attitude and to speak of other responses as behavior—hence, the roots of the so-called *attitude–behavior* problem. The mischief perpetrated by this confusion is pervasive and fundamental. As typically conceptualized, *attitude* has been viewed as a predisposition to respond positively or negatively to some object, act, or situation; thus, any behavioral measure of the construct is, of necessity, inferential. *One* way of arriving at inferences about people's attitudes is by obtaining evaluative verbal reports; if I want to know Editor Cushman's attitude about this Afterword, I can ask him. But in addition, I can observe other behaviors: I can check how many times he cites the work in his own writings, or I can try to determine how frequently he mentions the material in his classes. If he writes unsolicited letters to colleagues singing the praises of my arguments, or if he nominates the chapter for some national award, I can use such behaviors for arriving at inferential assessments of his attitude. If he says he likes the Afterword but does not nominate it for a national award, it would be patently absurd, on at least two counts, for me to assert that an inconsistency exists between his attitude and his behavior. First, such a claim implies that I somehow have direct access to Editor Cushman's attitude, when in fact, all I have are two behavioral indicants of it. Second, the example underscores the fact that no necessary inconsistency exists between the two behaviors; Editor Cushman may like many of the chapters he reads each year but not well enough to nominate them all for national awards.

What I have just said is neither new nor earthshaking. In what I believe to be the best conceptual paper ever written about the attitude construct, Campbell (1963) crisply and eloquently exposes the muddled thinking inherent in the attitude–behavior problem, as well as provides an alternative way of thinking about the issue. Different classes of responses, reasons Campbell, have different response thresholds; no one ever assumed that persons should be willing to go to jail or to die for every cause that they verbally support. Although talk is not always cheap, it usually involves fewer costs than incarceration or self-immolation. Yet when the talk consists of responses to Likert or semantic differential scales, this commonsense fact apparently escapes many persuasion researchers. Instead, these verbal responses mysteriously become *the* attitude, a reifying leap that is difficult to comprehend.

In a more recent controversial paper, Larson and Sanders (1975) have questioned the utility of the predispositional approach to persuasion and have suggested that the function of persuasion might be viewed more fruitfully as the appropriate alignment of behavior in various social situations. Despite some problems with the paper, their basic suggestion has much to recommend it: A science of persuasion which seeks to provide guidelines for prediction and control in our daily communicative transactions must be primarily concerned with how people behave, not with their affective dispositions. Yet the hue and cry aroused by Larson and Sanders' paper (e.g., Steinfatt & Infante, 1976) underscores the heavy commitment of many persuasion researchers to the hegemony of the attitude construct, a commitment that probably ensures continued attempts to map cognitive structures and continued preoccupation with such pursuits as the attitude–behavior problem.

With but occasional exception, the primacy of cognitive mapping and the importance of the attitude construct are taken for granted by the contributors to this volume. To be sure, there is considerable lively, interesting dialogue about how to proceed with persuasive matters, but the utility of the attitude link in the message–attitude–behavior chain is seldom questioned. For instance, Craig (Chapter 8) counsels researchers not to rely on intuition to determine "which attitudes go with which behaviors," but then suggests they should turn to the systematic study of *accounts* (i.e., information about attitude–behavior relationships gained from respondents themselves and then systematically analyzed). Such a procedure would, in Craig's view, yield insights concerning attitude–behavior syndromes of various populations.

To the degree that Craig's analysis is correct, however, it also implies an alternative possibility: Theories of persuasion that rely heavily on the construct of attitude may remain relatively weak in terms of their practical predictive utility. If it is difficult or impossible to make intuitive judgments about attitude–behavior relationships, persuaders who wish to predict from message inputs to behavioral responses are faced with the task of conducting frequent account censuses of relevant target audiences, an unrealistic undertaking in many everyday persuasive transactions. For example, even such a relatively simple transaction as trying to persuade a group of college undergraduates to give some time to a research project requires that the persuader take into account a potentially complex syndrome of related attitudes, some of which might trigger participative behavior and others which might not. If the persuader were to engage in intensive interviews with the students, content analyze their responses to determine the relevant attitude–behavior syndromes, and only then prepare the appropriate persuasive messages; the term would be ended and the research would remain uncompleted.

Of course, one could argue that when armed with the syndromes, the persuader would be able to enter next term's class and achieve a smashing rate of participation. This would be true only if two conditions were met: First, that the syndromes manifest relatively high invariance from term-to-term; second, that a dominant syndrome exists, which permits the use of a standard message for the entire class. This second condition is both more problematic and more troublesome, since should numerous syndromes exist, the accounts of the new term's students would have to be examined to determine which ones are to receive which messages. Moreover, this example creates fewer difficulties than some which might have been used, for it permits the possibility of a recurring persuasive situation with somewhat similar target audiences. Suppose, instead, that the persuasive goal consists of getting a salesman to lower the price of a late model car by $200. Here the problems involved in obtaining and analyzing accounts before encoding a persuasive message are formidible, if not impossible.

Returning to the research participation example, some additional considerations may help to illustrate the point I wish to emphasize. First, having been frequently involved in such a persuasive situation, it is clear to me that the persuader is much more concerned about students signing up for, and arriving at, a research session than in their uttering positive comments about the values of participating in communication research. To be sure, the two sets of behaviors are often related, but the acid persuasive test lies in the former behaviors, not the latter. Furthermore, when attempting to design persuasive messages, the strategies selected are usually based on some analysis of certain objective features of the persuasive situation. By far the most frequently employed strategy, the proffering of rewards and punishments, rests on the following assessment:

1. In this persuasive situation, the persuader exerts some means of control over the persuadees (i.e., the persuader has the *power* to reward or punish the persuadees for engaging or not engaging in certain behaviors).
2. Given this circumstance, a message emphasizing the potential rewards or punishments associated with compliance is likely to elicit the desired behavior.

Obviously, statements about attitudes and attitude change are notably absent from this assessment.

Since preoccupation with the attitude construct is deep-seated and pervasive, it is easy to imagine persuasion theorists triumphantly exclaiming that the preceding analysis rests entirely on a set of assumptions about the persuadees' attitudes regarding authority, power, rewards, punishments, and other related matters. In a sense, this is true; the habits of ordinary language and the half-century hegemony of the attitude construct are not easily overcome. But from the perspective of theory construction, some important changes in conceptual priorities have occurred. Instead of stressing the relationship between cognitive states (attitudes) and message strategies, the primary link concerns the relationship between certain objective characteristics of the persuasive situation (in this case, the means of control available to the persuader) and the persuader's choice of appropriate message strategies. Furthermore, the specified consequent of the relationship—in research vernacular, the dependent variable—is a specific set of responses (participating in the research) of the kind frequently sought in everyday persuasive transactions, and of the nature that relative persuasive success can be evaluated without recourse to cognitive mapping.

In proposing these possible changes in conceptual priorities, I know I risk the charge of imposing a fruitless radical behaviorism—or even more pejoratively, a "behavioristic pretentiousness"—on persuasion research. Although I believe the radical behavioristic approach to studying persuasion merits more attention than it has received, my intent is not to urge this perspective as the only fruitful way of developing persuasion theories, but rather to demonstrate some alternatives to the present fixation on attitudes and attitude change. Careful examination of the necessary conditions for effectively using various message strategies offers yet another potential avenue for developing useful insights concerning persuasive prediction and control. For instance, persuasive practitioners often allude to "accumulating and spending chips." Chips are accumulated by doing favors and contributing support to other potentially useful parties, a practice closely akin to the *pregiving* compliance-gaining strategy mentioned by Marwell and Schmitt (1967). After chips have been accumulated, persuasive attempts aimed at these parties often rely on a *debt* strategy (i.e., the parties are induced to behave in certain ways by subtle or not-so-subtle reminders that they "owe" the persuader the sought-after compliant behavior). Development of a typology of such message strategies, along with the necessary antecedent conditions for their effective use, could produce a set of related empirical generalizations—that is, a theory of persuasion—that avoids some of the pitfalls inherent in cognitive mapping.

The preceding discussion reveals a largely neglected aspect concerning the attitude construct itself: *In many persuasive situations, the crucial attitudes may not be those relating to a particular substantive issue or a specific topic but rather certain normative predispositions regarding the appropriate ways of conducting social relationships.* If one is trying to persuade a colleague on the curriculum committee to vote for the addition of a new course, the colleague's attitudes about the particular course (or for that matter, about course proliferation in general, or economic inefficiency and waste in the university) well may be of less import than his or her attitudes about the desirability of returning favors and keeping social accounts balanced. Social exchange theories rest on such "tit for tat" considerations, yet surprisingly, relatively little attention has been directed at these theories in the persuasion literature.

Indeed, it could reasonably be argued that the chapters showing the least concern for dealing with attitude in its traditional conceptual trappings offer the greatest promise for expanding our understanding of the persuasion process, at least so far as understanding enhances potential prediction and control. For example, whereas Woelfel's theory is based on mapping the relative position of concepts in cognitive space, his approach largely ignores the conventional wisdom regarding the affective predispositional nature of attitudes; in fact, his measurement system is grounded in distance rather than affective intensity. Moreover, as a study by Barnett, Serota, and Taylor (1976) demonstrates, application and test of Woelfel's theory moves from response-based measures of the initial distance between a set of concepts, to the selection of message strategies aimed at changing these distances in a manner congruent with the persuasive intent; and finally, to a behavioral measure (in this case, voting for a particular political candidate) of persuasive success. Although one could always label the entire process an instance of attitude change, such a step would be taking liberties with the traditional meaning of the construct, so much so that it seems useful to conceive of the theory as a different conceptual and operational animal than typical attitude-change theories.

In a similar vein, the discussion of structural–functionalism by Fontes, Shelby, and O'Connor (Chapter 10) minimizes the role of attitudes in facilitating or inhibiting persuasive success, focusing instead on the relationship between information and subsequent behavior. To be sure, a committed disciple of the traditional paradigm could argue that the function of information is to shape or change attitudes, which in turn leads to behavioral compliance or persuasive success. Such a rebuttal, however, overlooks two possibilities: First, there are undoubtedly cases where persons have no firmly established attitudes about a given matter but can be induced to comply with the persuader's desires through the presentation of specific information; second, in some instances provision of specific information may trigger the desired behavior even if it is counter attitudinal (e.g., I may have markedly negative attitudes about attending administrative cocktail parties but still show up if I discover that my dean believes attendance is desirable). Indeed, making me aware of this information may constitute a much more effective persuasive strategy than any prolonged campaign to change my affective posture about administrative cocktail parties.

Even two of the authors who make exceptionally strong cases for incorporating intervening variables into their theories seem to view the attitude construct somewhat atypically. In arguing that the hierarchical arrangement of attitudes influences the relative efficacy of persuasive messages; Poole (Chapter 7), like Woelfel (Chapter 3), emphasizes cognitive structure and concept positioning rather than affective intensity per se. And in developing his stochastic model of persuasion, Hewes (Chapter 2) does not even employ *attitude* as one of his five key variables. Moreover, when alluding to the basic triad, he frequently uses the terminology "message–*intervening variable*-behavior," rather than "message–attitude–behavior." As Cushman and McPhee note in Chapter 1, Hewes focuses on the expectations that people have regarding their behaviors and on the impact that messages have on these expectations. As far as I can tell, the notion of expectations is not synonymous with the notion of attitudes, at least not as the latter term is usually conceptualized.

Another way of characterizing such chapters as those of Woelfel, Poole, Hewes, and Seibold is to say that they focus on the *process* of information processing rather than the *construct* of attitude. For those students of communication who view intervening variables as an indispensable explanatory ingredient of persuasion theories, this shift in focus affords some real advantages. In particular, it assumes that postmessage behaviors will be used as the primary measure of persuasive effectiveness, with information processing viewed as a set of related antecedent variables, which function to inhibit or facilitate behavioral change. Such a theoretic posture is less likely to lead the persuasion student down blind alleys in search of some elusive solution to the attitude–behavior problem.

Thus, this Afterword ends on an optimistic note. Though I have expressed skepticism about the utility of the attitude construct, my reservations relate primarily to the way the construct has been typically conceptualized. Since, in addition to their theoretical and methodological advances, many of the present contributors have broken new conceptual ground, the possibility of gaining greater understanding about the effects of persuasion—that is, increasing the potential for prediction and control—is certainly enhanced. Though it is too early to determine the substantive payoffs of these diverse theoretical contributions, they indeed mark some exciting paths for persuasion researchers to follow.

REFERENCES

Allport, G. W. Attitudes. In C. M. Murchison (Ed.), *Handbook of social psychology*. Worcester, Mass.: Clark University Press, 1935. Pp. 798–844.

Barnett, G. A., Serota, K. B., & Taylor, J. A. Campaign communication and attitude change: A multidimensional analysis. *Human Communication Research*, 1976, *2*, 227–244.

Campbell, D. T. Social attitudes and other acquired behavioral dispositions. In S. Koch (Ed.), *Psychology: A study of a science* (Vol. 6). New York: McGraw–Hill, 1963. Pp. 94–172.

Festinger, L. Behavioral support for opinion change. *Public Opinion Quarterly*, 1964, *28*, 404–418.

Larson, C., & Sanders, R. Faith, mystery, and data: An analysis of "scientific" studies of persuasion. *Quarterly Journal of Speech*, 1975, *61*, 178–194.

Marwell, C., & Schmitt, D. R. Dimensions of compliance-gaining behavior: An empirical analysis. *Sociometry*, 1967, *30*, 350–364.

Steinfatt, T. M., & Infante, D. A. Attitude–behavior relationships in communication research. *Quarterly Journal of Speech*, 1976, *62*, 267–278.

Author Index

Davis, H., 103
Dawes, R. M., 152
DeCharms, R., 221
DeFleur, M. L., 6, 13, 58, 196, 201, 210, 213, 216, 221, 263, 275
Delia, Jesse G., 22, 118, 120, 122, 125, 126, 128, 130, 131, 132, 134, 137, 138, 140, 141, 143, 170, 171, 172, 188
Derman, C., 66
Descartes, R., 294
Deutscher, I., 197, 210
DeVries, D., 73
Dillehay, R. L., 210, 213
Doob, L., 203
Dubin, R., 2
Duncan, O., 44, 206, 247
Dunnette, M. D., 205
Durkheim, E., 113
Dutton, J., 142, 211, 212

E

Eagly, A. H., 2, 7, 10, 196, 200, 211, 234
Edison, N., 113
Ehrlich, H. J., 210, 212, 228
Einstein, A., 44, 89, 90
Eiser, J. R., 156
Ellis, B., 98
Evans-Hewes, D., 50, 57, 64, 72, 75

F

Fazio, R. H., 13, 184, 212, 213, 232, 233
Festinger, L., 205, 214, 321
Feyerabend, P., 43
Fields, J., 212
Fillmore, C. J., 153
Fink, E. L., 113
Fishbein, M., 2, 5, 8, 9, 10, 11, 12, 13, 14, 18, 19, 36–37, 49, 51, 54, 55, 73, 75, 79, 118, 119, 120, 122, 127, 129, 130, 135, 136, 137, 138, 139, 140, 141, 142, 155, 156, 157, 161, 166, 167, 168, 171, 172, 178, 179, 183, 187, 188, 196, 198, 200, 202, 203, 204, 210, 211, 212, 213, 214, 218, 219, 220, 226, 227, 232, 245, 260, 261, 263, 264, 274, 275, 277, 278, 279, 280, 281, 298
Fischoff, B., 179
Fiske, D. W., 225
Flay, B. R., 52, 57, 68, 214, 215

Folger, R., 7, 17, 24–25, 38, 52, 201
Fontes, N., 32–33, 38, 306, 307, 326
Foote, N., 93
Frideres, J., 212, 213, 228
Fridja, N. H., 185

G

Galanter, E., 173
Galileo, 90
Gauss, K. F., 90
Gergen, K., 52
Gillespie, D. F., 143
Gillham, J., 95, 109, 112
Ginsberg, R., 50, 64
Gleser, L., 66
Goffman, E., 103
Goldberg, A., 79
Goldberger, A., 206, 227
Goldman, A. I., 173, 174, 204, 205
Gonyea, A. H., 121, 122, 134
Gordon, T., 113
Gragg, R. L., 160
Green, J. A., 196, 212, 232, 263
Green, P., 101
Greeno, J., 50
Greenwald, A. C., 74, 183, 210
Gruder, C., 57
Guardalabene, N., 306, 307
Guthrie, W. K. C., 292

H

Hackman, J. R., 167, 170
Hage, J., 2, 200
Haight, L., 52
Halama, J., 57
Halliday, D., 103
Hale, C. L., 121
Haller, A., 93, 221, 228
Hamblin, R., 95, 98
Hanson, N. R., 43, 44
Harré, R., 6, 7, 17, 30, 205, 206, 283, 284, 285
Hass, R., 135, 214
Hauser, R., 227
Hawkes, A., 50, 64
Hays, W., 98, 258
Heberlein, T. A., 205, 211, 213, 264
Heider, F., 123, 125, 221, 316
Heise, D., 159, 160, 206

Subject Index

DATE DUE

0.12 81	
19 '83	
10.29.86	
2.24 88	
MAY 0 4 1997	
NOV 0 8 2004	

BRODART, INC.   Cat. No. 23-221